MANAGEMENT SCIENCE IN HOSPITALITY AND TOURISM

Theory, Practice, and Applications

Advances in Hospitality and Tourism

MANAGEMENT SCIENCE IN HOSPITALITY AND TOURISM

Theory, Practice, and Applications

Edited by
Muzaffer Uysal, PhD
Zvi Schwartz, PhD
Ercan Sirakaya-Turk, PhD

APPLE
ACADEMIC
PRESS

Apple Academic Press Inc. | Apple Academic Press Inc.
3333 Mistwell Crescent | 9 Spinnaker Way
Oakville, ON L6L 0A2 | Waretown, NJ 08758
Canada | USA

©2017 by Apple Academic Press, Inc.

First issued in paperback 2021

Exclusive worldwide distribution by CRC Press, a member of Taylor & Francis Group
No claim to original U.S. Government works

ISBN 13: 978-1-77463-297-0 (pbk)
ISBN 13: 978-1-926895-71-0 (hbk)

Library and Archives Canada Cataloguing in Publication

Management science in hospitality and tourism : theory, practice, and applications / edited by Muzaffer Uysal, PhD, Zvi Schwartz, PhD, Ercan Sirakaya-Turk, PhD.

(Advances in hospitality and tourism book series)
Includes bibliographical references and index.
ISBN 978-1-926895-71-0 (hardcover).--ISBN 978-1-4822-2347-7 (pdf)
1. Hospitality industry--Management. 2. Tourism--Management. I. Uysal, Muzaffer, author, editor II. Sirakaya-Turk, Ercan, author, editor III. Schwartz, Zvi, author, editor IV. Series: Advances in hospitality and tourism book series

TX911.3.M27M3557 2016   647.94068   C2016-903213-2   C2016-903214-0

Library of Congress Cataloging-in-Publication Data

Names: Uysal, Muzaffer, editor. | Schwartz, Zvi, editor. | Sirakaya-Turk, Ercan, editor.
Title: Management science in hospitality and tourism : theory, practice, and applications / [edited by] Muzaffer Uysal, PhD, Zvi Schwartz, PhD, Ercan Sirakaya-Turk, PhD.
Description: Warentown, New Jersey : Apple Academic Press Toronto, 2015. | Series: Advances in hospitality and tourism | Includes bibliographical references and index.
Identifiers: LCCN 2016020824 | ISBN 9781926895710 (hardcover : alk. paper)
Subjects: LCSH: Hospitality industry--Management. | Tourism--Management.
Classification: LCC TX911.3.M27 M295 2015 | DDC 647.94068--dc23
LC record available at https://lccn.loc.gov/2016020824

Apple Academic Press also publishes its books in a variety of electronic formats. Some content that appears in print may not be available in electronic format. For information about Apple Academic Press products, visit our website at **www.appleacademicpress.com** and the CRC Press website at **www.crcpress.com**

ABOUT THE EDITORS

Muzaffer Uysal, PhD

Muzaffer Uysal, PhD, is a Professor of tourism and hospitality management at Virginia Tech, Pamplin College of Business in the Department of Hospitality and Tourism Management. He has extensive experience in the travel and tourism field, has worked on several tourism management and marketing projects, and conducted tourism workshops and seminars in more than 30 countries. He is a member of International Academy for the Study of Tourism, the Academy of Leisure Sciences, and serves as co-editor of *Tourism Analysis: An Interdisciplinary Journal*. He has also authored and co-authored a significant number of articles, five monographs, and eight books related to tourism research methods, tourist service satisfaction, tourism and quality-of-life, creating experience value in tourism, and scales in tourism and hospitality settings. Dr. Uysal has also received a number of awards for Research, Excellence in International Education, Teaching Excellence, and best paper awards. His current research interests center on tourism demand/supply interaction, tourism development, and QOL research. E-mail: samil@vt.edu

Zvi Schwartz, PhD

Zvi Schwartz, PhD, is a Professor in the Department of Hospitality Business Management in the Alfred Lerner College of Business and Economics at the University of Delaware. Prior to joining the University of Delaware, Dr. Schwartz was the J. Willard and Alice S. Marriott Senior Faculty Fellow for Hospitality Finance and Revenue Management in the department of Hospitality and Tourism Management at Virginia Tech where he served as the director of graduate programs, and an associate professor at the University of Illinois. Prior to joining academia, he had over a decade of lodging industry experience as a manager and an entrepreneur. His scholarly research and industry consulting focus on the core technical and strategic elements of the revenue management cycle: forecasting, optimization, and monitoring, as well as strategic pricing, and consumer and firm decisions in advanced reservation environments. E-mail: zvi@udel.edu

Ercan Sirakaya-Turk, PhD

Ercan Sirakaya-Turk, PhD, is a Professor and the Associate Dean for Research, Grants, Graduate and International Programs in the College of Hospitality, Retail and Sports Management at the University of South Carolina. He received his PhD from Clemson University, South Carolina, USA. In 2007, he spent a year in Saint Petersburg, Russia as a Fulbright scholar teaching at FINEC Saint Petersburg State University of Economics and Finance. Before joining USC, he worked as an associate professor at Texas A&M University and as an assistant professor at the Pennsylvania State University. Ercan is the writer of one of the most influential articles in tourism. He also published a significant number of articles in the area of tourism destination marketing and developmental policy in prestigious tourism and business journals such as the *Annals of Tourism Research, Journal of Travel Research, Journal of Business Research,*and *Tourism Analysis*. Dr. Sirakaya-Turk is the founding Editor-in-Chief for *e-Review of Tourism Research*, and the current Co-Editor-In-Chief for *Tourism Analysis*. He teaches tourism, marketing, tourism economics, and advanced research methods classes, conducts grant and statistics workshops for faculty and doctoral students, provides individual consultation in research and grants, and approves all grant activity going forward from his college. Email: ercan@hrsm.sc.edu

ADVANCES IN HOSPITALITY AND TOURISM BOOK SERIES

Editor-in-Chief:

Mahmood A. Khan, PhD

Professor, Department of Hospitality and Tourism Management,
Pamplin College of Business, Virginia Polytechnic Institute and State University,
Falls Church, Virginia, USA
email: mahmood@vt.edu

BOOKS IN THE SERIES:

Hospitality Marketing and Consumer Behavior: Creating Memorable Experiences
Editor: Vinnie Jauhari, PhD

Women and Travel: Historical and Contemporary Perspectives
Editors: Catheryn Khoo-Lattimore, PhD, and Erica Wilson, PhD

Wilderness of Wildlife Tourism
Editor: Johra Kayeser Fatima, PhD

CONTENTS

LIST OF CONTRIBUTORS

Frank Wogbe Agbola, PhD
Associate Professor, Newcastle Business School, University of Newcastle, SRS 152, University Drive, Callaghan, NSW 2308, Australia. E-mail: frank.agbola@newcastle.edu.au

Albert G. Assaf, PhD
Associate Professor, Isenberg School of Management, University of Massachusetts-Amherst, 90 Campus Center Way, 209A Flint Lab, Amherst, MA 01003, USA. E-mail: assaf@isenberg.umass.edu

Guy Assaker, PhD
Associate Professor, Hospitality & Marketing, Hospitality & Marketing, School of Business, Lebanese American University, Byblos, Lebanon. E-mail: guy.assaker@lau.edu.lb

Rodolfo Baggio, PhD
Professor, Department Economics and Tourism, Dondena Center for Research on Social Dynamics, Bocconi University, Via Röntgen, 1, 20146 Milan, Italy. E-mail: rodolfo.baggio@unibocconi.it

Cherylynn Becker, PhD
Associate Professor of Management, University of Southern Mississippi, Gulf Coast, College of Business, 730 East Beach Boulevard, Long Beach, MS 39560, USA. E-mail: Cheri.becker@usm.edu

Neeraj Bharadwaj, PhD
Assistant Professor, Department of Marketing and Supply Chain Management, University of Tennessee, Knoxville, TN, USA. E-mail: nbharadw@utk.edu

Jason Li Chen, PhD
Research Associate, School of Hospitality and Tourism Management, University of Surrey, Guildford GU2 7XH, United Kingdom. E-mail: l.chen@surrey.ac.uk

Eli Cohen, PhD
Department of Management, Ben Gurion University of the Negev, Beersheba, Israel. E-mail: elico@bgu.ac.il; Ehrenberg Bass Institute of Marketing Science, University of South Australia, Adelaide, SA, Australia. E-mail: eli.cohen@unisa.edu.au

Giacomo Del Chiappa, PhD
Department of Economics and Business, University of Sassari and CRENOS, Via Muroni, 25, 07100 Sassari, Italy. E-mail: gdelchiappa@uniss.it

Tarik Doğru, PhD
Assistant Professor, School of Hospitality Administration (SHA), Boston University, 928 Commonwealth Avenue, Boston, MA 02215, USA. E-mail: tarikdogru@gmail.com

Daniel R. Fesenmaier, PhD
Professor and Director, National Laboratory for Tourism & eCommerce, Eric Friedheim Tourism Institute, Department of Tourism, Recreation and Sport Management, University of Florida, Gainesville, FL 32611, USA. E-mail: drfez@ufl.edu

Aliza Fleischer, PhD
Associate Professor, Department of Agricultural Economics and Management, Hotel, Food Resources and Tourism Management Program, Hebrew University of Jerusalem, Jerusalem, Israel. Address: P.O. Box 12, Rehovot 7610001, Israel. E-mail: aliza.f@mail.huji.ac.il

Sandro Formica, PhD, JD
Managing Self & Others, Leadership, and Personal Empowerment, Florida International University Biscayne Bay, 3000 N.E. 151 Street, North Miami, FL 33181, USA. Email: sformica@fiu.edu. Address: P.O. Box 190501, Miami, FL 33119, USA. E-mail: sandro@sandroformica.com

Rob Hallak PhD
School of Management, UniSA Business School, University of South Australia, City West Campus, Adelaide, SA 5001, Australia. E-mail: Rob.Hallak@unisa.edu.au

SooCheong (Shawn) Jang, PhD
Professor, School of Hospitality and Tourism Management, Purdue University, Marriott Hall, 900 W. State Street, West Lafayette, IN 47907, USA. E-mail: jang12@purdue.edu

Ersem Karadag, PhD
Associate Professor, Robert Morris University, Massey Hall, #311, Moon Township, PA 15108, USA. E-mail: karadag@rmu.edu

Larissa Koupriouchina, MSc
Research Fellow in Pricing and Revenue Management, Senior Lecturer in Revenue Management, Hotelschool The Hague, Hospitality Business School, Brusselselaan 2, 2587 AH, The Hague, The Netherlands. E-mail: l.koupriouchina@hotelschool.nl.

Matthew Krawczyk
Research Associate, Virginia Tech, 12600 Foxridge Lane Apt. F Blacksburg, VA 24060, USA. E-mail: mattjk@vt.edu

Gang Li, PhD
School of Hospitality and Tourism Management, University of Surrey, Guildford GU2 7XH, United Kingdom. E-mail: g.li@surrey.ac.uk

Larry Lockshin, PhD
Ehrenberg Bass Institute of Marketing Science, University of South Australia, Adelaide, SA, Australia. E-mail: larry.lockshin@unisa.edu.au

Bing Pan, PhD
Associate Professor, Department of Hospitality and Tourism Management, School of Business, College of Charleston, Charleston, SC 29424-001, USA. E-mail: bingpan@gmail.com

Jeong-Yeol Park, PhD
Assistant Professor, Rosen College of Hospitality Management, University of Central Florida, 9907 Universal Blvd., Orlando, FL 32819, USA. E-mail: Jeong-Yeol.Park@ucf.edu

Zvi Schwartz, PhD
Professor, Department of Hospitality Business Management, Alfred Lerner College of Business & Economics, University of Delaware, 14 W. Main Street, Raub Hall, Newark, DE 19716, USA. E-mail: zvi@udel.edu

D. D. Sierag
PhD Student, Centrum Wiskunde & Informatica (CWI), Stochastics Department, Amsterdam, The Netherlands; VU University Amsterdam, Faculty of Exact Sciences, Science Park 123, 1098 XG, Amsterdam, The Netherlands.

Ercan Sirakaya-Turk, PhD
College of Hospitality, Retail and Sport Management, University of South Carolina, Columbia, SC 29208, USA. E-mail: ERCAN@hrsm.sc.edu

Haiyan Song, PhD
Chair Professor of Tourism and Associate Dean (Research), The School of Hotel and Tourism Management, The Hong Kong Polytechnic University, 17 Science Museum Road, TST East, Kowloon, Hong Kong. E-mail: haiyan.song@polyu.edu.hk

Jason Stienmetz
Research Coordinator, National Laboratory for Tourism & eCommerce, University of Florida, Gainesville, FL, USA. E-mail: Jason.stienmetz@ufl.edu

Muzaffer Uysal, PhD
Professor of Hospitality and Tourism Management, 362 Wallace Hall (0429), 295 West Campus Drive, Department of Hospitality and Tourism Management, Virginia Tech, Blacksburg, VA 24061, USA. E-mail: samil@vt.edu

J. I. Van der Rest, PhD
Associate Professor of Business Administration, Department of Business Studies, Institute of Tax Law and Economics, Leiden Law School, Steenschuur 25, 2311 ES Leiden, The Netherlands. E-mail: j.i.van.der.rest@law.leidenuniv.nl.

Timothy Webb
Research Associate, Virginia Tech, 2507 Capistrano St. Blacksburg, VA 24060, USA. E-mail: Timdw89@vt.edu

Zheng Xiang, PhD
Assistant Professor, The Department of Hospitality and Tourism Management, Pamplin College of Business, Virginia Tech. 362 Wallace Hall -295 West Campus Drive, Blacksburg, VA 24061, USA. E-mail: philxz@vt.edu

Yang Yang, PhD
Assistant Professor, School of Tourism and Hospitality Management, Temple University, Philadelphia, PA, USA. E-mail: yangy@temple.edu

Tianshu Zheng, PhD
Associate Professor, Department of Apparel, Events, and Hospitality Management, Iowa State University, Ames, IA, USA. E-mail: tianshu.zheng@outlook.com

LIST OF ABBREVIATIONS

ABMs	agent-based models
ACSI	American customer satisfaction index
ADR	average daily rate
A-GPS	assisted GPS
AHP	analytic hierarchy process
ANN	artificial neural networks
AR	autoregressive
ARI	Average Rate Index
ARIMA	autoregressive integrated moving average
ARR	average room rate
AVE	average variance extracted
BIBD	balanced incomplete block design
BIC	Bayesian information criterion
BLS	Bureau of Labor Statistics
BSC	balanced scorecard
BWS	best–worst scaling
CBS	Central Bureau of Statistics
CGE	computable general equilibrium
CM	competitiveness monitor
CM	contribution margin
CPOR	cost per occupied room
CRM	customer relationship management
CRS	computerized reservation systems
CSA	covariance structure analysis
CSE	competitive share effect
CVBs	convention and visitors bureaus
DEA	data envelopment analysis
DF	Dickey–Fuller
DI	destination image
DMOs	destination marketing organizations
DMS	destination management system
DV	dependent variable
ESE	entrepreneurial self-efficacy
eWoM	electronic word of mouth

FE	fixed effects
FS	family size
GDP	gross domestic product
GDS	global distribution system
GMRAE	geometric mean relative absolute error
GOP	gross operating profit
GopPar	gross operating profit per available room
I	integrated
IME	industrial mix effect
IT	information technology
IVs	independent variables
KPI	key performance indicators
LCE	Lyapunov characteristic exponent
LL	log likelihoods
LOS	length of stay
LVs	latent variables
MA	moving average
MAE	mean absolute error
MAPE	mean absolute percentage error
Market Occ	market occupancy
MASE	mean absolute scaled error
MdAE	median absolute error
MdAPE	median absolute percentage error
MdRAE	median relative absolute error
ME	mean error
MFP	multi-factor productivity
MGC	marketer-generated content
MIMIC	multiple indicator multiple cause
ML	maximum likelihood
MOA	motivation, opportunity, and ability
MPE	mean percentage error
MPI	Market Penetration Index
MRAE	mean relative absolute error
MSE	mean square error
NAICS	North American Industry Classification System
NGE	national growth effect
NITN	Northern Indiana Travel Network
NOP	net operation profit
OLS	ordinary least squares

OTA	online travel agency
PI	place identity
PLS	partial least squares
PLS-SEM	Partial Least Squares Structural Equation Modeling
PMS	property management systems
PPP	purchasing power parity
REBUS	response-based segmentation techniques
RelMAE	relative mean absolute error
RevPAC	revenue per available customer
RevPAR	revenue per available rooms
RGI	Revenue Generation Index
RM	revenue management
RMdSPE	root median square percentage error
RMS	restaurant management systems
RMSE	root mean square error
RMSPE	root mean square percentage error
ROA	return on assets
ROE	return on equity
ROI	return on investment
SDL	service dominant logic
SEM	structural equation modeling
SEM	structural equation modeling
SF	stochastic frontier
SFC	support for community
SIC	standardized industrial classification
sMAPE	symmetric mean absolute percentage error
sMdAPE	symmetric median absolute percentage error
SSA	shift–share analysis
SSM	shift–share model
TE	technical efficiency
TFP	total-factor productivity
TQM	total quality management
TrevPar	total revenue per available room
TrevPAR	total revenue per available room
TSA	tourism satellite accounts
TSI	tourist satisfaction index
TTSA	Travel and Tourism Satellite Accounts
UGC	user-generated content
UNESCO	United Nations Educational, Scientific and Cultural Organization

UNWTO	United Nations World Tourism Organization
VIF	variance inflation factor
WDI	World Development Indicators
WEF	World Economic Forum
WHCjt	World Heritage Cultural sites
WHNjt	World Heritage Natural sites
WTTC	World Travel and Tourism Council

PREFACE

Decision makers and researchers need to be more creative and innovative than ever in solving problems and developing unique approaches to solutions in the highly dynamic tourism and hospitality sectors. Researchers need to use scientific methods and approaches at their disposal more effectively. An examination of existing studies in our academic world reveals that there has been a significant increase in applications of management science and quantitative analysis in tourism and hospitality settings and operations. However, research that utilizes management science and quantitative analysis with decision aided approaches is rather sporadic in tourism and hospitality journals.

The academic scope of management science in today's world is interdisciplinary and covers a wide array of research areas such as data analytics and data mining, decision support and analysis, data envelopment analysis (DEA), forecasting, revenue management, game theory, logistics, supply chain management, mathematical modeling, optimization, probability and statistics, risk management, project management, simulation, network modeling and transportation, and industrial engineering and design. Regardless of the nature of tools and approaches we may have, the aim should be to use rational, systematic, science-based techniques to generate new information and enable managers to improve their capacity to make effective decisions.

In today's highly dynamic business environment, we expect an increased demand for a wider use of management science approaches to research and business solutions. This trend will continue in the future. With this backdrop depicting the importance of management science applications in the field of tourism and hospitality, we developed this book. We expect that this volume will contribute to the growing body of knowledge in the field and encourage researchers to further advance the scope and coverage of this stream of research with appropriate applications in tourism and hospitality operations. Extant management science applications in the field of tourism and hospitality are limited in number and sporadic, thus needing further concerted efforts and attention from tourism and hospitality researchers. Therefore, this book contains key writings by a group of outstanding researchers on the applications of management science in tourism and hospitality in a single resource.

The goal is not to cover every possible subject under the knowledge domain of management science, but rather bring a group of topics to the forefront of our research agenda that would exemplify the best work of our contributors and provide a portfolio of applications that represent the issues of the field. We believe that this book will be of great interest not only to students of tourism and hospitality, but also to researchers and practitioners. Enjoy it!

Muzaffer Uysal, Zvi Schwartz,
and Ercan Sirakaya-Turk
(Editors)

CHAPTER 1

MANAGEMENT SCIENCE APPLICATIONS IN TOURISM AND HOSPITALITY

MUZAFFER UYSAL[1], ZVI SCHWARTZ[2] and
ERCAN SIRAKAYA-TURK[3]

[1]*Department of Hospitality and Tourism Management, Virginia Tech, 362 Wallace Hall (0429), 295 West Campus Drive, Blacksburg, VA 24061, USA. E-mail: samil@vt.edu*

[2]*Department of Hospitality Business Management, Alfred Lerner College of Business & Economics, University of Delaware, 14 W. Main Street, Raub Hall, Newark, DE 19716, USA. E-mail: zvi@udel.edu*

[3]*College of Hospitality, Retail and Sport Management, University of South Carolina, Columbia, SC 29208, USA. E-mail: ercan@hrsm.sc.edu*

CONTENTS

1.1   INTRODUCTION

The field of tourism and hospitality has witnessed remarkable academic achievements in the last four decades. The degree of complexity in knowledge generation and fast data accumulation are posing new challenges (Mayer-Schonberger & Cukier, 2013, Rivera & Pizam, 2015). Today, decision makers and researchers must function more efficiently in real time and need to be more creative and innovative in solving problems and developing unique approaches to solutions in this highly dynamic and ever-increasingly competitive business environment. At the same time, the pace of data generation and research not only creates new opportunities for researchers, but also influences the manners in which researchers conduct empirical studies. For example, with a conventional theory-driven study, the researcher develops and conceptualizes his/her hypotheses based on relevant literature, supported by theory and reasonable argument, and then tests and verifies the hypotheses by the use of samples and appropriate tools and techniques. On the other hand, the richness of big data in today's world allow the researcher to proceed without a priori set of conditions on the content of data and reveal patterns and structures that may be reflective of the industry and market structure. Furthermore, the convergence of quantitative and qualitative approaches, supported by solid and verifiable research findings, linear and nonlinear data analyses, and utilization of mixed methods in research and development, have enabled researchers to offer science-based solutions to today's complex problems. Baggio (2008) argues that a shift in management attitude is needed, and that dynamic and adaptive methods may be better suited and sought to deal with today's complex tourism and hospitality systems.

1.2   MANAGEMENT SCIENCE APPLICATIONS

Researchers agree that tourism and hospitality systems need to be analyzed as dynamic complex, ever-evolving systems, comprised of interdependent factors that are not always linearly related to each other. Researchers also need to continuously develop and incorporate new frames of approaches and tools that are augmented with both linear and nonlinear techniques and analysis as a function of demand and supply interactions in tourism and hospitality.

There exists a plethora of interdisciplinary and multidisciplinary approaches and tools grounded in management theories, marketing and consumer behavior, economics, statistics, management science, transportation and network systems, and computing science. We must use scientific methods and approaches at our disposal. An examination of existing studies in our academic world reveals that there has been a significant increase in applications of management science and quantitative analyses in tourism and hospitality settings and operations (e.g., Toh, 1985, 1986; Bitran & Gilbert, 1996; Ingold, McMahon-Beattie, & Yeoman, 2000; Wöber, 2002; Schwartz & Cohen, 2003; Cooper, 2005; Barros, 2005; Talluri & Van Ryzin, 2005; Schwartz, 2006; Barros & Santos, 2006; Chen, 2007; Reynolds & Thompson, 2007; Wu, Hsiao, & Tsali, 2008; Pullman & Rodgers, 2010; Assaf, Barros, & Josiassen, 2010; Assaf & Agbola, 2011; Hara, 2011; Baggio & Klobas, 2011; Zheng & Gu, 2011; Hayes & Miller, 2011; Song, 2012; Zheng et al., 2012; Fantazy, Kumar, & Kumar, 2012; Guo et al., 2012; Assaf & Agbola, 2014). These efforts are recently augmented with benchmarking studies that cover performance comparison, gap identification, competitive analysis, and best practices (e.g., Assaf & Dwyer, 2013; Kozak, 2003; Wöber, 2002; Pyo, 2001). Obviously, these applications are not limited to tourism and hospitality publications. A closer look at some of the recent issues of various management science and operation research journals also reveals that several aspects of tourism and hospitality issues dealing with destinations, airlines (e.g., Assaf & Gillen, 2012; Smith, Leimkuhler, & Darrow, 1992), hotels (e.g., Sun and & Lu, 2005; Baum & Ingram, 1998), fast food (Love & Hoey, 1990), theme parks, sport areas, national parks (e.g., Schwartz, Stewart, & Buckland, 2012), demand for travel, revenue management (e.g., Kimes, 2011) and yield management (e.g., Toh & Dekay, 2002; Badinelli, 2000; Baker & Collier, 1999; Schwartz, 1998; Bitran & Mondschein, 1995; Kimes, 1989), and measurement (Jones, 2000; Huyton & Thomas, 2000; Whelan-Ryan, 2000) are subjects for academic investigation and research, further signaling the heightened interest in management science applications to the field of tourism and hospitality. Thus, this book is developed to house key writings by a group of outstanding contemporary researchers and colleagues. We believe that the readers will enjoy it as a single reference source.

In the 1970s, we saw early applications of management science tools and techniques grounded in operations research. These techniques allowed us to assess potential for tourism and recreation development, to determine investment policy (Gearing, Swart, & Var, 1973) measure attractiveness of places as destinations; allocate resources and creating efficiency in performance and productivity, and generate sound information and intelligence in order to aid and improve decision making (e.g., Swart, Var, & Gearing, 1978; Cesario, 1969, 1975).

One of the most comprehensive books that followed a quantitative approach with different management science techniques to tourism planning and development was "Planning for Tourism Development: Quantitate Approaches" (1976) by Gearing, Swart, and Var. This particular book was the first attempt from the perspective of management science approach to quantify and measure the notion of touristic attractiveness by constructing a multi-attribute utility function. The results of the procedure were then used to support the planning activities for the 65 geographic areas in Turkey. The level of attractiveness of a given geographic unit was also tied to a consequence of carrying out a specific development project. The change in touristic attractiveness was then used as a surrogate measure for net foreign exchange earnings. The tools utilized to enhance the study results were all about optimization. Since then, we have seen a good number of research projects on the topic in different tourism settings and countries (e.g., Ritchie & Zins, 1978; Tang & Rochananond, 1990; Nyberg, 1995; Lundgren, 2004; Cracolici & Nijkamp, 2008, Iatu & Bulai, 2011; Lee, Qu, & Huang, 2009).

The type of research that utilized management science and quantitative analysis with judgment-aided approaches in the field of tourism and hospitality has appeared not on a regular basis, but rather sporadically in tourism and hospitality and allied journals. From the mid-1970s to the early-1980s, there was limited research that focused on management science applications in tourism and hospitality (e.g., Var, Beck, & Loftus, 1977; Liberman & Yechiali, 1978; Gapinski & Tuckman, 1978). From the 1980s to the 1990s, we witnessed an increase in research that utilized management science tools, and since then the trend has shown an upward movement in research (Zhang, Song, & Huang, 2009; Liu, Tzeng, & Lee, 2012). This trend is likely to continue in the future. As Wöber (2002) in his well-received book "Benchmarking in Tourism and Hospitality Industries: The Selection of Benchmarking Partners" points out that some of the management science-based business performance measurements, gap identification, solutions, and studies of best practices will continue to grow and gain further attention in the field of tourism and hospitality.

One of the most recent treatises of management science applications in tourism and hospitality was created by Gu Zheng (2004) who guest-edited a special issue titled "Management Science Applications in Tourism and Hospitality" which was co-published simultaneously in the *Journal of Travel and Hospitality Marketing* (16, 2/3, 2004) and as a monograph. This volume contains eight pieces that focus on destination benchmarking with a multi-criteria approach (Wöber & Fesenmaier, 2004); restaurant productivity assessment (Reynolds, 2004), data envelopment in hotel productivity (Hu & Cai, 2004); data envelopment analysis (DEA) for benchmarking productivity in the hotel sector (Sigala, 2004); modeling demand with decision-rules-based approach (Law, Goh, & Pine, 2004) and forecasting hotel occupancy (Law, 2004); forecasting in short-term planning with a casino buffet restaurant (e.g., Hu, Chen, & McCain-Chen, 2004); and destination-positioning decisions with perception analysis (Dolnicar & Grabler, 2004). Most of these papers provide context-specific implications for decision makers and some directions for future research. Although the scope of the applications and issues presented in the monograph are limited in its coverage and topics, the volume certainly contributes to the growing body of the scholarly tourism and hospitality literature.

The academic scope of management science in today's world is rather interdisciplinary and not always necessarily quantitative. The topics dealt with may include such areas as data analytics and data mining, decision support and analysis, DEA, forecasting, revenue management, game theory, logistics, supply chain management, mathematical modeling, optimization, probability and statistics, risk management, project management, simulation, network modeling and analysis, transportation forecasting models, and industrial engineering and design. Regardless of the nature of tools and approaches we may have, the aim is to use rational, systematic, and science-based techniques to generate knowledge and improve decisions of all kinds.

One of the streams of research that has attracted a great deal of systematic attention from researchers is in the area of forecasting and demand estimation at different spatial levels and assessment of economic impacts of tourism and hospitality activities (e.g., Seward & Spinrad, 1982; Johnson & Thomas, 1992; Witt & Witt, 1992; Jones & Munday, 2008; Dwyer, Forsyth, & Dwyer, 2010), tourism and yield management and measurement (Dwyer et al., 2006; Ingold, McMahon-Beattie, & Yeoman, 2000). This may be attributed largely to the fact that economic implications of demand for travel and hospitality products and services are enormous and also have policy and resource allocation implications. This stream of research has been extensively examined since the early-1980s and will continue in the future.

The first book on tourism demand-estimation models was published by Brian Archer (1976) in the 1970s, and since then we have seen a good number of well-received books (e.g., Johnson & Thomas, 1992; Frechtling, 1996; Romilly, Liu, & Song, 1998; Croes, 2000; Wong & Song, 2002; Witt & Witt, 1992) published in the field of tourism and hospitality as researchers continue to do research with improved and advanced approaches to further shed light on the complexity of demand estimation and forecasting methods (e.g., Yu & Schwartz, 2006; Song, Witt, & Li, 2009).

In recent years, we have also seen a number of studies that focus on measuring performance and gap identification, monitoring performance in tourism and hospitality settings (e.g., Pyo, 2001; Wöber, 2002). Most of these developmental efforts resulted in generating and developing goal- and context-oriented indexes and index scores that are generally used to measure and monitor regional tourism activity, lodging and accommodation use, investment performance, restaurant growth and opportunity, room comfort, and tourist intensity and development (e.g., Bond & McDonald, 1978; Keogh, 1984; Pearce & Elliott, 1983; Uysal & McDonald, 1989; Hinch, 1990; Backman, Uysal, & Backman, 1992; Oppermann, 1992; Potts & Uysal, 1992; Uysal, Oh, & O'Leary, 1995; Gu, 1994; Huan & O'Leary, 1999; Reynolds & Biel, 2007; Beck et al., 2010). A few of these indices and measures are similar to financial performance measures and business ratios that are common tools to finance and accounting fields. A recent special issue of *Tourism Analysis* (Vol 19, no. 4, 2014) on "Performance Measurement and Management in Tourism" was guest-edited by Frederick Dimanche. This particular issue included eight pieces that help to advance our understanding and practice of tourism performance measurement and management, either at the destination or at the organizing level (Dimanche, 2014). It is stressed that in order to be effective, the tourism enterprise needs to go from measurement to management, challenging us to seek and implement ways to improve organizational performance with available tools and approaches, whether it be quantitative or qualitative and or a combination of the two approaches to developing performance measures. This stream of research is an area that will continue to be important and requires further research.

In today's highly dynamic business environment, there will be an increased demand for a wider use of performance measurement methods under the stream of benchmarking research. We hope to see more efforts directed toward this line of research. With this backdrop depicting the notion of management science applications in the field of tourism and hospitality, we edited this book, hoping that it contributes to the growing body of knowledge in the field and encourage researchers to further advance the scope and coverage of this stream of research with appropriate implications.

Another area of research that enjoys a great deal of systematic research attention has occurred in the area of revenue management. The practice of optimizing revenue and profit in capacity constrained sections of the tourism industry such as airlines, hotels, car rentals, and other has gained prominence in the past 30 years. The three elements of a typical revenue management cycle include forecasting, setting controls, and monitoring (AHLA, 1994). They are all well served by advanced theories and models in management science. First, consider the multiple horizons repeated forecasting in this challenging dynamic, granular level advanced reservation setting. It requires the application of uniquely designed and creative approaches to forecasting such as the pickup models and the forecasting combinations of advanced reservation with established historical/actual demand patterns (e.g., Schwartz & Hiemstra, 1997). The forecasting task is further complicated because the data are subject-to-patterns "distortion." As the field of revenue management progresses, an increasing portion of the data reflects revenue management response to observed and predicted demand levels, and shifts, as well as game theoretic behavior of competing companies and customers, both contributing to the challenge of making efficient use of the data to generate accurate demand predictions (e.g., Schwartz 1996, 1997, Schwartz & Cohen, 2003). The controls setting phase is about setting prices and allocating units to prices and to distribution channels in a manner that will optimize revenues and profits. This is a classic area of management science applications where early simple optimization efforts included mathematical programing which was replaced in recent years with more appropriate expected marginal revenue type of optimization and overbooking models. The third phase of monitoring is perhaps the most neglected at this time and calls for most attention from management science researchers. We are yet to develop appropriate tools to assess the true contribution of various revenue management policies and practices and correctly assess the accuracy of various forecasting efforts. Of particular interest are the questions of performance measurements (revenue vs. profits) given the shift toward total revenue management, the increasing role and influence of customers' sentiment and their online activity, and the emergence of big data and text analytics as major influencers on the type and level of revenue management activities.

As seen from this general review of exiting research, publications covering management science applications in the field of tourism and hospitality are limited in number and sporadic in comparison to the attention afforded to tourism marketing and development issues of the field. So, what is the contribution of this book?

1.3　CONTRIBUTION OF THIS BOOK

Our main goal for this book is to serve as a reference from the unique perspective of management science applications in tourism and hospitality settings, and to keep researchers and decision makers abreast with new developments as they impact our approaches to solutions and decision making.

Our goal is not to cover every possible subject that may fall under the realm of management science but rather offer a selection of topics that would exemplify the best work of our contributors and provide a portfolio of applications that represents the issues of the field of tourism and hospitality. We believe that this book will be of great interest to students of tourism and hospitality. In addition, hospitality and tourism researchers and practitioners may find the book very useful in understanding the richness of management science applications and their associated management implications in the field of tourism and hospitality.

1.4   OVERVIEW OF THE CONTENTS

More than 30 outstanding scholars representing several countries contributed their work to this book. We have invited those researchers who have the knowledge and expertise to share their work under the umbrella of the focus of the book, "Management Science in Hospitality and Tourism: Theory, Practice and Applications." They infuse their passion into their writings when communicating their expertise regarding their respective topics. The field of tourism and hospitality is dynamic and complex. While introducing the chapters, we paraphrased summary points of the chapters to some extent and relied on what our contributors provided rather generously. With this acknowledgement, we introduce the chapters in the following section.

Chapter 2 "Complex Tourism Systems: A Quantitative Approach" by Rodolfo Baggio and Giacomo Del Chiappa argues that tourism destinations are also complex dynamic systems; knowing their structural and dynamic characteristics is certainly needed to reach an effective governance that in turn can allow to obtain sustainable growth and destination competitiveness. The aim of this chapter is to briefly present and discuss the most common and used techniques, such as agent-based modeling, nonlinear analysis of time series, and network analysis, their main aims and tools. Further, the chapter provides information on the requirements of these techniques in terms of data collection and software applications. In doing this, examples from recent literature are described, and implications for a "good governance" practice are suggested. Finally, the chapter ends with a number of suggestions for future research.

Chapter 3 "Monitoring and Forecasting Tourist Activities with Big Data" by Bing Pan and Yang Yang provides a conceptual framework that connects the types of big data with stages of travel. The chapter reviews literature on the use of big data sources in the tourism industry, including data gathered from search queries, Web analytics, customer reviews, location tracking data, and social media. Most existing studies have focused on building behavioral models and validating correlational relationships between travel behavior and big data. The chapter states that research on personalization, optimization, and resource allocation is lacking, and studies involving forecasting with big data for specific properties or businesses are also rare. Nonetheless, the combination of multiple data sources possesses a huge potential to dramatically improve the accuracy of forecasting and monitoring. The authors of the chapter indicate that although privacy concerns and business boundaries may limit the widespread adoption, application, and sharing of big data, as the related technology matures and big data productivity increases, its full impact and significance for the tourism industry will emerge.

Chapter 4 "Micro-Marketing and Big Data Analytics: An Information System for Destination Marketing Management" by Daniel R. Fesenmaier, Neeraj Bharadwaj, Jason Stienmetz, and Zheng Xiang presents that in recent years, the ability of marketers to create a "market of one" has improved substantially as information technology has enhanced our capacity to understand consumers with a variety of ways to collect, manage, analyze, and interpret massive amounts of data. However, destination marketing organizations seem to be lagging behind the curve of technological innovations due to their inability to adapt and lack of control over the marketplace. This chapter describes a destination management system (DMS) that combines micro-marketing concepts with big data analytics in order to meet the needs of visitors to a destination more effectively and efficiently. The chapter first discusses the paradigm shift in destination marketing from mass marketing to micro-marketing and the technological foundations that support this transition. Then, it outlines a DMS called the Northern Indiana Travel Network specifically designed for the Northern Indiana Tourism Development Commission which is in charge of tourism development and marketing for a region located in the northern part of the State of Indiana. Finally, the discussion focuses on the unique characteristics of micro-markets in tourism and the potential for integrating big data analytics into the practice of destination management.

In Chapter 5 "Best-Worst Scaling Method: Application to Hospitality and Tourism Research," Eli Cohen and Larry Lockshin point out that many tourism and hospitality studies apply rating scales (such as Likert-type scales of 1–5 or 1–7) to each attribute to measure consumers' preferences. Provided that the rating scales are interval in nature, then the analyses of the data are straightforward, but the results can be biased. The authors of the chapter stress that respondents do not use ratings the same way across respondents and people may limit their responses to certain parts of a rating scale. This is more accentuated across countries and cultures. Another issue is that ratings of attributes measured independently often result in scores, which are too similar or too difficult to interpret. Respondents rate each attribute separately without considering the association with the other attributes and are not forced to make trade-offs between the relative importances of attributes. The chapter presents the method of Best Worst Scaling, as a new method of forced choice and its application. Furthermore, the chapter uses examples in tourism and restaurant issues to demonstrate the method and its advantages that overcome the limitations of other methods of measurements such as Likert-type rating methods.

In Chapter 6 "Using Partial Least Squares Structural Equation Modeling (PLS-SEM) in Tourism Research," Rob Hallak and Guy Assaker explain the variance-based procedure of SEM known as Partial Least Squares Structural Equation Modeling (PLS-SEM) which remains new to tourism research despite its rapid growth in other business disciplines. The chapter illustrates the advantages of PLS-SEM in examining models where the assumptions for applying traditional (covariance based) SEM methods are not met. In particular, the authors of the chapter argue that PLS-SEM works best when: (1) the aim is prediction, the phenomenon investigated is relatively new, and measurement models need to be developed; (2) the conditions relating to sample size, independence, or normal distribution are not met; (3) the relationships between the indicators and latent factors must be modeled in different modes (i.e., formative and reflective measurement models); and (4) the model is complex with a large number of latent constructs and/or includes higher order molecular and molar models. The chapter further presents the necessary criteria and "rules of thumb" for analyzing model validity for both the outer (measurement) models, as well as the inner (structural models). A working example of PLS-SEM analysis is illustrated through examining a structural model of tourism entrepreneurship performance. This explains how PLS-SEM is used to evaluate models with higher order, reflective, and formative constructs. The chapter concludes with recommendations on the future application of PLS-SEM in tourism research.

In Chapter 7 "Quantity and Quality Issues in Demand for Tourism" Aliza Fleischer submits that total vacation expenditure will increase with an increase in income but in order to understand the impact on the industry, there is a need to disentangle the expenditure into its components. The method developed by the author of this chapter and her colleagues (2008, 2011) enables this disentanglement and provides an understanding of what might be the changes in vacation expenditures when households enjoy an increase in income cross-section. The comparison conducted in this chapter provides a further insight into the two aforementioned studies that were conducted by her and her colleagues; namely, a temporal aspect of what happens over time not only cross-sectional change. Policy makers and managers in the travel and tourism industry can be assisted in their decision-making process by better understanding that an increase in income generates a rise in vacation expenditures but at a decreasing rate. The proposition is that the wealthier the household becomes, the less is the increase in income expenditures on vacation. However, when decision makers have to decide whether to upgrade the tourism services or expand their facilities they have to take into consideration the shift in income elasticities from quantity to quality and thus the option of upgrading is gaining weight compared to expanding.

Chapter 8 "Time Series Models for Capacity Management in the Hospitality Industry" by Tianshu Zheng provides researchers and industry practitioners with easy-to-follow step-by-step instructions of using several effective and efficient time-series analysis and forecasting methods to facilitate their capacity management-related research and decision making. In addition to explaining some fundamental time-series forecasting concepts such as seasonality and autocorrelation, this chapter also uses real data from the hospitality and tourism industry to demonstrate the procedures of using Simple Moving Average Method, Single Exponential Smoothing Method, Multiplicative Hold-Winters Method, Regression, and Box–Jenkins Procedure. These methods are capable of modeling a variety of time series in the hospitality and tourism industry for capacity management purpose and producing satisfactory forecasts. In addition, this chapter suggests future studies on combined methods that will potentially improve forecasting accuracy.

In Chapter 9 "An Extended Gravity Model: Applying Destination Competitiveness," Jeong-Yeol Park and SeeCheong (Shawn) Jang argue that due to the substantial growth of tourism, various studies have employed different forms of gravity models. However, previous models had limitations in terms of generalizing their results. This is primarily due to their focus on specific regions or variables for special events or components of tourism. Thus, the primary objective of this chapter is to present an extended gravity model that can more generally explain tourism flows. The method followed in the chapter adopted components of destination competitiveness as complementary variables and a panel data framework to include the cross-sectional and time effects in the model. The result shows that the proposed model has greater explanatory power than traditional gravity models. Additionally, along with gravity variables, destination competitiveness components, such as natural and cultural resources, general and tourism infrastructure, price competitiveness, and openness, have significant effects on tourism flows.

Chapter 10 "Efficacy of Static Shift Share Analysis in Measuring Tourism Industry's Performance in South Carolina" by Tarik Doğru and Ercan Sirakaya-Turk demonstrates the efficacy and the application of a static shift–share analysis (SSA) in examining the performance of tourism industry in South Carolina, USA. SSA is a popular model that is frequently used in the fields of economics, political economy, marketing, geography, and urban studies. It is a relatively simple method for describing regional economic growth, measuring policy effects, and forecasting future growth of a region. This method measures the change of a region's performance relative to the nation over a given period. The chapter concludes with policy and strategy recommendations for South Carolina on future tourism development.

Chapter 11 "Destination Attractiveness Based on Supply and Demand Evaluations," by Sandro Formica and Muzaffer Uysal presents a model to explain and measure the determinants of tourist attractiveness of a destination by measuring supply and demand indicators. The guiding principle of the chapter foundation is that the overall tourist attractiveness of a destination is dependent upon the relationship between the availability of existing attractions and the perceived importance of such attractions. The method uses qualitative and quantitative statistical analyses to inventory, group, and measure the existing attraction portfolio and its perceived importance. The findings confirm that tourist regions are not created equal and reveal significant spatial differences in terms of resource availability and actual perception of these resources. The proposed framework could be used as a decision-making tool in planning, marketing, and developing appropriate resource allocation strategies.

Chapter 12 "Overbooking Research in the Lodging Industry: From Origins in Airlines to What Lies Ahead" by Matthew Krawczyk, Timothy Webb, Zvi Schwartz, and Muzaffer Uysal presents a review of hotel over-booking literature, showing the progression of research into the present day. Evolving from the airline industry, overbooking research in the lodging industry has seen substantial development in its related empirical models. Beginning with a dynamic programming approach, previous works have shifted in focus over time to address heuristics, simulations, Yield Management principles, and customer perceptions of overbooking practices. Analysis of this development serves to give present-day researchers a more thorough comprehension of the research foundations of overbooking in the lodging industry. Major works are discussed with their main contributions to our understanding of overbooking models. A few of the models that represent some of the most fundamental shifts in the stream of literature are also presented. The current state of knowledge concerning the area is discussed, as well as some conclusions about what the future holds.

Chapter 13 "Evaluating Forecasting Performance: Accuracy Measures and their Application in Hospitality" by Larissa Koupriouchina, Jean-Pierre van der Rest, Zvi Schwartz, and Dirk Sierag points out that although forecasting is crucial in hotel revenue management, not enough attention is given to the question of how forecasting quality should be systematically and consistently evaluated or what accuracy measures should be used in hotel revenue management research and practicum. This chapter demonstrates how various, widely-used, forecasting accuracy measures are calculated and presents known and recorded advantages and disadvantages of each measure. This characterization is based on both theoretical considerations and empirical observations from both the general literature on forecasting and using the authors' own data from hotel revenue management operations. Finally, the chapter cautions against unconsidered usage of measures by illustrating how different measures may generate contradictory results and lead to misjudgment in evaluating forecasting accuracy.

In Chapter 14 "Frontier Approaches for Performance Measurement in the Hospitality and Tourism Industries" Albert Assaf and Frank Agbola review the parametric and nonparametric frontier methods for efficiency measurement and illustrate their advantages and disadvantages. The chapter provides researchers in tourism and hospitality with guidance on how to estimate these methods using an interesting application on Australian hotels. Furthermore, the chapter discusses the various software available and the advantages and limitations of each type. The results from the chapter application clearly illustrates the need for tourism studies to compare between the efficiency results derived from various frontier approaches in order to validate the findings. The authors also discuss various situations in which one approach is better than the other and highlighted some weaknesses in existing studies. The chapter ends with some discussed latest methodological advances in the area and provides some guidance for future research in the field of hospitality and tourism.

Chapter 15 "Managing tourist satisfaction: An index approach" by Jason Li Chen, Gang Li and Haiyan Song introduces the tourist-satisfaction index approach as a framework to manage tourist satisfaction at different levels. The chapter reviews the development of the theoretical framework of the tourist-satisfaction index. The applications of the index framework are demonstrated through case studies. In the chapter, the tourist-satisfaction in-dex framework is a dual-model system. The first model is designed to evalu-ate tourist satisfaction and its antecedents and consequences at a particular-service level and generate a satisfaction index at this level of service. The second model aims to aggregate the tourist satisfaction at the previous level and produce an aggregate-satisfaction index. It is argued that the tourist-satisfaction index framework can be applied across various levels of service encounters, such as departments, firms, service sectors, source markets, and destinations. The framework is able to track changes in service performance over time. The authors of the chapter indicate that monitoring the dynamic changes of the tourist-satisfaction index scores can help evaluate the success and effectiveness of relevant business strategies and government policies.

Chapter 16: "Toward Increased Accuracy in Productivity Measurement: Evidence-Based Analytics" Cherylynn Becker argues that in spite of over 100 years of research, the relationships among workforce productivity, organizational profitability, and the impact of various management activi-ties implemented to increase productivity remain fuzzy. Evidence-based management and analytics have emerged to offer a new model for exam-ining these relationships. The chapter focuses on a review of productivity research over the last century and identifies the key issues associated with measurement that have undermined efforts to establish meaningful values for labor productivity in existing research or support-hypothesized relation-ships. Examples from hospitality studies are highlighted. Explanations are provided to illustrate how the newer models associated with evidence-based management and analytics are positioned to overcome the deficiencies of the past. The chapter also presents the prevalent approaches used by hospitality firms and hospitality researchers to assess productivity and organizational performance and explains how the newer concepts of evidence-based man-agement and human resources analytics have the potential to offer improved insights to aid managerial decision making.

Finally, Chapter 17 "Performance Measures and Use in Hospitality" by Ersem Karadag focuses on the most common financial and nonfinancial mea-surement tools used in the hospitality industry. These measurement tools are presented in two categories: financial and nonfinancial measurement tools. Companies use financial measurement tools, often called key performance indicators, to measure, manage, and communicate operational results. The traditional management accounting literature advocates the use of financial performance measures as the basis of many decisions. On the other hand, the use of nonfinancial performance measures is rather relatively new. Managers and other stakeholders have been utilizing financial measures for a long time, but globalization, competitive forces, market dynamics, and deregulation in the airline industry have changed the business environment and forced companies to seek out and utilize nonfinancial tools. Nonfinancial measures usually derive from nonfinancial resources, such as guest satisfaction, employee satisfaction, competitiveness, customer loyalty, service quality, customer retention rate, innovation, social responsibility, etc. The author of the chapter argues that there is a strong correlation between the quality of managerial decisions and selected performance measurement tools. Performance metrics are vital tools in any organization to build accountability and motivate managers to meet pre-established goals or standards. Without utilizing performance measurement tools, a company is unable to make successful plans, control the operation and measures organizational effectiveness.

ACKNOWLEDGMENTS

A book like this would not have been possible without the generous and full support from our esteemed colleagues around the world. We thank all the contributors and are grateful for sharing their time, talent, and expertise in writing their valuable chapters. We are also grateful for the support and encouragement of Apple Academic Press and Series Editor Dr. Mahmood Khan for helping to shape this book to reach its current form. Finally, we thank our family members for their constant support.

KEYWORDS

- management science
- theory and applications
- tourism and hospitality
- quantitate analysis
- forecasting
- performance measures
- yield management
- revenue management

REFERENCES

AHLA. *Revenue Management: A Technology Primer*. American Hotel & Lodging Association: Lansing, MI, 1994.

Archer, B. H. *Demand Forecasting in Tourism*. University of Wales Press: Bangor, Wales, 1976.

Assaf, A. G.; Agbola, F. W. Modelling the Performance of Australian Hotels: A DEA Double Bootstrap Approach. *Tourism Econ.* **2011,** *17*(1), 73–89.

Assaf, A.; Barros, C. P.; Josiassen, A. Hotel Efficiency: A Bootstrapped Metafrontier Approach. *Int. J. Hosp. Manage.* **2010,** 29(3), 468–475.

Assaf, A. G; Gillen, D. Measuring the Joint Impact of Governance Form and Economic Regulation on Airport Efficiency. *Eur. J. Oper. Res.* **2012,** *220*(1), 187–198.

Assaf, A. G.; Dwyer, L. Benchmarking International Tourism Destinations. *Tourism Econ.* **2013,** *19*(6), 1233–1247.

Assaf, A. G.; Josiassen, A. Identifying and Ranking the Determinants of Tourism Performance: A Global Investigation. *J. Travel Res.* **2012,** *51*(4), 388–399.

Assaf, A. G.; Agbola, F. W. Efficiency Analysis of the Australian Accommodation Industry: A Bayesian Output Distance Function. *J. Hospitality Tourism Res.* **2014,** *38*(1), 116–132.

Backman, K. F.; Uysal, M.; Backman, S. J. Index Number: A Tourism Managerial and Policy-Making Tool. *J. Appl. Recreation J.* **1992,** *17*(2), 158–177.

Badinelli, R. D. An Optimal, Dynamic Policy for Hotel Yield Management. *Eur. J. Oper. Res.* **2000,** *121*(3), 476–503.

Baggio, R. Symptoms of Complexity in a Tourism System. *Tourism Anal.* **2008,** *13*(1), 1–20.

Baggio, R.; Klobas, J. *Quantitate Methods in Tourism: A Handbook*. Channel View Publications: Bristol, 2011.

Baker, T. K.; & Collier, D. A. A Comparative Revenue Analysis of Hotel Yield Management Heuristics. *Decision Sci.* **1999,** *30*(1), 239–263.

Barros, C. A. P.; Santos, C. A. The Measurement of Efficiency in Portuguese Hotels Using Data Envelopment Analysis. *J. Hospitality Tourism Res.* **2006,** *30*(3), 378–400.

Barros, C. P. Measuring Efficiency in the Hotel Sector. *Ann. Tourism Res.* **2005,** *32*(2), 456–477.

Baum, Joel A. C.; Ingram, P. Survival-Enhancing Learning in the Manhattan Hotel Industry, 1898–1980. *Manage. Sci.* **1998,** *44*(7), 996–1016.

Beck, J.; Knutson, B.; Kim, S. Y.; Cha, J. M. Developing the Dimensions of Activities Important to Successful Revenue Management Performance: An Application of the Lodging Industry. *Int. J. Revenue Manage.* **2010,** *4*(3/4), 268–283.

Bitran, G. R.; Gilbert, S. M. Managing Hotel Reservations with Uncertain Arrivals. *Oper. Res.* **1996,** *44*(1), 35–49.

Bitran, G. R.; Mondschein, S. V. An Application of Yield Management to the Hotel Industry Considering Multiple Day Stays. *Oper. Res.* **1995,** *43*(3), 427–443.

Bond, M. E.; McDonald, B. Tourism Barometers: The Arizona Case. *J. Travel Res.* 1978, *17*, 14–17.

Cesario, F. J. Operations Research in Outdoor Recreation. *J. Leisure Res.* **1969,** *1*, 33–51.

Cesario, F. J. A New Method for Analyzing Outdoor Recreation Trip Data. *J. Leisure Res.* **1975,** *7*(3), 200–215.

Chen, C. F. Applying the Stochastic Frontier Approach to Measure Hotel Managerial Efficiency in Taiwan. *Tourism Manage.* **2007,** *28*(3), 696–702.

Cooper, C. Knowledge Management and Tourism. *Ann. Tourism Res.* **2005,** *33*(1), 47–64.

Cracolici, M. F.; Nijkamp, P. The Attractiveness and Competitiveness of Tourist Destinations: A Study of Southern Italian Regions. *Tourism Manage.* **2008,** *30*, 336–344.

Croes, R. R. *Anatomy of Demand in International Tourism: The Case of Aruba*. Van Gorcum: The Netherlands, 2000.

Dimanche, F. Introduction: Performance Measurement and Management in Tourism. *Tourism Anal.* **2014,** *19*(4), 397–399.

Dolnicar, S.; Garbler, K. Applying City Perception Analysis (CPA) for Destination Positioning Decisions. In *Management Science Applications in Tourism and Hospitality*; Zheng, G., Ed.; The Haworth Hospitality Press, Inc.: Binghamton, NY, 2004; pp 99–112.

Dwyer, L.; Forsyth, D.; Dwyer, D. *Tourism Economics and Policy*. Channel View Publications: Bristol, U.K., 2010.

Dwyer, L.; Forsyth, P.; Fredline, L.; Jago, L.; Deery, M.; Lundie, S. *Concepts of Tourism Yield and their Measurement*. CRC for Sustainable Tourism Pty Ltd: Australia, 2006.

Fantazy, K.; Kumar, V.; Kumar, U. Supply Management Practices and Performance in the Canadian Hospitality Industry. *Int. J. Hospitality Manage.* **2012,** *29*, 685–693.

Frechtling, D. C. *Practical Tourism Forecasting*. Butterworth-Heinemann: London, U.K., 1996.

Gapinski, J. H.; Tuckman, H. P. Amtrak, Auto-Train, and Vacation Travel to Florida: Little Trains that Could. *Manage. Sci.* **1978,** *24*, 1109–1116.

Gearing, C.; Swart, W.; Var, T. *Planning for Tourism Development: Quantitate Approaches*. Preager Publishers: New York, 1976.

Gearing, C.; Swart, W.; Var, T. Determining the Optimal Investment Policy for the Tourism Sector of a Developing Country. *Manage. Sci.* **1973,** *20*, 487–497.

Gu, Z. Hospitality Investment Return, Risk and Performance Indexes: A Ten Year Examination. *Hospitality Res. J.* **1994,** *17*(3), 17–26.

Guo, Y.; Ling, L.; Dong, Y.; Liang, L. Cooperation Contract in Tourism Supply Chains: The Optimal Pricing Strategy of Hotels for Cooperative Third Party Strategic Websites. *Ann. Tourism Res.* **2012,** *41*, 20–41.

Hara, T. *Quantitative Tourism Analysis*. Butterworth-Heinemann: London, U.K., 2011.

Hayes, D. K.; Miller, A. *Revenue Management for the Hospitality Industry*. Wiley: New York, 2011.

Hinch, T. D. A Spatial Analysis of Tourist Accommodation in Ontario. *J. Appl. Recreation J.* **1990,** *15*(4), 239–264.

Hu, B.; Cai, L. A. Hotel Labor Productivity Assessment: A Data Envelopment Analysis. In *Management Science Applications in Tourism and Hospitality*; Zheng, G., Ed.; The Haworth Hospitality Press, Inc.: Binghamton, NY, 2004; pp 27–38.

Hu, C.; Chen, M.; McCain-Chen, S. L. (2004). Forecasting in Short Term Planning and Management for Casino Buffet Restaurant. In *Management Science Applications in Tourism and Hospitality*; Zheng, G., Ed.; The Haworth Hospitality Press, Inc.: Binghamton, NY, 2004; pp 79–98.

Huan, T. C; O'Leary, J. T. *Measuring Tourism Performance*. Sagamore Publishing: Champaign, IL, 1999.

Huyton, J. R.; Thomas, S. Application of Yield Management to the Hotels Industry. In *Yield Management: Strategies for the Service Industries*, Ingold, A., McMahon-Beattie U., Yeoman I., Eds.; Continuum, New York, 2000; pp 256–270.

Iatu, C.; Bulai, M. New approach in Evaluating Tourism Attractiveness in the Region of Moldavia. *Int. J. Energy Environ.* **2011,** *2*(5), 165–174.

Ingold, A.; McMahon-Beattie, U.; Yeoman, I., Eds. *Yield Management: Strategies for the Service Industries*. Continuum: New York, 2000.

Johnson, P.; Thomas, B. 1992. *Choice and Demand in Tourism*. Mansell: New York, NY.

Jones, C.; Munday, M. Tourism Satellite Accounts and Impact Assessments: Some Considerations. *Tourism Anal.* **2008,** *13*(1), 53–70.

Jones, P. Defining Yield Management and Measuring its Impact on Hotel Performance. In *Yield Management: Strategies for the Service Industries*, Ingold A., McMahon-Beattie U., Yeoman I., Eds.; Continuum: New York, 2000; pp 85–97.

Keogh, B. The Measurement of Spatial Variations in Tourist Activity. *Ann. Tourism Res.* **1984,** *11*, 267–282.

Kimes, S. E. Yield management: A Tool for Capacity-Considered Service Firms. *J. Oper. Manage.* **1989,** *8*(4), 348–363.

Kimes, S. E. The Future of Hotel Revenue Management. *J. Revenue Pricing Manage.* **2011,** *10*(1), 62–72.

Kozak, M. *Destination Benchmarking: Concepts, Practices and Operations*. CABI: U.K., 2003.

Law, R. Initially Testing an Improved Extrapolative Hotel Room Occupancy Rate Forecasting Technique. In *Management Science Applications in Tourism and Hospitality*; Zheng, G., Ed.; The Haworth Hospitality Press, Inc.: Binghamton, NY, 2004; pp. 71–78.

Law, R.; Goh, C.; Pine, R. Modeling Tourism Demand: A Decision Rules Based Approach. In *Management Science Applications in Tourism and Hospitality*; Zheng, G., Ed.; The Haworth Hospitality Press, Inc.: Binghamton, NY, 2004; pp 61–70.

Lee, C.-F.; Qu, W.-M. O.; Huang, H.-I. Study of Destination Attractiveness through Domestic Visitors' Perspectives: The Case of Taiwan's Hot Springs Tourism Sector. *Asia-Pacific J. Tourism Res.* **2009,** *14*(1), 17–38.

Liberman, V.; Yechiali, U. On the Hotel Overbooking Problem—An Inventory system with Stochastic Cancelations. *Manage. Sci.* **1978,** *24*, 1117–1126.

Liu, C. H.; Tzeng, G. H., & Lee, M. H. Improving Tourism Policy Implementation—The Use of Hybrid MCDM Models. *Tourism Manage.* **2012,** *33*, 413–426.

Love, R. R.; Hoey, J. M. Management Science Improves Fast-Food Operations. *Interface* **1990,** *20*(2), 21–29.

Lundgren, A. Micro-simulation Modelling of Domestic Tourism Travel Patterns in Sweden. *The 7th International Forum on Tourism Statistics*, Stockholm, Sweden, June 9–11, 2004.

Mayer-Schonberger, V.; Cukier, K. *Big Data*. Mariber Books: Boston, MA, 2013.

Nyberg, L. Determinants of the Attractiveness of a Tourism Region. In *Tourism Marketing and Management Handbook*; Witt S. F.; Moutinho L., Eds.; Prentice Hall: Hertfordshire, 1995, pp 29–38.

Oppermann, M. Travel Dispersal Index. *J. Tourism Stud.* **1992,** *3*(1), 44–49.

Pearce, D. G.; Elliott, J. M. C. The Trip Index. *J. Travel Res.* **1983,** *22*(1), 6–9.

Potts, T.; Uysal, M. Tourism Intensity as a Function of Accommodations. *J. Travel Res.* **1992,** *31*(2), 40–43.

Pullman, M.; Rodgers, S. Capacity Management for Hospitality and Tourism: A Review of Current Approaches. *Int. J. Hospitality Manage.* **2010,** *29*, 177–187.

Pyo, S., Ed. *Benchmarks in Hospitality and Tourism.* Routledge: London, U.K., 2001.

Reynolds, D. (2004). An Exploratory Investigation of Multiunit Restaurant Productivity Assessment Using Data Envelopment Analysis. In *Management Science Applications in Tourism and Hospitality*; Zheng, G., Ed.; The Haworth Hospitality Press, Inc.: Binghamton, NY, 2004; pp 19–26.

Reynolds, D.; Biel, D. Incorporating Satisfaction Measures into a Restaurant Productivity Index. *Int. J. Hospitality Manage.* **2007**, *26*(2), 352–361.

Reynolds, D.; Thompson, G. M. Multiunit Restaurant Productivity Assessment Using Three-Phase Data Envelopment Analysis. *Int. J. Hospitality Manage.* **2007**, *26*(1), 20–32.

Ritchie, B. J. R., & Zins M. Culture as a Determinant of the Attractiveness of a Tourist Region. *Ann. Tourism Res.* **1978**, *5*(2), 252–267.

Romilly, P.; Liu X. M.; Song Y. Economic and Social Determinants of International Tourism Spending: A Panel Data Analysis. *Tourism Anal.* **1998**, *3*(1), 3–16.

Rivera, M. A., & Pizam, A. (2015). Advances in hospitality research: "from Rodney Dangerfield to Aretha Franklin". *International Journal of Contemporary Hospitality Management*, 27(3), 362–378.

Schwartz Z. A Dynamic Equilibrium Pricing Model: A Game Theoretic Approach to Modeling Conventions' Room Rates. *Tourism Econ.* **1996**, *2*(3), 251–263.

Schwartz Z. Game Theory: Mathematical Models Provide Insights into Hospitality Industry Phenomena. *J. Hospitality Tourism Res.* **1997**, Special issue: *Adv. Res. Methods Hospitality Res.*, *21*(1), 48–70.

Schwartz Z.; Hiemstra, S. Improving the Accuracy of Hotel Reservations Forecasting: Curves Similarity Approach. *J. Travel Res.* **1997**, *36*(1), 3–14.

Schwartz, Z. The Confusing Side of Yield Management: Myths, Errors, and Misconceptions. *J. Hospitality Tourism Res.* 1998, 22(4), 413–430.

Schwartz, Z. Advanced Booking and Revenue Management: Room Rates and the Consumers' Strategic Zones. *Int. J. Hospitality Manage.* **2006**, *25*(3), 447–462.

Schwartz, Z.; Cohen, E. Hotel Revenue Management with Group Discount Room Rates. *J. Hospitality Tourism Res.* **2003**, *27*(1), 24–47.

Schwartz, Z.; Stewart, W.; Buckland, E. Visitation at Capacity-Constrained Tourism Destinations: Exploring Revenue Management at a National Park. *Tourism Manage.* **2012**, *33*(3), 500–508.

Seward, S. B.; Spinrad, B. K. *Tourism in the Caribbean: The Economic Impact.* International Development Research Center: Ottawa, Canada; 1982.

Sigala, M. Using Data Envelopment Analysis for Marketing and Benchmarking Productivity in the Hotel Sector. In *Management Science Applications in Tourism and Hospitality*; Zheng, G., Ed.; The Haworth Hospitality Press, Inc.: Binghamton, NY, 2004; pp 39–60.

Smith, B. C.; Leimkuhler, J. F.; Darrow, R. Yield Management at America Airlines. *Interface* **1992**, *22*(1), 8–31.

Song, H. *Tourism Supply Chain Management.* Routledge: London, U.K., 2012.

Song, H.; Witt, S. F.; Li, G. *The Advanced Econometrics of Tourism Demand.* Routledge: Oxon, U.K., 2009.

Sun, S.; Lu, W. M. Evaluating the Performance of the Taiwanese Hotel Industry Using a Weight Slacks-Based Measure. *Asia-Pacific J. Oper. Res.* **2005**, *22*(04), 487–512.

Swart, W.; Var, T.; Gearing, C. Operation Research Applications to Tourism. *Ann. Tourism Res.* 1978, October/December, 414–428.

Talluri, K. T.; Van Ryzin, G. J. *The Theory and Practice of Revenue Management.* Springer Science + Media, Inc.: New York, 2005.

Tang, J. C.; Rochanahond, N. Attractiveness as Tourist Destination: A Comparative Study of Thailand and Selected Countries. *Soc.-Econ. Plann. Sci.* **1990**, *24*(3), 229–236.

Toh, R. S. An Inventory Depletion Overbooking Model for the Hotel Industry. *J. Travel Res.* **1985**, *23*(4), 24–30.

Toh, R. S. Coping with No-Shows, Late Cancellations and Oversales: American Hotels out-do the Airlines. *Int. J. Hospitality Manage.* **1986,** *5*(3), 121–125.

Toh, R. S.; Dekay, F. Hotel Room-Inventory Management: An Overbooking Model. *Cornell Hotel Restaurant Admin. Q.* **2002,** *43*(4), 79–90.

Uysal, M.; McDonald, D. C. Visitor Segmentation by Trip Index. *J. Travel Res.* **1989,** *27*(3), 38–42.

Uysal, M.; Oh, H. C.; O'Leary, J. T. Seasonal Variation in Propensity to Travel in the US. *J. Tourism Syst. Quality Manage.* **1995,** *1*(1), 1–13.

Var, T.; Beck, R. A.; Loftus, P. Determination of Tourist Areas in British Columbia. *J. Travel Res.* **1977,** *15*(Winter), 23–29.

Whelan-Ryan, F. Yield Management and the Restaurant Industry. In *Yield Management: Strategies for the Service Industries*, Ingold A., McMahon-Beattie U., Yeoman I., Eds.; Continuum: New York, 2000; pp 270–288.

Witt, S. F.; Witt, C. A. *Modeling and Forecasting Demand in Tourism*. Academic Press Limited: London, U.K., 1992.

Wöber, K. W. *Benchmarking in Tourism and Hospitality Industries: The Selection of Benchmarking Partners*. CABI Publishing: U.K., 2002.

Wöber, K. W.; Fesenmaier, D. R. A Multi-Criteria Approach to Destination Benchmarking: A Case Study of State Tourism Adverting Programs in the United States. In *Management Science Applications in Tourism and Hospitality*; Zheng, G., Ed.; The Haworth Hospitality Press, Inc.: Binghamton, NY, 2004; pp 1–18.

Wong, K. K. F.; Song, H. Eds. *Tourism Forecasting and Marketing*. The Haworth Hospitality Press, Inc.: Binghamton, NY, 2002.

Wu, W. Y., Hsiao, S. W., & Tsai, C. H. Forecasting and Evaluating the Tourist Hotel Industry Performance in Taiwan Based on Grey Theory. *Tourism Hospitality Res.* **2008,** *8*(2), 137–152.

Yu, G.; Schwartz, Z. Forecasting Short Time-Series Tourism Demand with Artificial Intelligence Models. *J. Travel Res.* **2006,** *45*(2), 194–203.

Zhang, Y.; Song, H.; Huang, G. Q. Tourism Supply Chain Management: A New Research Agenda. *Tourism Manage.* **2009,** *30*, 345–355.

Zhen, G., Ed. *Management Science Applications in Tourism and Hospitality*. The Haworth Hospitality Press, Inc.: Binghamton, NY, 2004.

Zheng, T.; Gu, Z. Shanhai's High-end Hotel Overcapacity in 2011 and Beyond: How Bad It Could be and Why? *Tourism Anal.* **2011,** *16*, 571–581.

Zheng, T.; Bloom, B. A. N.; Wang, X.; Schrier, T. How Do Less Advanced Forecasting Methods Perform on Weekly Revpar in Different Forecasting Horizons Following the Recession? *Tourism Anal.* **2012,** *17*, 459–472.

CHAPTER 2

COMPLEX TOURISM SYSTEMS: A QUANTITATIVE APPROACH

RODOLFO BAGGIO[1] and GIACOMO DEL CHIAPPA[2]

[1]*Master in Economics and Tourism, Dondena Center for Research on Social Dynamics, Bocconi University, Via Runtgen, 1, 20146 Milan, Italy. E-mail: rodolfo.baggio@unibocconi.it*

[2]*Department of Economics and Business, University of Sassari and CRENoS, Via Muroni, 25, 07100 Sassari, Italy. E-mail: gdelchiappa@ uniss.it*

CONTENTS

2.1 INTRODUCTION

Tourism systems, and tourism destinations in particular, can be defined in many ways and using different approaches (Pearce, 2014); however, it is widely recognized that they can be considered as being complex dynamic systems composed of different entities (companies, associations, etc.) and resources interacting in nontrivial and complicated ways for satisfying needs and wishes of its *users* (Baggio, Scott, & Cooper, 2010b).

From a management point of view, tourism destinations may be considered as being strategic business units (Bieger, 1998), thus representing the main unit of analysis (Framke, 2002) and the main target for the implementation of tourism policies (Pearce, 2014). The analysis of structural and dynamic characteristics of tourism destinations enables to understand broad issues which affect tourism and to better take into account the relationships between its different components (Page & Connell, 2006).

Destinations are essentially socioeconomic networks, comprising an ensemble of dynamically interacting stakeholders, jointly producing the experience for the travelers to consume (Baggio et al. 2010b; Del Chiappa & Presenza, 2013); therefore, the harmonization and coordination of these stakeholders is a fundamental element for their governance (Bregoli & Del Chiappa, 2013). The effectiveness of governance highly impacts on the development of tourism destinations (Moscardo, 2011), and ensures a balanced and continuing sustainable growth, and is fundamental for the destination competitiveness.

Managing and governing a complex system is notoriously a daunting task that requires a sound knowledge of the structural and dynamic characteristics of the system. This knowledge can be obtained by using a number of different methods based on the idea that a systemic holistic view is more suitable than traditional reductionist approaches; this perspective is rooted in the research tradition of what is today known as *complexity science*.

Many proposals have been put forward for the investigation of complex systems and some have been successfully applied to tourism destinations. The objective of this chapter is to briefly present and discuss the most common and used techniques (agent-based modeling, nonlinear analysis of time series and network analysis). In doing this, examples from recent literature will be provided, and implications for a "good governance" practice will be suggested.

2.2   COMPLEX TOURISM SYSTEMS

A complex system is an entity composed of a set of elements interacting with each other and with the external environment in dynamic nonlinear ways. The most common and universally recognized characteristics of complex systems are as follows (Brodu, 2009):

- the number (and types) of elements and the number of relationships between them are nontrivial (i.e., not too small but not necessarily huge);
- the relationships between the different parts of the system and with its environment are nonlinear;
- the system has a memory or includes feedback and adapts itself by changing its configuration according to its history or feedback;
- the system can be influenced by, or can adapt itself to, its environment (the system is open) in unexpected and nontrivial ways; and
- the system is highly sensitive to initial conditions.

The system evolves continuously redefining its configuration and functions; it may exhibit an intricate mix of ordered and disordered behaviors and show emergent phenomena which are generally surprising and, at times, extreme. Depending on certain conditions the system may also exhibit a chaotic behavior (Bertuglia & Vaio, 2005).

The analysis of complex systems needs different approaches from those traditionally used. When a system is sufficiently simple, it can be analyzed by decomposing it; its parts are examined individually and the outcomes are recomposed in order to derive the characteristics of the whole. The same method (known as reductionist) can be theoretically adopted even when a huge number of elements are present provided the relationships are linear. However, when a system is complex, or in time frames in which the system undergoes abrupt and critical transitions, a reductionist approach is unable to give meaningful results (Baggio, 2013). As a consequence, we do not have a definite 'metric' able to measure the phenomena we want to study. It is possible, however, to understand the properties of collective phenomena because in most situations they do not depend on the exact microscopic details of the processes involved. Rather, for many questions it is sufficient to consider only the most important features of single elements, and sometimes only higher level features such as symmetries, dimensionality, or conservation laws play a relevant role for the global behavior. In order to generate quantitative statements, and to relate the statistical laws to the microscopic properties of the system, these models need to be calibrated with empirical data measured from real systems (Castellano, Fortunato & Loreto, 2009).

We study a system, a tourism destination in our case, because we want to predict its behavior in the future and assess the possibility to intervene in some way in order to drive the system toward a certain configuration (or state). As complex system, a tourism destination would need a high number of variables for its description; in technical words, the system is embedded in a high-dimensional space (the many variables) called phase space. One point in this space represents a certain configuration of the system. If the system evolves, all the different points form a path which represents the dynamical evolution of the system. In its evolution, a system can assume several different configurations, often identified by the values of some pa-rameter (order parameter) that differentiate its behavior. One or more of the variables can be modified (endogenously or exogenously) and the system's reaction may be more or less strongly affected by these modifications. In a complex or chaotic system these changes may result in the system undergo-ing some kind of abrupt transformation, shown as jumps or discontinuities in the phase space paths. These critical phase transitions are the points where no full knowledge or predictability of the system is possible (Baggio, 2008).

In its dynamic evolution the system may go from a completely ordered and stable phase to one in which the dynamic behavior is so heavily depen-dent on small variations of the initial conditions that, although deterministi-cally shaped, appears completely irregular: the chaotic phase. The region at the boundary of these phases, known as the *edge of chaos*, is a region of complexity (e.g., Waldrop, 1992). In this region, small variations in the conditions can lead to unpredictable and unrepeatable outcomes. New prop-erties or structures can emerge and it is difficult to determine accurately how a manager can act or to what extent there is a possibility to effectively steer the system. Yet, this is an important phase: one that ensures adequate dynamicity for allowing the growth of the system or for giving it sufficient robustness to resist shocks.

As a living organism, a complex system, a tourism destination in our case, is always a dynamic entity; it reaches a stable static equilibrium only when it is dead (e.g., Ulgiati & Bianciardi, 1997). Predictability and tractability of the system depend on what type of evolution occurs in the time frame considered and on the time scale, or spatial scale, used for the investigation. Ideally we may want to project it on a lower dimensional space with fewer variables. Several techniques exist that allow this projection, but, obviously, the lower the space dimension, the higher the information lost. Whether this is acceptable or not will depend on whether the approximation made is still able to provide a meaningful description of the system (Sornette, 2008). Many diverse methods have been proposed for the analysis of a complex system and the toolbox of the complexity scientist is today quite crowded. Many of them originate from the work of 19th century scientists, but, since they rely on quite extensive calculations, only modern computational facilities have made it possible to use them in practical contexts.

As can be easily guessed, a complex system such as a tourism destination is difficult to be managed and governed. Due to its strong self-organization capabilities, a rigid deterministic, authoritarian style can be ineffective or even disruptive for the system. When direct and linear cause and effect relationships lose full validity, long-term planning is almost impossible. There may be a need for strong rules or policies, but given the inherent unpredictability (or low predictability) the most important element is to develop the capability to change them dynamically, to react in short times to all the changes that may occur in the system and in the external environment, to monitor the effects generated by the decisions made and use these to re-orient the future actions (Farrell & Twining-Ward, 2004). Further, when a tourism destination is considered, it is possible to adopt the idea that systems do not only adapt to their environments, but help creating them (Stacey, 1996).

Despite these difficulties, it is still possible to manage and understand complex systems, at least at some level. Large-scale behaviors might still be foreseeable if it is possible to describe the overall dynamics of the system including the presence of any preferred evolutionary paths. Once these have been identified, it can be possible to determine whether changes in some specific parameter can produce sudden shifts in behavior, or at least establish a probability distribution for their occurrence (Hansell, Craine, & Byers, 1997). Short-term predictions allow identification of the main evolutionary paths and small corrections to the system behavior that may be effective in avoiding undesired regimes.

2.3   THE STUDY OF COMPLEX SYSTEMS: A METHODOLOGICAL OVERVIEW

According to Amaral and Ottino (2004), we can group the approaches for studying a complex system in three main classes: statistical physics, nonlinear dynamics, and network theory.

2.3.1   STATISTICAL PHYSICS

Statistical physics is one of the fundamental fields of physics, and employs statistical methods for addressing physical problems that concern systems with a large number of components. It provides a rigorous framework for relating the microscopic properties of individual "particles" to the macroscopic ones of objects and system observed in everyday life. Statistical physics is the strong theoretical framework that *justifies* all the methods discussed here for the study of a complex system. Specifically, one important outcome is the possibility to use discrete models such as individual–based models and agent-based models (ABMs) (e.g., Baggio, 2011a). The fundamental assumption is that a phenomenon can be modeled numerically in terms of some appropriate algorithm, usually implemented as a computer program, rather than with analytical expressions.

2.3.2   NONLINEAR DYNAMICS

The main feature of complex systems is the nonlinearity of the interactions among the components. The equations describing its behavior can be solved only in very rare cases. Poincaré's (1883) work on the impossibility to fully describe analytically a gravitational system containing more than three bodies is considered the starting point of a study tradition in nonlinear dynamics. Since then, a number of mathematical techniques have been developed to approximate the solutions of the differential equations used to describe such systems. However, only the availability of modern powerful computers has made it possible to find solutions since, in almost all cases, they are obtained by numerical approximations. Much of the mathematics of chaos theory, for example, involves the repeated iteration of simple formulas, which would be impractical to do otherwise (e.g., Gharajedaghi, 2006).

2.3.3   NETWORK SCIENCE

A complex system can be described as a network of interacting elements. Understanding the structure and the dynamics of the relationships and the interactions among the elements in a complex system is a key step to comprehend its structure and dynamic behavior. The collective properties of dynamic systems composed of a large number of interconnected parts are strongly influenced by the topology of the connecting network.

A network is made of nodes or vertices, which can be used to represent the system's elements, and links or edges, which usually correspond to the interactions or relationships between the elements. In this context, networks represent the structure of complex systems, but a network can also be used to represent the dynamics or the functions of a complex system (e.g., when interpreting nodes as states and links as transitions). Thus, a network analysis can be applied to the structure and the function of a complex entity. Understanding the relationship between structure and function is one of the major open questions in any discipline, which can, often, be examined by looking at how changes in the structure (topology) of a network affects its state (Baggio et al. 2010b; Baggio, Scott, & Cooper, 2013; da Fontoura et al., 2011; Dominici & Levanti, 2011; Newman, 2010).

2.4 MAIN ISSUES IN THE APPLICATION OF COMPLEXITY SCIENCE

Two issues are relevant when approaching the study of a complex system. The first concerns the choice of methods to be used, the second regards the collection of the data needed for the analysis.

As far as the first issue is concerned, it should be noted that when studying complex system the traditional dichotomy between qualitative and quantitative methods, each with its own advantages and disadvantages (e.g., Veal, 2006), is meaningless and can even be dangerous. No matter how sophisticated and effective the techniques used can be; they have little value when applied to a complex system without coupling them with sound physical interpretations. Adopting the language of social science, this means that a thorough knowledge of the object of analysis is crucial to obtain meaningful outcomes from both a theoretical and a practical point of view. A pure qualitative investigation risks missing or misinterpreting important factors, because the quantitative analysis often provides rather unexpected outcomes. This is even more relevant when employing numerical simulation techniques. If correctly used, simulations are a powerful tool, but the basic assumptions must represent as faithfully as possible the reality and a good comprehension of what will be simulated is crucial.

A reliable model, especially when dealing with a complex system, needs continuous interactions between researchers and empirical issues (Silvert, 2001). For those interested or involved in managing a destination, the combination of both traditional qualitative evaluations and quantitative measurements can give more strength to the decisions made and better inform the actions and policies needed (e.g., Baggio et al. 2010a; Pearce, 2014). Finally, a good integration of quantitative and qualitative methods can help in a substantial way in finding different, new and more effective ways to better understand systems and phenomena under study (Gummesson, 2007; Olsen, 2004).

The second issue faced when analyzing complex systems is related to the quality and the quantity of data needed. Obviously, data quality is important, as ignoring even small variations can hide effects that may develop rapidly to important consequences, and approximate evaluations risk inhibiting a full recognition of the nonlinear effects that characterize complex dynamic systems (Batini & Scannapieco, 2006). More than that, however, the quantity of observations can be a crucial issue. Indeed, as it will be better explained in the next sections, some techniques (e.g., those using time series) are 'data hungry'. They ask for a large number of data points, typically not widely available in the tourism arena (e.g., Baggio & Sainaghi, 2011). Other methods (e.g., network analysis) call for a possibly complete set of data, representing fully the system examined. As a matter of fact, due to the strong nonlinearity and non-normality of the quantities involved, traditional sampling methods are mostly meaningless and the likelihood to overlook or disregard important factors is quite high (e.g., Kossinets, 2006).

2.5   THE ANALYSIS OF COMPLEX TOURISM SYSTEMS

This section is dedicated to the main methods used for analyzing and assessing complex or chaotic characteristics in a tourism system.

2.5.1   NONLINEAR ANALYSIS OF TIME SERIES

The object of study in nonlinear dynamics is a time series that contains a certain number of quantities related to some behavior of the system under investigation. In tourism studies, logging of arrivals, overnight stays, or other similar quantities are usually used for depicting the history of a destination, predicting its future development, and interpreting its evolution (e.g., Butler, 1980).

Here, a time series is seen as the representation of the system's behavior and is used to assess a number of traits about the nature and the extent of the complexity or chaoticity of the system.

Most of the methods give reliable and meaningful results only with relatively *long* series (typically more than some thousand values); unfortunately datasets of this size are not very common in tourism studies. The frequency with which data are collected is another relevant aspect; if it is too low, an interesting dynamic pattern may be lost, while if it is too high, the number of values risks increasing the computational time needed without need. Only the experience will guide researchers and practitioners toward the "ideal" solution; "this is more an art than a science, and there are few sure-fire methods. You need a battery of tests, and conclusions are seldom definitive" (Sprott, 2003, p. 211). Despite this, an accurate use of the techniques available has shown to provide a wealth of interesting insights into the structural and dynamic patterns of complex and chaotic systems (e.g., Baggio & Sainaghi, 2011).

When dealing with a time series, trend and seasonality components may corrupt the outcomes of the measurements by adding strong effects to the recording of system's internal dynamics (e.g., Clegg, 2006); in order to remove these effects the series needs to be filtered. However, many classical techniques make some type of "linear" assumptions, which may be not fully appropriate in the case of a complex system, it is better to use some method which uses directly the data without any "external" intervention (such as defining the length of a season). An example of this method is the Hodrick–Prescott filter (Hodrick & Prescott, 1997), a nonparametric, nonlinear algorithm which acts as a tunable bandpass filter controlled by a parameter λ. The effect is the identification of long-term trend components without affecting too much short-term fluctuations. High values for λ give a smooth long-term component (in the extreme cases: $\lambda = \infty$ produces a line, $\lambda = 0$ leaves intact the observed values). The literature suggests as optimal choice λ the values: 14,400, 260,100, and 6250,000 for monthly, weekly, and daily data, respectively (e.g., Baggio & Klobas, 2011). Once filtered, the series can be examined to assess whether it originates from a linear or a nonlinear or chaotic process. A common procedure is the Brock, Dechert, and Scheinkman (BDS) test that checks whether a given signal is deterministic (chaotic) or stochastic (Brock, Dechert, Scheinkman & LeBaron, 1996).

A chaotic system is characterized by a great sensitivity to initial conditions; in other words, it has a long memory. This attribute can be assessed by adopting a method due to Harold Edwin Hurst (Hurst, 1951). The mathematical definition of long-memory processes calls for the evaluation of the autocorrelation function $p(k)$ of the time series (k is the lag). When long memory is present, $p(k)$ decays following a power law: $p(k) \sim k^{\alpha}$. The quantity $H = 1 - \alpha/2$ is called Hurst exponent and its value ranges between 0 and

1. If $H = 0.5$, the time series is similar to a random walk; when $H < 0.5$, the time series is antipersistent (i.e., if values increase, it is more probable that they will decrease in subsequent periods, and vice versa); if $H > 0.5$, the time series is persistent (if the time series increases, it is more probable that it will continue to increase). Values higher than 0.5 therefore characterize systems with a long memory and thus show a tendency to be chaotic. The calculation of H can be performed by using a number of different methods, again, all having their specificities, power, and reliability in different conditions (e.g., Clegg, 2006). The Hurst exponent can also been used as a measure of complexity: the lower its value, the higher the complexity of the system (Giuliani, Colafranceschi, Webber, & Zbilut, 2001).

An attractor in the phase space is, as sketched above, a trajectory of stability for a complex system. The tendency of a system to follow one of these paths can clearly provide interesting information about its dynamics, and provide one more measure of the sensitive dependence on initial conditions, that is of its chaotic (or potentially chaotic) behavior. In the study of the stability of motion of a low-dimensional physical system, Aleksandr Mikhailovich Lyapunov (1892) proposed a way to assess the rate of convergence between two orbits when one of them had been perturbed. The quantities calculated, called Lyapunov exponents, depend on the equations of the orbits (e.g., the system's path and a reference orbit) and on the dimension of the phase space in which the system is embedded. The largest exponent [Lyapunov characteristic exponent (LCE)] gives the most important information on the system's motion. When LCE < 0, orbits converge in time and the system is insensitive to initial conditions. If LCE > 0, the distance grows exponentially in time, and the system tends to go away from the stable attractor and exhibits sensitive dependence on initial conditions. In the case of a real system, for which we have a time series representing it, it is possible to calculate LCE by using some numerical methods (e.g., Wolf, Swift, Swinney, & Vastano, 1985).

When using these methods, it is important to have a null model in order to help the interpretation of the results (here we do not have a clear hypothesis to test via a p-value). In chaos theory, one well-known system of such kind is the one described by Lorenz (1963). A series obtained from some solution of his equations is a good null model; since the Lorenz equations are in the three-dimensional space one of the components needs to be used.

As said, all these methods are used by means of a computer application. A useful list of programs is the following:

- Hodrick—Prescott filter: Matlab script by W. Henao, available at: http://www.mathworks.com/matlabcentral/fileexchange/ 3972-hodrick -prescott-filter
- BDS test: Matlab script by L. Kanzler, available at: http://econpapers. repec.org/software/bocbocode/t871803.htm
- Hurst exponent: Matlab scripts by C. Chen, available at: http://www. mathworks. com/matlabcentral/fileexchange/19148-hurst-parameter- estimate
- Lyapunov characteristic exponent: Matlab script by S. Mohammadi, available at: http://ideas.repec.org/c/boc/bocode/t741502.html
- Lorenz time series: Matlab scripts by E. A. Wan , available at: http:// www.bme.ogi.edu/~ericwan/data.html

All the outcomes of the analyses described here need a sound qualitative interpretation in order to provide useful insights. These methods, although not frequently used in tourism studies, have anyway provided some interesting results from both a theoretical and a practical point of view. Basically, they assess the extent to which a destination system (or even a single stakeholder) is dynamically stable, thus allowing a better choice of the actions that could be adopted without contrasting with the self-organization tendencies of the system. In turn, this guarantees a higher probability to be effective (e.g., Baggio & Sainaghi, 2011).

2.5.2 AGENT-BASED MODELING

ABMs are useful tools for the simulation of a complex system. Applications exist in many fields of physical, chemical, biological, and social sciences; propagation of fire, predator–prey models diffusion of diseases, demographic phenomena or the evolution of natural, and artificial organizations can be represented with ABMs (e.g., Baggio & Baggio, 2013).

In ABMs, agents are programmed in order to obey predetermined rules, reacting to certain environmental conditions, interact between themselves, and be able to learn and adapt (Gilbert & Terna, 2000). The interactions are asynchronous and the global behavior emerges as a cumulative result of these local interactions. A researcher using computer simulated ABMs to represent real systems uses a model-building process that can be outlined as follows (Galán et al. 2009):

- conceptualize the system defining the research question and identifying the crucial variables along with their interrelations;
- find a set of formal specifications that is able to fully characterize the conceptual model;
- code and implement by using an appropriate development environment.

The resulting model is iterative, every agent receives input from the environment, processes it, and acts generating a new environmental input until a pre-determined condition is met (e.g., time limit, all agents in a given condition, etc.).

For the development of ABMs, a number of software applications exist that use relatively simple scripting languages and provide all the facilities needed to run the model and to record the outcomes; NetLogo (ccl.northwestern.edu/netlogo) is one of these. However, an ABM can be implemented with any programming language.

Validating, verifying, and evaluating ABMs is a crucial task, since simulation behaviors are difficult to grasp at first. For this purpose, several criteria have been proposed. The first one is an assessment of its reliability by allowing for different separate implementations and a subsequent comparison of the results. Taber and Timpone (1996) propose three steps for the validation of a numerical simulation model that can be rendered as answers to the following questions:

- Do the results of a simulation correspond to those of the real world (when data are available)?
- Does the process by which agents and the environment interact correspond to the one that happens in the real world (when they are known)?
- Is the model coded correctly so that it is possible to state that the outcomes are a result solely of the model assumptions (i.e., is the computer program free from evident errors)?

In the tourism field, AMBs have been used for different purposes. On one hand, they have been implemented for studying certain processes or examining certain phenomena such as the analysis of the effects of asymmetric information digital market on buyers and sellers' satisfaction and earnings is an example (Baggio & Baggio, 2013). On the other hand, ABM systems have been created to analyze and predict tourism related phenomena in tourism destinations (e.g., Baggio, 2011a; Johnson & Sieber, 2010).

2.5.3   NETWORK ANALYSIS

Tourism destinations can be considered as socioeconomic networks, with groups of interacting players that are related one to another. Literature has provided an extensive set of mathematical tools for analyzing networks and the graphs they represent. Realizing that a social or economic group can be represented by detailing the stakeholders of the group and their mutual relationships, sociologists have used some of these methods to explore their patterns of relations (Freeman, 2004).

Today, the network science toolbox can rely on several metrics (e.g., da Fontoura Costa et al. 2007; Newman, 2010) obtained by combining those coming from the social network analysis tradition with those developed in more recent mathematical studies. The main measurements that can be used to fully characterize topology and behaviors of a complex network are as follows:

- *degree*: the number of links each node has, and degree distribution, the statistical distribution of links and *degree distribution:* the statistical distribution of the number (and sometimes the type) of the linkages among the network elements;
- *assortativity*: the correlation between the degrees of neighbor nodes;
- *average path length*: the mean distance (number of links) between any two nodes and *diameter*, the maximal shortest path connecting any two nodes;
- *closeness*: the mean weighted distance (i.e., the shortest path) between a node and all other nodes reachable from it;
- *betweenness*: the extent to which a node falls between others on the shortest paths connecting them;
- *clustering coefficient*: the concentration of connections of a node's neighbors: it provides a measure of the heterogeneity of the local density of links;
- *eigenvector*: calculated by using the matrix representation of a network and its principal eigenvector, and based on the idea that a relationship to a more interconnected node contributes to the own centrality to a greater extent than a relationship to a less well interconnected node. One variation of this measure is the well-known *PageRank*;
- *efficiency* (at a local or global level): which can be interpreted as a measure of the capability of the system to exchange information over the network;

- *modularity*: the quality of a partition of the network into modules or communities. High values of modularity are found when the connections between the nodes within modules are denser than those between nodes belonging to different modules (Fortunato, 2010).

At a local (nodal) level the metrics described assume, often, the meaning of importance attributed to the single actors (they are also called centrality measures). Actors can be important if they have many connections (friends) or can quickly reach all other actors in the network (closeness) or are a bridge or information broker between different parts of the network (betweenness), or because their local neighborhoods are well connected (clustering coefficient). Moreover the actor's importance can be greater if the connections are set, even indirectly, toward the other most important elements of the network (eigenvector, PageRank). Several software programs allow calculating the main metrics. Some of them (such as NodeXL, Pajek, Gephi, Ucinet, etc.) can be used for general purposes, while some others have been developed for specific tasks, or are libraries to be used by some programming language (e.g., Matlab, R, or Python).

Network analyses in tourism have highlighted a series of interesting outcomes. The first application concerns the topological characterization and the identification of the structural peculiarities of a tourism destination (Baggio et al. 2010b; Bendle & Patterson, 2008; Del Chiappa & Presenza, 2013; Grama & Baggio, 2014; Presenza & Cipollina, 2010; Scott, Cooper & Baggio, 2008). An effective assessment of the characteristics of the network would require to adopt this structural perspective with the relational one so that how the inter-organizational relationships influence the way different nodes can interact and collaborate with each other can be analyzed as well (Del Chiappa & Presenza, 2013). These empirical studies unveiled complex structures with power-law degree distributions, very low density of connections, low clusterization, and negative degree–degree correlations (i.e., highly connected nodes tend to link low-degree elements). These latter features have been interpreted as symptom of the well-known tendency of tourism stakeholders to avoid forms of collaboration or cooperation. The related metrics (clustering and assortativity coefficients) have thus been proposed as quantitative measurements for these characteristics (Baggio, 2007; da Fontoura Costa & Baggio, 2009). This is an important result, because the identification of strategic weaknesses in the cohesiveness of the destination can be addressed by policy and management approaches (Erkuş-Öztürk & Eraydın, 2010).

A modularity analysis has uncovered that some form of aggregations exist in a destination, even if not very well defined or highly significant. However, this community structure goes beyond preset differentiations (by geography or type) of the agents. In other words, companies of the same type (e.g., hotels), or in the same geographical area, tend to connect with some other company which runs a different business or are located in different localities (Baggio, 2011b).

Network analysis methods have been applied also to the virtual network of the websites belonging to destination's stakeholders, with results that are similar to those obtained by studying the real destination network (Baggio, 2006, 2007; Baggio, Scott, & Wang, 2007; Piazzi, Baggio, Neidhardt, & Werthner, 2012). This has allowed to gauge the level of utilization of advanced communication technologies among the actors in a destination and measure the extent to which they exploit (or waste) resources universally deemed to be crucial for today's survival in a highly competitive globalized market. Moreover, it has been possible to show the structural integration between the virtual and the real components in a destination. This gives more strength to the idea that a digital ecosystem needs to be fully considered when dealing with tourism activities at a destination (Baggio & Del Chiappa, 2014b).

The substantial similarity of the main topological characteristics, coupled with considerations on the mechanisms with which corporate websites are interlinked, has then suggested the important conjecture that the World Wide Web can provide an efficient and effective way to gather significant samples of networked socioeconomic systems to be used for analyses and simulations (Baggio et al. 2010b).

One more interesting outcome is the possibility to identify the most relevant members in a destination: those who are reputed to give the most important contribution to the tourism activities (Cooper, Scott & Baggio, 2009; Presenza & Cipollina, 2010). Also some important features such as the creativity and innovation potential of the destination or the productive performance of single stakeholders have been related to the network configuration through some of its quantitative peculiarities (Baggio, 2014; Sainaghi & Baggio, 2014).

An advantage of a network representation of a complex system is that it is possible to perform numerical simulations. Different configurations can be conceived and several dynamic processes simulated in order to better understand how these configurations influence the behavior of the whole destination system.

Information and knowledge flows in a destination network are relevant determinants of the *health* of the system. Productivity, innovation and growth are strongly influenced by them, and the way in which the spread occurs affects the speed by which individual actors perform (Argote & Ingram, 2000). A common technique to study the problem is based on an analogy with the diffusion of a disease (Hethcote, 2000), which can be implemented using a network as substrate. It has been shown, in fact, that the structure of the network is highly influential in determining the unfolding of the process (López-Pintado, 2008). These methods have been used in tourism to show the effects of possible modifications in the network structure on the extent and the speed of information diffusion or knowledge sharing (Aubke, Wöber, Scott, & Baggio, 2014; Baggio & Cooper, 2010). Based on this strand of research and on the one on digital ecosystem, Baggio and Del Chiappa (2014a) assessed the opinion and consensus dynamics in tourism destinations and proved that a structurally strong cohesion between the real and the virtual components of a destination do exist. It could be argued that current research on diffusion models is still limited; future efforts would be useful to deepen the knowledge in this area (Baggio, 2011c).

2.6 CONCLUSION

This chapter showed how the analysis and management of tourism destinations can benefit from adopting principles and methods rooted in the interdisciplinary approach of *complexity science*. To do this, some of the most common and used techniques were presented, describing, for each of them, aims, tools, and software that can be used to apply them along with the requirements for data collection. Specifically, three different families of methods were considered: agent-based modeling, nonlinear analysis of time series, and network analysis; these are summarized, along with their main purpose in Table 2.1.

This contribution also underlined that mixing qualitative and quantitative methods and simultaneously considering the real and virtual components of tourism destinations would be beneficial in supporting researchers and practitioners in their attempt to obtain a better picture of the structure, the evolution, the outcomes, and the governance of the system as a whole.

Finally, the need for an additional refinement of the described methods, both from a theoretical and practical point of view, was highlighted, thus calling for further research and empirical investigations in order to validate

TABLE 2.1 Methods for the Analysis of Complex Dynamic Systems.

Method	Data used	Main purpose
Agent-based models	Actors (single entities) Rules that define local interactions between agents	Simulation of large scale behaviors Production of scenarios
Nonlinear analysis of time series	Time series of systems' observable characteristics	Diagnosis of complex and/or chaotic dynamics
Network analysis	Graph of actors and relationships	Structural characteristics of the system Basis for dynamic processes

them. As stated by San Miguel et al. (2012: 268), however, the challenge is strong and includes:

> "data gathering by large-scale experiment, participatory sensing and social computation, and managing huge distributed dynamics and heterogeneous databases; moving from data to dynamical models, going beyond correlations to cause-effect relationships, understanding the relationship between simple and comprehensive models with appropriate choices of variables, ensemble modeling and data assimilation, and modeling systems of systems of systems with many levels between micro and macro; and formulating new approaches to prediction, forecasting, and risk, especially in systems that can reflect on and change their behavior in response to predictions, and systems whose apparently predictable behavior is disrupted by apparently unpredictable rare or extreme events."

This also suggests that these new promising approaches can be effectively used to more deeply investigate the dynamics and evolution of tourism destinations and the dynamic processes, such as consensus building and knowledge creation and diffusion that occur on them.

KEYWORDS

- complexity science
- tourism destination governance
- agent-based modeling
- nonlinear time series analysis
- network analysis

REFERENCES

Amaral, L. A. N.; Ottino, J. M. Complex Networks—Augmenting the Framework for the Study of Complex Systems. *Eur. Phys. J. B.* **2004**, *38*, 147–162.

Argote, L.; Ingram, P. Knowledge Transfer: A Basis for Competitive Advantage in Firms. *Organ. Behav. Hum. Decis. Process.* **2000**, *82*(1), 150–169.

Aubke, F.; Wöber, K.; Scott, N.; Baggio R. Knowledge Sharing in Revenue Management Teams: Antecedents and Consequences of Group Cohesion. *Int. J. Hospital. Manage.* **2014**, *41*, 149–157.

Baggio, J. A. Agent-based Modeling and Simulations. In *Quantitative Methods in Tourism: A Handbook*; Baggio, R., Klobas, J., Eds.; Channel View: Bristol, UK, 2011a; pp 199–219.

Baggio, R. Complex Systems, Information Technologies and Tourism: A Network Point of View. *Inf. Technol. Tourism.* **2006**, *8*(1), 15–29.

Baggio, R. The Web Graph of a Tourism System. *Physica A.* **2007**, *379*(2), 727–734.

Baggio, R. Symptoms of Complexity in a Tourism System. *Tourism Anal.* **2008**, *13*(1), 1–20.

Baggio, R. Collaboration and Cooperation in a Tourism Destination: A Network Science Approach. *Curr. Issues Tourism.* **2011b**, *14*(2), 183–189.

Baggio, R. The Mechanism for Spreading Online Reputation. *Acad. Turistica.* **2011c**, *3*(2), 7–15.

Baggio, R. Oriental and Occidental Approaches to Complex Tourism Systems. *Tourism Plann. Dev.* **2013**, *10*(2), 217–227.

Baggio, R. Creativity and the Structure of Tourism Destination Networks. *Int. J. Tourism Sci.* **2014**, *14*(1), 137–154.

Baggio, R.; Baggio, J. A. Modeling Information Asymmetries in Tourism. In *Tourism Marketing: On Both Sides of the Counter*; Kozak, M., Lebe, S. S., Andreu, L, Gnoth, J.; Fyall, A., Eds.; Cambridge Scholars Publishing: Newcastle upon Tyne, UK, 2013; pp 156–174.

Baggio, R.; Cooper, C. Knowledge Transfer in a Tourism Destination: The Effects of a Network Structure. *Serv. Ind. J.* **2010**, *30*(10), 1–15.

Baggio, R.; Del Chiappa, G. Opinion and Consensus Dynamics in Tourism Digital Ecosystems. In *Information and Communication Technologies in Tourism 2014 (Proceedings of the International Conference in Dublin, Ireland, January 21–24, 2014)*; Xiang, Z., Tussyadiah, I., Eds.; Springer: Berlin-Heidelberg, 2014a; pp 327–338.

Baggio, R.; Del Chiappa, G. Real and Virtual Relationships in Tourism Digital Ecosystems. *Inf. Technol. Tourism.* **2014b**, *14*(1), 3–19.

Baggio, R.; Klobas, J. *Quantitative Methods in Tourism: A Handbook*; Channel View: Bristol, UK, 2011:.

Baggio, R.; Sainaghi, R. Complex and Chaotic Tourism Systems: Toward a Quantitative Approach. *Int. J. Contemp. Hospital. Manage.* **2011**, *23*(6), 840–861.

Baggio, R., Scott, N.; Cooper, C. Improving Tourism Destination Governance: A complexity Science Approach. *Tourism Rev.* **2010a**, *65*(4), 51–60.

Baggio, R.; Scott, N.; Cooper, C. Network science—A Review Focused on Tourism. *Ann. Tourism Res.* **2010b**, *37*(3), 802–827.

Baggio, R.; Scott, N.; Cooper, C. Using Network Analysis to Improve Tourist Destination Management. In *Trends in European Tourism Planning and Organisation Systems*; Costa, C.; Panyik, E.; Buhalis, D., Eds.; Channel View: Clevedon, UK, 2013; pp 278–288.

Baggio, R.; Scott, N.; Wang, Z. What Network Analysis of the WWW Can Tell us About the Organisation of Tourism Destinations. *Proceedings of the CAUTHE 2007, Sydney, Australia, 11–14 February*, 2007.

Batini, C.; Scannapieco, M. *Data Quality: Concepts, Methods and Techniques*; Springer: Berlin, 2006.

Bendle, L. J.; Patterson, I. Network Density, Centrality, and Communication in a Serious Leisure Social World. *Annals of Leisure Research* **2008**, *11*(1–2), 1–19.

Bertuglia, C. S.; Vaio, F. *Nonlinearity, Chaos, and Complexity: The Dynamics of Natural and Social Systems*; Oxford University Press: Oxford, 2005.

Bieger, T. Reengineering Destination Marketing Organisations–The Case of Switzerland. *Revue de Tourisme* **1998**,*53*(3), 4–17.

Bregoli, I., Del Chiappa, G. Coordinating Relationships among Destination Stakeholders: evidence from Edinburgh (UK), *Tourism Anal.* **2013**, *18*(2), 145–155.

Brock, W. A.; Dechert, W. D.; Scheinkman, J. A.; LeBaron, B. A Test for Independence Based on the Correlation Dimension. *Econ. Rev.* **1996**, *15*(3), 197–235.

Brodu, N. A Synthesis and a Practical Approach to Complex Systems. *Complexity* **2009**, *15*(1), 36–60.

Butler, R. W. The Concept of a Tourist Area Cycle of Evolution: Implications for Management of Resources. *Can. Geographer* **1980**, *24*(1), 5–12.

Castellano, C.; Fortunato, S.; Loreto, V. Statistical Physics of Social Dynamics. *Rev. Mod. Phys.* **2009**, *81*(2), 591–646.

Clegg, R. G. A Practical Guide to Measuring The Hurst parameter. *Int. J. Simulation* **2006**, *7*(2), 3–14.

Cooper, C.; Scott, N.; Baggio, R. Network Position and Perceptions of Destination Stakeholder Importance. *Anatolia* **2009**, *20*(1), 33–45.

da Fontoura Costa, L.; Baggio, R. The Web of Connections between Tourism Companies: Structure and Dynamics. *Phys. A* **2009**, *388*, 4286–4296.

da Fontoura Costa, L.; Oliveira, O. N.; Travieso, G.; Rodrigues, F. A.; Villas Boas, P. R.; Antiqueira, L.; Viana, M. P.; Correa Rocha, L. E. Analyzing and Modeling Real-World Phenomena with Complex Networks: A Survey of Applications. *Adv. Phys.* **2011**, *60*(3), 329–412.

da Fontoura Costa, L.; Rodrigues, A.; Travieso, G.; Villas Boas, P. R. Characterization of Complex Networks: A Survey of Measurements. *Adv. Phys.* **2007**, *56*(1), 167–242.

Del Chiappa, G.; Presenza, A. The Use of Network Analysis To Assess Relationships Among Stakeholders Within A Tourism Destination: An Empirical Investigation On Costa Smeralda-Gallura, Italy. *Tourism Anal.* **2013**, *18*(1), 1–13.

Dominici, G.; Levanti, G. The Complex System Theory for the Analysis of Inter-Firm Networks: A Literature Overview and Theoretic Framework. *Int. Bus. Res.* **2011**, *4*(2), 31–37.

Erkuş-Öztürk, H.; Eraydın, A. Environmental Governance for Sustainable Tourism Development: Collaborative Networks and Organisation Building in the Antalya Tourism Region. *Tourism Manage.* **2010**, *31*, 113–124.

Farrell, B. H.; Twining-Ward, L. Reconceptualizing Tourism. *Ann. Tourism Res.* **2004**, *31*(2), 274–295.

Fortunato, S. Community Detection in Graphs. *Phys. Rep.* **2010**, *486*(3-5), 75–174.

Framke, W. The Destination as a Concept: A Discussion of the Business-related Perspective versus the Socio-cultural Approach in Tourism Theory. *Scand. J. Hospital. Tourism* **2002**, *2*(2), 92–108.

Freeman, L. C. *The Development of Social Network Analysis: A Study in the Sociology of Science*; Vancouver Empirical Press: Vancouver, 2004.

Galán, J. M.; Izquierdo, L. R.; Izquierdo, S. S.; Santos, J. I.; del Olmo, R.; López-Paredes, A.; Edmonds, B. Errors and Artefacts in Agent-Based Modelling. *J. Artificial Soc. Soc. Simulation* **2009**, *12*(1), 1.

Gharajedaghi, J. *Systems Thinking: Managing Chaos and Complexity–A Platform for Designing Business Architecture* (2nd ed.), Elsevier: Amsterdam, 2006.

Gilbert, N.; Terna, P. How to Build and Use Agent-Based Models in Social Science. *Mind Soc.* **2000**, *1*(1), 52–72.

Giuliani, A.; Colafranceschi, M.; Webber, C. L. J.; Zbilut, J. P. A Complexity Score Derived from Principal Components Analysis of Nonlinear Order Measures. *Phys. A* **2001**, *301*, 567–588.

Grama, C.-N.; Baggio, R. A Network Analysis of Sibiu County, Romania. *Ann. Tourism Res.* **2014**, *47*(1), 89–93.

Gummesson, E. Case Study Research and Network Theory: Birds of a Feather. *Qual. Res. Organ. Manage.* **2007**, *2*(3), 226–248.

Hansell, R. I. C.; Craine, I. T.; Byers, R. E. Predicting Change in Non-linear Systems. *Environ. Monit. Assess.* **1997**, *46*, 175–190.

Hethcote, H. W. The Mathematics of Infectious Diseases *SIAM Rev.* **2000**, *42*(4), 599–653.

Hodrick, R. J.; Prescott, E. C. Postwar U.S. Business Cycles: An Empirical Investigation. *J. Money Credit Bank.* **1997**, *29*(1), 1–16.

Hurst, H. E. Long-Term Storage of Reservoirs: An Experimental Study. *Trans. Am. Soc. Civil Eng.* **1951**, *116*, 770–799.

Johnson, P. A.; Sieber, R. E. An Individual-Based Model of Tourism Dynamics. *Tourism Anal.* **2010**, *15*(5), 517–530.

Kossinets, G. Effects of Missing Data in Social Networks. *Soc. Networks* **2006**,*28*(3), 247–268.

López-Pintado, D. Diffusion in Complex Social Networks. *Games Econ. Behav.* **2008**, *62*(2), 573–590.

Lorenz, E. N. Deterministic Nonperiodic Flow. *J. Atmos. Sci.* **1963**, *20*, 130–141.

Moscardo, G. The Role of Knowledge in Good Governance for Tourism. In *Tourist destination governance: Practice, theory and issues* Laws, E., Richins, H., Agrusa, J., Scott, N. Eds., CABI: Wallingford, UK, 2011, pp 67–80.

Newman, M. E. J. *Networks—An introduction*. Oxford University Press: Oxford, 2010.

Olsen, W. Triangulation in Social Research, Qualitative and Quantitative Methods Can Really be Mixed. In *Developments in Sociology: An Annual Review* Holborn, M. Ed., Causeway Press: Ormskirk, UK, pp 103–121, 2004.

Page, S. J.; Connell, J. *Tourism: A Modern Synthesis* (2nd ed.); Thomson; London, 2006.

Pearce, D. G. Toward an Integrative Conceptual Framework of Destinations. *J. Travel Res.* **2014**, *53*(2), 141–153.

Piazzi, R.; Baggio, R.; Neidhardt, J.; Werthner, H. Destinations and the Web: A Network Analysis View. *Inf. Technol. Tourism,* **2012**, *13*(3), 215–228.

Poincaré, H. Sur certaines solutions particulières du problème des trois corps. *Comptes Rendus de l'Académie des Sciences, Paris,* **1883**, *97*, 251–252.

Presenza, A.; Cipollina M. Analysing Tourism Stakeholders Networks. *Tourism Rev.* **2010**, *65*(4), 17–30.

Sainaghi, R.; Baggio, R. Structural Social Capital and Hotel Performance: Is There a Link? *Int. J. Hospital. Manage.* **2014**, *37*, 99–110.

San Miguel, M.; Johnson, J. H.; Kertesz, J.; Kaski, K.; Díaz-Guilera, A.; MacKay, R. S.; Loreto, V.; Érdi, P.; Helbing, D. Challenges in Complex Systems Science. *Eur. Phys. J. Spec. Top.* **2012**, *214*, 245–271.

Scott, N.; Cooper, C.; Baggio, R. Destination Networks—Four Australian Cases. *Ann. Tourism Res.* **2008**, *35*(1), 169–188.

Silvert, W. Modeling as a Discipline. *Int. J. Gen. Sys.* **2001**, *30*(3), 261–282.

Sornette, D. Interdisciplinarity in Socio-Economics, Mathematical Analysis and Predictability of Complex Systems. *Socio-Econ. Rev.* **2008**, *6*(4), 734–745.

Sprott, J. C. *Chaos and Time-Series Analysis*. Oxford University Press: Oxford, 2003; p. 211.

Stacey, R. D. *Complexity and Creativity in Organizations*. Berrett-Koehler: San Francisco, 1996.

Taber, C. S.; Timpone, R. J. *Computational Modeling*; Sage: Thousand Oaks, CA, 1996.

Ulgiati, S.; Bianciardi, C. Describing States and Dynamics in far from Equilibrium Systems. Needed a Metric within a System State space. *Ecol. Modell.* **1997**, *96*(1–3), 75–89.

Veal, A. J. *Research Methods for Leisure and Tourism: A Practical Guide* (3rd ed.); Financial Times—Prentice Hall/Pearson Education: Harlow, UK, 2006.

Waldrop, M. *Complexity: The Emerging Science and the Edge of Order and Chaos*; Simon and Schuster: London, 1992.

Wolf, A.; Swift, J. B.; Swinney, H. L.; Vastano, J. A. Determining Lyapunov Exponents from a Time Series. *Physica D.* **1985**, *16*, 285–317.

CHAPTER 3

MONITORING AND FORECASTING TOURIST ACTIVITIES WITH BIG DATA

BING PAN[1] and YANG YANG[2]

[1]*Department of Hospitality and Tourism Management, School of Business, College of Charleston, Charleston, SC 29424-001, USA. E-mail: bingpan@gmail.com*

[2]*School of Tourism and Hospitality Management, Temple University, Philadelphia, PA, USA. E-mail: yangy@temple.edu*

CONTENTS

3.1   INTRODUCTION

The tourism industry, by nature, is information-intensive (Poon, 1993): the variety of services it involves, the intangible and perishable nature of its many products, and the inseparable relationship between its production and consumption requires the generation, storage, co-ordination, and analysis of information (Nyheim, McFadden, & Connolly, 2004). This characteristic indicates that the tourism industry can benefit greatly from the fast evolution of information technology (IT). Indeed, many adoptions of IT, from Property Management Systems (PMS) and Restaurant Management Systems (RMS), designed for optimizing production and increasing efficiency, to the Internet revolution, which disrupted many industries related to tourism, have demonstrated the co-evolution between the tourism industry and IT. In particular, so-called big data has become the latest manifestation of this co-evolution and will create more opportunities and challenges for the industry.

"Big data" refers to the large amount of IT data generated every day and that may be beyond the processing capabilities of traditional databases (Mayer-Schonberger & Cukier, 2013). This demands new ways of storing, retrieving, and analyzing the data. Moore's Law dictates that our computer speed will double every 18–24 months (Schaller, 1997). As a result, our capability to capture, store, and process data will keep increasing exponentially, while the cost will keep decreasing. More importantly, the burst of big data symbolizes a paradigm change as industries can develop new business insights that do not come from the sampling and surveying of one's customers, but from the aggregated digital footprints of their behavior (Mayer-Schonberger & Cukier, 2013).

Big-data revolution also indicates that the causal relationship between particular data points and a business' revenue or profit is no longer the central focus; instead, it is the correlation that matters. With only a correlational relationship, one can use the data as benchmark measurements, forecasting performance, and optimizing business operations. Also, when merging a large amount of data from a wide variety of sources, one can gain insight on unexpected patterns that might not be otherwise disclosed by a limited number of conventional sources.

Recent scholars have used search engine traffic, website traffic, and social media content to monitor and predict tourist activities and sentiments. This chapter will review relevant studies in different fields. The authors will provide a conceptual framework on leveraging various sources of big data to monitor and forecast tourist activities and discuss the potential sources for big-data forecasting.

3.2   CONCEPTUAL FRAMEWORK

A tourist is a person on the move spatially; today's tourists will likely carry many technology gadgets with him or her and use them to interact with IT resources in the tourism industry. Thus, a tourist will generate and contribute a tremendous amount of data: for example, tourism website's analytics data, a hotel mobile app's log data, call center logs, the amount of foot traffic in the city, the sales records of travel services, search engine query volumes, social media mentions, location data from cell phones, GPS and photos, etc. All of these are potential indicators of a tourist's likes and dislikes, motivations, travel planning behavior, and actual travel and stay experience.

Combining these indicators together can make the data even more powerful and telling. Figure 3.1 shows a behavioral framework connecting the types of big data sources and a tourist's behavior. Different types of data will be available and useful in different stages of traveling: For example, tourists may perform searches before, en route to, or after arriving at a destination, while mobile positions are most useful in determining the location of the visitors while he or she is en route or at the destination. These assorted types of information are useful in monitoring and forecasting tourists' activities in different ways. The following section specifically discusses these information types, their usage, the results from past studies, and the potential for monitoring and forecasting tourist activities.

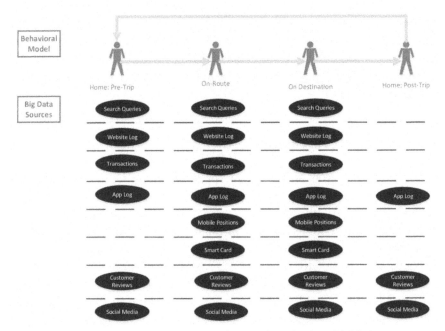

FIGURE 3.1   A Behavioral Model of Forecasting Tourist Behavior with Big Data

3.3   TYPES OF BIG DATA FOR MONITORING, UNDERSTANDING, AND FORECASTING TOURISTS' BEHAVIOR

Traditional forecasting methods usually hinge on historical data and a stable economic structure (Pan, Wu, & Song, 2012). Thus, dramatic change in economic structure may decrease the accuracy of these forecasting models. Big data has great potential in the short-term forecasting of dramatic and changing behavior. This section discusses different types of big data and their usefulness in monitoring and forecasting tourist activities.

3.3.1   SEARCH QUERIES

Searching is the most popular activity on the Internet in the United States (Purcell, 2011). The queries typed in search engines reflect users' interests, informational needs, attitude, and feelings. Most tourists use search engines to look for information; thus, the traces of their search activities could be used to monitor and predict their travel behavior. For example, Pan, Litvin, and O'Donnell (2007)investigated information needs for accommodations, as reflected by search engine queries. Xiang and Pan (2011) studied how users search information for a destination city.

A few researchers have been using search engine queries for forecasting travel demand. Choi and Varian (2012) adopted the Google Trends index for Hong Kong in a time series method. Their model increased the forecasting accuracy for monthly volumes of visitors from the top nine origin countries to Hong Kong. Gawlik, Kabaria, and Kaur (2011) improved Choi and Varian (2012)'s algorithm by considering query-specific data, and they proposed a method for selecting relevant queries, leading to a significant improvement in forecasting accuracy. Similarly, Pan, Wu, and Song (2012) adopted search queries for a US destination and improved the forecasting accuracy for local hotel occupancy rates based on the traditional time series method. Yang, Pan, Evans, and Lv (2015) further demonstrated that Baidu queries are more useful than Google in forecasting visitor volumes to a destination in China. Bangwayo-Skeete and Skeete (2015) used Google Trends data with an Autoregressive Mixed-Data Sample Method and helped increase the forecasting accuracy of five popular tourist destinations in the Caribbean.

3.3.2   WEB ANALYTICS DATA

When visitors land on a website, their browsers communicate with the Web server continuously. The website owner can use page-tagging and web-log analysis to track visitor behavior (Clifton, 2010).

Researchers have used Web traffic data to predict business revenues, including the revenue of Internet companies from 1998 to 2000 (Trueman, Wong, & Zhang, 2001). Lazer, Lev, and Livnat (2001) correlated Internet traffic data with portfolio returns of publicly traded Internet companies. Their results showed that higher Web traffic for those companies correlated with higher returns. In the tourism field, Yang, Pan, and Song (2014) used a local Destination Marketing Organization's web traffic to forecast each local hospitality industry's average occupancy. The results highlighted the significant predictive power of DMOs' Web traffic data: these data provided a 7% to 10% increase in accuracy when forecasting hotel occupancy four to eight weeks in advance.

3.3.3   GPS LOGS AND MOBILE POSITIONING

The understanding of the spatial–temporal pattern of tourist movement reveals vital insights for tourism infrastructure planning, tourist route design,
and tourism capacity management (Shoval, Isaacson, & Chhetri, 2013). The
widespread adoption of several spatial–temporal digital tracking technologies provides various types of big data to further understand this pattern of
tourists at different scales (Shoval & Isaacson, 2007). Even though GPS
data sets are fairly popular in studies with a small size of participation-based
tourist sample (Shoval et al., 2013), there are very few large data sets of GPS
logs used for tourist tracking. Gang et al. (2013) recognized the potential to
utilize taxi GPS logs to study tourist movement by focusing on traces starting from and/or ending at tourist attractions.

Since modern tourists use mobile phones and smartphones at different
stages of their travel (Wang, Xiang, & Fesenmaier, 2014), another type of
big data—mobile positioning data—became greatly useful in highlighting
hotspots of tourist activities and understanding tourists' data traces (Shoval et
al., 2013). Shoval and Isaacson (2007) compared different methods for tracking tourist movement, such as cell-tower tracking, Assisted GPS (A-GPS),
and Wi-Fi. Even though non-GPS mobile positioning data have been found
to be less accurate than GPS log data (Shoval & Isaacson, 2007),due to the
difficulty of data access caused by confidentiality concerns, mobile positioning data offer several notable advantages, such as lower data collection
cost, a larger volume of data, functionality in indoor environments, and less
sample selection bias due to the non-participatory nature of surveyors (Ahas,
Aasa, Mark, Pae, & Kull, 2007).

Asakura and Iryo (2007)designed a route topology index based on mobile
positioning in order to understand the topological characteristics of tourist
behavior. A group of researchers from Estonia utilized a nationwide roam-
ing mobile dataset of the Estonian GSM network to study the seasonality
of tourism hotspots (Ahas et al., 2007), destination loyalty of visitors (Tiru,
Kuusik, Lamp, & Ahas, 2010), space–time flows of tourists (Ahas, Aasa,
Roose, Mark, & Silm, 2008), market segmentation of repeat visitors (Vadi et
al., 2011), and travel distance of visitors (Nilbe, Ahas, & Silm, 2014). Based
on a rich mobile positioning dataset, Tiru, Saluveer, Ahas, and Aasa (2010)
also designed an online tourism monitoring tool for Estonia. Di Lorenzo,
Reades, Calabrese, and Ratti (2012) extracted the information from people's
past trajectory histories reflected in mobile positioning data, and predicted
the location of a person over time.

3.3.4 BLUETOOTH AND INFRARED TRACKING

In this digital age, with the popularity of Bluetooth-enabled devices (smartphones, laptops, tablets, and headsets), Bluetooth tracking technology has been used to further understand tourists' spatial–temporal movement patterns on a small scale (Versichele et al., 2014; Versichele, Neutens, Delafontaine, & Van de Weghe, 2012). Versichele et al. (2012)used this tracking technology to understand visitor movement at the Ghent Festivities, and Versichele et al. (2014) demonstrated a visit pattern map by mining the big data of citywide Bluetooth tracking in Ghent, Belgium. An Alge-Timing system with infrared technology has also been introduced to monitor the movement of people within a park (O'Connor, Zerger, & Itami, 2005).

3.3.5 CUSTOMER REVIEWS

The Internet has become a major distribution channel for hotel sales (Connolly, Olsen, & Moore, 1998). The growing use of social media allows tourists to post their travel-related information and connect with others on a shared platform (Leung, Law, van Hoof, & Buhalis, 2013). Social media have been widely embraced by tourists through a large variety of social media websites, such as customer reviews, blogs/microblogs, online communities, and media sharing sites.

Electronic word of mouth (eWoM) about hotels is an important source for hotel guests to alleviate information asymmetry disadvantage when making booking decisions, and this source of information is expected to be more convincing and reliable than other information they can obtain on gauging the quality of hotels (Öğüt & Onur Taş, 2012). Sparks and Browning (2011) found that a high level of perceived trust in online reviews is associated with positively framed information and with numerical ratings that focus on interpersonal services. In general, there are two research streams to leverage the big data of customer reviews: The causal model of customer reviews and performance, and data mining of reviews.

For the first stream of research, several studies employed econometric models to decipher the causal relationship between online customer reviews and hotel performance measures. Ye, Law, and Gu (2009) found that a high score in average customer rating from Ctrip.com boosts the sales of Chinese city hotels, whereas a high level of discrepancy in customer reviews (variance of rating) reduces sales. Öğüt and Onur Taş (2012) also discovered the positive relationship between customer rating from the online travel agency, Booking.com, and online sales of hotels in Paris and London. Andersson (2010) obtained consumer feedback information on Singapore's hotels across six attributes from HotelTravel.com, and an analysis revealed that a higher room price is associated with higher customer numeric ratings on "standard of room", "hotel facilities", and "food and beverage". Zhang, Ye, and Law (2011) show that, among four types of customer ratings from TripAdvisor.com, the ratings of "room quality" and "location" are significantly correlated with room price for hotels in New York. By using the hotel review data from Booking.com, Yacouel and Fleischer (2012) found that hotels with a higher average score from reviewers charge a price premium. Based on the review data from the online meta-booking engine trivago.com, Schamel (2012) also reached a similar finding: Consumer rating is positively associated with room rate for both weekend and midweek hotel stays.

For the second stream of research, since the reviews posted online incorporate customers' opinions and attitudes subjectively expressed in natural language text, they are hard to summarize in a single or multiple numeric ratings. Data mining becomes a promising tool to better understand embedded tourists' experiences in an efficient and accurate way. To better analyze the attitudes of customers in their reviews, Pekar and Shiyan (2008) adapted the opinion-mining technique to extract patterns embedded in the customer reviews from Epinions.com. Ye, Zhang, and Law (2009) conducted opinion mining on traveler reviews from Yahoo! Travel. Li, Ye, and Law (2012) text-mined the traveler reviews from a third-party website, Daodao. com, in China, and found six categories of factors influencing customer satisfaction.

In addition, in their efforts to propose a ranking system for hotels based on numerical values, Ghose, Ipeirotis, and Li (2012) parsed customer reviews from Travelocity.com and TripAdvisor.com using text-mining techniques. Liu, Law, Rong, Li, and Hall (2013) used sentiment mining to impute the missing value in the traveler review dataset from TripAdvisor.com, and then they utilized association rule mining to investigate how satisfaction and expectations vary for customers with different trip modes. Capriello, Mason, Davis, and Crotts (2013) compared different methods for mining tourists' sentiment and found that manual content coding, corpus-based semantic methods, and stance-shift analysis provide robust and similar results. Li, Law, Vu, and Rong (2013) used another data-mining technique, the Choquet Integral, to look into the hotel selection preferences of inbound travelers to Hong Kong with customer review data from TripAdvisor. Brejla and Gilbert (2014) text-mined customer reviews from CruiseCritic.com, and recognized patterns of co-creation of cruise value. In addition, Johnson, Sieber, Magnien, and Ariwi (2011) demonstrated the use of automated Web harvesting in extracting review data from Travel Review to better monitor tourists' experience. Zhang, Ye, Song, and Liu (2013) also investigated the structure of customer satisfaction and dissatisfaction with cruiseline services using the review data from CruiseCritic.com. Lastly, moving beyond data mining, Korfiatis and Poulos (2013) designed a demographic recommended system using online reviews from Booking.com as inputs.

3.3.6   OTHER USER-GENERATED CONTENT

Large amounts of user-generated content (UGC) have become available through social media (Lu & Stepchenkova, 2014), and they provide valuable information to better understand tourists' behavior and experience (Tussyadiah & Fesenmaier, 2009), attitudes and preferences (Magnini, Crotts, & Zehrer, 2011), and public images of tourist destinations (Choi, Lehto, & Morrison, 2007). Akehurst (2009) argued that UGC is more credible and trustworthy than other conventional marketing communications. Sharda and Ponnada (2008) introduced a Blog Visualizer to present the most relevant and useful blogs for tour planning.

Quantitative content analysis has been frequently utilized to analyze UGC by keyword counting and text characteristic measuring (Carson, 2008; Wenger, 2008). Pan, MacLaurin, and Crotts (2007) employed semantic network analysis to understand Charleston, South Carolina's destination image from the UGC on travel blogs. Moreover, several studies introduced netnography and netblographyas methods to use available UGC to decipher the interpretation of places, people, and situations by tourists (Hsu, Dehuang, & Woodside, 2009; Woodside, Cruickshank, & Dehuang, 2007). Kwok and Yu (2013) studied restaurant-related social media messages on Facebook and found that, compared to sales and marketing messages, conversational messages are endorsed by Facebook users. Stepchenkova and Zhan (2013) analyzed online user-generated photography, a particular type of UGC, to understand Peru's image as a tourist destination. Pang et al. (2011) proposed a framework to summarize a tourist destination by mining different aspects of both textual and visual UGC on tourist destinations.

Recently, with the development of reliable and accessible smartphones with built-in GPS antennas, tourists are able to share their UGC on smartphones with high-precision geo-referenced data, such as geo-referenced Twitter sharing and geo-tagged photos. This type of data offers several advantages to track tourists' movement patterns. First, it provides additional data on tourists' travel histories and their profiles (Kádár & Gede, 2013). Second, the data alleviates the sample selection bias of surveyed tourists, which is inherently embedded in the conventional tourist survey (Girardin, Fiore, Ratti, & Blat, 2008). Girardin et al. (2008) investigated the geo-referenced information of photos taken by tourists from the photo-sharing website Flickr and geo-visualized tourist hotspots and travel trajectories. To better understand visitors' travel patterns in nature protected areas, Orsi and Geneletti (2013) used the visitor flow information embedded in geo-tagged photographs to estimate a gravity model. Kádár (2014) validated the accuracy of Flickr geo-tagged photos by comparing them with tourism statistical data and found a high level of correlation between them. He argued that tourists are more likely to take multiple photos of complex urban or architectural structures. Vu, Li, Law, and Ye (2015) introduced a framework to understand tourist travel behavior using geo-tagged photos and proposed a Markov chain model for travel pattern mining. On a larger scale, Hawelka et al. (2014) show the usefulness of geo-located Twitter data as a proxy for country-to-country tourist/visitor flows, and these data provide information that is similar to official international tourism statistics.

3.3.7 TRANSACTION DATA

Now, with the development of computer-based electronic funds transfer systems, credit cards from different points of origin are widely accepted around the world. As a result, the credit card has become a popular travel companion, and tourists have achieved increased mobility around the world (Weaver, 2005). Morrison, Bose, and O'Leary (1999) retrieved transaction data from a credit card service's marketing database to understand the demographic, socioeconomic, and psychographic characteristics of cardholders who used their cards to engage in hotel transactions. Moreover, credit card transaction data can be geo-coded by the address of card terminals. More importantly, the financial value of transactions provides important information on visitors' expenditures. By using bank card transactions data, Sobolevsky et al. (2014) investigated the mobility patterns of foreign visitors within Spain by network analysis and gravity models. They concluded that this type of data is particularly useful in understanding large-scale mobility.

After the introduction of computerized reservation systems into the tourism and hospitality industry, transaction data from hotel reservations and bookings became important in forecasting hospitality demand and understanding the travel patterns of hotel guests (Sato, 2012). To better understand the pre-purchase comparison behavior of online customers, Chatterjee and Wang (2012) used online transaction data and clickstream data, and they examined the relationship between customers' comparison search dispersion and purchase probability for flights, rental cars, and hotels. Weaver (2008) pointed out the potential use of another type of big data: tourist-reward-points data. These huge datasets enable airlines, hotels, and casinos to get a more comprehensive picture of preferences and behaviors of their customers.

Different from other types of data sources, transaction data are the results of product purchases and could also be used to monitor and forecast other types of spending. For example, transaction data for airline tickets could be used to predict future hotel purchases and attraction attendance. ForwardKeys (ForwardKeys.com) is a company that mines global distribution system transaction data, and a few hotel companies and destinations have adopted its products for analytical and forecasting purposes (ForwardKeys, 2014).

3.3.8   APP LOGS

Large amounts of log data for mobile apps are available through smartphone application software, which runs in the background of mobile operating systems and transmits the records of user activities to the app server. The log data captured by the software, as an alternative to other automated data collection methods, provide detailed records of location, voice calls, SMS messages, data usage, and application usage (Bouwman, de Reuver, Heerschap, & Verkasalo, 2013; Hamka, Bouwman, de Reuver, & Kroesen, 2014).

Schaller, Harvey, and Elsweiler (2014) utilized the log data of an Android app, consisting of all user interactions and positional data from the app, to predict visits to a cultural event in Munich. Hamka et al. (2014) conducted a psychographic and demographic segmentation of mobile users based on the log data from smartphone measurement software. Vlassenroot, Gillis, Bellens, and Gautama (2014) used several tracking applications installed on Android phones to mine the travel patterns of smartphone users. Passive trip logging keeps the log data from the GPS, the signals from nearby cell towers and Wi-Fi networks, and the data from the accelerometer. Heerschap, Ortega, Priem, and Offermans (2014) demonstrated another example of using app log data for tourism statistics in the Netherlands. The smartphone measurement software registers time and location every 5 min, and this allowed a heat map of travel behavior to be generated.

3.3.9 SMART CARDS

Smart cards have been introduced for automated fare collection systems, such as those used to automate ticketing systems for public transportation (Yue, Lan, Yeh, & Li, 2014). More recently, smart card systems have been used to provide payment functions for various business-like restaurants, grocery stores, and healthcare services. Hotel guests can also swipe smart cards for different activities within a resort. In the field of transportation research, big data from smart cards has been used to understand the transport flow patterns of city residents and predict their future spatial movement trajectories (Pelletier, Trépanier, & Morency, 2011). After conducting a geo-demographic analysis based on transit smart card data, Páez, Trépanier, and Morency (2011) highlighted potential business opportunities for many hospitality business establishments. Moreover, Li, van Heck, and Vervest (2006) demonstrated a method for dynamic pricing strategies based on smartcard data from the travel industry. As a type of smartcard, the destination card, which offers free/discounted admission to various activities and attractions within a destination, has been found to be particularly useful in understanding the intra-destination movements of tourists (Zoltan & McKercher, 2014).

3.4 CONCLUSIONS

In conclusion, many types of big data, from a variety of sources, are available to monitor and predict tourist behavior. Travelers generate different types of big data in various travel stages: searches and web visits prior to the trip, GPS locations and transaction during the trip, and social media mentions during and after the trip. The different lag structure determines their distinct utility values: Many are useful for real-time tracking at the destination, while others are instrumental in forecasting future tourist activities. For example, search engine queries and website traffic have been used for forecasting purposes, while GPS data and social media content are used more often for real-time position and service quality monitoring.

3.4.1 FUTURE RESEARCH

However, many limitations exist for these reviewed studies. For example, search engine queries and web traffic are useful in helping forecast tourist volumes and hotel occupancy for a destination. However, no studies hither to have adopted these data to forecast the revenue or customer numbers for a specific hospitality or tourism business. Researchers have embraced mobile data for monitoring activities, but no studies have focused on predicting users' spatial behavior based on mobile data. It is the latter that will provide great potential for tourism industry management in order to reduce crowding and to strategically allocate resources. Bluetooth tracking can offer accurate data of visitors' whereabouts because of a unique ID for visitor identification. However, the investment in the required infrastructure will be prohibitive on a large scale, whereas GPS systems use only a few satellites to cover the entire surface of the earth. Very few studies on causal relationship between reviews and business performance have been conducted, so does forecasting the latter from the former. App log data are specific to an application and, thus, wide sharing is limited. Privacy concerns might also prohibit businesses sharing their data. However, individual businesses or organizations may be able to mine the application data to track visitors' behavior and predict their activities.

Thus, there are five future directions of the usage of big data analytics for hotel and tourism industry:

1. Understanding tourist behavior. For example, big data can provide insights on tourists' likes and dislikes; the way tourists plan their stay; the time when they start booking their hotel rooms; the service weaknesses that impact hotel occupancy and revenue;
2. Forecasting tourist activities and the future performance of tourism businesses. The likelihood that one will have an overbooked hotel, whether or not one needs to hire more hourly staff, the amount of increase in occupancy one can expect in the following weeks;
3. Personalizing of service and improving customer experience. Tourism businesses can target each individual guest's likes and dislikes and focus on a market size of one;
4. Optimizing business operations. The discovery of the key predictors of a hotel's occupancy and revenue; the design of marketing and operation strategy to improve performance in those key predictors.
5. Allocating resources and facilities at destinations. By understanding tourists' spatial–temporal movement patterns and their preferences, tourist destinations are better able to propose more specific planning strategies to satisfy tourist needs and, hence, to maximize potential revenue.

First, past studies have been focusing on the first and second directions on understanding and forecasting; to our knowledge, directly connecting big data with personalization, optimization, and resource allocation are still rare, if there is any. Future studies could focus on studying big data along with its direct applications in personalization, optimization, and e-resource allocation. It calls for more experimental studies which directly test the insights of big data with changes of business operations. Second, almost all studies have focused on a single source of big data, either search engine queries or web traffic, the combination of different data sources possess great potential in increasing forecasting accuracy. Scholars should focus on more utilization of different data sources on monitoring and forecasting. Third, the current studies have focused on the level of a destination, and research on an individual business or organization is still lacking, probably due to a lack of data. This review calls for more collaboration between individual businesses and researchers on fully taking advantages of big data analytics to increase their revenue and profit.

In general, research at the crossroads of the tourism industry and big data is still limited: Most studies focus on identifying correlation and causal relationships. Forecasting with big data for specific properties or businesses is rare. Furthermore, the combination of multiple data sources possesses huge potential and dramatically raises the accuracy of forecasting and monitoring. Privacy concerns and the business boundaries may also limit the wide adoption and application and sharing of big data.

Many off-the-shelf tools for these purposes have emerged, including solutions from Datameer, Solace Systems, and Metric Insights, but these are general tools and still in an early stage of development and adoption. These platforms assist researchers in extracting data from diverse sources and analyzing them by using a dashboard-like user interface. Many commercial or free statistical and data mining software solutions, such as SAS, R, Python, and Oracle, provide additional tools, but they are not designed with simplified tourism analysis in mind, and they may be cumbersome for use for this purpose.

From a macro-level perspective, the research and applications of big data in the tourism industry are still at an early stage. Like the adoption and application of other information technologies and byproducts, we expect that big data will likely go through a preliminary phase in which it receives considerable attention and focus before the related technology starts to mature and its productivity starts to increase. Once this occurs, the utilization and application of big data will show its full impact and significance. Hoteliers and tourism professionals who moved quickly and were early adopters of big data will enjoy a competitive advantage. However, with the further development of data and tools, and more research on its application in the hospitality and tourism field, the use of big data will inevitably increase beyond these early adopters, and the market will eventually produce effective tools that are accessible throughout the industry. The evolution of data, tools, and our understanding of this phenomenon will converge, and real increase in productivity and applicable insight, as a result, will occur.

KEYWORDS

- **monitoring**
- **forecasting tourist activities**
- **big data**
- **web analytic**
- **customer reviews**

REFERENCES

Ahas, R.; Aasa, A.; Mark, Ü.; Pae, T.; Kull, A. Seasonal Tourism Spaces in Estonia: Case Study with Mobile Positioning Data. *Tourism Manage.* **2007,** *28*(3), 898–910.

Ahas, R.; Aasa, A.; Roose, A.; Mark, Ü.; Silm, S. Evaluating Passive Mobile Positioning Data for Tourism Surveys: An Estonian Case Study. *Tourism Manage.* **2008,** *29*(3), 469–486.

Akehurst, G. User Generated Content: The Use of Blogs for Tourism Organisations and Tourism Consumers (English). *Serv. Bus.* **2009,** *3*(1), 51–61.

Andersson, D. E. Hotel Attributes and Hedonic Prices: An Analysis of Internet-Based Transactions in Singapore's Market for Hotel Rooms (English). *Ann. Reg. Sci.* **2010,** *44*(2), 229–240.

Asakura, Y.; Iryo, T. Analysis of Tourist Behaviour Based on the Tracking Data Collected Using a Mobile Communication Instrument. *Transp. Res. Part A: Policy Pract.* **2007,** *41*(7), 684–690.

Askitas, N.; Zimmermann, K. Google Econometrics and Unemployment Forecasting. *Appl. Econ. Q.* **2009,** *55*(2), 107–120.

Bangwayo-Skeete, P.; Skeete, R. W. Can Google Data Improve the Forecasting Performance of Tourist Arrivals? Mixed-Data Sampling Approach. *Tourism Manage.* **2015,** *46*, 454–464.

Baram-Tsabari, A.; Segev, E. Exploring New Web-Based Tools to Identify Public Interest in Science. *Public Understand. Sci.* **2011,** *20*(1), 130–143.

Bouwman, H.; de Reuver, M.; Heerschap, N.; Verkasalo, H. Opportunities and Problems with Automated Data Collection via Smartphones. *Mobile Media Commun.* **2013,** *1*(1), 63–68.

Brejla, P.; Gilbert, D. An Exploratory Use of Web Content Analysis to Understand Cruise Tourism Services. *Int. J. Tourism Res.* **2014,** *16*(2), 157–168.

Capriello, A.; Mason, P. R.; Davis, B.; Crotts, J. C. Farm Tourism Experiences in Travel Reviews: A Cross-comparison of Three Alternative Methods for Data Analysis. *J. Bus. Res.* **2013,** *66*(6), 778–785.

Carson, D. The 'Blogosphere' as a Market Research Tool for Tourism Destinations: A Case Study of Australia's Northern Territory. *J. Vacation Mark.* **2008,** *14*(2), 111–119.

Chatterjee, P.; Wang, Y. Online Comparison Shopping Behavior of Travel Consumers. *J. Qual. Assur. Hospitality Tourism* **2012,** *13*(1), 1–23.

Choi, H.; Varian, H. Predicting the Present with Google Trends. *Econ. Rec.* **2012,** *88*(s1), 2–9.

Choi, S.; Lehto, X. Y.; Morrison, A. M. Destination Image Representation on the Web: Content Analysis of Macau Travel Related Websites. *Tourism Manage.* **2007,** *28*(1), 118–129.

Clifton, B. *Advanced Web metrics with Google analytics: Sybex*, 2010.

Connolly, D. j.; Olsen, M. D.; Moore, R. G. The Internet as a Distribution Channel. *Cornell Hotel Restaurant Admin. Q.* **1998,** *39*(4), 42–54.

Di Lorenzo, G.; Reades, J.; Calabrese, F.; Ratti, C. Predicting Personal Mobility with Individual and Group Travel Histories. *Environ. Plann. B: Plann. Des.* **2012,** *39*(5), 838–857.

ForwardKeys. *ForwardKeys—Applied Traveller Intelligence for Tactical Marketers—DMO, Hoteliers, Merchants, etc.*, 2014 (retrieved from http://forwardkeys.com/revenue-management/article/quantified-occupancy-forecasts.html).

Gang, P.; Guande, Q.; Zhaohui, W.; Daqing, Z.; Shijian, L. Land-Use Classification Using Taxi GPS Traces. *Intell. Transp. Syst., IEEE Trans.* **2013,** *14*(1), 113–123.

Gawlik, E.; Kabaria, H.; Kaur, S. Predicting Tourism Trends with Google Insights, 2011. Retrieved from http://cs229.stanford.edu/proj2011/GawlikKaurKabaria-PredictingTouris mTrendsWithGoogleInsights.pdf.

Ghose, A.; Ipeirotis, P. G.; Li, B. Designing Ranking Systems for Hotels on Travel Search Engines by Mining User-Generated and Crowdsourced Content. *Mark. Sci.* **2012,** *31*(3), 493–520.

Ginsberg, J.; Mohebbi, M. H.; Patel, R. S.; Brammer, L.; Smolinski, M. S.; Brilliant, L. Detecting Influenza Epidemics Using Search Engine Query Data. *Nature* **2009,** *457*(7232), 1012–1014.

Girardin, F.; Fiore, F. D.; Ratti, C.; Blat, J. Leveraging Explicitly Disclosed Location Information to Understand Tourist Dynamics: A Case Study. *J. Location Based Serv.* **2008,** *2*(1), 41–56.

Hamka, F.; Bouwman, H.; de Reuver, M.; Kroesen, M. Mobile Customer Segmentation Based on Smartphone Measurement. *Telematics Inform.* **2014,** *31*(2), 220–227.

Hand, C.; Judge, G. Searching for the Picture: Forecasting UK Cinema Admissions Using Google Trends Data. *Appl. Econ. Lett.* 2012, *19*(11), 1051–1055.

Hawelka, B.; Sitko, I.; Beinat, E.; Sobolevsky, S.; Kazakopoulos, P.; Ratti, C. Geo-located Twitter as Proxy for Global Mobility Patterns. *Cartogr. Geog. Inf. Sci.* **2014,** *41*(3), 260–271.

He, W.; Zha, S.; Li, L. Social Media Competitive Analysis and Text Mining: A Case Study in the Pizza Industry. *Int. J. Inf. Manage.* **2013,** *33*(3), 464–472.

Heerschap, N.; Ortega, S.; Priem, A.; Offermans, M. *Innovation of Tourism Statistics Through the Use of New Big Data Sources*. Paper Presented at the Global Forum on Tourism Statistics, Prague, 2014.

Hsu, S. Y.; Dehuang, N.; Woodside, A. G. Storytelling Research of Consumers' Self-Reports of Urban Tourism Experiences in China. *J. Bus. Res.* 2009, *62*(12), 1223–1254.

Johnson, P. A.; Sieber, R. E.; Magnien, N.; Ariwi, J. Automated Web Harvesting to Collect and Analyse User-Generated Content for Tourism. *Curr. Issues Tourism* 2011, *15*(3), 293–299.

Kádár, B. Measuring Tourist Activities in Cities Using Geotagged Photography. *Tourism Geogr.* **2014,** *16*(1), 88–104.

Kádár, B.; Gede, M. Where do Tourists Go? Visualizing and Analysing the Spatial Distribution of Geotagged Photography. *Cartographica: Int. J. Geogr. Inf. Geovisual.* **2013,** *48*(2), 78–88.

Korfiatis, N.; Poulos, M. Using Online Consumer Reviews as a Source for Demographic Recommendations: A Case Study Using Online Travel Reviews. *Expert Syst. Appl.* **2013,** *40*(14), 5507–5515.

Kwok, L.; Yu, B. Spreading Social Media Messages on Facebook: An Analysis of Restaurant Business-to-Consumer Communications. *Cornell Hospitality Q.* **2013,** *54*(1), 84–94.

Lazer, R.; Lev, B.; Livnat, J. Internet Traffic and Portfolio Returns. *Finan. Anal. J.* **2001,** *57*(3), 30–40.

Leung, D.; Law, R.; van Hoof, H.; Buhalis, D. Social Media in Tourism and Hospitality: A Literature Review. *J. Travel Tourism Market.* **2013,** *30*(1–2), 3–22.

Li, G.; Law, R.; Vu, H. Q.; Rong, J. Discovering the Hotel Selection Preferences of Hong Kong Inbound Travelers Using the Choquet Integral. *Tourism Manage.* **2013,** *36*(0), 321–330.

Li, H.; Ye, Q.; Law, R. Determinants of Customer Satisfaction in the Hotel Industry: An Application of Online Review Analysis. *Asia Pac. J. Tourism Res.* **2012,** *18*(7), 784–802.

Li, T.; van Heck, E.; Vervest, P. Dynamic Pricing Strategies for Yield Improvement with Smart Card Adoption in the Dutch Travel Industry. In *Information and Communication Technologies in Tourism 2006*; Hitz, M., Sigala M., Murphy J., Eds.; Springer: Vienna, 2006; pp 234–234.

Liu, S.; Law, R.; Rong, J.; Li, G.; Hall, J. Analyzing Changes in hotel Customers' Expectations by Trip Mode. *Int. J. Hospitality Manage.* **2013,** *34*(0), 359–371.

Lu, W.; Stepchenkova, S. User-Generated Content as a Research Mode in Tourism and Hospitality Applications: Topics, Methods, and Software. *J. Hospitality Marketing Manage.* **2014,** null–null.

Magnini, V. P.; Crotts, J. C.; Zehrer, A. Understanding Customer Delight: An Application of Travel Blog Analysis. *J. Travel Res.* **2011,** *50*(5), 535–545.

Mayer-Schonberger, V.; Cukier, K. *Big Data: A Revolution that Will Transform how We Live, Work, and Think*: Eamon Dolan/Houghton Mifflin Harcourt, 2013.

Morrison, A. M.; Bose, G.; O'Leary, J. T. Can Statistical Modeling Help with Data Mining. *J. Hospitality Leisure Marketing* 1999, *6*(4), 91–110.

Nilbe, K.; Ahas, R.; Silm, S. Evaluating the Travel Distances of Events Visitors and Regular Visitors Using Mobile Positioning Data: The Case of Estonia. *J. Urban Technol.* **2014,** *21*(2), 91–107.

Nyheim, P. D.; McFadden, F. M.; Connolly, D. J. *Technology Strategies for the Hospitality Industry*; Prentice-Hall, Inc., 2004.

O'Connor, A.; Zerger, A.; Itami, B. Geo-Temporal Tracking and Analysis of Tourist Movement. *Math. Comput. Simul.* **2005,** *69*(1–2), 135–150.

Öğüt, H.; Onur Taş, B. K. The Influence Of Internet Customer Reviews on the Online Sales and Prices in Hotel Industry. *Ser. Ind. J.* **2012,** *32*(2), 197–214.

Orsi, F.; Geneletti, D. Using Geotagged Photographs and GIS Analysis to Estimate Visitor Flows in Natural Areas. *J. Nature Conser.* **2013,** *21*(5), 359–368.

Páez, A.; Trépanier, M.; Morency, C. Geodemographic Analysis and the Identification of Potential Business Partnerships Enabled by Transit Smart Cards. *Transp. Res. Part A: Policy Prac.* **2011,** *45*(7), 640–652.

Pan, B.; Litvin, S. W.; O'Donnell, T. E. Understanding Accommodation Search Query Formulation: The First Step in Putting 'Heads in Beds'. *J. Vacation Marketing* **2007,** *13*(4), 371–381.

Pan, B.; MacLaurin, T.; Crotts, J. C. Travel Blogs and the Implications for Destination Marketing. *J. Travel Res.* **2007,** *46*(1), 35–45.

Pan, B.; Wu, D. C.; Song, H. Forecasting Hotel Room Demand Using Search Engine Data. *J. Hospitality Tourism Technol.* **2012,** *3*(3), 196–210.

Pang, Y.; Hao, Q.; Yuan, Y.; Hu, T.; Cai, R.; Zhang, L. Summarizing Tourist Destinations by Mining User-Generated Travelogues and Photos. *Comput. Vision Image Understand.* **2011,** *115*(3), 352–363.

Pekar, V.; Shiyan, O. Discovery of Subjective Evaluations of Product Features in Hotel Reviews. *J. Vacation Mark.* **2008,** *14*(2), 145–155.

Pelletier, M.-P.; Trépanier, M.; Morency, C. Smart Card Data Use in Public Transit: A Literature Review. *Transp. Res. Part C: Emerg. Technol.* **2011,** *19*(4), 557–568.

Poon, A. *Tourism, Technology and Competitive Strategies*; Wallingford, CT: CAB International, 1993.

Purcell, K. Search and Email Still Top the List of Most Popular Online Activities. *Pew Research Internet Project: Report*, 2011 (retrieved from http://www.pewinternet.org/2011/08/09/search-and-email-still-top-the-list-of-most-popular-online-activities/).

Sato, A. H. Patterns of Regional Travel Behavior: An Analysis of Japanese Hotel Reservation Data. *Int. Rev. Financial Anal.* **2012,** *23*(0), 55–65.

Schaller, R.; Harvey, M.; Elsweiler, D. Detecting Event Visits in Urban Areas via Smartphone GPS Data. In *Advances in Information Retrieval*; de Rijke M., Kenter, T., de Vries, A., Zhai, C., de Jong, F., Radinsky, K., Hofmann, K., Eds.; Springer International Publishing, 2014; Vol. 8416, pp 681–686.

Schaller, R. R. Moore's Law: Past, Present and Future. *IEEE Spectrum* **1997,** *34*(6), 52–59.

Schamel, G. Weekend vs. midweek stays: Modelling Hotel Room Rates in a Small Market. *Int. J. Hospitality Manage.* **2012,** *31*(4), 1113–1118.

Sharda, N.; Ponnada, M. Tourism Blog Visualizer for Better Tour Planning. *J. Vacation Mark.* **2008,** *14*(2), 157–167.

Shoval, N.; Isaacson, M. Tracking Tourists in the Digital Age. *Ann. Tourism Res.* **2007,** *34*(1), 141–159.

Shoval, N.; Isaacson, M.; Chhetri, P. GPS, Smartphones, and the Future of Tourism Research. *The Wiley Blackwell Companion to Tourism*, 2013, pp 251–261.

Sobolevsky, S.; Sitko, I.; Tachet des Combes, R.; Hawelka, B.; Murillo Arias, J.; Ratti, C. *Money on the Move: Big Data of Bank Card Transactions as the New Proxy for Human Mobility Patterns and Regional Delineation. The Case of Residents and Foreign Visitors in Spain.* Paper Presented at the Big Data (BigData Congress), 2014 IEEE International Congress on, 2014, June 27 2014–July 2 2014.

Song, H.; Witt, S. F.; Li, G. *The advanced econometrics of tourism demand*: Routledge 2008.

Sparks, B. A.; Browning, V. The Impact of Online Reviews on Hotel Booking Intentions and Perception of Trust. *Tourism Manage.* **2011,** *32*(6), 1310–1323.

Stepchenkova, S.; Zhan, F. Visual Destination Images of Peru: Comparative Content Analysis of DMO and User-Generated Photography. *Tourism Manage.* **2013,** *36*(0), 590–601.

Tiru, M.; Kuusik, A.; Lamp, M. L.; Ahas, R. LBS in Marketing and Tourism Management: Measuring Destination Loyalty with Mobile Positioning Data. *J. Location Based Serv.* **2010,** *4*(2), 120–140.

Tiru, M.; Saluveer, E.; Ahas, R.; Aasa, A. The Positium Barometer: A Web-Based Tool for Monitoring the Mobility of Tourists. *J. Urban Technol.* **2010,** *17*(1), 71–89.

Tnooz. *Google's 2014 Travel Study: App Mania has Ebbed, Yet Booking by Smartphone is Still Hot,* 2014 (retrieved from http://www.tnooz.com/article/google-research-travel-marketers-traveler-shopping-behavior/).

Trueman, B.; Wong, M. F.; Zhang, X. J. Back to basics: Forecasting the Revenues of Internet firms. *Rev. Accounting Stud.* **2001,** *6*(2–3), 305–329.

Tussyadiah, I. P.; Fesenmaier, D. R. Mediating Tourist Experiences: Access to Places via Shared Videos. *Ann. Tourism Res.* **2009,** *36*(1), 24–40.

Vadi, M.; Vedina, R.; Karma, K.; Kuusik, A.; Tiru, M.; Ahas, R.; et al. Innovation in Destination Marketing. *Baltic J. Manage.* **2011,** *6*(3), 378–399.

Versichele, M.; de Groote, L.; Claeys Bouuaert, M.; Neutens, T.; Moerman, I.; Van de Weghe, N. Pattern Mining in Tourist Attraction Visits Through Association Rule Learning on Bluetooth Tracking Data: A case Study of Ghent, Belgium. *Tourism Manage.* **2014,** *44*(0), 67–81.

Versichele, M.; Neutens, T.; Delafontaine, M.; Van de Weghe, N. The Use of Bluetooth for Analysing Spatiotemporal Dynamics of Human Movement at Mass Events: A Case Study of the Ghent Festivities. *Appl. Geogr.* **2012,** *32*(2), 208–220.

Vlassenroot, S., Gillis, D., Bellens, R., & Gautama, S. The Use of Smartphone Applications in the Collection of Travel Behaviour Data (English). *Int. J. Intell. Transp. Syst. Res.* **2014,** 1–11.

Vosen, S.; Schmidt, T. A Monthly Consumption Indicator for Germany Based on Internet Search Query Data. *Appl. Econ. Lett.* **2012,** *19*(7), 683–687.

Vu, H. Q.; Li, G.; Law, R.; Ye, B. H. Exploring the Travel Behaviors of Inbound Tourists to Hong Kong Using Geotagged Photos. *Tourism Manage.* **2015,** *46*(0), 222–232.

Wang, D.; Xiang, Z.; Fesenmaier, D. R. Adapting to the Mobile World: A model of Smartphone Use. *Ann. Tourism Res.* **2014,** *48*(0), 11–26.

Weaver, A. 'Passports to Pleasure': Credit Cards and Contemporary Travel. *Int. J. Tourism Res.* **2005,** *7*(3), 151–159.

Weaver, A. When Tourists Become Data: Consumption, Surveillance and Commerce. *Curr. Issues Tourism* **2008,** *11*(1), 1–23.

Wenger, A. Analysis of Travel Bloggers' Characteristics and Their Communication about Austria as a Tourism Destination. *J. Vacation Mark.* **2008,** *14*(2), 169–176.

Woodside, A. G.; Cruickshank, B. F.; Dehuang, N. Stories Visitors Tell about Italian Cities as Destination Icons. *Tourism Manage.* **2007,** *28*(1), 162–174.

Wu, L.; Brynjolfsson, E. The Future of Prediction: How Google Searches Foreshadow Housing Prices and Sales. *Available at SSRN 2022293,* 2009.

Xiang, Z.; Pan, B. Travel Queries on Cities in the United States: Implications for Search Engine Marketing for Tourist Destinations. *Tourism Manage.* **2011,** *32*(1), 88–97.

Yacouel, N.; Fleischer, A. The Role of Cybermediaries in Reputation Building and Price Premiums in the Online Hotel Market. *J. Travel Res.* **2012,** *51*(2), 219–226.

Yang, X.; Pan, P.; Evans, J. A.; Lv, B. Forecasting Chinese Tourist Volume with Search Engine Data. *Tourism Manage.* **2015,** 46, 386–397.

Yang, Y.; Pan, B.; Song, H. Predicting Hotel Demand Using Destination Marketing Organization's Web Traffic Data. *Journal of Travel Research* **2014,** *53*(4), 433–447.

Ye, Q.; Law, R.; Gu, B. The Impact of Online User Reviews on Hotel Room Sales. *Int. J. Hospitality Manage.* **2009,** *28*(1), 180–182.

Ye, Q.; Zhang, Z.; Law, R. Sentiment Classification of Online Reviews to Travel Destinations by Supervised Machine Learning Approaches. *Expert Syst. Appl.* **2009,** *36*(3, Part 2), 6527–6535.

Yue, Y.; Lan, T.; Yeh, A. G. O.; Li, Q. Q. Zooming into Individuals to Understand the Collective: A Review of Trajectory-Based Travel Behaviour Studies. *Travel Behav. Soc.* **2014,** *1*(2), 69–78.

Zhang, Z.; Ye, Q.; Law, R. Determinants of Hotel Room Price: An Exploration of Travelers' Hierarchy of Accommodation Needs. *Int. J. Contemp. Hospitality Manage.* **2011,** *23*(7), 972–981.

Zhang, Z.; Ye, Q.; Song, H.; Liu, T. The Structure of Customer Satisfaction with Cruise-Line Services: An Empirical Investigation Based on Online Word of Mouth. *Curr. Issues Tourism* **2013,** 1–15.

Zoltan, J.; McKercher, B. Analysing Intra-Destination Movements and Activity Participation of Tourists Through Destination Card Consumption. *Tourism Geographies* **2014,** 1–17.

CHAPTER 4

MICRO-MARKETING AND BIG DATA ANALYTICS: AN INFORMATION SYSTEM FOR DESTINATION MARKETING MANAGEMENT

DANIEL R. FESENMAIER[1], NEERAJ BHARADWAJ[2],
JASON STIENMETZ[3] and ZHENG XIANG[4]

[1]National Laboratory for Tourism & eCommerce, Eric Friedheim Tourism Institute, Department of Tourism, Recreation and Sport Management, University of Florida, Gainesville, FL 32611, USA. E-mail: drfez@ufl.edu

[2]Department of Marketing and Supply Chain Management, University of Tennessee, Knoxville, TN, USA. E-mail: nbharadw@utk.edu

[3]National Laboratory for Tourism & eCommerce, University of Florida, Gainesville, FL, USA. E-mail: Jason.stienmetz@ufl.edu

[4]The Department of Hospitality and Tourism Management, Pamplin College of Business, Virginia Tech. 362 Wallace Hall-295 West Campus Drive, Blacksburg, VA 24061, USA. E-mail: philxz@vt.edu

CONTENTS

4.1   INTRODUCTION

Creating markets of "one" has been a longstanding mantra for marketing (Peppers & Rogers, 1996), especially as the Internet has evolved from a push perspective to one largely based upon co-creation (Vargo & Lusch, 2004, 2008). Importantly, the ability of marketers to achieve this goal has improved substantially over the past few years as information technology has enhanced our capacity to understand consumers with a variety of ways to collect, manage, analyze, and interpret massive amounts of data (Lazer et al., 2009). "Big data analytics" has now taken a front seat in enabling firms, including those in the travel and tourism industry, to become intimately involved with their customers (Davenport, Mule, & Lucker, 2011; Manyika et al., 2011; McAfee & Brynjolffson, 2012). Indeed, recent articles in the popular press and elsewhere (e.g., Duhigg, 2012; Lindberg, 2013) highlight the degree to which firms have begun to invest in building comprehensive profiles of their customers and developing information systems capable of communicating with them in highly personalized ways. Within the context of tourism, hotels, airlines, restaurants, and theme parks have made marked progress in designing systems needed to customize their products so as to appeal to very specialized markets (Poon, 1993). However, destination marketing organizations (DMOs), which are essentially the marketing agents for cities and regions throughout the world, face enormous challenges due to the continuing evolution of technology, their inability to adapt, and their lack of control over the marketplace (Gretzel, Fesenmaier, & O'Leary, 2006; Fesenmaier & Xiang, 2014). At the same time, DMOs have direct access to their customers as travelers need to visit the destination in order to consume the place, and which offers numerous opportunities for them to gain a deeper understanding of visitor behavior.

Within this context, the goal of this chapter is to describe a destination management system (DMS) that will have the capabilities to combine micro-marketing concepts with big data analytics in order to meet the needs of visitors to a destination more effectively and efficiently. There are several benefits of such a system in that: (1) it is dynamic and can quickly respond to changing interests of visitors; (2) it is connected to the industry when enables them to maintain a customer focus; (3) it will result in increased revenue and visitor satisfaction; and (4) it will help distribute revenue throughout the destination rather than benefiting only the dominant firms/organizations.

4.2 FROM MASS MARKETING TO MICRO-MARKETING FOR TOURIST DESTINATIONS

There was a sea of change in tourism marketing led by the publication of the *Experience Economy* by Pine and Gilmore (1999). While the concept of experience was brought into focus within tourism marketing only, recently, the tourism industry had long recognized the importance of experience in understanding tourism behavior (e.g., Jakle, 1985; Gunn, 1988; Urry, 1990). More recently, the tourism literature recognizes the importance context defined as the nature of place (in a spatial context), the nature of the visitor or visitor group, the nature of the social settings (both physical and virtual), and more recently, the role of communications systems in creating the visitor experience. Parallel to this development in destination marketing, our understanding of tourism services has grown to incorporate the general marketing literature within the framework of "services dominant logic" as proposed by Vargo and Lusch (2004, 2008); they argued that services are essentially different than goods and therefore the economic models of exchange and marketing should differ. Examples of the emergence of the service dominant logic (SDL) within tourism setting include the initial success of themed restaurants such as the Rainforest Café, the growth of highly niche marketed hotels and resorts, the dominance of systems such as TripAdvisor whereby the experiences of the travelers provide the core product. SDL is epitomized by the success of Disneyworld in that they have designed "mass market products" which are now highly individualized (i.e., personalized). As such, these products support and derive value from their customers across the entire range of tourism experiences. Furthermore, this new paradigm has led to a new area of so-called service design or within tourism, "experience design", which aims to unify the basic concepts proposed by Gunn (1988) in Vacationscape, the concepts of servicescape and the basic principles of event design.

Learning from the success of these firms, tourism marketing organizations have also shifted their focus from a traditional marketing and advertising approach whereby they promote the destination in a variety of forms such as permission marketing and customer relationship management to a new approach that emphasizes personalization with individual's experiences in mind. In large part, this shift was accomplished by a systematic restructuring of DMOs whereby they changed from focusing on external marketing to building capacity within the organization and the destination in order to support visitors in very different ways, enabling DMOs to realize the catchphrase "markets of one." This has been exemplified by the increasingly sophisticated, persuasive design of destination websites, the use of search engine optimization strategies and destination recommendation systems, and the realization that success is led by the innovativeness of their partnerships and their efforts in "long tail" marketing (Anderson, 2006).

More recently, scholars have reconceptualized the destination where the core concept is based upon "tourist activated networks" wherein visitors to an area define the nature of the experience through their choices of places visited (Gnoth & Jaeger, 2007; Kracht & Wang, 2010; Meriläinen & Lemmetyinen, 2011; Steinmetz & Fesenmaier, 2015). This suggests that destinations can be conceptualized as a self-organizing network that are connected through visitor values, perceptions, geographies, and trip characteristics (Wang & Fesenmaier, 2007; Zach & Gretzel, 2011) and might be better described by the notion proposed by Gretzel (2010) and elaborated by Fesenmaier and Xiang (2014) as "traveling-the-network." In particular, they argue that traveling-the-network implies wherein value creation is no longer limited to the physical act of experiencing a tourism destination. Hence, digital assets such as information and the information processing capabilities of tourism firms, and the numerous information spaces (e.g., DMO websites) and channels (e.g., online travel agencies and travel search engines) that support the basic information needs for travel should also be considered as key elements of destination value creation. The Internet is no longer a monolithic ecommerce platform; instead, it offers countless networks and platforms vying for the traveler's attention and spending power by supporting information seeking and transactions (Xiang, Wöber, & Fesenmaier, 2008).

Also, traveling-the-network has resulted in new visitor behavior whereby travelers tend to "extend" daily life into travel, become much more involved in creating and controlling the tourism experience by sharing with others, are more involved and creative as they seek authentic experiences, and today's travelers tend to adapt much better to local settings by using various forms of mobile technology (Gretzel, 2010; Gretzel et al., 2006; MacKay & Vogt, 2012; Wang, Park, & Fesenmaier, 2012). Therefore, with the understanding that each traveler's destination experience is unique, DMO's should not focus on creating and controlling the tourism experience itself, but rather emphasize developing the capabilities of the destination that are needed to facilitate the visitor's co-creation of their individual destination experiences (Fig. 4.1).

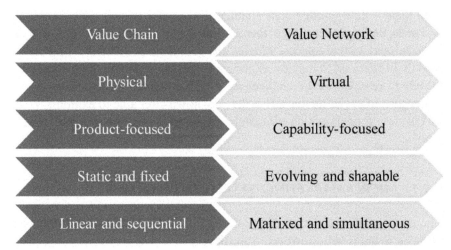

Value Chain	Value Network
Physical	Virtual
Product-focused	Capability-focused
Static and fixed	Evolving and shapable
Linear and sequential	Matrixed and simultaneous

FIGURE 4.1   Changing paradigm of destination value creation (adapted from Freeman & Liedtka, 1997).

The traditional perspective implies that relationships among destination actors are largely static and fixed, though this viewpoint must be challenged (Beritelli, Bieger, & Laesser, 2014). Traveling-the-network implies that there are an infinite number of combinations of touch points (or paths) that can be taken through a destination (Zack & Gretzel, 2011). This suggests that there is a complex pattern to visitor activities that exists within a destination, and that understanding visitor paths through this system of destination firms is essential. Further, recognizing that each destination experience is unique, it also becomes valuable to understand if any patterns emerge in the ways in which visitors experience the destination or "activate" the network of destination firms (Zack & Gretzel, 2011). These paths, though often preplanned, can also be considered flexible or shapeable and are often changed as travelers encounter unanticipated opportunities or constraints to their destination experience (Hwang & Fesenmaier, 2011).

Traveling-the-network also implies that the value chain paradigm must be updated from a linear and sequential conceptualization to understand that the destination value creation process is matrixed and simultaneous. That is, destination value is not created through a series of dyadic interactions between travelers and individual destination firms, but rather as a constellation of service providers whose relationships are not only with the travelers, but also with each other's impact of the value created within a destination (Tax, McCutcheon, & Wilkinson, 2013). Another important aspect of the travel in the network metaphor is that technology-supported networks are mobile, with today's cutting-edge apps enabling travelers to search for information and make decisions on-the-go, thereby simultaneously creating value in both physical and virtual spaces. Finally, the foundations created by investing heavily in adapting to the new experience marketing paradigm have enabled DMOs to respond to the challenges of technological changes such as the emergence of social media in that they are now better able to exploit a range of business models which ultimately create value for the destination as a whole.

4.2.1 MICRO-MARKETING SYSTEM DEVELOPMENT

The concept of micro-marketing is not new; indeed, it has been done for decades. What is new, however, is the degree to which marketers access data about people and the information systems as well as analytical tools that have been developed to enable them to identify specific individuals with the potential to buy certain products and the ability of the firm to meet their needs. Within the context of tourism, there are a variety of strategies for developing detailed information about travelers. One of the best strategies within the travel industry takes advantage of what might be described as "story boards" wherein potential travelers/visitors are asked to go through some process of selection; they also might be referred to as "recommender systems" (see Fesenmaier, Wöber, & Werthner, 2006). Prominent examples of this approach include the online travel agency Expedia where travelers input some information regarding date and destinations and they are then invited to make selections among various options relating to flights, accommodations, etc. (Goyal, Hancock & Hatami, 2012). Other examples include menus at restaurants and rides at theme parks where the choices (and routes) are food–attractions–rides during a given period of time. Interestingly, however, most tourism destinations have not progressed to this stage of micro-marketing wherein they can actually create an offer or "seamless package" of products and services to potential visitors which represents a personalized experience at the destination (Tax, McCutcheon & Wilkinson, 2013; Zach & Gretzel, 2011). Indeed, while most destinations are comparable in many ways to a theme park or museum, destination marketers do not manage the destination as a comprehensive or cohesive "package" of experiences similar to how Disney might (Sfandla & Björk, 2013; Wang & Fesenmaier, 2007).

There is a clear distinction between micro-marketing and providing personalized services (personalization). A number of studies have shown that there are significant trade-offs between the benefits of personalized products, the costs related to personalization and the ability to appreciate a certain level of personalization. This research indicates that consumers prefer and are willing to pay a premium for personalized products but it requires active and sometimes extensive (i.e., intrusive) customer participation. Additionally, this research suggests that many individuals prefer a limited choice set when they have limited knowledge or preference structures. For instance, one study shows that standardized offerings are better suited (than customized ones) for novices (Bharadwaj, Naylor, & ter Hofsetede, 2009). Furthermore, tailored segments may lead to a better product (i.e., experience) based upon aggregated preferences rather than individual preferences (Goyal et al., 2012). As such, this literature suggests that products designed for micro-markets, rather than totally personalized products, are highly effective and efficient marketing strategies.

The availability of the so-called big data makes micro-marketing possible with not only a technical basis, but also a paradigm change in terms of how we approach and understand reality (Lazer et al., 2009). Goyal at al. (2012) argued that: "Sophisticated sales organizations are combining and crunching the mountains of data now available about customers, competitors, and their own operations to dice up their existing sales regions into dozens or hundreds of "micro-markets" and identify new-growth hot spots" (p. 81). Further, they demonstrated that there are a variety of strategies that can be used to identify micro-markets. Davenport et al. (2011) indicate that these systems often involve the integration of a number of data describing the consumer and include basic consumer trends and personal demographic information but substantially enriched with behavioral information including spending patterns, etc. Perhaps the most widely recognized example of the application of data mining and target marketing is where Target, a major retailer in the United States, developed a system to identify women that are expecting a baby and then creating offers that are specifically tailored to this change in family status (Duhigg, 2010). With the growing capabilities to gain access to a variety of visitor data, it is argued that micro-marketing offers the potential to help tourism organizations and destinations to bring about significant change to the way they market their destination, which in turn, moves their marketing practices to a new higher level.

Recent studies suggest that that one of the most effective strategies for developing a micro-marketing system for tourism destination is to use data describing actual behavior including the places (including sequence) travelers visit, destination attributes and the websites within the destination, information about the visitor and the destination accessible on various social media sites, as well as feedback from visitors as they respond to offers during the visit to the destination (Steinmetz & Fesenmaier, 2015). Further, this research indicates that individual places within the destination provide efficient access to the visitor such that they can be approached through various marketing channels. Additionally, this research suggests that a micro-market focused DMS which is based upon a tourism activated network structure enables the destination to track visitor patterns so as to build a reasonably complete understanding of visitor behavior, manage visitor interaction and experiences through on-site program, channels, etc. and support relationships between and among all the firms (and organizations) within the destination. Therefore, the notion of tourist activated network provides the conceptual foundation for the development of micro-marketing systems for destinations (Zheng & Fesenmaier, 2014). The following section describes a proposed micro-marketing DMS for the Northern Indiana tourist region in the United States.

4.3   DESIGN METHOD: THE NORTHERN INDIANA TRAVEL NETWORK (NITN)

The current project focuses on developing a micro-marketing DMS, namely the Northern Indiana Travel Network (NITN), for the Northern Indiana Tourism Development Commission which is responsible for tourism development and marketing for a region that includes seven counties across the northern portion of the state (see Fig. 4.2). This region is located directly east of Chicago along the Interstate 80–90 corridor and includes the Indiana Dunes National Seashore (located on Lake Michigan) which attracts millions of visits from Chicago and the Midwest part of the United States; also, this region is notable for the city of South Bend and Notre Dame University

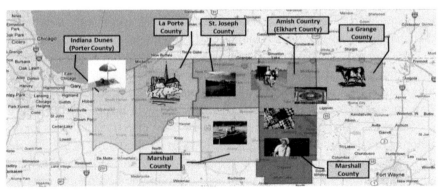

FIGURE 4.2   Area included in case study.

and is home to one of the largest Amish communities in the United States. Finally, it includes 17 main tourist attractions including an outlet mall, a casino, popular cultural–historic venues, a variety of festivals as well as popular restaurants which provide the basis for understanding and assessing the network structure of visitation to the area.

A four-step process was employed in developing the system (see Fig. 4.3). The first step was a Destination Visitor Analysis, whereby we conduct a survey of visitors to the area with the goal to identify a number visitor micro-segments and then to create "offers" which will be used as "seeding information" for the system; these micro-segments (and offers) are initially based upon the places visited, visitor expenditures, satisfaction, previous visitation to the area and visitor demographics. The second step in NITN is the travel pattern analysis whereby visitation patterns within Northern Indiana are further analyzed to identify the key drivers which may be used to encourage visitors when using on-the-go information; this analysis adopts

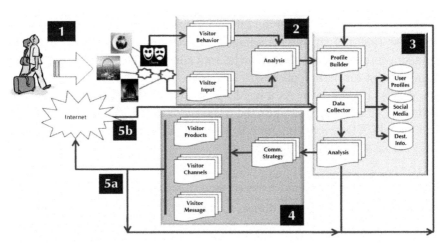

FIGURE 4.3 Proposed micro-marketing DMS.

the approach proposed by Steinmetz and Fesenmaier (2015) that can be used for deconstructing value construction based upon the network relationships among visitor touch points (i.e., the places, events, etc. which comprise the visit to the destination). The third phase in the development of the destination marketing system focuses on integrating dynamics to reflect various seasonal changes in visitors as well as the potential to encourage individual visitors (within a particular micro-market) to adopt new behaviors. The key sources of data for this engine include various social media channels and visitor responses to "offers" made by the system; again, these offers or recommendations are essentially "experiments" which can be used to further refine the models used to direct communication with visitors. The final step in the development of NITN is implementation and evaluation which includes a plan to roll out the system as well as the methodology to evaluate the validity and merit of the system. Each of these steps are described below.

4.3.1 STEP 1. DESTINATION ANALYSIS

The data used for the study were drawn from conversion studies for eight regional convention and visitors bureaus (CVBs) located in Northern Indiana and obtained from a total of nine survey waves during September 2011 to September 2014 (a total of 17 sub-studies and the aggregated data). An online survey packet was sent to a total of 53,950 individuals who had requested travel information from each CVB during the time period of this study. The survey employed the following three-step process to increase the response rate: (1) an initial invitation was sent out; (2) 4 days later a reminder was delivered to those who had not completed the survey; and (3) the final request for participation was sent out to those who had not completed the survey 1 week later. As a result, a total of 5700 usable responses were returned (10.6% response rate); the response rates for each survey wave and individual CVBs vary from 3.5% to 12.0% (CVBs) and for each wave, from 7.7% to 12.4% (see in Table 4.1).

TABLE 4.1   Descriptive Characteristics of Samples Used in This Study.

County[a]	Samples (N)	Responses (n)	Response rate (%)	Survey wave	Samples (N)	Responses (n)	Response rate (%)
C1	16,313	1866	11.4	W1	1889	116	6.1
C2	11,780	1029	8.7	W2	6051	561	9.3
C3	2930	289	9.9	W3	5860	607	10.4
C4	17,847	1720	9.6	W4	4541	380	8.4
C5	8201	658	8.0	W5	11,834	1204	10.2
C6	2963	104	3.5	W6	9246	712	7.7
C7	2121	173	8.2	W7	5031	455	9.0
C8	4866	586	12.0	W8	6773	843	12.4
				W9	8425	822	9.8
Total	53,950	5700	10.6	Total	53,950	5700	10.6

Research (e.g., Becken & Gnoth, 2004; Jeng & Fesenmaier, 2002; Woodside & Dubelaar, 2002) indicates that numerous factors (e.g., trip characteristics, demographic characteristics, seasonality) influence travelers' decision making and behaviors at the destination. In particular, McKercher, Shoval, and their colleagues (e.g., Lew & McKercher, 2006; Shoval & Isaacson, 2009) have focused on the typology of tourist movement and a spatial–temporal pattern at the destination, but often lack of empirical evidence concerning either antecedent and consequences of tourist mobility. This study extends earlier studies by incorporating the concept of tourist mobility into the foundation of traveler's decision-making process and experiences at the destination. The results of this study help to describe the entire process of tourism experiences such as trip planning, a movement pattern at the destination, and experiences of tourism behaviors.

In the first step of the development process, this study described the nature of visitors to Northern Indiana. The results (see Table 4.2) indicate that

TABLE 4.2   Basic Characteristics of Northern Indiana Visitors.

	Total %		Total %		Total %
Gender		Timing of travel planning		Past Experience in the past 3 year	
Male	46.8	<1 month	39.8	Once	60.9
Female	53.2	2 months	22.2	2 times	15.3
Highest education		3 months	15.0	3–5 times	14.8
High school level	18.5	4 months	4.7	6–10 times	6.2
College level	61.8	5 months	3.1	11 or more times	2.8
Graduate level	15.2	More than 6 months	15.2		
Etc.	4.5			Party size	
Age		Length of Trip		One	32.1
Less than 20	5.0	Day Trip	.1	Two	30.7
21–30	33.3	One Night	3.7	3–5 Persons	25.2
31–40	27.1	Two Nights	21.6	6 or more persons	12.0
41–50	18.5	Three to Five Nights	45.0		
51–60	11.1	Six to Ten Nights	13.0	Trip Purpose	
61 and above	5.0	11 or more nights	16.6	Pleasure	49.7
				Shopping	11.7
				VFR	11.4
				Business	25.0
				Other	2.1

in large part the group is relatively older, well educated, have visited the destination at least once in the past 3 years, and spend 3–5 days traveling to places within the mid-west United States. Further analyses show that there are a number of smaller visitor segments that vary in terms of these basic visitor characteristics and which suggest that may be easily targeted, depending upon the capacity of the attractions, restaurants, events, etc. within the destination to "adjust" their product offerings.

4.3.2   STEP 2. TRAVEL PATTERN ANALYSIS

A series of analyses using Chi-squared tests, ANOVA, and multiple regression analysis were conducted to assess differences in visitor expenditures, visitor satisfaction, and the actual places visited based upon the total number of places visited (see Table 4.3). Then, analyses were conducted to assess differences in visitor expenditures based by the places visited and the number of visits. Last, analyses were conducted to identify and assess the impact of the linkages between destinations on visitor expenditures. The results of these analyses confirm that the pattern of travel, that is, the network structure of tourism attractions, within Northern Indiana has substantial impact on visitor expenditure and trip satisfaction. The mean number of places visited was 1.96 with a range of 0 (0.5%) to 7 or more (5.5%); there were 218

TABLE 4.3 Distribution of Destination Bundles.

Number of places visited	Destination bundles				Visitors	
	Total	%	potential	% of bundle	Total	%
0 places	1	0.5	1	100.0	56	7.8
1 place	14	6.4	17	82.4	210	29.4
2 places	49	22.5	136	36.0	208	29.1
3 places	57	26.1	680	8.4	115	16.1
4 places	41	18.8	2,380	1.7	57	8.0
5 places	32	14.7	6,188	0.5	43	6.0
6 places	12	5.5	12,376	0.1	13	1.8
7 places or more	12	5.5	109,294	0.0	12	1.7
Total	**218**	100.0	131,072	0.2	714	100.0

Number of places = 17, number of visitors = 710, number of visits to places = 1,367
Mean number of places = 1.96, number of combinations = 218

different combinations of trip patterns within the potential of approximately 22,000. The results of these analyses were significant ($\alpha < 0.01$), indicating that the important variables that can be used to evaluate the usefulness of the micro-targeting system (i.e., visitor expenditure, satisfaction and repeat behavior) are driven by a range of variables including number of places visited. This finding is important in that it sets the stage for further enhancement of the system using "social data" including online comments regarding the popularity of places, ratings of experiences, etc. (Table 4.4).

TABLE 4.4   Average Overall Expenditure and Visitor Satisfaction and No. of Places Visited.

Number of places visited	N	Mean expenditure	Satisfaction
0	45	$472.40	3.17
1	188	$453.72	3.50
2	187	$574.32	3.59
3	97	$756.70	3.79
4	51	$725.94	4.00
5	33	$817.61	3.85
6	11	$1,258.36	4.18
More than 7	10	$883.00	4.45
Overall	**622**	**$601.34**	**3.62**

A third set of analyses integrated information regarding the travel party (i.e., number of persons, age, and mobility), motivations and perceptions and aspects of the trip (i.e., trip length, places visited, and order of visit) into three separate multiple regression analyses using visitor expenditures, satisfaction, and likelihood to return as dependent variables, separately. The dependent variables are value as measured by visitor $, satisfaction, likelihood to return (Table 4.5):

$$\text{Value} = b_0 + b_{i,1-17}X_i + b_{k,1-17}X_{i,1-17} \times X_{j,1-17}$$

1. Main effects—dummy (0/1) variables representing 17 attractions in the region
2. Interaction terms—dummy (0/1) variables representing the connections between the attractions
3. Exogenous variables

   1. Prior experience
   2. Distance traveled
   3. Distance to alternative attractions

TABLE 4.5 Marginal Value of Visitors to Northern Indiana Attractions.

	1	2	3	4	5	6	7	8	9	10	11	12	13	14	15	16	17
1	66.47	1627.33	121.10	-392.10	—	76.65	8.91	-27.14	431.42	208.40	-55.72	-9.63	-37.33	293.78	37.49	-289.51	-1310.80
2		-182.82	—	3.43	—	64.53	-103.89	1103.45	522.75	-828.21	0.98	—	-636.72	271.35	—	—	-993.15
3			756.69	-335.38	—	6097.71	1030.61	-633.82	-461.66	296.82	682.24	-319.98	-7439.36	—	-209.60	575.00	162.85
4				-21.63	890.41	-206.76	1641.70	-136.18	498.49	329.55	-183.78	-7616.62	252.02	—	-205.37	362.27	—
5					1851.17	-1461.56	1475.88	-160.59	-1641.41	-2091.94	-1655.38	-700.86	-2290.00	-52.62	390.78	143.54	-331.65
6						-5.39	-176.47	-255.81	-886.85	145.10	354.88	9.20	309.94	-323.69	—	—	—
7							192.98	-144.01	-99.59	-243.22	137.31	-32.52	337.66	—	-88.50	0.00	—
8								-76.11	127.10	143.29	71.70	284.89	907.41	—	61.65	-127.55	—
9									-60.70	146.80	779.25	244.48	767.72	—	-760.23	-354.95	-34.95
10										-36.04	-793.33	-665.21	-243.38	-744.86	129.56	681.55	178.77
11											6.40	-90.25	12.38	-105.65	-5.90	-500.88	391.15
12												19.02	-376.84	-119.62	180.04	571.54	—
13													-363.55	34.30	525.25	894.36	—
14														139.77	-96.31	-577.09	—
15															68.65	236.10	588.31
16																315.94	-2390.29
17																	189.64

Dependent variable = Overall visitor expenditure; independent variables = places visited.

Model R^2 = 0.298 (F-value 1.585 sig = 0.000), constant = $462.82; values are in $.

4.3.3   STEP 3. GOING DYNAMIC

The third step in the development process focused on adding visitor data obtained through tracking visitors through website use, use of mobile systems, visitor volumes, comments on social media, and responses to communication programs (see Fig. 4.4). Recent research focusing on travel recommender systems and on social media indicates that this information provides a very detailed understanding of current and potential travelers (Gonzalez, Lopez & de la Rosa, 2003; Gretzel, Mitsche, Hwang, & Fesenmaier, 2004), and that it can be easily integrated into such systems. In particular, the data contained within the primary component of the NITN (see Step 2) can provide essential information in terms of (1) the demographics of visitors to the area including age, gender, and family status; (2) user preferences for attractions, restaurants, etc.; and (3) the channels and other modalities visitors use to learn about and sharing this information. As shown in Fig. 4.4, this basic information is captured, stored, and then analyzed so as to provide a detailed description of the micro-segments within the existing travel market. Additionally, information is collected from a range of travel and travel-related websites in order to identify important trends in the area, the region

FIGURE 4.4   Connections between the Northern Indiana attractions.

and the nation. These trends include various aspects that somehow impact travel including general economic, social, and political events and are stored in a second database. A third source of information focuses on various aspect of the destination including detailed assessments of the quality of the local area including attractions, restaurants, accommodations, events, and traffic (including roads), etc.

Recent studies (Leung & Bai, 2013; Chan & Guillet, 2011; Huang, 2011; Xiang & Gretzel, 2010) have suggested that social media is not only an important information search tool for tourists, but also one of the key marketing tools for destination management organizations. Today, UGC and marketer-generated content on social media has increasingly influenced destination awareness and subsequent decisions on destination selection, and it is capable of providing unprecedentedly up-to-date and diversified formats of information to travel consumers (Goh et al., 2013; Tussyadiah & Fesenmaier, 2009). However, as highlighted by Gretzel et al. (2006), one of the challenges that DMOs continue to face is technical change. While more DMOs continue to adopt social media as one of their marketing tools, the majority are just beginning to realize the power of social media; however, Leung and Bai (2013) argues that the tourism industry has made slow progress in responding to the business opportunities brought on by social media. Discussing DMOs adoption of social media, Hays et al. (2013) argued that DMOs are still at the beginning stages of understanding and experimenting in using social media to promote their destinations, and that most DMOs struggle to assess the return on investment of their social media strategies.

Recent studies of social media and destination marketing indicate that the most commonly used metric is the number of social media followers the DMO has (Hays et al., 2013). In addition to measuring audience size, other key metrics commonly employed by DMOs include number of user comments (i.e., brand engagement) and the valence of user comments (i.e., word-of-mouth) (Hays et al., 2013). While metrics based on brand awareness, brand engagement, and word-of-mouth can be used as indicators of firm equity value, and can also provide insights for evaluating mimetic strategies of building a community or social network centered on the DMO, they are less effective in determining the real value of social media as a marketing tool used in advertising strategies; however, recent research has considered development of metrics which focus on social media's direct impact on consumer behavior. For example, Leung and Bai (2013) applied the motivation, opportunity, and ability theory and the concept of involvement in exploring travelers' behaviors in hotel social media pages (Facebook and Twitter). The results of the study showed that travelers' motivation and opportunity have positive relationships with their social media involvement in hotel social media pages. Further, as argued by Pike (2004), the most important role of social media is marketing and therefore the development of social media metrics which can evaluate marketing effectiveness is needed for the DMO as they work to enhance destination image, increasing industry profitability, reducing seasonality, and ensuring long-term funding.

The analytics and marketing engines are used to integrate the data described above into a composite segmentation program wherein a series of detailed micro-segments—small aggregated groups of visitor types—are developed to reflect a variety of different visitors so as to drive: (1) the development of specific tourism products within the region; (2) the channels that can best be used to communicate with the visitors before, during and after visiting the area; and (3) the messages that describe the specific aspects of the visitor experience which will be highlighted within the marketing effort. Importantly, this engine is dynamic in that it is fully integrated within the overall system so it can learn from its successes and failures within each of these aspects of the targeting strategy. This is tracked within the destination and by soliciting feedback as in Step 4.

4.3.4 STEPS 4. DEVELOPMENT AND EVALUATION

Implementation of NITN will be achieved over the next 2 years as visitor data is collected and archived. The evaluation of the proposed system in integrated fully within both the data collection and analytics engines. In particular, the various metrics collected within each of the engines discussed above inform (i.e., create the basic for) the identification of the most "efficient" micro-markets and their response to the various offers. Of course, overall evaluation of the proposed system will include information regarding: (1) the number (and percent) of visitors targeted; (2) the amount of money and time spent at the proposed offered "products"; (3) the degree (i.e., number and percent) to which alternative—lesser known—"products" are included within the proposed products; (4) visitor perceptions in terms of trust, intrusiveness, etc. of the marketing effort; and (5) the overall satisfactory of visitor with their experiences at the destination. While online sources now dominate the information search behavior of most travelers, it is important to note that online and offline information channels complement each other in such a way that online information search strategies may be followed up with offline search strategies (Ho, Lin, & Chen, 2012). Based on this literature, it is expected that the social media channels that a traveler is exposed to will have an influence on the advertisement response for each main travel facet. It is argued that this model can easily be extended to evaluate the effectiveness of this system of channels as part of an overall destination marketing strategy.

4.4   DISCUSSION

Many forces of change have heavily impacted all facets of travel and tourism. Travel today differs substantially from travel 50 years ago when mass tourism began in earnest. For example, recent studies in tourism and elsewhere (e.g., MacKay & Vogt, 2012; Turkle, 2011; Tussyadiah & Zach, 2012; Wang & Xiang, 2012) suggest that there are now important structural changes in travel behavior in that, in large part due to today's Internet and mobile technologies, travelers tend to extend daily life into travel, become more involved in creating the tourism experience, and are more and creative as they seek authentic experiences. As such, tourism experience is becoming increasingly controlled and defined by individual travelers. It seems that micro-marketing combined with big data analytics has come of age to offer a better approach to understanding the consumer market as well as to developing more effective strategies to engage with the today's visitors to tourist destinations.

Future research on micro-marketing in tourism must take into consideration several important characteristics of today's traveler markets due to the continuous influence of technology. First, micro-markets in tourism are primarily connected with information technology as the penetration rate of the Internet has reached to a maximum level of saturation (see http://www. pewinternet.org/). The Internet is the predominant information source for travel information (TIA, 2011). Therefore, instead of simply seeing travelers as users of technology, they can be considered as active players in technology-supported networks. Thus, the Internet is no longer a monolithic eCommerce platform; instead, it offers countless networks and platforms vying for the traveler's attention and spending power by supporting information seeking and transactions (Xiang, Wöber, & Fesenmaier, 2008). Indeed, it may be of primary importance for marketers to focus on understanding how travelers navigate these information spaces and channels within the network structure in order to build and anticipate their upcoming travel plans and experiences.

Second, today's micro-segments are social and community-based. Indeed, the explosive growth of Web 2.0 with a variety of tools and platforms that support consumer-generated content has further transformed the Internet into the networks for social interactions (Xiang & Gretzel, 2010). Facebook, Twitter, YouTube, and Pinterest are quintessential Web 2.0 applications in that they are developed as novel ways to facilitate exchange of information and social networking. Particularly in travel and tourism, websites such as TripAdvisor and Yelp are social spaces wherein word-of-mouth is created, distributed, and shared among peer travellers and consumers. As a result, tourism marketing is no longer a practice of advertising and promotion; rather, the focus now has shifted to participating in and being part of the online conversations (Sigala, Christou, & Gretzel, 2012). This gives much weight on incorporating the social Web into the tourism micro-marketing practice.

Third, today's micro-segments are also mobile because the smartphone and numerous travel-related apps offer all kinds of tools for travelers to search for information and to make decisions on-the-go (Zack & Gretzel, 2011). For many people, a mobile phone is far beyond a communication tool or an accessory of daily lives, and it has become an inseparable part of his/her life or even body (Turkle, 2011; Wang & Fesenmaier, 2012). As such, the ubiquitous presence of these devices in people's lives potentially intensifies and encourages the participation in mobile social networking. This implies that tourism micro-marketing must be built upon a solid understanding of social connectivity and dynamic decision making within mobile contexts.

These changes in travel behavior are mirrored by a host of new approaches that have been developed to take advantage of the inherent quality of travel. Today's travelers are creators of data through the multitude of "touch points" within the trip whereby travelers leave traces behind them due to product searches, reviews and purchases, the sharing of experiences with family and friends, and from reports in the news. Also, the emergence of "geo-location" data enables businesses to identify movement patterns, preferences, and levels of loyalty within a destination. Micro-marketing has been a "dream" for marketing destinations for a long time but because travel is inherently fragmented, few DMO have been able to create an effective system. The proposed approach fully integrates marketing theory and data-driven analyses into a dynamic micro-segment model which supports the visitor while enabling the DMO to increase revenue and visitor satisfaction and plays a central role in coordinating relationships within the industry. Importantly, it is dynamic in that is capable of learning about visitors by first creating and promoting very specific touristic products using various channels and messages but then retailoring these channels and messages through a series of "trails" or "experiments."

KEYWORDS

- micro-marketing
- big data analytics
- destination marketing organization (DMOs)
- travel network
- destination marketing

REFERENCES

Anderson, C. *The Long Tail: Why the Future of Business is Selling Less of More*. Hachette Digital, Inc.: New York, NY, 2006.

Becken, S.; Gnoth, J. Tourist Consumption Systems among Overseas Visitors: Reporting on American, German, and Australian Visitors to New Zealand. *Tourism Manage.* **2004,** *25*(3), 375–385.

Beritelli, P.; Bieger, T.; Laesser, C. The New Frontiers of Destination Management Applying Variable Geometry as a Function-based Approach. *J. Travel Res.* **2014,** *53*(4), 403–417.

Bharadwaj, N.; Naylor, R. W.; Ter Hofstede, F. Consumer Response to and Choice of Standardized versus Customized Systems. *Int. J. Res. Market.* **2009,** *26*(3), 216–227.

Chan, N. L.; Guillet, B. D. Investigation of Social Media Marketing: How Does the Hotel Industry in Hong Kong Perform in Marketing on Social Media Websites? *J. Travel Tourism Mark.* **2011,** *28*(4), 345–368.

Davenport, T. H.; Mule, L. D.; Lucker, J. Know What Your Customers Want Before They Do. *Harvard Bus. Rev.*, **2011,** *89*(12), 84–92.

Duhigg, C. How Companies Learn Your Secrets. *New York Times*. February 16, **2010**.

Fesenmaier, D. R.; Wöber, K. W.; Werthner, H., Eds. *Destination Recommendation Systems: Behavioral Foundations and Applications*. CABI: U.K., 2006.

Fesenmaier, D. R.; Xiang, Z. Tourism Marketing From 1990 to 2010: Two Decades and a New Paradigm. In *the Routledge Handbook of Tourism Marketing*; McCabe, S., Ed.; Routledge: London and New York, 2014; pp 549–560.

Freeman, E.; Liedtka, J. Stakeholder Capitalism and the Value Chain. *Eur. Manage. J.* **1997,** *15*(3), 286–296.

Gnoth, J.; Jaeger, S. Destinations as Networking Virtual Service Firms. *Int. J. Excell. Tourism, Hospitality, Catering* **2007,** *1*(1), 2–18.

Gonzalez, G.; Lopez, B.; de la Rosa, J. Smart User Models for Tourism: A Holistic Approach for Personalized Tourism Services. *Inf. Technol. Tourism* **2003,** *6*(4), 273–286.

Goyal, M.; Hancock, M. Q.; Hatami, H. Selling into Micromarkets. *Harvard Bus. Rev.* **2012,** *July–August*, 79–86.

Gretzel, U. Travel in the Network: Redirected Gazes, Ubiquitous Connections and New Frontiers. In *Post-global Network and Everyday Life*; Levina, M., Kien, G., Eds.; Peter Lang: New York, 2010; pp. 41–58.

Gretzel, U.; Fesenmaier, D. R.; O'Leary, J. T. The Transformation of Consumer Behaviour. In *Tourism Business Frontiers, Butterwork–Heinemann*; Buhalis, D., Costa, C., Eds.; 2005; pp. 9–18.

Gretzel, U.; Mitsche, N.; Hwang, Y.-H.; Fesenmaier, D. R. Tell Me Who You Are and I Will Tell You Where to Go: Use of Travel Personalities in Destination Recommendation Systems. *Inf. Technol. Tourism* **2004,** *7*(1), 3–12.

Gunn, C. A. *Vacationscape: Designing Tourist Regions*, 2nd ed., Van Nostrand Reinhold: New York, 1988.

Hwang, Y. H.; Fesenmaier, D. R. Unplanned Travel Decisions. *Tourism Geogr.* **2011,** *13*(3), 398–416.

Jakle, J. *The Tourist: Travel in the Twentieth-Century North America,* The University of Nebraska Press: Lincoln, 1985.

Jeng, J.; Fesenmaier, D. R. Conceptualization of the Travel Planning Hierarchy: A Review of Recent Developments. Tourism Anal. **2002,** *7*(1), 15–32.

Kracht, J.; Wang, Y. Examining the Tourism Distribution Channel: Evolution and Transformation. *Int. J. Contemp. Hospitality Manage.* **2010,** *22*(5), 736–757.

Lazer, D.; Pentland, A. S.; Adamic, L.; Aral, S.; Barabasi, A. L.; Brewer, D.; et al. Life in the Network: The Coming Age of Computational Social Science. *Science (New York, NY)* **2009,** *323*(5915), 721.

Leung, X. Y.; Bai, B. How Motivation, Opportunity, and Ability Impact Travelers' Social Media Involvement and Revisit Intention. *J. Travel Tourism Mark.* **2013,** *30*(1–2), 58–77.

Lew, A.; McKercher, B. Modeling Tourist Movements: A Local Destination Analysis. *Ann. Tourism Res.* **2006,** *33*(2), 403–423.

Lindberg, P. J. *What your Hotel Knows About You.* http://www.cnn.com/2013/02/26/travel/what-your-hotel-knows/ (accessed February 26, 2013).

MacKay, K.; Vogt, C. Information Technology in Everyday and Vacation Contexts. *Ann. Tourism Res.* **2012,** *39*(3), 1380–1401.

Manyika, J.; Chui, M.; Brown, B.; Bughin, J.; Dobbs, R.; Roxburgh, C.; Byers, A. H. *Big Data: The Next Frontier for Innovation, Competition, and Productivity.* McKinsey Global Institute, 2011.

McAfee, A.; Brynjolfsson, E. Big Data: The Management Revolution. *Harvard Bus. Rev.* **2012,** *October,* 61–68.

Meriläinen, K.; Lemmetyinen, A. Destination Network Management: A Conceptual Analysis. *Tourism Rev.* **2011,** *66*(3), 25–31.

Peppers, D.; Rogers, M. *The One to One Future.* Currency: New York, NY, 1996.

Pine II, B. J.; Gilmore, J. H. *The Experience Economy.* Harvard Business Press: Cambridge, 1999.

Poon, A. *Tourism, Technology, and Competitive Strategies.* CAB Publishing: Oxon, UK, 1993.

Sfandla, C.; Björk, P. Tourism Experience Network: Co-Creation of Experiences in Interactive Processes. *Int. J. Tourism Res.* **2013,** *15*(5), 495–506. DOI: 10.1002/jtr.1892.

Shoval, N.; Isaacson, M. *Tourist Mobility and Advanced Tracking Technologies.* Routledge: London, 2009.

Sigala, M.; Christou, E.; Gretzel, U. *Social Media in Travel, Tourism and Hospitality: Theory, Practice and Cases.* Sage: Thousand Oaks, CA, 2012.

Tax, S. S.; McCutcheon, D.; Wilkinson, I. F. The Service Delivery Network (Sdn): A Customer-Centric Perspective of the Customer Journey. *J. Serv. Res.* **2013,** 16(4), 454–470.

TIA. *Travelers' Use of the Internet*. Travel Industry Association of America: Washington, DC, 2011.

Turkle, S. *Alone Together: Why We Expect More From Technology and Less From Each Other*. Basic Books: New York, 2011.

Tussyadiah, I. P.; Fesenmaier, D. R. Mediating Tourist Experiences: Access to Places Via Shared Videos. *Ann. Tourism Res.* **2009,** *36*(1), 24–40.

Tussyadiah, I. P.; Zach, F. The Role of Geo-based Technology in Place Experiences. *Ann. Tourism Res.* **2012,** *39*(2): 780–800.

Urry, J. *The Tourist Gaze*. Sage: Thousand Oaks, CA, 1990.

Vargo, S. L.; Lusch, R. F. Evolving to a New Dominant Logic for Marketing. *J. Mark.* **2004,** *68*(1), 1–17.

Vargo, S. L.; Lusch, R. F. Service-Dominant Logic: Continuing the Evolution. *J. Acad. Mark. Sci.* **2008,** *36*(1), 1–10.

Wang, D.; Xiang, Z. The New Landscape of Travel: A Comprehensive Analysis of Smartphone Apps. In *Information and Communication Technologies in Tourism 2012*; Fuchs, M., Ricci, F., Cantoni, L., Eds.; Springer-Verlag Wien: Wien, 2012.

Wang, Y.; Fesenmaier, D. R. Collaborative Destination Marketing: A Case Study of Elkhart County, Indiana. *Tourism Manage.* **2007,** *28*(3), 863–875.

Woodside, A. G.; Dubelaar, C. A General Theory of Tourism Consumption Systems: A Conceptual Framework and an Empirical Exploration. *J. Travel Res.* **2002,** *41*(2), 120–132.

Xiang, Z.; Gretzel, U. Role of Social Media in Online Travel Information Search. *Tourism Manage.* **2010,** *31*(2), 179–188.

Xiang, Z.; Wöber, K.; Fesenmaier, D. R. Representation of the Online Tourism Domain in Search Engines. *J. Travel Res.* **2008,** *47*(2), 137–150.

Zach, F.; Gretzel, U. Tourist-Activated Networks: Implications for Dynamic Bundling and En Route Recommendations. *Inf. Technol. Tourism* **2011,** *13*(3), 229–238.

BEST–WORST SCALING METHOD: APPLICATION TO HOSPITALITY AND TOURISM RESEARCH

ELI COHEN[1,2] and LARRY LOCKSHIN[3]

[1]*Department of Management, Ben Gurion University of the Negev, Beersheba, Israel. E-mail: elico@bgu.ac.il*

[2]*Ehrenberg Bass Institute of Marketing Science, University of South Australia, Adelaide, SA, Australia. E-mail: eli.cohen@unisa.edu.au*

[3]*Ehrenberg Bass Institute of Marketing Science, University of South Australia, Adelaide, SA, Australia. E-mail: larry.lockshin@unisa.edu.au*

CONTENTS

5.1   INTRODUCTION

Tourism has become increasingly global and the demand and competition for international tourism as a key component of local economies has increased rapidly in the last decade. The growth rate of international tourist arrivals (overnight visitors) in 2013 was 5% and the total export earnings generated by international tourism increased in 2013 to US$ 1159 billion. This amount includes expenditures by international visitors for accommodation, food and beverages, entertainment, and other services and goods (World Tourism Organization, 2014). This growth of tourism exceeded the long-term trend estimation of 3.8% for the period of 2010–2020. Tourism is ranked fifth of the worldwide export categories, after fuel, chemicals, food, and automotive products, but it is ranked first in many developing countries (World Tourism Organization, 2014). As a result, researchers are trying to explore international tourist expectations and preferences to provide better, more competitive tourism services and enhance guest hospitality experiences. Usually, studies are carried out in a specific country or region within the country to identify the crucial factors to provide added value and or gain advantage over competition. However, comparing studies or generalizing the results is not applicable or straightforward as culturally-based expectations are different across countries and even in different regions within the same country.

One of the most important tasks in improving the quality of a service or product in a hospitality environment is learning about customers' preferences. Without measuring what customers like and dislike, or more importantly, the relative importance of these likes and dislikes, academics and managers cannot make improvements. It is just as important to be able to prioritize these improvements, because it is most efficient to focus on those that will produce the biggest improvement in satisfaction and repeat business.

Many marketing researchers use traditional surveys to measure consumers' perceptions and preferences, where subjects are asked to use rating scales to provide their preferences for each attribute, for example, using a 1–7 scale to rate the service in a restaurant, the quality of the food, the cleanliness of the restaurant, and other features that the researcher is interested to explore. Analyses of the data are usually straightforward using simple statistical procedures. However, this assumes that the rating scales are interval scales. Treating the category ratings as equal interval scales has numerous limitations.

A significant limitation of the rating approach is that the respondents rate each feature separately without considering the association with other features, namely, respondents are not forced to make trade-offs between the relative importance of different features. Overall, the relative importance of each attribute is derived based on the average across all respondents. Furthermore, it is common that respondents consider all attributes as "important" (or "not important") and hence, it is not possible to draw reliable conclusions concerning the relative importance of issues or attributes.

Another limitation of rating scales is different people or different cultures often use different parts of the scale. Hence, the results of surveys using a Likert-type scale are subject to a range of biases resulting in scores or ratings, which are too similar or too difficult to interpret. There is empirical evidence showing that residents of different countries differ significantly in their responses (see e.g., Bachman & O'Malley, 1984; Baumgartner & Steenkamp, 2001; Chen et al., 1995; Dolnicar & Grün, 2007; Yeh et al., 1998). Cohen (2003) also claimed that segmentation studies in international markets produce differences, which may be due to differences in scale usage rather than to real differences in consumers' preferences. As a result, the conclusions of international studies based on rating scales may be biased.

Another method used to evaluate the relative importance of attributes is ranking. The method requires respondents to rank attributes in terms of the importance of a specific characteristic, for example quality of service, or food type in terms of preference. The task is relatively easy for respondents to complete, if the number of attributes is small. As the number of attributes increases the task becomes exhausting for respondents. There are ways to rank many attributes, but the task becomes over complicated.

Finn and Louviere (1992) suggested the Best–Worst Scaling (BWS) method to overcome several limitations of the rating scales. The attributes are presented in various combinations, based on experimental designs, and the subjects are forced to make trade-offs between the items and to choose the most preferred item (called "most" or "best") and the least preferred item ("least" or "worst") in a set of items, called "choice sets." The method provides better discrimination between the attributes and it helps to overcome many of the limitations of scale-based surveys (e.g. see Crask & Fox, 1987; Cohen, 2009; Finn & Louviere, 1992; Hein et al., 2008).

The BWS methodology has been recently used in different areas such as social sciences, food, and health care (e.g., Auger et al., 2007; Cohen, 2009; Cohen & Neira, 2003; Dekhili et. al., 2011; Lee et al., 2008; Lockshin & Cohen, 2011; Lusk & Briggeman, 2009). Flynn et al. (2007) present an application of the Best–Worst approach to health care to understand whether waiting time is more important than quality of care. Auger et al. (2004) tested country differences related to attitudes of individuals with respect to social and ethical issues such as human rights, child labor, animal rights, and recyclable material. Consumers' preferences for minced pork patties were studied by Jaeger et al. (2008). The BW method also has been used to evaluate the importance of food values such as naturalness, taste, safety, origin, environmental impact and other factors (Lusk & Briggeman, 2009). Lockshin & Cohen (2011) used BWS to segment wine consumers in eleven countries based on their choices of wines in wine stores. Dekhili et al. (2011) implemented the BW method to explore the importance of origin cues of olive oil in two countries, France and Tunisia. However, there is limited research in hospitality and tourism that applies the BW method. For example, Lockshin et al. (2011) examined what factors influenced restaurants in five star hotels in Beijing in the choice of wines for the restaurant's wine list. An example of using BWS in wine tourism was presented by Cohen et al. (2011). They applied the BWS method to compare the preferences of potential wine tourists in France and in Israel.

The aim of this chapter is to describe the BWS method, to demonstrate the implementation of the method and to provide more information on the design and analysis of the data derived by surveys based on the Best–Worst method. The BWS method is demonstrated by empirical examples in hospitality and tourism, which presents the steps necessary to design and analyze a Best–Worst study. The advantage of BWS and its ability to compare attributes using BW scores will be shown. BWS offers a direct and relatively easy to implement method for overcoming the issues related to surveying and comparing consumers, whether from different countries and cultures or merely in different segments in the same country, compared to the traditional methods for such research.

5.2   DESIGNING BEST WORST SURVEYS AND DATA ANALYSES

The first step in the design of the survey is to decide what are the important attributes that to be compared. The list of important attributes usually comes from prior research or from focus groups and interviews. If an important attribute is missing, then the results will only be accurate for comparing those attributes actually included. Once the total attributes to be compared are decided, then the researchers search for a design using that number of attributes. The design should be balanced, that is, all attributes should be presented to respondents with the same frequency across the whole design to avoid biasing of the results. Also, each attribute should appear an equal number of times with every other attribute. Any Balanced Incomplete Block Design (BIBD) might be used to assign the attributes into choice sets. One advantage of BIBDs is that large numbers of items can be studied in order to get the full ranking of all items in a relatively small number of subsets. The simplest design is the one where each item appears only once with each other. Comparing each item with each other item more frequently increases the internal validity of the survey, but makes it longer and more repetitive for the respondent. For BWS, each respondent is asked to choose from each choice set, the item he/she considered most important (Best) and the least important (Worst). Practice with Best Worst designs seems to indicate that 4–6 items per choice set is optimal for most respondents and most tasks. Based on our experience, respondents can typically undertake up to 15 choice sets in 1 survey.

5.3   EXAMPLES OF BEST–WORST STUDIES

5.3.1   *IMPORTANCE OF WINE TOURISM FEATURES*

The tourism experience is often a part of an overall "bundle-of-benefits," which includes visits to the region, staying at a resort or a hotel, culinary tourism, wine tourism, enjoying scenery and participating in other activities, and local attractions (Charters & Ali-Knight, 2000, 2002; Cohen & Ben-Nun, 2009; Dodd, 1995; Hall et al., 2000; Mitchell & Hall 2004). What is really important for tourists? How do the tourists rate their preferences? These questions and many others might be the basis of many tourism studies regarding the perceptions of the tourists.

An example of using the BW method is demonstrated using wine tourism data collected in Israel. A survey was based on 7 features that were chosen as the most relevant out of 42 winery and wine region features. (These attributes were presented by Cohen & Ben-Nun, 2009.) The seven features were organized in choice sets, and respondents were asked to choose the most and least important feature in each choice set with regard to their decision to visit a winery or a wine region. The features were organized in tables (choice sets) using BIBD type (7, 4, 4, and 2). In this way, the seven features were used to construct seven tables (choice sets), each table contains four features, each feature appears four times across all tables and occurred twice with each other feature. The subjects had to choose from each table, representing one of the seven choice sets, the feature they considered most important and the least important feature when he/she considers choosing a wine tourism destination. Table 5.1 presents the design of the wine tourism features in the seven choice sets and Figure 5.1 presents an example of a choice set. The first choice set includes features number 1, 3, 7, and 5; the second choice set includes features number 6, 7, 2, and 3, and so on. The feature number is assigned randomly.

TABLE 5.1   Balanced Incomplete Blocks Design Seven Wine Tourism Features.

Choice set No.	7,4,4,2			
	Feature No.			
1	1	3	7	5
2	6	7	2	3
3	5	2	1	6
4	7	5	6	4
5	4	6	3	1
6	3	4	5	2
7	2	1	4	7

Please consider the following features when planning a visit to a wine region. For each of the following tables, tick the ONE reason that MOST influenced your choice and the ONE that LEAST influenced your choice.

Least/Worst	Feature	Most/Best
☐	Attractive view	☐
☐	Easy to get information	☐
☐	A range of activities in the region	☐
☐	Staff are polite and welcoming	☐

FIGURE 5.1   An example of a Best Worst choice set as presented to respondents

The analysis starts with summing the number of times each attribute is chosen as best and the number of times it is chosen as worst. The Best minus Worst score (B–W) for each item is calculated, and then for each respondent we have seven new variables of the B–W score, one for each item. As each item appears four times in this design (see Table 5.1), each attribute could be chosen four times as best, as the maximum, and none as worst or vice versa, that is, four times as worst and none as best. Consequently, the B–W scores for each attribute for individual can range from +4 to −4. Frequencies beyond this range indicate error(s) in the data. Positive values of Best minus Worst means that the given attribute was chosen more frequently as "Best" than "Worst" and vice versa. The average B–W score is calculated by dividing the totals of B–W scores by the number of respondents. The ranking of the attributes for all the subjects in the survey is obtained by ordering the Best–Worst score of each attribute. The result provides a scale that is about 95% as accurate as using multinomial logit to model the same data (Auger et al., 2004; Marley and Louviere, 2005).

Table 5.2 presents the average B–W scores of the wine tourism features that are considered by the respondents before visiting a winery or a wine region. We can easily see the most important features and which are of least importance. All the attributes that received a positive B–W average score are those which perceived as more important on average for people in this study when they consider visiting a winery or a wine region.

TABLE 5.2   Importance of Wine Tourism Features ($n = 265$, Ranked by B–W Score).

#	Feature	Total Best	Total Worst	B–W score	Average B–W score	SQRT (B/W)	Relative importance (%)
1	Activities related to the wine region	440	90	350	1.32	2.32	100
7	A range of activities in the region	410	144	266	1.00	1.83	76
4	Attractive view	383	237	146	0.55	1.45	58
3	Staff polite and welcoming	218	194	24	0.09	1.27	48
2	Staff are familiar with the history of region	182	339	−157	−0.59	1.02	33
6	Easy to get info on the winery and the region	147	321	−174	−0.66	0.98	31
5	Option of guided tours	75	530	−455	−1.72	0.80	17

It is obvious that overall, the most important feature is the "activities related to the wine region" followed by "a range of activities in the region." The least important feature is the "possibility to participate in guided tours within the region." Using Analysis of Variance and post-hoc analysis (e.g., LSD comparison of means) might show significant differences among the attributes, if differences exist.

Applying a 1–5 Likert-type scale in the same survey showed that the most important feature is "attractive view" (mean = 3.98) followed by "activities related to wine region" (mean = 3.92) and "staff polite and welcoming" (mean = 3.87). No significant differences were observed among these three features. It is obvious that the BWS method better discriminates the importance of the features.

Another way to compare attribute importance is to derive ratio scores by taking the square root of total Best/total Worst (adding 0.5 or any small number to the total Worst score avoids dividing by zero). The resulting coefficient measures the probability of being chosen as best overall compared to the most important item benchmark of 100% (Auger et al., 2007; Flynn et al., 2007; Lee et al., 2008, Marley & Louviere, 2005). The square root of (B/W) for all attributes (sqrt(B/W)) is scaled by a factor such that the most important attribute with the highest sqrt(B/W) becomes 100. All attributes can then be compared to each other by their relative sqrt(B/W) ratio. The result is interpreted as X% (e.g., 70%) as likely to be chosen best as the most important. The results are presented in Table 5.2.

The most important feature for the potential wine tourists is "activities related to the wine region." The relative importance of "attractive view" is only 58% as important and the "option of guided tour" is only 17% as important relative to the "activities related to the wine region" (Table 5.2). Using the square root of B/W avoids having negative scores, which can be misinterpreted as negative reasons, but are merely less important than the positive scores.

5.4   IMPORTANCE OF ISSUES IN RESTAURANTS

Another example is based on a study on the importance of restaurants' issues. Respondents were asked to choose the Best and the Worst issue while considering eating in a restaurant. The BW design was adopted from Finn and Louviere (1992), which contains 12 sets of choices. The design ensured that each issue appeared 6 times across all the choice sets. Hence, the range of Best and Worst scores is between −6 to +6. The level of importance for each choice was determined by subtracting the number of times the issue was least important (Worst) from the number of times it was most important (Best) in all choice sets, divided by the number of respondents (average B−W score). Table 5.3 presents the results of the study carried out in Australia based on 211 respondents with 7 attributes. It can be easily seen that "food handling and food safety" is the most important issue based on BWS and ranked far above "offering consistent standards of food" which has a relative importance of 42% compared to "food handling and food safety." The next most important issue is "A wide variety of choices on the menu" with relative importance of 22% compared to "food handling and food safety."

The results of the same items using a Likert-type scale show that the most important issue is "offering low-fat entrees" followed by "food handling and food safety," which were rated 4.81 and 4.51, respectively. The following two issues are "offering consistent standards of food" and "a wide variety of choices on the menu" which were rated as 4.15 and 4.09, respectively. It is obvious that even though significant differences might observed among the results, it is not simple to draw conclusions about the relative importance of each issue, since the ratings are so close together. Likert-type scaling measures each attribute or issue in isolation, so it is impossible to discern which should be a priority for management.

TABLE 5.3   Importance of Restaurants' Issues ($n = 211$, Ranked by B–W Score).

Restaurant issue	Average B–W	Relative importance (%)	Likert score
Food handling and food safety	2.45	100	4.51
Offering consistent standards of food	0.99	42	4.15
A wide variety of choices on the menu	0.30	22	4.09
Offering a variety of alcoholic beverages	−0.45	14	3.71
Offering vegetarian entrees or meat alternatives	−1.18	11	2.88
Providing ingredient list for all menu items on request	−2.24	6	2.98
Offering low-fat entrees	−3.81	3	4.81

5.5   SEGMENTATION

Marketers usually apply demographic or other a-priori characteristics trying to explore possible differences among different segments, for example, between males and females, among age groups, education level, etc. However, segments might exist based on latent characteristics of the respondents, that is, "latent segments" or "latent clusters." Lockshin and Cohen (2011), for example, showed that there are three similar clusters of wine consumers in all 11 countries where the research was carried out, rather than 11 country-based segments as might be expected considering that each country represents a different culture. The three segments reveal different ways consumers choose wines: cognitive-based (using the brands or regions), assurance-based (using scores, medals or recommendations), and in-store promotion-based. The same segments were found in each country, but the size of each segment and its importance differed by country.

We used Latent GOLD software, version 4.0 (Vermunt and Magidson, 2005) to estimate a latent class cluster model based on the individual scores, using both B–W scores and Likert scores. We estimated models ranging from two to four clusters. The criteria for choosing the best model are the log likelihoods (LL) and the Bayesian Information Criterion (BIC) of each. Decreasing BIC (closer to zero) and increasing LL indicate improving fit. The choice of the optimum cluster number is then based on the fewest number of interpretable clusters (Cohen & Neira, 2003; Ruta et al., 2008) with appropriate LLs and BICs.

5.6 COMPARING LATENT CLUSTERING RESULTS USING BWS AND LIKERT-TYPE SCALING

We use the restaurant data to demonstrate the power of BWS in latent clustering. We compared the latent segments of respondents derived from BW and Likert-scale data (using Latent GOLD software). The Best model fit using BW scaling is a three-cluster solution and it shows strong loadings on each cluster with no cross-loadings (Table 5.4). The first cluster represents respondents who are mainly concerned about food handling and food safety; the respondents in the second cluster focus mainly on the consistency of the food; and the third cluster look at the variety of choices in the menu. The Likert-type scaling data did not show any discrimination as the clusters include overlapping attributes. Cluster 3 includes all the attributes, cluster

TABLE 5.4 Latent Class Cluster Parameter of the Restaurants Study, BW and Likert-Type Scaling.

Restaurant issue	Best–Worst scaling			Likert-type scaling		
	Cluster1	Cluster2	Cluster3	Cluster1	Cluster2	Cluster3
Food handling and food safety	1.826	−0.624	−1.203	−1.095	−1.607	2.702
Offering consistent standards of food	−0.005	**0.412**	−0.407	−1.268	−1.040	**2.307**
A wide variety of choices on the menu	−0.301	0.125	**0.175**	−0.552	−0.673	**1.225**
Offering a variety of alcoholic beverages	0.007	**0.202**	−0.209	−0.308	−0.393	**0.702**
Offering vegetarian entrees or meat alternatives	−0.143	−0.149	**0.291**	−0.161	−1.190	**1.351**
Providing ingredient list for all menu items on request	−0.155	−0.206	**0.361**	**0.295**	−0.792	**0.497**
Offering low-fat entrees	−0.037	−0.355	**0.392**	**0.410**	−0.591	0.181

2 does not include any of them and cluster 1 includes only two attributes which are already in cluster 3, hence the classification of the attributes is impossible and no discrimination of the respondents was observed. It is obvious that discrimination with this data set is possible only when using the BW scaling method.

5.7 CONCLUSION

One of the popular methods to measure consumers' preferences is using surveys where subjects are asked to rate or rank their preferences for each attribute on a given scale. Although the rating tasks are easy for respondents to complete and easy to analyze, the rating scale approach has several limitations. One of the limitations is that researchers assume that the rating scales are interval scales and hence it is straightforward to apply simple statistical analyses. The average ratings of the attributes are then compared based on the assumption that the rating scaling method is an interval scale. Furthermore, the attributes are rated independently by the respondents and not rated relative to the other attributes in the questionnaire. Hence, there are no trade-offs among the attributes and the relative importance of an attribute to the others is not easy to understand.

It has been shown in this chapter that trying to discriminate among consumers using rating scales might not be possible as some consumers might like almost every attribute or consider most of the attributes as important or might dislike every attribute. Such responses do not provide adequate discrimination and it is not possible to draw reliable conclusions concerning the importance of attributes. Consumers in different cultures may use different parts of the rating scales, so the results of surveys of different populations are subject to a range of biases resulting in scores or ratings, which are too similar or too difficult to interpret. As many tourism and hospitality activities are international and multicultural, the conclusions of international studies based on rating scales may be biased. As shown in this chapter, BWS method provides a better discrimination of items within and among different populations.

The BWS method is an approach that has much to offer researchers in tourism and hospitality. The method overcomes most of the limitations of rating and ranking methods and it has several advantages compared to other scaling methods. The respondents are provided choice sets with several items, and they are forced to choose the best/most important and the worst/least important item from each set. As there is only one option to choose an attribute as "best"/"most" important/preferred or "worst"/"least" important there is no bias in the choice. The key issue for implementation BWS is to design a series of choice sets that include all the items of interest and possible comparisons an equal number of times for each respondent.

The BWS method provides the ranking of the items in the study and allows the researcher to measure the relative importance of each attribute to the other as a ratio-level scale based on the probability of choosing each attribute. The method yields a score of Best–Worst for each attribute that can be analyzed using any multivariate procedure without further standardization of the data. The B/W score of each attribute is almost perfectly correlated with the probability of choosing the attribute as important and can be directly compared to other attributes.

There are several limitations to the method. First, it becomes complicated to analyze many attributes (above 15) in a single survey. Furthermore, respondents can perceive the survey as boring as there are many repeated items across all choice sets, even with a small number of items or choice sets. However, our experience suggests that it is relatively easy for respondents to answer 15 choice sets or less, using a paper questionnaire.

In this chapter, we cited scholars who implemented BWS in various fields of research, such as food purchasing and consuming, food values, healthcare issues, social sciences, ethical issues, wine choice, and more. Specialized software to collect and analyze data have been developed, though the initial analysis can be done in Excel© and other analyses can be made in any multivariate software. We highly recommend that tourism and hospitality researchers and managers, especially those using multiple country samples, consider the advantages of BWS in future studies.

KEYWORDS

- **Best–Worst Scaling**
- **rating scale**
- **choice sets**
- **tourism**
- **hospitality**
- **choice behavior**

REFERENCES

Auger, P.; Devinney, T. M.; Louviere, J. J. Consumer's Social Beliefs—An International Investigation Using Best Worst Scaling Methodology. Working Paper, University of Melbourne, Melbourne Business School: Melbourne, Victoria, AU, 2004.

Auger, P.; Devinney, T. M.; Louviere, J. J. Using Best Worst Scaling Methodology to Investigate Consumer Ethical Beliefs across Countries. *J. Bus. Ethics* **2007**, 70, 299–326.

Bachman, J. G.; O'Malley, P. M. Yea-Saying, Nay-Saying, and Going to Extremes: Black-White differences in Response Style. *Public Opin. Q.* **1984**, *48*(2), 491–509.

Baumgartner, H.; Steenkamp, J. B. E. M. Response styles in marketing research: A Cross National Investigation. *J. Mark. Res.* **2001**, *38*(2), 143–156.

Charters, S.; Ali-Knight, J. Wine Tourism—A Thirst for Knowledge?. *Int. J. Wine Mark.* **2000**, *12*(3), 70–80.

Charters, S.; Ali-Knight, J. Who is the Wine Tourist?. *Tourism Manage.* **2002**, *23*, 311–319.

Chen, C.; Lee, S.; Stevenson, H. W. Response Style and Cross-Cultural Comparison of Rating Scales among East Asian and North American Students. *Psychol. Sci.* **1995**, *6*(3), 170–175.

Cohen, E. Applying Best-Worst Scaling to Wine Marketing. *Int. J. Wine Bus. Res.* **2009**, *21*(1), 8–23.

Cohen, E.; Ben-Nun, L. The Important Dimensions of Wine Tourism Experience from Potential Visitors' Perception. *Tourism Hospitality Res.* **2009**, *9*(1), 20–31.

Cohen, J.; Cohen, E.; Ben-Nun, L. What Influences Potential Wine Tourists?. *Proceedings of the 5th Annual Conference American Association of Wine Economists (AAWE)*, Bolzano, Italy, June 22–25, 2011. (Available from http://www.wine-economics.org/bolzano/ Bolzanoregistration/aawe2011.unibz.it/en/registration/scientificprogramfull.html).

Cohen, S. H. Maximum Difference Scaling: Improved Measures of Importance and Preference for Segmentation, Sawtooth Software Conference Proceedings, Sequim, WA, 2003.

Cohen, S. H.; Neira, L. Measuring Preference for Product Benefits Across Countries: Overcoming Scale Usage Bias with Maximum Difference Scaling, ESOMAR 2003 Latin America Conference Proceedings. Amsterdam: The Netherlands, 2003.

Crask, M. R.; Fox, R. J. An Exploration of the Interval Properties of Three Commonly Used Marketing Research Studies: A Magnitude Estimation Approach. *J. Mark. Res. Soc.* **1987**, *29*(3), 317–339.

Dekhili, S.; Sirieix, L.; Cohen, E. How Consumers Choose Olive Oil: The Importance of Origin Cues. *Food Qual. Preference* **2011**, *22*, 757–762.

Dodd, T. Opportunities and Pitfalls of Tourism in a Developing Wine Industry. *Int. J. Wine Mark.* **1995**, *7*(1), 5–16

Dolnicar, S.; Grün, B. Cross-Cultural Differences in Survey Response Patterns. *Int. Mark. Rev.* **2007**, *24*(2), 127–143.

Finn, A.; Louviere, J. J. Determining the Appropriate Response to Evidence of Public Concerns: the Case of Food Safety. *J. Public Policy Mark.* **1992**, *11*(1), 12–25.

Flynn, T. N.; Louviere, J.; Peters, T. J.; Coast, J. Best Worst Scaling: What It Can Do for Health Care Research and How to Do It. *J. Health Econ.* **2007**, *26*, 171–189.

Hall, C. M.; Longo, A. M.; Mitchell, R.; Johnson, G. Wine Tourism in New Zealand. In *Wine tourism around the world: Development, Management and Markets*; Hall, C. M., Sharples, L., Cambourne, B., Macionis, N., Eds.; Elsevier: Oxford, 2000; pp 150–176.

Hein, K. A.; Jaeger, S. R.; Carr, B. T.; Delahunty, C. M. Comparison of Five Common Acceptance and Preference Methods. *Food Qual. Preferences* **2008**, *19*, 651–661.

http://dtxtq4w60xqpw.cloudfront.net/sites/all/files/pdf/unwto_barom14_02_apr_excerpt_0.
pdf).

Jaeger, S. R.; Jorgensen, A. S.; Aaslyng, M. D.; Bredie, W. L. P. Best-Worst Scaling: An
Introduction and Initial Comparison with Monadic Rating for Preference Elicitation with
Food Products. *Food Qual. Preference* **2008,** *19*, 579–588.

Lee, J. A.; Soutar, G.; Louviere, J. The Best–Worst Scaling Approach: An Alternative to
Schwartz's Values Survey. *J. Personality Assess.* **2008,** *90*(4), 335–347.

Lockshin, L.; Cohen, E. Using Product and Retail Choice Attributes for Cross-National
Segmentation. *Eur. J. Mark.* **2011,** *45*(7/8), 1236–1252.

Lockshin, L.; Cohen, E.; Zhou, X. What influences Five-star Beijing Restaurants in Making
Wine Lists?. *J. Wine Res.* **2011,** *22*(3), 227–243.

Lusk, J. L.; Briggeman, B. Food Values. *Am. J. Agric. Econ.* **2009,** *91*(1), 184–196.

Marley, A. A. J.; Louviere, J. J. Some Probabilistic Models of Best, Worst, and Best Worst
Choices. *J. Math. Psychol.* **2005,** *49*, 464–480.

Mitchell, R.; Hall, C. M. The post-visit Consumer Behaviour of New Zealand Winery
Visitors. *J. Wine Res.* **2004,** *15*(1), 39–50.

Ruta, E.; Garrod, G; Scarpa, R. Valuing Animal Genetic Resources: A Choice Modelling
Application to Indigenous Cattle in Kenya. *Agric. Econ.* **2008,** 38, 89–98.

Vermunt, J. K.; Magidson, J. , *Technical Guide for Latent GOLD 4.0: Basic and Advanced.*
Belmont Massachusetts: Statistical Innovations Inc., 2005.

World Tourism Organization UNWTO. *World Tourism Barometer*, Vol. 12, April 2014 (ac-
cessed on August 15, 2014 (Yeh, L. L.; Kim, K. O.; Chompreeda, P.; Rimkeeree, H.; Yau, N.
J. N.; Lundahl, D. S. Comparison in Use of the 9-Point Hedonic Scale between Americans,
Chinese, Koreans, and Thai. *Food Qual. Preferences* **1998,** *9*(6), 413–419.

CHAPTER 6

USING PARTIAL LEAST SQUARES STRUCTURAL EQUATION MODELING (PLS-SEM) IN TOURISM RESEARCH

ROB HALLAK[1] and GUY ASSAKER[2]

[1]*School of Management, UniSA Business School, University of South Australia, City West Campus, Adelaide, SA 5001, Australia. E-mail: Rob.Hallak@unisa.edu.au*

[2]*Hospitality & Marketing, School of Business, Lebanese American University, Byblos, Lebanon. E-mail: guy.assaker@lau.edu.lb*

CONTENTS

6.1 INTRODUCTION

Structural equation modeling (SEM) emerged from the need to measure latent constructs while simultaneously testing the relationships among these constructs within a single framework of analysis (Bollen, 1989). The use of SEM in tourism studies has grown rapidly in recent years (e.g., Assaker, Esposito Vinzi, & O'Connor, 2010, Hallak, Assaker, & Lee, 2015, Nunkoo, Ramkissoon, & Gursoy, 2013). It is used to examine a broad spectrum of research including destination image (DI), tourist loyalty, destination competitiveness, tourism entrepreneurship, resident attitudes, etc. (see, Nunkoo et al., 2013 for a comprehensive review). While there are several approached to SEM, tourism researchers have largely utilized the traditional covariance-based (CB-SEM) method to examine the validity and fit of theoretical derived measurement and structural models (Jöreskog, 1973, 1978). This is partly due to the large volume of articles and books that explain this method and the popularity of CB-SEM software programs such as LISREL and AMOS (Chin, Peterson, & Brown, 2008). However, "the full benefits of SEM in tourism research can be achieved only if it is used correctly" (Nunkoo et al. 2013, p. 759). The CB-SEM approach is based on a number of stringent assumptions that need to be met in order to support a model's validity:

- CB-SEM model must have a strong theoretical foundation where all components of the model (including the measurement model(s) and the structural model) are directed by theory.
- The data is multivariate normal.
- A large sample size (depending on the size of the model) is needed (Henseler, et al., 2009).
- The latent constructs are operationalized as 'reflective' constructs (Diamantopoulos & Siguaw, 2006).

Another limitation of CB-SEM concerns model identification and model complexity. CB-SEM typically employs a full information maximum likelihood (ML) estimation process that yields parameter estimates that minimize the discrepancy between the implied covariance matrix and the observed covariance matrix. To compute parameter estimates and the implied covariance matrix, the number of observations (known parameters in the model) should be greater than, or at least equal to, the number of structural relationships among all constructs and their indicators as well as measurement errors (Kline, 2011). The more complex is the model, the more parameters are to be estimated. This increases the chance of non-convergence and improper solutions (Boomsma & Hoogland, 2001).

The required assumptions for CB-SEM analysis are sometimes "over-looked" by researchers, not only in tourism but also in other disciplines including marketing, psychology, and the social sciences. Nunkoo et al. (2013: p.769) argue that tourism researchers "seem to have adopted the practices and malpractices in use of SEM from other disciplines". They give evidence on how the assumption of multivariate normality of data is often overlooked in tourism studies. Theoretical models developed and examined in tourism may be "new" and hence exploratory in nature; thus, using a confirmatory approach to testing theory can be problematic (Kline, 2011). In such cases, alternative methods of SEM such as variance-based partial-least squares (PLS-SEM) may be more appropriate.

The use of PLS-SEM is well established in disciplines such as strategic management (Hulland, 1999), management information systems (Urbrach & Ahlemann, 2010), and marketing (Reinartz, Krafft, & Hoyer, 2004). However, its adoption in tourism research remains at the early stages (Assaker & Hallak, 2012). A review of 196 SEM papers published over the past 5 years in *Tourism Management, Tourism Analysis*, and *Journal of Travel Research* found only 29 (15%) utilized PLS-SEM. However, the number of tourism studies utilizing PLS-SEM has increased substantially since 2011 (Assaker et al., 2014). PLS has been used in tourism research to predict tourism demand (Mazanec & Ring 2011), destination competitiveness (Assaker et al., 2014), and loyalty (Song et al. 2011). It has also been used to operationalize several other constructs in tourism research, such as service quality (Howat & Assaker, 2012), service evaluation (Huang et al., 2014), and tourist satisfaction with hospitality services (Ekinci, Dawes, & Massey, 2008).

In this chapter we explain the PLS-SEM method and illustrate its application in a tourism modeling context. We examine how PLS-SEM can be used to examine complex models where the phenomenon is new and exploratory, where the sample size is small, examine models with formative and reflective constructs, as well as higher order models. We also present an empirical example of PLS-SEM in the context of examining a model of tourism entrepreneurship, illustrating the process, the output, and their interpretations. Finally, we discuss recent advancements in PLS-SEM and present directions for its future use in tourism research.

6.2   PLS-SEM BASICS

PLS-SEM is a partial information method that maximizes the explained variance of all dependent variables based on how these variables relate to their neighboring constructs (Wold, 1982, 1985). It uses an iterative algorithm in which the parameters are calculated with a series of least squares regressions after explicitly creating construct scores by weighting the sums of items underlying each construct (Chin et al., 2008). The term "partial" thus emanates from the fact that the iterative procedure involves separating the parameters rather than estimating them simultaneously (Hulland, 1999).

PLS-SEM follows a two-step process that starts with an iterative estimation of latent variables (LVs) scores. To do so, the method estimates an outer and inner weight using the PLS algorithm. The weights are obtained based on how the structural and measurement models are specified. This requires an iterative procedure in which two kinds of approximations for the LVs are estimated until the weight estimates converge. The two types of approximations, referred to as the "inside" and "outside" weights calculations, relate to the inner relations and outer relations. The algorithm starts with an arbitrary initial weight used to calculate an outside approximation of the LVs. Then, the inner relations among LVs are considered in order to calculate the inside approximations. Here, the researcher can choose among three possible scenarios, called weighting schemes, to perform this approximation: (1) centroid, (2) factor, or (3) path scheme. After the inside approximations are obtained, the algorithm turns again to the outer relations and new weights are calculated considering how the indicators are related to their constructs by Mode A (reflective) or Mode B (formative). Mode A implies simple linear regressions between the construct and its reflecting indicators since the construct is assumed to affect each indicator separately. Mode B implies multiple linear regressions between the construct and the set of indicators since the indicators are assumed to affect the construct on a collective basis. The simple or multiple regression coefficients are then used as new weights for the outside approximation. The process continues iteratively until the weights converge; that is, until the change in the outer weights between two iterations drops below a predefined limit (Henseler et al., 2009).

The second step of the process calculates the parameters of the structural and the measurement models. The structural coefficients, also known as path coefficients, are calculated by ordinary least squares regression between the LVs. There are as many regressions as there are endogenous LVs. The parameters of a measurement model (loading coefficients) are also estimated by least squares regressions by taking into account the mode used (A = reflective, or B = formative).

6.3 PLS-SEM PURPOSE AND APPLICATION

PLS-SEM can be used to achieve four major purposes. First, it is advantageous when the researcher is trying to explore, rather than confirm, theory. It is useful when the phenomenon being investigated is relatively new and the measurement models are at the exploratory stage (Wold, 1985). Second, PLS-SEM can be used to examine structural models in cases of small samples and when the multivariate normality of the data cannot be supported (Chin & Newsted, 1999). Third, it allows the unrestricted computation of models comprised of "reflective" and "formative" measurement models (Diamantopoulos & Winklhofer, 2001). Fourth, PLS-SEM can examine large, complex models comprised of several latent and manifest variables, as well as hierarchical models with first-order and second-order latent constructs (Wold, 1985). Thus, PLS can overcome the identification issues, non-convergence, limitations and assumptions associated with CB-SEM (Krijnen, Dijkstra, & Gill, 1998).

6.3.1 EXPLORATORY/PREDICTIVE RESEARCH

As CB-SEM is based on a full information procedure, models with newly developed constructs, or where the measurement items cross-load on other LVs, can bias other estimates in the model. PLS-SEM, on the other hand, is less affected as the weights developed for each construct consider only neighboring constructs to which they are structurally connected. This is why it is best suited for examining models investigating a relatively new phenomenon. The use of PLS to "confirm theory" should be treated with caution as the analysis does not determine the goodness-of-fit indices that CB-SEM produces.

6.3.2 SMALL SAMPLE SIZE AND MULTIVARIATE NORMALITY ISSUES

CB-SEM requires a large sample size for the analysis. Some suggest that a minimum of 200 cases is needed; however, the sample size requirements are also dependent on the complexity of the model and the number of free parameters (Boomsma & Hoogland, 2001). Sample size is less of a problem in PLS. As a rule of thumb, the sample size for PLS-SEM models should be at least 10 times the number of indicators of the scale with the largest number of formative indicators, or, 10 times the largest number of structural paths directed at a particular construct in the inner path model (Barclay et al., 1995). PLS-EM can also overcome the problems associated with non-normal data. Evidence suggests that PLS-SEM estimates are more accurate and less biased than ML estimates in cases where the data is skewed (Reinartz et al., 2009; Vilares, Almeida, & Coelho, 2010).

6.3.3   FORMATIVE MEASUREMENT MODELS

PLS-SEM is particularly effective when the structural model includes both reflective and formative measurement models. While classic theory assumes that latent constructs are reflective, this is not always the case and failing to consider the reflective/formative specification of latent construct may result in model misspecification (Bollen, 2007). Misspecifications can bias estimations of inner model parameters and lead to inaccurate assessment of relationships (Jarvis et al., 2003). A formative construct is *formed* through a combination of the respective measures where changes in the indicators cause changes in the latent factor (Jarvis et al., 2003). For example, consider the latent construct of "Customer Complaints" as it applies in tourism research. Measuring complaints includes (1) the frequency of complaining to a store manager; (2) incidence of telling friends and relatives about a bad service experience; (3) likelihood of reporting the supplier to a consumer complaint agency; (4) likelihood of pursuing legal action against the supplier. In such cases, the Customer Complaints LV represents a *formative,* rather than a *reflective* construct. It is formative since a high score on one observed variable would affect the latent construct, but would not necessarily affect the other observed variables. Thus, customer complaints should be modeled as a (typically linear) combination of its indicators plus a disturbance term (see Diamantopoulos & Siguaw, 2006).

Jarvis et al. (2003) stipulate five criteria for determining the formative scheme for a LV:

- The indicators are viewed as defining characteristics of the LV.
- Changes in the indicators are expected to cause changes in the LV.

- Changes in the LV are not expected to cause changes in the indicators.
- A change in the value of one of the indicators is not necessarily expected to be associated with a change in all of the other indicators (i.e., measurement items are not necessary correlated to each other).
- Eliminating an indicator may alter the conceptual domain of the LV.

Although examining formative measures in CB-SEM is possible and has been well documented (e.g., Joreskog & Sorbom, 1996), attempts to model formative indicators explicitly in a CB-SEM analysis have been shown to lead to identification problems (MacCallum & Browne 1993).

6.3.4 COMPLEX MODELS AND HIGHER ORDER MOLAR AND MOLECULAR CONSTRUCTS

PLS-SEM is capable of examining large, complex models with numerous observed and LVs. It is also robust in examining hierarchical models comprising higher (second) order constructs. The tourism construct of DI is often considered to be a higher order factor that comprises several first-order attribute factors including entertainment, recreation, accessibility, general environment, etc., each measured through a number of observed items (see, Kim & Yoon, 2003). PLS-SEM can also analyze both *molar* and *molecular* models. Molecular constructs are higher order constructs with arrows (paths) directed toward the respective first-order constructs. A higher order *molar* construct is the opposite; direction of the paths starts from the first-order constructs to the higher second-order constructs (Rindskopf & Rose, 1988).

6.4 MODEL ASSESSMENT AND VALIDATION

The validation of PLS-SEM models involves a two-step process: (1) assessing the *outer* (measurement) model; and (2) assessing the *inner* (path) model. The reliability and validity of the outer models need to be established before the inner model is examined (Chin, 1998; Henseler et al., 2009). Since measurement models in PLS-SEM can be reflective or formative, the process for validating these models is different.

6.4.1 ASSESSING REFLECTIVE MEASUREMENT (OUTER) MODELS

Reflective measurement models are examined for their (1) unidimensionality, (2) reliability (internal consistency), (3) convergent validity, and (4) discriminant validity (Lewis et al., 2005). Unidimensionality refers to how well the indicators of an LV relate to each other (Gerbing & Anderson, 1992). Exploratory factor analysis (EFA) is needed to establish whether the measurement items load on their latent factors. The number of selected factors is determined by the number of factors with an eigenvalue >1.0 (based on standardized data). Loading coefficients for each observed variable (indicator) >0.6; are considered "high" (Gefen & Straub, 2005). In the case of higher order models, EFA is first performed on each lower order factor in order to compute aggregate scores for that factor; it is then performed on all aggregate scores from the different factors to test the unidimensionality of the higher order factor—all lower order factors should load with a high coefficient on only one factor with an eigenvalue >1.0.

Reliability (internal consistency) of the measurement models is determined through the Cronbach's α and Composite Reliability tests. The Composite Reliability is preferred as it draws on the standardized loadings and measurement error for each item (Chin, 1998). As a rule of thumb, values <0.60 suggest poor reliability (Nunnally & Bernstein, 1994). In the case of higher order factors, Cronbach's α and the Composite Reliability measure are based on the "secondary loadings"—that is, the standardized loadings and measurement error for each lower order factor underlying the higher order factor (Wetzels et al., 2009).

Convergent validity is the degree to which individual items reflecting a construct converge (or explain that construct well), as compared to items measuring different constructs. This is examined through the Average Variance Extracted (AVE) index (Fornell & Larcker, 1981). An AVE >0.50 suggests that a latent constructs is, on average, able to explain more than 50% of the variance of its indicators (Chin, 1998). A high AVE provides support that the indicator variables are truly representative of the latent construct. Convergent validity is also examined through the significance of the indicator loadings which can be tested using resampling methods, such as bootstrapping (Efron & Tibshirani, 1993) or jackknifing (Miller, 1974).

Discriminant validity represents the extent to which measures of a given construct differ from measures of other constructs in the same model. This is determined by calculating the shared variance between two constructs and verifying that the result is lower than the AVE for each individual construct (Fornell & Larcker, 1981). Each latent construct should share greater variance with its assigned indicators than with any other latent constructs. Discriminant validity can be determined by examining cross-loadings of each latent construct's indicators with all the other constructs (Chin, 1998). If each indicator's loading is higher for its designated construct and each construct loads highest with its assigned items, then the discriminant validity of the model is supported. In the case of higher order models, discriminant validity is determined when the lower order factors are "distinct" enough to be conceptualized as separate dimensions of the higher order construct (Wetzels et al., 2009; Becker et al., 2012). Table 6.1 summarizes the model assessment guidelines.

6.4.2 ASSESSING FORMATIVE MEASUREMENT MODELS

The validity of formative measurement models is assessed in terms of *content validity* across two levels: (1) indicator and (2) construct (Henseler et al., 2009).

6.4.2.1 INDICATOR LEVEL

The estimated weights of formative measurement models should be significant at $p < 0.05$. These are computed through bootstrapping (Efron & Tibshirani, 1993) or jack-knifing (Miller, 1974). The standardized path coefficients (β) should >0.10 (Lohmöller, 1989), although some suggest $\beta > 0.20$ is more sound (Chin, 1998). In addition, the Variance Inflation Factor (VIF) is used to determine the degree of multicollinearity among the formative indicators (Cassel & Hackl, 2000; Fornell & Bookstein, 1982). This examines the extent to which an indicator's variance is explained by the other indicators of the same construct. As a rule of thumb, VIF values should be <10 (Diamantopoulos & Siguaw, 2006). In the case of higher order models, the β for the paths between the lower order factor(s) and the high-order construct should be >0.10, and $p < 0.05$.

TABLE 6.1 Guidelines for Assessing Reflective/Formative Measurement Models.

Validity type	Criterion	Reflective measurement models	
		Description	**Suggested literature**
Unidimensionality	Exploratory factor analysis (EFA)	Measurement items should load with a high coefficient on only one factor, and this factor is the same for all items that are supposed to measure it. The number of selected factors is determined by the numbers of factors with an Eigenvalue exceeding 1.0. Loading is usually considered high if the loading coefficient is above 0.600	Gefen and Straub (2005), Gerbing and Anderson (1992)
Internal consistency reliability	Cronbach's alpha	Measures the degree to which the indicators belong together. Alpha values ranges from 0 (completely unreliable internal consistency) to 1 (perfectly reliable consistency). For confirmative research: CA > 0.700	Cronbach (1951), Nunnally and Bernstein (1994)
	Composite reliability (CR)	Alternative to Cronbach's alpha, allows indicators to be unequally weighted. Proposed threshold value for confirmative research: CR > 0.700	
Convergent validity	Indicator loadings	Measures how well the indicators explain their corresponding LV. Values should be significant at the 0.050 level and higher than 0.70. The significance can be tested using bootstrapping or jack-knifing	Chin (1998), Gerbing and Anderson (1988)
	Average variance extracted (AVE)	Attempts to measure the amount of variance that an LV component captures from its indicators relative to the amount due to measurement error. Proposed threshold value: AVE > 0.500	
Discriminant validity	Cross-loadings	Cross-loadings are obtained by correlating the loadings of each item with all latent variables. If the loading of each indicator is higher for its designated construct than for any of the other constructs, it can be inferred that the models' constructs differ sufficiently from one another	Chin (1998, 2008), Fornell and Larcker (1981)

TABLE 6.1 (Continued)

Validity type	Criterion	Reflective measurement models	
		Description	**Suggested literature**
	Fornell–Larcker criterion	Requires an LV to share more variance with its assigned indicators than with any other LV. Accordingly, the AVE of each LV should be greater than the LV's highest squared correlation with any other LV	
Validity type	**Criterion**	Formative measurement models	
		Description	**Suggested literature**
Indicators content validity	Indicator weights	Significance at the 0.050 level suggests that an indicator is relevant for constructing the formative index and, thus demonstrates a sufficient level of validity. Some authors also recommend path coefficients greater than 0.100 or 0.200	Chin (1998), Lohmöller (1989)
Constructs content validity	Nomological validity	Means that relationships between the formative construct and other models' constructs, which are well known through prior literature, should be strong and significant	Henseler et al. (2009), Straub et al. (2004)
	Multicollinearity/variance inflation factor (VIF)	Variance inflation factor can be used to test for multicollinearity among manifest variables in a formative block. As a rule of thumb, VIF < 10 indicates the absence of harmful collinearity among indicators, suggesting that each indicator contribute significantly to its formative block	Mackenzie et al. (2005)

6.4.2.2   CONSTRUCT LEVEL

The content validity of the formative construct is established through nomo-logical validity. This determines whether the formative construct behaves as initially hypothesized within a system of related constructs. The hypoth-esized relationships between the formative construct and other constructs in the path model should be strong and significant (Henseler et al., 2009). The achieved explained variance (R^2) of the endogenous constructs is used primarily to determine whether a theoretically sound formative factor was appropriately operationalized (Diamantopoulos & Winklhofer, 2001) (see Table 6.1).

6.4.3   ASSESSING THE STRUCTURAL (INNER) MODEL

Once the validity of the measurement (outer) models are established, the structural (inner) model can be analyzed. The primary criterion for inner model assessment is the coefficient of determination (R^2) which represents the amount of a latent factor's explained variance to its total variance, for each endogenous LV. Chin (1998) describes R^2 values of 0.67, 0.33, and 0.19 in PLS-SEM as substantial, moderate, and weak, respectively. As a general rule an $R^2 > 0.20$ is needed in to establish validity (Vinzi et al., 2010).

A second approach to testing model validity concerns the standardized path coefficients between the latent constructs. Paths between latent con-structs should be both statistically significant ($p < 0.05$) and theoretically sound. Standardized path coefficients (β) between two constructs should be >0.10 in order for the path to account for a certain impact in the way the two constructs are linked and for it to be retained in the model (Huber et al., 2007). The significance of the path coefficients may be calculated using resampling techniques. The *effect size* of each path in the inner model can be calculated through the Cohen's $f2$ (Cohen, 1988). The *effect size* is the in-crease in R^2 of the latent construct to which the path is connected, relative to the latent construct's proportion of unexplained variance (that is, relative to the proportion of variance of the endogenous LV that remains unconsidered) (Chin, 1998). Cohen's $f2$ values of 0.02, 0.15, and 0.35 signify small, me-dium, and large effects, respectively, on endogenous latent constructs (Chin, 1998; Cohen, 1988).

Finally, validity of the inner model can be determined through the *cross-validated redundancy measure*—the model's ability to predict the endog-enous LV's indicators (Wold, 1982). The Stone–Geisser's Q^2 (Stone, 1974;

Geisser, 1975) can be computed using blindfolding procedures (Tenenhaus et al., 2005) to create estimates of residual variances. Positive Q^2 values confirm the model's strength in predicting the endogenous constructs. However, this is only applicable to reflective constructs (Table 6.2).

6.5   EXAMPLE OF PLS-SEM IN TOURISM

This section will demonstrate the analysis of a tourism structural model using PLS-SEM. The model is drawn from Hallak, Brown, & Lindsay (2012), who empirically examined the relationships among tourism entrepreneurs' place identity (PI), entrepreneurial self-efficacy (ESE), support for community (SFC), and enterprise performance. Hallak et al. (2012) validated their model using CB-SEM following a two-step approach of (1) validating the measurement model (confirmatory factor analysis); (2) validating the structural model. According to theory, the constructs of place identity (PI) and entrepreneurial self-efficacy (ESE) are both multi-dimensional, higher order constructs. In order to conduct their analysis, Hallak et al. (2012) used "parceling" to transform the higher order constructs into latent factors whereby the dimensions of PI and ESE could represent the manifest variables. This step was necessary to reduce the number of variables in the model, thereby reducing the model's complexity so as to ensure convergence of the results under CB-SEM.

In this example, we demonstrate how PLS-SEM can be used to examine the structural relationships among full higher order molecular models, without the need for parceling. Figure 6.1 presents the theoretically derived structure model to be examined using PLS-SEM. The model consists of (1) higher order molecular exogenous variable—Place Identity (PI_HO)—which comprises five first-order latent factors and their indicators (PI_F1 to PI_F5); (2) higher order molecular mediator variable—Entrepreneurial Self-Efficacy (ESE_HO)—which comprises six first-order latent factors and their indicators (ESE_F1 to ESE_F6); (3) a formative latent mediating variable—SFC, (4) An endogenous reflective construct–Enterprise Performance.

TABLE 6.2 Guidelines for Assessing Inner/Structural Models.

Validity type	Criterion	Description	Suggested literature
Structural predictive hypothesis	Path coefficients	Path coefficients between the LVs should be analyzed in terms of their algebraic sign, magnitude, and significance. The significance can be tested using bootstrapping or jack-knifing	Chin (1998), Ringle (2006)
Model validity	Coefficient of determination (R2)	R2 Measure the explained variance of an LV relative to its total variance. Values of 0.67, 0.33, or 0.19 for endogenous latent variables in the inner path model are described as substantial, moderate, or weak	Cohen (1988), Stone (1974), Geisser (1975), Fornell and Cha (1994)
	Effect size (f2)	Measures if an independent LV has by itself a substantial impact on a dependent LV. Values of 0.020, 0.150, and 0.350 indicate the predictor variable's weak, medium, or large effect in the structural model	Cohen (1988), Stone (1974), Geisser (1975)
	Predictive relevance (Q2)	The Q2 statistic measures the predictive relevance of the model in terms of manifest variables. A tested model has more predictive relevance the higher Q2 is. The proposed threshold value is Q2 > 0	Cohen (1988), Stone (1974), Geisser (1975)

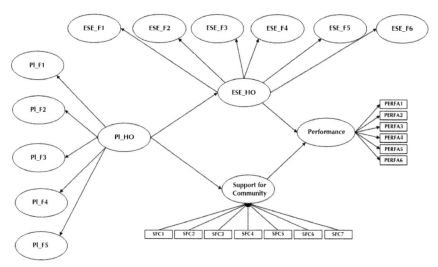

FIGURE 6.1 Place identity–performance: higher order model.

The model is analyzed using PLS-SEM through the software package XL-STAT v. 2011. The two-step process discussed earlier was followed: (1) validating the outer model and (2) fitting the inner model (Chin, 1998). For the outer model analysis, the EFA results demonstrate that all reflective constructs are unidimensional, with each represented by one factor with an eigenvalue >1. In addition, all loadings performed well inside each block (loadings > 0.6), further supporting the unidimensionality (Kaiser, 1974). The Cronbach's α and Dillon–Goldstein's ρ (Composite Reliability) for all constructs were robust and well above the lower limit of 0.7 (Nunnally & Bernstein, 1994), indicating high-scale reliability for each of the reflective constructs (PI_F1 to PI_F5, ESE_F1 to ESE_F6, Performance) as well as for the higher order molecular PI and ESE factors.

The convergent validity of the reflective constructs was also supported as nearly all factor loadings exceeded the 0.7 threshold (see Table 6.3); thus, on average more than 50% of the AVE was due to the underlying construct (Hulland, 1999). Furthermore, the bootstrap test showed high significance levels for all loadings (bootstrap-based empirical 95% confidence interval does not include zero; see Table 6.3).

With respect to discriminant validity, the average shared variance of each lower order reflective construct and its indicators should exceed the shared variance with every other construct of the model (Fornell & Larcker, 1981). This was the case in the model where the root of AVE for the PI1 to PI5,

ESE1 to ESE6, and Performance was greater than the correlation coefficient of that construct with every other construct of the model (Table 6.4).

For the formative SFC construct, at the indicator level the results of the bootstrap tests showed high significance levels for SFC indicators (SFC1 to SFC6) (critical ratios >2) (see Table 6.3). Moreover, the VIF for the SFC indicators shows levels <10 for each of the indicators. Thus, these indicators are not highly correlated and are retained in the measurement model. The achieved explained variance (R^2) of the endogenous construct (Performance) also surpassed the minimum required threshold (see Fig. 6.2), further supporting content validity at the construct level and suggesting that the formative SFC construct was appropriately operationalized (Diamantopoulos & Winklhofer, 2001).

For the inner model, the R^2 results demonstrate that a substantial part of the variance of the endogenous latent constructs could be explained by the model (Fig. 6.2). In particular, the cross-sectional regressions (for ESE, SFC, and performance: 0.112, 0.126, and 0.251, respectively) provided an explained variance of approximately 20%. Thus, the nomological validity of the model was considered to be acceptable. In addition, the bootstrapping results including 1000 iterations of resampling demonstrated that all standardized path coefficients (β) >0.1 and significant ($p < 0.05$).

TABLE 6.3 Outer Model: First-Order and Higher Order Latent Variables with Reflective Indicators, and Formative SFC Latent Variable.

Latent variable	Manifest variables label	Standardized loadings	Critical ratio (CR)	Lower bound (95%)	Upper bound (95%)	Average variance extracted (AVE)
PI_F1	PI1	0.856	51.929	0.815	0.888	0.612
	PI2	0.878	56.846	0.837	0.905	
	PI3	0.823	31.506	0.761	0.866	
	PI4	0.513	7.896	0.385	0.645	
PI_F2	PI5	0.565	9.650	0.417	0.700	0.698
	PI6	0.901	88.161	0.875	0.922	
	PI7	0.917	96.832	0.897	0.936	
	PI8	0.905	87.310	0.876	0.924	
PI_F3	PI9	0.743	21.467	0.659	0.806	0.637
	PI10	0.828	40.411	0.783	0.866	
	PI11	0.873	56.835	0.843	0.906	
	PI12	0.740	24.703	0.668	0.801	

Latent variable	Manifest variables label	Stan-dardized loadings	Critical ratio (CR)	Lower bound (95%)	Upper bound (95%)	Average vari-ance extract-ed (AVE)
PI_F4	PI13	0.855	65.955	0.827	0.886	0.664
	PI14	0.793	27.018	0.726	0.843	
	PI15	0.801	33.041	0.738	0.847	
	PI16	0.807	31.036	0.746	0.860	
PI_F5	PI17	0.840	48.809	0.803	0.878	0.741
	PI18	0.776	19.462	0.668	0.840	
	PI19	0.913	71.618	0.882	0.938	
	PI20	0.908	72.524	0.884	0.933	
ESE_F1	ESE1	0.814	31.886	0.760	0.869	0.639
	ESE2	0.862	45.675	0.812	0.894	
	ESE3	0.862	54.300	0.829	0.893	
	ESE4	0.777	28.813	0.711	0.834	
	ESE5	0.817	32.576	0.755	0.859	
	ESE6	0.784	26.339	0.720	0.849	
	ESE7	0.665	11.282	0.479	0.770	
ESE_F2	ESE8	0.835	30.767	0.772	0.882	0.715
	ESE9	0.879	40.476	0.815	0.912	
	ESE10	0.879	51.667	0.830	0.909	
	ESE11	0.785	31.790	0.726	0.836	
ESE_F3	ESE12	0.862	37.071	0.805	0.903	0.794
	ESE13	0.932	89.049	0.903	0.954	
	ESE14	0.877	51.075	0.835	0.910	
ESE_F4	ESE15	0.887	44.311	0.837	0.921	0.769
	ESE16	0.872	39.206	0.814	0.910	
	ESE17	0.871	42.711	0.820	0.916	
ESE_F5	ESE18	0.900	53.239	0.865	0.934	0.834
	ESE19	0.918	63.260	0.883	0.948	
	ESE20	0.922	75.413	0.895	0.946	
ESE_F6	ESE21	0.868	46.682	0.831	0.903	0.828
	ESE22	0.926	78.801	0.899	0.947	
	ESE23	0.934	106.234	0.913	0.950	
Performance	PERFA1	0.864	42.401	0.806	0.906	0.765

TABLE 6.3 *(Continued)*

Latent variable	Manifest variables label	Stan-dardized loadings	Critical ratio (CR)	Lower bound (95%)	Upper bound (95%)	Average vari-ance extract-ed (AVE)
	PERFA2	0.866	36.235	0.797	0.906	
	PERFA3	0.848	35.250	0.788	0.896	
	PERFA4	0.904	73.926	0.879	0.932	
	PERFA5	0.932	96.588	0.909	0.951	
	PERFA6	0.827	31.979	0.757	0.891	
PI_HO	PI_F1	0.633	14.082	0.315	0.492	0.559
	PI_F2	0.886	32.853	0.751	0.840	
	PI_F3	0.857	28.674	0.682	0.795	
	PI_F4	0.896	34.769	0.772	0.844	
	PI_F5	0.828	25.437	0.611	0.747	
ESE_HO	ESE_F1	0.832	25.790	0.612	0.768	0.563
	ESE_F2	0.786	21.900	0.500	0.730	
	ESE_F3	0.747	19.351	0.457	0.661	
	ESE_F4	0.815	24.159	0.575	0.749	
	ESE_F5	0.744	19.178	0.463	0.658	
	ESE_F6	0.791	22.270	0.547	0.720	
Support for community (formative)	SFC1	0.815	9.102	0.525	0.911	–
	SFC2	0.578	3.733	0.104	0.784	
	SFC3	0.636	4.439	0.148	0.841	
	SFC4	0.862	8.616	0.520	0.958	
	SFC5	0.686	5.178	0.270	0.906	
	SFC6	0.626	5.083	0.285	0.797	
	SFC7	0.688	5.551	0.386	0.823	

TABLE 6.3   *(Continued)*

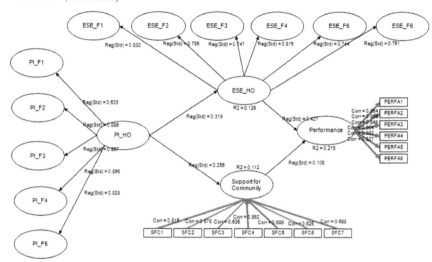

FIGURE 6.2   Higher order model results.

In addition, the Cohen's f^2 for the different paths in the inner model were all >0.02 (PI → SFC = 0.045; PI → ESE = 0.185; SFC → Performance = 0.032; and ESE → Performance = 0.222), suggesting satisfactory effects for the endogenous latent constructs. Finally, the Stone–Geisser Q^2 values for all reflective constructs and the higher order molecular PI and ESE factors were also computed using blindfolding procedures (Tenenhaus et al., 2005). They were found to be larger than zero, suggesting predictive relevance in explaining the endogenous LVs being evaluated (Henseler et al., 2009).

The above example illustrates the usability of PLS-SEM in examining complex, hierarchical models that comprise reflective and formative constructs. The interrelationships between the higher order constructs were examined without the need for parceling (as would be the case in CB-SEM). The analysis demonstrates the structural relationships among the constructs in the model and presents the variance explained in the endogenous variable (performance).

6.6   CONCLUSION

This chapter explained the variance-based procedure of SEM known as PLS-SEM, which remains new to tourism research despite its rapid growth in other business disciplines. We illustrated the advantages of PLS-SEM in

TABLE 6.4 Discriminant Validity: First-Order Latent variables with Reflective Indicators (Squared Correlations for any Pair of Latent Variables <AVE).

	Performance	PI_F1	PI_F2	PI_F3	PI_F4	PI_F5	ESE_F1	ESE_F2	ESE_F3	ESE_F4	ESE_F5	ESE_F6	Mean communalities (AVE)
Performance	1	0.058	0.017	0.005	0.034	0.025	0.186	0.078	0.096	0.178	0.096	0.116	**0.765**
PI_F1	0.058	1	0.250	0.172	0.190	0.185	0.083	0.030	0.022	0.029	0.006	0.012	**0.612**
PI_F2	0.017	0.250	1	0.511	0.578	0.399	0.060	0.050	0.021	0.023	0.060	0.021	**0.698**
PI_F3	0.005	0.172	0.511	1	0.571	0.382	0.089	0.061	0.039	0.031	0.054	0.017	**0.637**
PI_F4	0.034	0.190	0.578	0.571	1	0.461	0.096	0.056	0.022	0.044	0.097	0.041	**0.664**
PI_F5	0.025	0.185	0.399	0.382	0.461	1	0.089	0.027	0.013	0.027	0.036	0.019	**0.741**
ESE_F1	0.186	0.083	0.060	0.089	0.096	0.089	1	0.304	0.231	0.425	0.248	0.234	**0.639**
ESE_F2	0.078	0.030	0.050	0.061	0.056	0.027	0.304	1	0.349	0.266	0.260	0.328	**0.715**
ESE_F3	0.096	0.022	0.021	0.039	0.022	0.013	0.231	0.349	1	0.316	0.183	0.373	0.794
ESE_F4	0.178	0.029	0.023	0.031	0.044	0.027	0.425	0.266	0.316	1	0.317	0.351	**0.769**
ESE_F5	0.096	0.006	0.060	0.054	0.097	0.036	0.248	0.260	0.183	0.317	1	0.384	**0.834**
ESE_F6	0.116	0.012	0.021	0.017	0.041	0.019	0.234	0.328	0.373	0.351	0.384	1	**0.828**
Mean communalities (AVE)	0.765	0.612	0.698	0.637	0.664	0.741	0.639	0.715	0.794	0.769	0.834	0.828	0

examining models where the assumptions for applying traditional CB-SEM approach are not met. In particular, we argued that PLS-SEM works best when: (1) the aim is prediction, the phenomenon investigated is relatively new, and measurement models need to be developed; (2) the conditions relating to sample size, independence, or normal distribution are not met; (3) the relationships among the indicators and latent factors must be modeled in different modes (i.e., formative and reflective measurement models); and (4) the model is complex with a large number of latent constructs and/or includes higher order molecular and molar models. The chapter presented the necessary criteria and "rules of thumb" for analyzing model validity for both the outer (measurement) models, as well as the inner (structural models). An example of PLS-SEM was presented by examining a model of tourism entrepreneurship performance. This explained how PLS-SEM is used to evaluate models with reflective and formative constructs, as well as higher order constructs.

The chapter presents important insights on the application of the PLS-SEM method in tourism and is particularly useful for researchers, doctoral students, as well as journal editors and reviewers. Future research in tourism could benefit from the application of PLS-SEM, especially in cases where constructs examined are multidimensional, and the models examined are hierarchical. Multidimensional constructs examined in tourism such as DI, Perceived Quality, Visitor Loyalty, or even Business Innovations can be examined in full (unparceled) through PLS modeling. The network of causal relationships among multidimensional constructs, and the predictive power of the model can be examined even when faced with sample size limitations. This creates new opportunities for complex modeling and new theory development in broad areas of tourism and hospitality research.

Our understanding of PLS-SEM and its application is continuously evolving. There are new advances such as response-based segmentation techniques PLS, which are designed to cater for a heterogeneous dataset (finite mixture partial least squares; Hahn et al., 2002; Sarstedt et al., 2011). Emerging PLS techniques include methods to test for the moderating effects on SEM models and multigroup analysis (Henseler & Chin, 2010). Tourism researchers can examine the validity of complex models across subgroups in the dataset, determining the invariance of the model and moderating effects caused by group characteristics (i.e., nationality, gender, attitudinal differences, etc.).

These advancements broaden the application of PLS-SEM as a method of analysis in tourism research and tourism modeling. We emphasize, however, that it is critical for researchers to understand the limitations of this 'soft-modeling' approach. It is not our intention to present PLS-SEM as the replacement for CB-SEM, given the strength of CB-SEM on testing theory CB-SEM and the availability of overall goodness-of-fit, which are still limited in PLS-SEM. Research utilizing PLS-SEM needs be explicit as to why this approach was chosen over CB-SEM. Our intent is to ensure that the method's value in tourism research and practice can be enhanced and expanded.

KEYWORDS

- **PLS-SEM**
- **tourism research**
- **measurement model**
- **structural model**
- **higher order molecular and molar models**

REFERENCES

Assaker, G.; Hallak, R. Examining a Supply-Side Predictive Model in Tourism using Partial Least Squares Path Modeling: An Empirical Analysis at the Country Aggregate Level. *Tourism Anal.* **2012**, *17*(5), 587–599.

Assaker, G.; Esposito Vinzi, V.; O'Connor, P. Structural Equation Modeling in Tourism Demand Forecasting: A Critical Review. *J. Travel Tourism Res.* **2010**, *Spring/Fall*, 1–27.

Assaker, G.; Hallak, R.; Vinzi, V.; O'Connor, P. An Empirical Operationalization of Countries' Destination Competitiveness Using Partial Least Squares Modeling. *J. Travel Res.* **2014**, *53*(1), 26–43.

Bagozzi, R. P. Structural Equation Models in Marketing Research: Basic Principles. In *Principles of Marketing Research*; Bagozzi, R. P., Ed.; Blackwell: Oxford, 1994; pp 317–385.

Barclay, D.; Higgins, C.; Thomson, R. The Partial Least Squares Approach (PLS) to Causal Modeling, Personal Computer Adoption and Use as an Illustration. *Technol. Stud.* **1995**, *2*(2), 285–309.

Becker, J.; Klein, K.; Wetzels, M. Hierarchical Latent Variable Models in PLS-SEM: Guidelines for Using Reflective-Formative Type Models. *Long Range Plann.* **2012**, *45*, 359–394.

Bollen, K. A. *Structural Equations with Latent Variables*. Wiley: New York, 1989.

Bollen, K. A. Interpretational Confounding is due to Misspecification, not to Type of Indicator: Comment on Howell, Breivik, and Wilcox (2007). *Psychol. Methods* **2007**, *12*, 219–228.

Boomsma, A.; Hoogland, J. J. The Robustness of LISREL Modeling Revisited. In *Structural Equation Modeling: Present and Future*; Cudeck, R., DuToit, S., Sorbom, D., Eds.; Scientific Software International: Chicago, IL, 2001; pp 139–168.

Cassel, C. M.; Hackl, P. On Measurement of Intangible Assets: A Study of Robustness of Partial Least Squares. *Total Qual. Manage.* **2000**, *11*(7), 897–907.

Chin, W. W. The Partial Least Squares Approach to Structural Equation Modeling. In *Modern Methods for Business Research*; Marcoulides, G. A. Ed.; Lawrence Erlbaum Associates: Mahwah, 1998; pp 295–336.

Chin, W. W.; Newsted, P. R., Ed. *Statistical Strategies for Small Sample Research*. Sage: Thousand Oaks, 1999.

Chin, W. W.; Peterson, R. A.; Brown, S. P. Structural Equation Modeling in Marketing: Some Practical Reminders. *J. Mark. Theory Pract.* **2008**, *16*(4), 287–298.

Cohen, J. *Statistical Power Analysis for the Behavioral Sciences.* Lawrence Erlbaum Associates: New Jersey 1988.

Cronbach, L. J. Coefficient Alpha and the Internal Structure of Tests, *Psychometrika* **1951**, *16*(3), 297–334.

Diamantopoulos, A.; Siguaw, J. A. Formative vs. Reflective Indicators in Organizational Measure Development: A Comparison and Empirical Illustration. *Br. J. Manage.* **2006**, *17*(4), 263–282.

Diamantopoulos, A.; Winklhofer, H. M. Index Construction with Formative Indicators: An Alternative to Scale Development. *J. Mark. Res.* **2001**, *38*(2), 269–277.

Efron, B.; Tibshirani, R. J. *An Introduction to the Bootstrap.* Chapman Hall: New York, 1993

Ekinci, Y.; Dawes, P. L.; Massey, G. R. An Extended Model of the Antecedents and Consequences of Consumer Satisfaction for Hospitality Services. *Eur. J. Mark.* **2008**, 42(1/2), 35–68.

Fornell, C. G.; Bookstein, F. L. Two Structural Equation Models: LISREL and PLS Applied to Consumer Exit-Voice Theory. *J. Mark. Res.* **1982**, *19*(4), 440–452.

Fornell, C.; Larcker, D. F. Evaluating Structural Equation Models with Unobservable Variables and Measurement Error. *J. Mark. Res.* **1981**, *18*, 39–50.

Gefen, D.; Straub, D. A Practical Guide to Factorial Validity Using PLS-Graph: Tutorial and Annotated Example. *Commun. AIS* **2005**, *16*, 91–109.

Geisser, S. The Predictive Sample Reuse Method with Applications. *J. Am. Stat. Assoc.* **1975**, *70*, 320–328.

Gerbing, D. W.; Anderson, J. C. Monte Carlo Evaluations of Goodness-Of-Fit Indices for Structural Equation Models. *Sociological Methods & Research*, 1992, *21*(2), 132-160.

Hahn, C.; Johnson, M. D.; Herrmann, A.; Huber, F. Capturing Customer Heterogeneity Using a Finite Mixture PLS Approach. *Schmalenbach Bus. Rev.* **2002**, *54*(3), 243–269.

Hallak, R.; Assaker, G.; Lee, C. Tourism Entrepreneurship Performance: The Effects of Place Identity, Self-Efficacy and Gender. *J. Travel Res.* **2015**, *54*(1), 36-51

Hallak, R.; Brown, G.; Lindsay, N. J. The Place Identity–Performance Relationship among Tourism Entrepreneurs: A Structural Equation Modelling Analysis. *Tourism Manage.* **2012**, *33*(1), 143–154.

Henseler, J.; Chin, W. W. A Comparison of Approaches for the Analysis of Interaction Effects Between Latent Variables Using Partial Least Squares Path Modeling. *Struct. Equ. Modeling: Multi. J.* **2010**, *17*(1), 82–109.

Henseler, J.; Ringle, C. M.; Sinkovics, R. R. The Use of Partial Least Squares Path Modeling in International Marketing. *New Challenges Int. Mark.: Adv. Int. Mark.* **2009**, *20*, 277–319.

Howat, G.; Assaker, G. The Hierarchical Effects of Perceived Quality on Perceived Value, Satisfaction, and Loyalty: Empirical Results from Public, Outdoor Aquatic Centres in Australia. *Sport Manage. Rev.* **2012**, *16*(3), 268–284.

Huang, S.; Weiler, B.; Assaker, G. Examining the Effects of Interpretive Guiding Outcomes on Tourist Satisfaction and Behavioural Intention: A Hierarchical Structural Model. *J. Travel Res.* **2014**, DOI: 10.1177/0047287513517426.

Huber, F.; Herrmann, A.; Frederik, M.; Vogel, J.; Vollhardt, K. *Kausalmodellierung mit Partial Least Squares—Eine anwendungsorientierte Einführung.* Gabler: Wiesbaden, 2007.

Hulland, J. Use of Partial Least Squares (PLS) in Strategic Management Research: A Review of Four Recent Studies. *Strat. Manage. J.* **1999**, *20*, 195–204.

Jarvis, C. B.; Mackenzie, S. B.; Podsakoff, P. M. A Critical Review of Construct Indicators and Measurement Model Misspecification in Marketing and Consumer Research. *J. Consum. Res.* **2003**, *30*(2), 199–218.

Jöreskog, K. G. A General Method for Estimating a Linear Structural Equation System. In *Structural Equation Models in the Social Sciences* Goldberger, A. S. Duncan, O. D. Eds., Academic Press: New York, 1973, pp 85–112.

Jöreskog, K. G. Structural Analysis of Covariance and Correlation Matrices. *Psychometrika* **1978**, *43*(4), 443–477.

Joreskog, K. G.; Sorbom, S. *LISREL 8: User's Reference Guide.* Scientific Software, 1996.

Joreskog, K. G.; Goldberger, A. S. Estimation of a Model with Multiple Indicators and Multiple Causes of a Single Latent Variable. *J. Am. Stat. Assoc.* **1975**, *70*, 631–639.

Kaiser, H. F. An Index of Factorial Simplicity. *Psychometrika* **1974**, *39*, 31–36.

Kim, S.; Yoon, Y. The Hierarchical Effects of Affective and Cognitive Components on Tourism Destination Image. *J. Travel Tourism Mark.* **2003**, *14*(2), 1–22.

Kline, R. B. *Principles and Practice of Structural Equation Modeling, 3rd edn.* Guidford Press: New York, 2011.

Krijnen, W. P.; Dijkstra, T. K.; Gill, R. D. Conditions for Factor (In) Determinacy in Factor Analysis. *Psychometrika* **1998**, *63*(4), 359–367.

Lewis, B. R.; Templeton, G. F.; Byrd, T. A. A Methodology for Construct Development in MIS Research. *Eur. J. Inf. Syst.* **2005**, *14*(4), 388–400.

Lohmöller, J.-B. *Latent Variable Path Modeling with Partial Least Squares.* Physica: Heidelberg, 1989.

MacCallum, R. C.; Browne, M. W. The Use of Causal Indicators in Covariance Structure Models: Some Practical Issues. *Psychol. Bull.* **1993**, *114*(3), 533–541.

Mazanec, J.; Ring, C. Tourism Destination Competitiveness: Second Thoughts on the World Economic Forum Reports. *Tourism Econ.* **2011**, *17*(4), 725–751.

Miller, R. G. The Jackknife—A Review. *Biometrika* **1974**, *61*, 1–15.

Nunally, J. *Psychometric Theory* (1st ed.). McGraw-Hill: New York, 1978.

Nunkoo, R.; Ramkissoon, H.; Gursoy, D. Use of Structural Equation Modeling in Tourism Research: Past, Present, and Future. *J. Travel Res.* **2013**, *52*(6), 759–771.

Nunnally, J. C.; Bernstein, I. H. *Psychometric Theory.* McGraw-Hill: New York, 1994.

Reinartz, W. J.; Haenlein, M.; Henseler, J. An Empirical Comparison of the Efficacy of Covariance-Based and Variance Based SEM. *Int. J. Market Res.* **2009**, *26*(4), 332–344.

CHAPTER 7

QUANTITY AND QUALITY ISSUES IN DEMAND FOR TOURISM

ALIZA FLEISCHER

Department of Agricultural Economics and Management, Hotel, Food Resources and Tourism Management Program, Hebrew University of Jerusalem, Jerusalem, Israel. E-mail: aliza.f@mail.huji.ac.il

CONTENTS

7.1   INTRODUCTION

Household total yearly expenses on vacations[1] are a result of some of the following independent and some interconnected decisions: (a) where to travel—long distance or short distance, (b) how to travel—that is, which mode of transportation to use, (c) what level of quality to choose in the travel mode—for example, fly business or coach, (d) how many total vacation days to take over the year, (e) how many vacations to take over the year, (f) what is the average length of the vacations; the last two decision can actually be seen as a decision to take multiple short vacations or a few long vacations, and (g) what level of accommodation to choose—for example, a five star hotel or a two star hotel. These decisions determine the total vacation expenses, how they are divided between travel and accommodation and the level of quality of each service. This chapter offers a theoretical and empirical framework enabling to disentangle the data of total household expenditure on vacation to its components and thus gain an insight into the different decisions made on vacations expenditure and the possible effect of changes in income and prices on these decisions. Moreover, based on two papers by Fleischer and Rivlin (2008) and Fleischer, Peleg, and Rivlin (2011), a comparison of the changes in income elasticities in Israel over a period of 8 years between 1999 and 2007 is conducted. This allows one to gain an insight into the changes in income elasticities not only from cross section data but also over time.

Understanding the aforementioned decisions taken by the households is important for owners, planners, managers, and decision makers in the travel and hospitality industries to plan their investments. Investments in these sectors are usually done in the long run and are not easily changed in the short run. For example, hotel owners have to make a decision where to invest—in expanding the facility or upgrading it. This long-run investment decision depends on what the hotel owners perceive as would be the shift in the demand. Are the hotel's customers expected to shift to higher quality accommodations or are they expected to take more vacation days. If the former were true then the decision would be to invest in upgrading the hotel to higher star standards; if the latter is true then the hotel owners would be better off in expanding the hotel and investing in building more rooms. Similar decisions have to be made by the airlines like whether to purchase

---

[1]In the context of this chapter, expenses on vacation include travel and accommodation expenditure, only. The main reason is that household expenditure surveys include mainly these items under vacation expenditures.

airplanes accommodating more travelers or to purchase airplanes that are more comfortable where air travelers can indulge in a different travel experience. Thus, it is important to forecast future trends in vacation consumption based on the present consumption patterns of households and the expected ones as key factors such as income and prices would change. The problem is that most of the data available on household-vacation expenditure are aggregated (in some cases travel and onsite expenses are disaggregated) over the period defined by the survey. Simple analysis of the data can give indication as to how changes in income and other household characteristics can affect total expenses but cannot give answers to the aforementioned issues. The approach offered in this chapter, including a theoretical model and an applied econometric model based on Fleischer et al. (2008, 2011), can provide answers to these questions. Although the available data is still aggregated, it is possible to deduce whether the households allocate funds to improve the level of quality of their vacation or increase the number of vacation days.

The reminder of the chapter includes a review of the pertinent literature then continues with a description of the models and their application to Israeli data. It concludes with possible managerial recommendations.

7.2 LITERATURE REVIEW

There are numerous empirical papers studying tourism demand in the tourism and applied economics literature. Most of these papers apply macroeconomics approach and analyze either flows of international tourist arrivals and/or departures or levels of tourist expenditures and/or receipts (Crouch, 1994; Lim 1997). A microeconomics approach is applied in this chapter with a focus on demand of households for vacation. Decrop's (2006) definition of vacation is loosely adapted, that is, vacation involves leisure tourism: vacationers can spend their vacation touring or staying in the same spot. Unlike Decrop (2006), however, we exclude the possibility of vacationing at home from our definition.

The different aspects of vacation decision-making are discussed at length in Decrop's (2006) book and in many other papers (e.g., Heung, Qu, & Chu, 2001; Litvin, Xu, & Kang, 2004; Duman & Mattila, 2005; Pan & Fesenmaier, 2006; Hyde & Laesser, 2009). Nonetheless, only a small group of papers analyze tourist demand based on cross-sectional, household vacation expenditure. These data allow these studies to focus on leisure travel or as it was alternatively termed vacation or holiday behavior. The underlying assumption in these studies is that prices are constant across households.

As a result the demand function, which describes the relationship between the quantity demanded and the price and income of the consumer, turns into an Engel curve. The Engel curve describes only the relationship between expenditure and income. Furthermore, price elasticities cannot be obtained and income elasticities are estimated under the assumption that prices do not vary. In the following examples of such studies, the income elasticities were estimated to be larger than one in most cases. This indicates that vacations are a luxury good and that household expenditures on tourism increase faster than income. Davies and Mangan (1992) use a UK family expenditure survey and estimated the midpoint income elasticity to be 2.1. Poor households had an elasticity of 4.0 and wealthy ones of 1.5. Similarly, Van Soest, and Kooreman (1987) and Melenberg and Van Soest (1996) studied the factors determining vacation expenditures in Dutch households. They also used crosssectional data, but unlike Davies and Mangan (1992), they took into consideration the fact that only a fraction of the households have nonzero expenditures. In the first Dutch study, it was found that vacations abroad are a luxury good with an income elasticity of 2.1, whereas domestic vacations are a basic good with an income elasticity of only 0.7 (Van Soest & Kooreman, 1987). In the latter study (Melenberg & Van Soest, 1996), using parametric and semi-parametric modeling, income elasticity was found to be 1.7. In other papers analyzing leisure and recreation expenditures based on crosssectional data (Costa, 1999; Weagley, 2004), similar findings of income elasticities larger than one have been reported. These aforementioned papers did not discuss the issue of length of stay; this is done by another group of studies presented in the following section.

The following group of studies focuses on the issue of a tourist's length of stay. Gokovali, Bahar, and Kozak (2007) analyzed determinants of vacation duration for tourists in Bodrum, Turkey. By employing survival analysis, they found that about 16 variables, among them nationality, education and income, are significantly associated with length of stay. A similar approach was used by Menezes, Moniz, and Vieira (2008) to examine the length-of-stay determinants for tourists in the Azores. Alegre and Pou (2006) took an economic approach to explain the continuous declining trend in vacation duration for tourists visiting the Balearic Islands. Their analysis was based on data collected by a survey of tourists' expenditures on the islands, taking into account their demographic and socioeconomic characteristics. The analysis was limited to the vacation on the islands themselves and thus cannot give a full picture of the household's holiday consumption.

Despite this accumulation of previous work, these tourism demand modeling studies have mostly neglected to distinguish between the quality and quantity components of tourism expenditures. Studies based on cross-sectional data make the implicit assumption that prices are constant across households. Accordingly, an income elasticity larger than one implies that if a household enjoys an increase in income it will increase its tourism expenditures more rapidly. However, since prices are assumed constant, the increase in expenditures reflects only an increase in the number of vacation days. It does not reflect changes in the quality of the vacations.

Furthermore, when the data allow to separate vacation expenditure into travel and on-site expenses, the trend toward shorter vacations observed by Alegre and Pou (2006) and the switch to higher quality holidays pointed out by Morgan (1991) can be explained. It is also possible to obtain the relationship between these trends and economic variables such as income and prices. This is mainly because the number of vacations is affected by, among other things, economic factors in the travel industry. Each vacation involves traveling and thus, for example, the emergence of low-cost carriers can affect number of vacations taken by a household. On the other hand, total number of vacation days is determined mainly by economic factors affecting the hospitality industry. Furthermore, change in income does not necessarily have the same impact on the number of vacations as on the total number of vacation days. The length of the vacation is the product of these two decisions. If a household decides to take more vacations but does not change the total number of vacation days during the survey year, the result is more, but shorter vacations. Thus, to understand where changes in the number of vacations and their duration are stemming from, a distinction has to be made between travel and on-site expenses.

The problem of obtaining prices from household expenditure surveys has been overcome in studies on demand for food (Cox & Wohlgenant, 1986; Deaton, 1988; Nelson, 1991; Dong, Shonkwiler, & Capps, 1998) and on rural tourism in Greece (Skuras, Petrou, & Clark, 2006). Additional data on the quantity consumed enabled researchers to obtain prices (unit values). Since expenditures are the product of a good's price and quantity, dividing expenditures by number of units consumed yields an average price per unit, termed in this study as unit value. The use of unit values enables an estimation of price elasticity and an unbiased estimation of income elasticity. It also enables the distinction between quality and quantity decisions for vacations consumed.

The unit value differs from the price of a homogeneous good if an aggregate commodity, such as vacation, is considered. Expenditure on vacations includes hotel nights consumed locally and abroad, travel, and other related recreational activities. Thus, vacation is a heterogeneous commodity and its unit price reflects differences in quality. For the purpose of this study, a unit of tourism consumption is one vacation day and a unit value is the average expenditure per vacation day. Accordingly, the unit value per day of vacation taken by a high-income household is probably higher than that paid for by a low-income family. A higher unit value per day of vacation reflects a household's decision to stay, for example, in a five-star hotel rather than a two-star hotel. Unlike prices of homogeneous goods, the unit value is not independent of income. This means that unit value as a price is endogenous to the household and it should be accounted for in the derivation of elasticities and in the estimation procedure.

In order to disentangle the aggregate data, it is necessary to start with a microeconomic theoretical model and develop it to an empirical model used on the data. The next section presents the theoretical models and their derived empirical models.

7.3 MODELS

Two types of models are presented here: Model 1 is applicable when data on household expenditures on vacations cannot be disentangled to travel and onsite expenses. Model 2 can be applied to a case where data on travel and onsite expenses can be separated.

7.3.1 MODEL 1

The model depicted in here was developed by Fleischer and Rivlin (2008). The utility maximization problem of a household is defined in the economic literature as follows:

$$U = U\left(x_1, x_2, \ldots x_R\right)$$

$$\text{s.t.} \quad \sum_{i=1}^{R} p_i x_i = Y \tag{7.1}$$

where x_i and p_i are the quantity and price of R elementary goods, respectively. Y is the household income. In the case of vacations, x_k is the number of vacation days the household spends at site k. For example x_1 can be three days in a five-star hotel and x_1 two days in a B&B. Prices of each of the elementary x's are given to the household and are not a function of its characteristics.

The household maximization of its utility (U) subject to income constraint results in the optimal basket of consumption goods.

For the purpose of our analysis, the same problem faced by the household in (7.1) is rewritten in terms of commodities (or alternatively aggregated goods). The elementary goods a household consumes can be aggregated to larger groups termed commodities, for example, "food," "clothing," "vacation." Continuing with the aforementioned example, the two vacations the household consumes, in the five-star hotel and the B&B, appear under the commodity "vacation." Equation (7.1) can then be expressed in terms of commodities as follows:

$$U = U(V, Z)$$
$$s.t. \quad \hat{p}_V V + Z = Y$$

$$(7.2)$$

where $V = \sum_{i \in G_V} q_i x_i$, q_i is the number of quality units in the aggregate-commodity vacation, G_V is the group of the elementary goods in this commodity. For example, q_i for a five-star hotel equals q_{5star} quality units; it is higher than for the B&B, which equals $q_{B\&B}$ units. V in this example equals $3q_{5star} + 2q_{B\&B}$ and can be interpreted as the number of quality units of vacation consumed by the household. Another way to obtain V is by multiplying q_V, the average level of quality per day by v_q number of vacation days ($V = q_V v_q$). The number of days of each vacation cannot be summed up because they differ in their quality. However, converting the vacation days into quality units enables their summation and the creation of a quantity measure of the aggregate commodity.

$\hat{p}_V$ is the price of one unit of vacation quality (Nelson (1991) defines it as a group-specific price-level indicator), and it relates to the elementary good prices in the commodity vacation in the following form: $p_i = \hat{p}_V q_i$. The price of Z, that is all other goods, is one.

Accordingly, the demand function for the aggregate-commodity vacation is:

$$V = V(\hat{p}_V, Y) = q_V v_q$$

$$(7.3)$$

where $q_V = \sum_{i \in G_V} q_i \left(x_i / \sum_{i \in G_V} x_i \right)$ and $v_q = \sum_{i \in G_V} x_i$.

The demand for V is a function of income (Y) and the price of unit of quality $\hat{p}$. It is also the product of the average level of quality per day and the number of vacation days (for details how this is derived see Appendix). This implies that different households have different "average quality" units.

The unit value, π_V, calculated by dividing total vacation expenditure E_V, by the number of vacation days, is expressed as follows:

$$\pi_V = \frac{E_V}{\sum_{i \in G_V} x_i} = \hat{p}_V q_V$$

(7.4)

The unit value is the average household vacation expenditure per day. It can also be interpreted as the weighted sum of quality units, all multiplied

by the exogenous price $\hat{p}_V$.

The unit value is comprised of two parts: the value of a unit of quality, which is exogenous to the consumer, and the weighted average level of quality, which is endogenous to the consumer. Two households can pay a different price for the same hotel because it can be of different quality: a room with a view is a higher quality product than a room without a view.

The income and price elasticities of variable X, η_x, and ε_x, respectively, are

$$\eta_V = \eta_{q_v} + \eta_{k_q}$$

(7.5)

$$\varepsilon_V = \varepsilon_{v_q} + \varepsilon_{q_v}$$

(7.6)

The income elasticity of demand for vacation η_V is the sum of the income elasticities of quantity and quality. A similar observation holds for the price elasticity. Deriving the elasticities for expenditure share $w = E_V / Y$ similarly yields the following relationships:

$$\eta_w = \eta_{E_V} - 1 = \eta_V - 1$$

(7.7)

$$\varepsilon_w = \varepsilon_{E_V} = \varepsilon_V + 1$$

(7.8)

These relationships allow an estimation of income (η_V) and demand (ε_V) elasticities by using w and π_V as the dependent variables.

For the empirical model we can re-specify Equation (7.3) as the following expenditure share function:

$$w = f\left(\ln \pi_V, \ln Y, A\right) \tag{7.9}$$

where A is a vector of household characteristics, including household size. This functional form is adapted following Dong et al. (1998) to facilitate the estimation of demand elasticities using the available expenditure share data.

7.3.2 EMPIRICAL MODEL AND ESTIMATION METHODOLOGY

The fact that only some of the households have nonzero vacation expenditures is accounted for in the empirical model by adding the following selection equation:

$$I^* = \alpha_0 + \alpha_1 \ln Y + \alpha_2 \ln FS + \alpha_3' M_1 + \alpha_4' S + u_1 \tag{7.10}$$

where Y is total expenditure, FS is family size, M_1 is a vector of a subset of household characteristics, and S is a vector of variables accounting for seasonality. The use of household total expenditures as a proxy for permanent income is commonly found in the literature (Deaton & Muellbauer, 1980; Fish, 1996). I^* is an unobserved variable. The observed variable, I, equals one when the household decided to take a vacation during the period of the survey and zero otherwise. Accordingly, Equation (11) takes on the following form:

$$I = \alpha_0 + \alpha_1 \ln Y + \alpha_2 \ln FS + \alpha_3' M_1 + \alpha_4' S + u_1 \tag{7.11}$$

The censored demand model is described by Equations (7.22) and (7.23) if $I = 1$.

$$\ln \pi_V = \beta_0 + \beta_1 \ln Y + \beta_2 \ln FS + \beta_3' M_2 + \theta_1 \lambda_1 + u_2 \} \quad \ln \pi_V > 0, \quad \text{if } I = 1 \tag{7.12}$$

$$w = \gamma_0 + \gamma_1 \ln Y + \gamma_2 \ln FS + \gamma_3' M_3 + \gamma_4 \ln \pi_V + \theta_2 \lambda_2 + u_3 \} \quad w > 0 \quad \text{if } I = 1 \tag{7.13}$$

where M_i, $i = 1,2,3$ are vectors of not necessarily identical subsets of household characteristic variables including household size, π_V is the unit value per day of vacation, w is the share of vacation expenditures out of all household expenditures, and $\lambda_{1,2}$ and $\theta_{1,2}$ are the selection variables and their coefficients, respectively. This functional form for demand systems has been used widely in the literature (e.g., Deaton & Muellbauer, 1980). One of the benefits of using it is that it neutralizes the impact of inflation and fluctuations in the exchange rate over the 13 months of the survey period.

7.3.3 INCOME AND DEMAND ELASTICITIES

Although data on V are not available, we can still estimate the income and price elasticity of the commodity vacation and its quality and quantity components using the parameters in estimations of Equations (7.12) and (7.13). The relationship between the estimated parameters and the elasticities are expressed in the following equations.

$$\eta_V = \eta_w + 1 = \frac{1}{w}\left[\gamma_1 + \phi_2 + \gamma_4\left(\beta_1 + \phi_1\right)\right] + 1 \tag{7.14}$$

where, $\phi_1 = d(\theta_1\lambda_1)/dY$ and $\phi_2 = d(\theta_2\lambda_2)/dY$.

The income elasticity of quality is of the following form:

$$\eta_{qv} = \eta_{\pi_V} = \frac{d\ln \pi_V}{d\ln Y} = \beta_1 + \phi_1 \tag{7.15}$$

Based on Deaton (1987) and Chung (2006), price elasticity can also be derived from the unit value and quality elasticity as follows:

$$\varepsilon_{v_q} = \frac{\left(\gamma_4 - w\right)\eta_{v_q}}{w\eta_{v_q} - \left(\gamma_4 - w\right)\eta_{qv}} \tag{7.16}$$

$$\varepsilon_{qv} = \varepsilon_{v_q}\frac{\eta_{qv}}{\eta_{v_q}} \tag{7.17}$$

According to Equation (6), ε_V is received by adding ε_{v_q} and ε_{qv}.

7.3.4 MODEL 2

The theoretical one-commodity model developed by Fleischer and Rivlin (2008) to depict households' vacation demand was adapted by Fleischer, Peleg, and Rivlin (2011) to a two-commodity model: travel and on-site services and is presented here. The model enables distinguishing between the quality and quantity of each of these services. An observed increase in vacationers' travel expenses can be due to an increase in the quality of the travel, for example, flying business instead of coach, or to an increase in the number of vacations. Similarly, an observed increase in vacationers' on-site expenditures can be due to two factors: a move to higher quality accommodations and activities on site, or an increase in the number of vacation days. Income and price elasticities for both quality and quantity of travel and on-site demand are derived from the following model.

The utility maximization problem of a household subject to budget constraints can be defined as follows:

$$U = U\left(d_1, d_2, \ldots d_n, v_1, v_2, \ldots v_k, z\right)$$

$$\text{s.t.} \quad \sum_{i=1}^{n} p_i d_i + \sum_{j=1}^{k} t_j v_j + z = Y \tag{7.18}$$

where d_i is the number of vacation days in vacation i, v_j is the number of vacations of type j, z is the rest of the goods and services the household consumes with a normalized price of one, p_i is the on-site price per day for vacation i, t_j is the price of traveling to vacation j, and Y is the household's income. Prices p_i and t_j depend on the quality of the service. In particular:

$$p_i = \hat{p}_d q_i^d \quad t_j = \hat{p}_v q_j^v \tag{7.19}$$

where q_i^d is the number of quality units consumed during one day of vacation i, q_j^v is the number of quality units of travel to vacation type j, and $\hat{p}_d, \hat{p}_v$ are the prices of a quality unit of vacation days and travel, respectively. The price of a quality unit can be viewed as a group-specific price-level indicator (Nelson, 1991).

By using the definition of price in Equation (7.19), the same problem faced by the household in Equation (7.18) can be rewritten in terms of quality units as follows:

$$U = U(D, V, z)$$

$$\text{s.t.} \quad \hat{p}_d D + \hat{p}_v V + z = Y \tag{7.20}$$

where $D = \sum_{i=1}^{n} q_i^d d_i$ is the total number of quality units consumed at the destination and $V = \sum_{j=1}^{k} q_j^v v_j$ is the total number of quality units consumed while traveling to vacation j. The number of vacation days cannot be summed up because they differ in quality as well as in travel to the vacation site. However, converting vacation days and travel into quality units enables their summation and the creation of a quantity measure of aggregate commodities D and V.

Solving the maximization problem in Equation (7.20) yields the following demand functions for the aggregate goods:

$$D = D(\hat{p}_d, \hat{p}_v, Y) = q_D d_q$$
$$V = V(\hat{p}_v, \hat{p}_d, Y) = q_V v_q \qquad (7.21)$$

where $q_D = \sum_i q_i^d \left(d_i / \sum_k d_k \right)$ and $q_V = \sum_j q_j^v \left(v_j / \sum_k v_k \right)$ are the weighted average quality units per day on site and per travel to vacation, respectively, $d_q = \sum_i d_i$ and $v_q = \sum_j v_j$ are the number of vacation days and the number of vacations, respectively (for details see Fleischer & Rivlin, 2008).

The unit values, π_D and π_V, are the average expenditure per day of vacation and per travel to vacation, respectively. They are calculated by dividing total on-site expenditure E_D by the number of vacation days, and by dividing total travel expenses E_V by the number of vacations:

$$\pi_D = \frac{E_D}{\sum_i d_i} = \hat{p}_d q_D$$
$$\pi_V = \frac{E_V}{\sum_j v_j} = \hat{p}_v q_V \qquad (7.22)$$

Unit values can also be interpreted as the weighted sum of quality units multiplied by the exogenous price $\hat{p}_d$ or $\hat{p}_v$.

The unit value is comprised of two parts: the price of a quality unit, which is exogenous to the consumer, and the weighted average level of quality, which is endogenous to the consumer. The endogeneity stems from the households' decision of how many units of quality to consume as a function of their socioeconomic characteristics.

The income and price elasticities of variable X, η_X, and ε_X, respectively, are

$$\eta_D = \eta_{q_D} + \eta_{d_q}$$

(7.23)

$$\eta_V = \eta_{q_V} + \eta_{k_q}$$

$$\varepsilon_D = \varepsilon_{d_q} + \varepsilon_{q_D}$$

(7.24)

$$\varepsilon_V = \varepsilon_{v_q} + \varepsilon_{q_V}$$

7.3.5 EMPIRICAL MODEL AND ESTIMATION METHODOLOGY

The empirical functional form is adopted following Fleischer and Rivlin (2008). This functional form facilitates the estimation of the demand elasticities in Equations (7.22) and (7.23) using the available expenditure share data and unit values from the household expenditure survey. Note that to generate the elasticities from the existing data, we had to assume zero cross-price elasticities. This implies that if travel costs are going up, households will take fewer vacations but will not change the total number of vacation days. This assumption does not affect the estimated own elasticities presented below since they do not depend on the cross elasticity. Moreover, cross elasticities are known to be much smaller than own elasticity in absolute terms in many empirical studies of demand (Deaton, 1987). Thus, we do not expect this assumption to have a strong impact on the results presented here.

The fact that only some of the households have nonzero vacation expenditures is accounted for in the empirical model by adding the following selection equation:

$$I^* = \alpha_0 + \alpha_1 \ln Y + \alpha_2 \ln FS + \alpha_3' M_1 + \alpha_4' S + u_1$$

(7.25)

where Y is total expenditure (as a proxy for permanent income), FS is family size, M_1 is a vector of a subset of household characteristics, and S is a vector of variables accounting for seasonality. I^* is an unobserved variable. The observed variable, I, equals one when the household decided to take a vacation during the period of the survey and zero otherwise. Accordingly, Equation (7.26) takes on the following form:

$$I = \alpha_0 + \alpha_1 \ln Y + \alpha_2 \ln FS + \alpha_3' M_1 + \alpha_4' S + u_1 \qquad (7.26)$$

The censored empirical demand model for on-site services is described by Equations. (7.27) and (7.28) if $I = 1$, and for vacation travel by Equations (7.29) and (7.30) if $I = 1$.

$$\ln \pi_D = \beta_0^D + \beta_1^D \ln Y + \beta_2^D \ln FS + \beta_3^D M_2 + \beta_4^D S + u_2 \} \qquad \ln \pi_D > 0, \quad \text{if } I = 1 \quad (7.27)$$

$$w_D = \gamma_0^D + \gamma_1^D \ln Y + \gamma_2^D \ln FS + \gamma_3^D M_3 + \gamma_4^D \ln \hat{\pi}_D + u_3 \} \qquad w_D > 0 \quad \text{if } I = 1 \quad (7.28)$$

$$\ln \pi_V = \beta_0^V + \beta_1^V \ln Y + \beta_2^V \ln FS + \beta_3^V M_4 + \beta_4^V S + u_4 \} \qquad \ln \pi_V > 0, \quad \text{if } I = 1 \quad (7.29)$$

$$w_V = \gamma_0^V + \gamma_1^V \ln Y + \gamma_2^V \ln FS + \gamma_3^V M_5 + \gamma_4^V \ln \hat{\pi}_V + u_5 \} \quad w_V > 0 \quad \text{if } I = 1 \quad (7.30)$$

where M_i, $i = 1,2,3,4,5$ are vectors of not necessarily identical subsets of household characteristic variables, π_D and π_V are the unit value per day of vacation and per vacation, respectively, w_D and w_V are the share of on-site and travel expenditures out of all household expenditures, respectively. This functional form for demand systems has been widely used in the literature.

7.3.6 INCOME AND DEMAND ELASTICITIES

Although data on V and D are not available, we can still estimate their income and price elasticities while distinguishing between quality and quantity components. Their elasticities are derived from the estimated parameters in Equations. (7.27)–(7.30). The relationship between the estimated parameters and the elasticities are expressed in the following equations.

$$\eta_D = \eta_{w_D} + 1 = \frac{1}{w_D}\left[\gamma_1^D + \gamma_4^D \beta_1^D\right] + 1 \qquad (7.31)$$

$$\eta_V = \eta_{w_V} + 1 = \frac{1}{w_V}\left[\gamma_1^V + \gamma_4^V \beta_1^V\right] + 1$$

The income elasticity of quality is of the following form:

$$\eta_{q_D} = \eta_{\pi_D} = \frac{d \ln \pi_D}{d \ln Y} = \beta_1^D \tag{7.32}$$

$$\eta_{q_V} = \eta_{\pi_V} = \frac{d \ln \pi_V}{d \ln Y} = \beta_1^V$$

η_{d_q} and η_{v_q} are calculated from Equationss. (7.23), (7.31), and (7.32).

The income elasticity of the length of the vacation, η_L, is derived from the two elasticities in Equation. (7.31):

$$\eta_L = \eta_{d_q} - \eta_{v_q} \tag{7.33}$$

Based on Deaton (1987) and Chung (2006), price elasticity can also be derived from the unit value and quality elasticity as follows:

$$\varepsilon_{d_q} = \frac{\left(\gamma_4^D - w_D\right)\eta_{d_q}}{w_D \eta_{d_q} - \left(\gamma_4^D - w_D\right)\eta_{q_D}} \tag{7.34}$$

$$\varepsilon_{v_q} = \frac{\left(\gamma_4^V - w_V\right)\eta_{v_q}}{w_V \eta_{v_q} - \left(\gamma_4^V - w_V\right)\eta_{q_V}}$$

$$\varepsilon_{q_D} = \varepsilon_{d_q}\frac{\eta_{q_D}}{\eta_{d_q}} \tag{7.35}$$

$$\varepsilon_{q_V} = \varepsilon_{v_q}\frac{\eta_{q_V}}{\eta_{v_q}} \tag{7.36}$$

7.4 APPLICATION

The two models were applied to two data sets of Israeli households. Model 1 was applied to a 1999 data set of a household expenditure survey (Fleischer

& Rivlin, 2008). At that period, the Israeli Central Bureau of Statistics (CBS) did not distinguish between travel and on-site expenses and published only the total expenditures on vacations. However, during 2007, the CBS decided to collect more detailed data on vacations distinguishing between travel and on-site expenses. This type of data enabled Fleischer, Peleg, and Rivlin (2011) to apply Model 2 and estimate much more detailed elasticities. Both estimates for the 1999 data and for the 2007 data are presented in Tables 7.1 and 7.2, respectively.

TABLE 7.1 Income and Price Elasticities for 1999 Data.

Income elasticities	Model 1 (w/o unit price)	Model 2 (with unit price)
η_V	1.43*	1.40*
η_{qV}	N.A.	0.67*
η_{v_q}	N.A.	0.73*
Price elasticities		
ε_V	N.A.	−0.63*
ε_{qV}	N.A.	−0.3*
ε_{v_q}	N.A.	−0.33*

*Significant at 5%. Standard errors of elasticities are derived using the delta method. Elasticities are calculated at mean value. N.A.: not applicable.

Source: Fleischer and Rivlin (2008).

These two estimates provided an opportunity to receive an overview of what happened to the different elasticities and thus the sensitivity to changes in income over the period of 8 years between the two surveys. It should be noted that real income per capita in Israel during this period increased by about 15%. A comparison of the elasticities in both periods presented in Table 7.3 reveals that income elasticity of the total vacation expenditures decreased between the two periods. In 1999, it was estimated to be 1.43 and in 2007, it decreased to 1.14[2]. This decline in income elasticity over the period when total income increased is an indication that vacations were becoming to be less of a luxury good with an increase in income. This can be taken to mean that an increase in income will not induce a big increase in vacation expenditures as it had in the past.

---

[2]This is the weighted average taking into consideration that 57% of the households took only a domestic vacation and 43% took for least one vacation abroad.

TABLE 7.2 Income and Price Elasticities by Vacation Destination for 2007 Data Set.

	Domestic vacations only	For at least one vacation abroad
Income elasticities		
η_{q_V} Quality of travel	−0.049	0.615*
η_{v_q} Number of vacations	0.328*	0.137*
η_V Total travel	0.279*	0.752*
η_{qD} Quality of on-site services	0.370*	0.919*
η_{d_q} Number of vacation days	0.050	0.065
η_D Total on-site	0.420*	0.984*
η_L Length of vacation	−0.277*	−0.072
Price elasticities		
ε_{q_V} Quality of travel	0.091	−0.635*
ε_{v_q} Number of vacations	−0.614*	−0.141*
ε_V Total travel	−0.523*	−0.776*
ε_{qD} Quality of on-site services	−0.725*	−0.903*
ε_{d_q} Number of vacation days	−0.098	−0.064
ε_D Total on-site	−0.823*	−0.967*

*, ** Significant at 5% and 10%, respectively.

Source: Fleischer et al. (2011).

TABLE 7.3 Comparison of Income Elasticities Between 1999 and 2007 Surveys.

Income elasticities	1999 data	2007 data*
η_V Total income elasticity	1.40	1.14
η_{qV} Quality income elasticity	0.67	0.84
η_{d_q} Quantity income elasticity	0.73	0.30

*In order to compare the 1999 and 2007 elasticities a weighted average of the 2007 estimations were calculated.

Sources: Fleischer et al. (2008, 2011).

An insight to the different components of the elasticity is obtained by disentangling the elasticity in 2007 into one for domestic vacation and for the households that took for a least one vacation abroad. The separation reveals that there is a big difference between the two types of vacations. Domestic vacation with an income elasticity of 0.67 is a normal good but not a luxury good, whereas a vacation abroad with an elasticity of 1.7 is clearly a luxury good. Thus although vacations in general are turning to be less of a luxury good there is still a big difference between domestic and international vacations.

Another interesting result revealed by comparing the two periods is the change in the quality and quantity income elasticities. The sensitivity of the total vacation expenditure to changes in income has decreased but the sensitivity of the level of quality of the vacation services to changes in income has increased (from 0.67 to 0.84), whereas the sensitivity of the number of vacations to changes in income has decreased (from 0.73 to 0.3) even more than total expenditures. This means that with an increase in income as it occurred during the 8 years between the two surveys the number of vacation days is almost not sensitive to changes in income. Namely, once a household has enough money to use the time available for vacation it reaches a ceiling of the number of vacation days. This ceiling might be determined by external constraints such as number of holidays or number of vacation days granted by employers, thus the household cannot continually increase vacation time at the same rate with increasing income. However, since the total vacation expenditure still rises faster than income this means that the households channel the increase in income to upgrade the tourism and travel services that they consume.

7.5   CONCLUSION

The method of distinguishing between the different components of the vacation income elasticities developed by Fleischer et al. (2008, 2011) provided an understanding of what might be the changes in vacation expenditures when households enjoy a cross-sectional increase in income. Previous studies revealed that total vacation expenditure will increase with an increase in income but in order to understand the impact on the industry there is a need to disentangle the expenditure into its components. The comparison conducted in this chapter provides a further insight into the two aforementioned studies of Fleischer et al. namely a temporal aspect of what happens over time not only cross-sectional change. Policy makers and managers in the travel and tourism industry can be assisted in their decision making process by better understanding that an increase in income generates a rise in vacation expenditures but at a decreasing rate. The wealthier the household becomes the less is the increase in income expenditures on vacation. However, when decision makers have to decide whether to upgrade the tourism services or expand their facilities they have to take into consideration the shift in income elasticities from quantity to quality and thus the option of upgrading is gaining weight comparing to expanding.

In this chapter, we concentrated on the relationship between changes in income and their impact on vacation expenditure. The income elasticities were calculated accordingly at the mean income value regardless of other attributes of the household population such as household size and structure. That is, the implicit assumption in the calculation of the trends in elasticities is that income would change but all the attributes of the household would stay the same. This is a strong assumption since these households' attributes have an effect on vacation expenditure, that is, empty nest older households will have different preferences for vacation spending than a younger full nest household. Thus, if the weight of these different households in the population changes over time than one should anticipate a shift in the household expenditures on vacation and possibly in the income elasticities. Thus, a future research should take into consideration other attributes of the households in order to receive a more comprehensive picture of the anticipated changes in household vacation expenditures.

Another limitation of this study is the issue of available vacation days. One of the reasons why households do not increase the total number of vacation days as fast as the level of quality of the vacation is because the former is limited. These are mainly people who work as employees and their number of vacation days is set. However, it should be noted that in some cases, employees who do not take all of their vacation days may be able to cash them in for additional income. For people who do not work or are self-employed, the number of available vacation days is not expected to be as binding a constraint as for salaried employees. However, people who are self-employed and enjoy high earnings have a high alternative cost for a day of vacation which makes their vacation more expensive than their lower earning counterparts. Our findings hold true for the whole sample, however, if we could distinguish between the households according to their limit of vacation days then we could safely assume that the more binding the constraint of number of vacation days, the more likely the households would be to increase their expenditure on quality rather than quantity. Such households would include those that have a very small number of vacation days or have already used most of them.

As a follow-up to this study, it would be interesting to determine whether these trends are intrinsic to Israeli vacationers or are more universal. Another complementary study might consider the limit of vacation days explicitly in the analysis, which would enable distinguishing between subsamples with and without limits to see how this affects their demand for vacations.

KEYWORDS

- **vacation expenditure**
- **quantity and quality issues**
- **demand for tourism**
- **household expenditure**
- **income elasticity**

REFERENCES

Alegre, J.; Pou, L. The Length of Stay in the Demand for Tourism. *Tourism Manage.* **2006**, *27*(6), 1343–1355.

Chung, C. Quality Bias in Price Elasticity. *Appl. Econ. Lett.* **2006**, *13*(4), 241–245.

Costa, D. L. *American Living Standards: Evidence from Recreational Expenditures. Working Paper* 7148, National Bureau of Economic Research, 1999.

Cox, T. L.; Wohlgenant, M. K. Prices and Quality Effects in Cross-Sectional Demand Analysis. *Am. J. Agric. Econ.* **1986**, *68*(2), 908–919.

Crouch, G. I. The Study of International Tourism Demand: A Review of Findings. *J. Travel Res.* **1994**, *33*(1), 12–23.

Davies, B.; Mangan, J. Family Expenditure on Hotels and Holidays. *Ann. Tourism Res.* **1992**, *19*(4), 691–699.

Deaton, A. Estimation of Own and Cross-Price Elasticities from Household Survey Data. *J. Econometrics* **1987**, *36*(1), 7–30.

Deaton, A. Quality, Quantity and Spatial Variation of Price. *Am. Econ. Rev.* **1988**, *78*(3), 418–430.

Deaton, A.; Muellbauer, J. *Economics and Consumer Behavior.* Cambridge University Press: Cambridge, 1980.

Decrop, A. *Vacation Decision Making.* CABI Publishing: Cambridge, 2006.

Dong, D.; Shonkwiler, J. S.; Capps, O. Estimation of Demand Functions Using Cross-Sectional Household Data: The Problem Revisited. *Am. J. Agric. Econ.* **1998**, *80*(5), 466–473.

Duman, T.; Mattila, A. S. The Role of Affective Factors on Perceived Cruise Vacation Value. *Tourism Management* **2005**, *26*(3), 311–323.

Fish, M. Current Income Versus Total Expenditure Measures in Regression Models of Vacation and Pleasure Travel. *J. Travel Res.* **1996**, *35*(2), 70–74.

Fleischer, A.; Rivlin (Byk), J. More or Better? Quantity and Quality Issues in Tourism Consumption. *J. Travel Res.* **2008**, *47*(3), 285–294.

Fleischer, A.; Peleg, G.; Rivlin (Byk), J. The Impact of Changes in Household Vacation Expenditures on the Travel and Hospitality Industries. *Tourism Manage.* **2011**, *32*(4), 815–821.

Gokovali, U.; Bahar, O.; Kozak, M. Determinants of Length of Stay: A Practical Use of Survival Analysis. *Tourism Manage.* **2007**, *28*(3), 736–746.

Heung, V. C. S.; Qu, H.; Chu, R. The Relationship Between Vacation Factors and Socio-Demographic and Traveling Characteristics: The Case of Japanese Leisure Travelers. *Tourism Manage.* **2001**, *22*(3), 259–261.

Hyde, K. F.; Laesser, C. A Structural Theory of the Vacation. *Tourism Manage.* **2009**, *30*(2), 240–248.

Lim, C. Review of International Tourism Demand Models. *Ann. Tourism Res.* **1997**, *24*(4), 835–849.

Litvin, S. W.; Xu, G.; Kang, S. K. Spousal Vacation-Buying Decision Making Revisited Across Time and Place. *J. Travel Res.* **2004**, *43*(2), 193–198.

Melenberg, B.; Van Soest, A. Parametric and Semi-Parametric Modeling of Vacation Expenditures. *J. Appl. Econ.* **1996**, *11*(1), 59–76.

Menezes, A. G.; Moniz, A.; Vieira, J. C. The Determinants of Length of Stay of Tourists in the Azores, *Tourism Econ.* **2008**, *14*(1), 205–222.

Morgan, M. Dressing Up to Survive. Marketing Majorca Anew. *Tourism Econ.* **1991**, *75*(August), 578–592.

Nelson, J. A. Quality and Quantity Aggregation in Consumer Demand for Food. *Am. J. Agric. Econ.* **1991**, *73*(4), 1204–1212.

Pan, B.; Fesenmaier, D. R. Online Information Search Vacation Planning Process. *Ann. Tourism Res.* **2006**, *33*(3), 809–832.

Skuras, D.; Petrou, A.; Clark, G. Demand for Rural Tourism: The Effects of Quality and Information. *Agric. Econ.* **2006**, *35*(1), 183–192.

Van Soest, A.; Kooreman, P. A Micro-Econometric Analysis of Vacation Behaviour. *J. Appl. Econ.* **1987**, *2*(3), 215–226.

Weagley, R. O; Huh, E. Leisure Expenditures of Retired and Near-Retired Households. *J. Leisure Res.* **2004**, *36*(1), 101–127.

CHAPTER 8

TIME SERIES MODELS FOR CAPACITY MANAGEMENT IN THE HOSPITALITY INDUSTRY

TIANSHU ZHENG

Department of Apparel, Events, and Hospitality Management, Iowa State University, Ames, IA, USA. E-mail: tianshu.zheng@outlook.com

CONTENTS

8.1   INTRODUCTION

Knowing the market and avoiding under- or over-supply is critical for effective demand and capacity management. However, the stochastic nature of the market made it challenging for practitioners to accurately forecast future market demand. Due to its uniqueness, time-series forecasting is an effective tool that provides accurate forecasts based on recognized patterns in historical data. A time series is an ordered sequence of data points measured at successive points in equally spaced time intervals. Time series is observed and analyzed in a variety of fields for various purposes. For example, in meteorology, rainfall and temperature can be studied and water levels of rivers can be predicted. In agriculture, annual crop production and market demand can be predicted. In healthcare, EEG and EKG tracings can be analyzed. In business and finance, stock prices and indices can be predicted. In management, business performance can be monitored and optimized.

Time series analysis is based on the fact that data points recorded over time have an internal structure. By examining the main characteristics of a time series such as autocorrelation, trend, and seasonal variations, a time-series model can be developed for forecasting purpose. There are two types of time series: continuous and discrete. Data that can be recorded continuously, such as radio waves and electric signals, are continuous. Data such as sales and number of customers are discrete. This chapter focuses on discrete time series recorded at equal time intervals.

Time-series analysis has not been commonly used in hospitality-related research recently. In fact, it has been underused. There are only a handful of studies on demand and capacity management adopted time-series approach in the past decade. Using plain language, this chapter provides an overview of some practical time series analyzing techniques and demonstrate their applications in the hospitality-related research. Particularly, this chapter provides easy to follow step-by-step demonstrations of performing those techniques for forecasting and assessing impact.

8.2   TIME SERIES FORECASTING

8.2.1   TIME SERIES DATA

Unlike other data sets, a time series has only one variable that is measured and recorded at successive points in equally spaced time intervals. Some time series in the hospitality industry are weekly average RevPAR, daily occupancy rate, daily casino slot coin-in, weekly casino table drop, daily number of guests served, daily stock price, etc. To model and analyze a time series, it is important to understand the unique characteristics of the data.

8.2.1.1   FOUR COMPONENTS

As described by Box, Jenkins, and Reinsel (2008) and Anderson, Sweeny, and Williams (2006), a time series has four components: trend, cycle, seasonal variation, and irregular fluctuations. Trend refers to the upward or downward movement of a time series. It shows the overall direction a business is heading over a period of time (e.g., sales increases or decreases over past several years). Cycle refers to the movements of a time series caused by the changes of external economic factors. It reflects expansions, peaks, and contractions in economic or business activities. Cyclical movements of a time series are around the trend levels. For example, it is expected that a new hotel will grow in future 5 years. However, the economy experiences a down turn 2 years after the hotel opens. The time series of monthly sales of this hotel will show overall upward trend in 5 years with a few downward movements after 24 months.

Irregular fluctuations are movements of a time series caused by unexpected events such as earthquakes, hurricanes, and strikes. Irregular fluctuations do not have recognized patterns. The impact of an unexpected event can be measured by examining the irregular fluctuations. For example, the impact of 2008 recession on weekly US RevPAR can be measured by examining the fluctuations of the time series.

Seasonal variations are unique patterns of a time series that repeat themselves annually. They are mainly caused by factors such as weather and holidays. Given that seasonality is one of the main characteristics of the hospitality industry, seasonal variations are particularly obvious in hospitality time-series data. Sales in winter months of a hotel in ski resort are higher than summer months and this pattern repeats every year. For most time series forecasting methods, data need to be deseasonalized before forecasting procedures can be performed. Anderson et al. (2006) introduced a simple and effective deseasonalizing procedure that uses seasonal indexes. Below is a step-by-step illustration of this procedure using average quarterly US RevPAR data from 2004 to 2007 listed in column 3 of Table 8.1.

TABLE 8.1   Deseasonalizing of Average Quarterly US RevPAR (2004–2007).

1	2	3	4	5	6	7	8
Year	Quarter	Average RevPAR ($)	Four-quarter moving average	Centered moving average	seasonal-irregular value	Seasonal indexes	Deseasonalized average RevPAR ($)
2004	1	49.44				0.98	50.45
	2	55.77	53.54			1.05	53.11
	3	58.42	54.51	54.02	1.08	1.07	54.60
	4	50.52	55.69	55.10	0.92	0.91	55.52
2005	1	53.33	56.91	56.30	0.95	0.98	54.42
	2	60.51	58.10	57.50	1.05	1.05	57.63
	3	63.27	59.59	58.85	1.08	1.07	59.13
	4	55.28	60.96	60.28	0.92	0.91	60.75
2006	1	59.31	61.94	61.45	0.97	0.98	60.52
	2	66.00	62.60	62.27	1.06	1.05	62.86
	3	67.16	64.78	63.69	1.05	1.07	62.77
	4	57.94	65.64	65.21	.089	0.91	63.67
2007	1	68.04	66.70	66.17	1.03	0.98	69.43
	2	69.41	67.46	67.08	1.03	1.05	66.10
	3	71.40				1.07	66.73
	4	61.00				0.91	67.03

Step 1: Calculating Four-Quarter Moving Average (column 4 of Table 8.1). To account for all seasonal variations and irregular fluctuations in the time series, one year of data should be included in the calculations (i.e., four-quarter moving average (MA) for quarterly data, 12-month MA for monthly data, 52-week MA for weekly data, etc.).

The first four-quarter MA is (49.44 + 55.77 + 58.42 + 50.52)/4 = 53.54.

The second four-quarter MA is (55.77 + 58.42 + 50.52 + 53.33)/4 = 54.51.

Step 2: Calculating Centered Moving Average (column 5 of Table 8.1). Centered MAs need to be calculated if the number of data points in a time series is an even number. In this example, since there are 16 quarters, the four-quarter MAs calculated in Step 1 do not correspond to the original time series. Therefore, centered MAs need to be calculated.

The first centered MA, (53.54 + 54.51)/2 = 54.02, is corresponding to the 3rd quarter of 2004.

The second centered MA, $(54.51 + 55.69)/2 = 55.10$, is corresponding to the 4th quarter of 2004.

Step 3: Calculating Seasonal Irregular Value (column 6 of Table 8.1). To identify the seasonal-irregular effect, seasonal-irregular values need to be calculated by dividing the original time series data points by corresponding centered MAs.

The first seasonal irregular value is $58.42/54.02 = 1.08$.

Step 4: Calculating Seasonal Index. Seasonal index needs to be calculated for each quarter by averaging corresponding seasonal-irregular values.

Seasonal Index for 1st quarter is $(0.95 + 0.97 + 1.03)/3 = 0.98$.
Seasonal Index for 2nd quarter is $(1.05 + 1.06 + 1.03)/3 = 1.05$.
Seasonal Index for 3rd quarter is $(1.08 + 1.08 + 1.05)/3 = 1.07$.
Seasonal Index for 4th quarter is $(0.92 + 0.92 + 0.89)/3 = 0.91$.

However, before the seasonal indexes can be used for deseasonalizing, adjustments may be needed if the average seasonal index is not 1.00 (i.e., the seasonal effects should even out through 1 year). In this case, since the average seasonal index equals 1 $((0.98 + 1.05 + 1.07 + 0.91)/4 = 1.00)$, no adjustments are needed.

The following formula can be used if adjustments are needed:

Adjusted Seasonal Index = Unadjusted Seasonal Index × (4/Sum of Unadjusted Seasonal Indexes).

Step 5: Deseasonalizaing. Dividing original time series (column 3 of Table 8.1) by seasonal indexes (column 7 of Table 8.1) or adjusted seasonal indexes to remove the seasonal and irregular components from the data. Deseasonalized quarterly RevPAR time series is listed in column 8 of Table 8.1.

After the forecasting procedure is performed on deseasonalized data, seasonal and irregular components need to be "added back" into the forecasts by multiplying each forecasted value with corresponding seasonal index.

8.2.1.2 AUTOCORRELATION

Autocorrelation, also known as lagged correlation or serial correlation, is the correlation of a variable with itself. It is the fundamental concept of time-series analysis as this relationship makes time series predictable. Autocorrelation in time series is the correlation of a time series with its own past and/or future values and time-series model fitting largely depends on the measures of this relationship. For example, today's RevPAR in a daily RevPAR time series is correlated to RevPARs in past a few days and is also correlated to RevPARs in future a few days. Therefore, future daily RevPAR can be predicted by examining and modeling a daily RevPAR time series.

8.2.2   FORECASTING METHODS

While performing time series forecasting, researchers and practitioners typically analyze and model the data in hand up to time T and use the model to forecast future data values beyond time T. The forecasting results are called out-of-sample forecasts, also known as *ex-ante* forecasts in economy and financial-related studies.

The main challenge of performing time-series forecasting is that actual observations are not available to verify the accuracy of the forecasts. Since it is not practical to wait until future observations become available to evaluate the model, the forecast ability of a model is usually assessed using the data in hand. To do so, a time series needs to be divided into *training set* and *test set*. The *training set* is used for analyzing and modeling, and the *test set* is used to evaluate and calibrate the forecast ability of the model. Once a model is developed, it is used to "forecast" the data values for the same timespan the *test set* covers. The "forecasted", or estimated data values are to be compared with the actual observations in the *test set* to determine the forecast ability of the model. The differences between the estimated data values and actual observations are called errors. The smaller the errors are, the better the model is and the more accurate the future forecasts will be. It is not uncommon that multiple models need to be developed and compared to find the one that produces the most accurate forecasts.

8.2.2.1   SMOOTHING METHODS

Smoothing methods are a group of relatively simple and easy-to-use time-series forecasting techniques. By eliminating the irregular fluctuations of a time series, smoothing methods are able to produce relatively accurate forecasts. Since the data needed are minimal and the procedures are easy to understand, smoothing methods are often used by practitioners for market forecasting. This section will introduce simple MA method, single exponential smoothing method, and Multiplicative Holt–Winters method.

8.2.2.2   SIMPLE MOVING AVERAGE METHOD

Simple MA method is the simplest smoothing method that uses the arithmetic average of the time-series data values from most recent n time periods in the data set to forecast the next data value. The method can be illustrated as

$$Y'_t = (Y_{t-1} + Y_{t-2} + L + Y_{t-n})/n$$

where Y_{t-1} is the actual data value in a time series at time period $t-1$ and Y'_t is the forecast of the time series data value for time period t. Since n, or the number of data value to be used for forecasting, directly affects the accuracy of the forecasts, it is critical to estimate an n that produces the most accurate forecast possible. Since different time series have different patterns, n needs to be estimated for every time-series forecasting.

Below is a simple example of time series forecasting of quarterly US RevPAR using simple MA method and quarterly data from 2006 to 2007. Raw data and deseasonalized data are listed in columns 3 and 8 of Table 8.1, respectively.

Step 1. Visual Inspection of the Data. The time series plot of quarterly US RevPAR from 2004 to 2007 shows very obvious seasonal variations. Therefore, the data need to be deseasonalized before they can be used for forecasting.

Step 2. Deseasonalizing. Demonstrated in Section 8.2.1.1.

Step 3. Calculating moving averages using deseasonalized data for model fitting (data listed in column 8 of Table 8.1). In this case, model fitting is a process of determining the optimal number of quarters to be included in MA calculations. First of all, the data set is divided into two parts. For the purpose of this example, the training set contains quarterly data from 2006 and the test set contains quarterly data from 2007. Using the data in training set, two-, three-, and four-quarter MA analyses are estimated for 2007 (i.e., the simple MA method is performed for $n = 2$, 3, and 4).

Below are the detailed step-by-step calculations for Two-Quarter Moving Average.

1st Q of 2007   = (Observed 3rd Q of 2006 + Observed 4th Q of 2006)/2
                  = (62.77 + 63.67)/2 = 62.55
2nd Q of 2007   = (Observed 4th Q of 2006 + Estimated 1st Q of 2007)/2
                  = (63.67 + 62.55)/2 = 60.25

3rd Q of 2007 $=$ (Estimated 1st Q of 2007 + Estimated 2nd Q of 2007)/2
$\qquad = (62.55 + 60.25)/2 = 61.40$

4th Q of 2007 $=$ (Estimated 2nd Q of 2007 + Estimated 3rd Q of 2007)/2
$\qquad = (60.25 + 61.40)/2 = 60.82.$

Below are the detailed step-by-step calculations for Three-Quarter Moving Average.

1st Q of 2007 $=$ (Observed 2nd Q of 2006 + Observed 3rd Q of 2006 + Observed 4th Q of 2006)/3
$\qquad = (62.86 + 62.77 + 63.67)/3 = 63.70$

2nd Q of 2007 $=$ (Observed 3rd Q of 2006 + Observed 4th Q of 2006 + Estimated 1st Q of 2007)/3
$\qquad = (62.77 + 63.67 + 63.70)/3 = 62.93$

3rd Q of 2007 $=$ (Observed 4th Q of 2006 + Estimated 1st Q of 2007 + Estimated 2nd Q of 2007)/3
$\qquad = (63.67 + 63.70 + 62.96)/3 = 61.52$

4th Q of 2007 $=$ (Estimated 1st Q of 2007 + Estimated 2nd Q of 2007 + Estimated 3rd Q of 2007)/3
$\qquad = (63.70 + 62.93 + 61.52)/3 = 62.72$

Below are the detailed step-by-step calculations for Four-Quarter Moving Average.

1st Q of 2007 $=$ (Observed 1st Q of 2006 + Observed 2nd Q of 2006 + Observed 3rd Q of 2006 + Observed 4th Q of 2006)/4
$\qquad = (60.52 + 62.86 + 62.77 + 63.67)/4 = 62.60$

2nd Q of 2007 $=$ (Observed 2nd Q of 2006 + Observed 3rd Q of 2006 + Observed 4th Q of 2006
$\qquad$ + Estimated 1st Q of 2007)/4
$\qquad = (62.86+62.77+63.67+62.60)/4 = 63.43$

3rd Q of 2007 $=$ (Observed 3rd Q of 2006 + Observed 4th Q of 2006 + Estimated 1st Q of 2007
$\qquad$ + Estimated 2nd Q of 2007)/4
$\qquad = (62.77 + 63.67 + 62.60 + 63.43)/4 = 62.78$

4th Q of 2007 $=$ (Observed 4th Q of 2006 + Estimated 1st Q of 2007 + Estimated 2nd Q of 2007
$\qquad$ + Estimated 3rd Q of 2007)/4
$\qquad = (63.67 + 62.60 + 63.43 + 62.78)/4 = 61.69$

Step 4. Using the *test set* to compare errors and select forecasting model (estimating *n* for simple MA method).

First of all, Sums of Squared Error are calculated for "forecasting" results (i.e., the estimated values) of Two-, Three-, and Four-Quarter MA methods, respectively. Table 8.2 illustrates the calculations using the results of Two-Quarter MA method. Specifically:

Column 5 = Column 3 − Column 2

Column 6 = Column 5^2

Mean Squared Error = Sum of Squared Error/4.

Using the same approach, the sums of square errors for Three-, and Four-Quarter MA results are calculated to be 22.15 and 24.48. In other words, Three-Quarter MA method produces the least amount of error. Therefore, to use Simple Moving Average method to forecast quarterly average US RevPAR beyond 2007, three data values should be used (i.e., *n* = 3) to produce the most accurate results.

TABLE 8.2   Calculations for "Forecasting" Errors in Two Quarter Moving Average.

1	2	3	4	5	6
Year	Quarter	Deseasonalized average RevPAR ($)	Two-quarter moving average	"Forecast-ing" error	Squared "fore-casting" error
2007	1	69.43	62.55	6.88	47.34
	2	66.10	60.25	5.85	34.22
	3	66.73	61.40	5.33	28.41
	4	67.03	60.82	6.21	38.56
			Sum of squared error		**148.53**
			Mean squared error		**37.12**

Step 5. Forecasting beyond 2007.

1st Q of 2008   = (2nd Q of 2007 + 3rd Q of 2007 + 4th Q of 2007)/3
= (66.10 + 66.73 + 67.03)/3 = 66.62

2nd Q of 2008 = (3rd Q of 2007 + 4th Q of 2007 + 1st Q of 2008)/3
= (66.73 + 67.03 + 66.62)/3 = 66.79

3rd Q of 2008 = (4th Q of 2007 + 1st Q of 2008 + 2nd Q of 2008)/3
= (67.03 + 66.62 + 66.79)/3 = 66.81

4th Q of 2008 = (1st Q of 2008 + 2nd Q of 2008 + 3rd Q of 2008)/3
= (66.62 + 66.79 + 66.81)/3 = 66.74

Since the deseasonalized data are used for forecasting, to reflect the seasonal nature of market demand, the seasonal effects need to be added into the forecasts for 2008 by multiplying with the quarterly indexes (listed in Table 8.3). Therefore, the quarterly averages US RevPAR are forecasted to be

1st Q of 2008 $= 66.62 \times 0.98 = 65.29$

2nd Q of 2008 $= 66.79 \times 1.05 = 70.13$

3rd Q of 2008 $= 66.81 \times 1.07 = 71.49$

4th Q of 2008 $= 66.74 \times 0.91 = 60.73.$

8.2.2.3   SINGLE EXPONENTIAL SMOOTHING METHOD

This is the simplest exponential smoothing method. It is essentially a Simple Moving Average method with weighted average of the last actual data value and the forecast of the last time period. Single Exponential Smoothing method can be illustrated as

$$Y'_t = \alpha Y_{t-1} + (1 - \alpha)Y'_{t-1}$$

where Y'_t is the forecast of the time series data value for time period t, Y_{t-1} is the actual observation in a time series for time period $t - 1$, and Y'_{t-1} is the forecast of time series value for time period $t - 1$.

For optimal forecasting, smoothing constant α needs to be estimated using a trial-and-error approach (Zheng, Bloom, Wang, & Schrier, 2012). Excel Solver can be used for estimating. The constraint to be used is $1 \geq \alpha \geq 0$ with the objective of Minimizing Mean Square Error.

8.2.2.4   MULTIPLICATIVE HOLT–WINTERS METHOD

This method extends Single Exponential Smoothing method by including levels, trends, and seasonal variations into the time series forecasting process. In addition to α, Multiplicative Holt–Winters method also use two other smoothing constants γ and δ to smooth the trend and seasonality in the data. Bowerman, Connell, and Koehler (2005) illustrated this method as follows:

$$Y'_t = (L_t + B_t) \times SN_t$$

where Y'_t = forecast of the time series for time period t, L_t = estimated level (i.e., mean) of the time series at the time period t, Bt = estimated growth rate (i.e., trend) of the time series at time period t, and SN_t = estimated seasonal factor at time period t.

L_t, B_t, and SN_t can be estimated using following equations:

$$L_t = \alpha(Y_t/SN_{t-1}) + (1 - \alpha)(L_{t-1} + B_{t-1})$$
$$B_t = \gamma\,(L_t - L_{t-1}) + (1 - \gamma)\,B_{t-1}$$
$$SN_t = \delta(Y_t/L_t) + (1 - \delta)SN_{t-1}$$

where Y_t = actual value in time series at time period t, α = level (i.e., mean) smoothing constant, γ = growth rate smoothing constant, and δ = seasonal smoothing constant.

The formulas suggest that the forecasting accuracy of Multiplicative Holt–Winters smoothing method is based on the values of the three smoothing constants. The three smoothing constants are related and their optimal values need to be estimated to ensure highest possible accuracy. Zheng, Farrish, and Wang (2012) suggested Excel Solver for estimating the optimal values. The three constraints to be used are $1 \geq \alpha \geq 0$, $1 \geq \gamma \geq 0$, and $1 \geq \delta \geq 0$. The objective is minimizing mean squared error.

8.2.2.5 SUMMARY

Although simple, smoothing methods are able to produce accurate forecasts by eliminating irregular fluctuations in a time series. As Makridakis et al. (1993) indicated, "The best methods were the simplest." Zheng et al. (2012) compared the performances of three smoothing methods (simple MA, single exponential smoothing, and Holt–Winters) with those of Box–Jenkins Procedure and Artificial Neural Networks in forecasting weekly US RevPAR in different forecasting time horizons up to 50 weeks beyond the training set and found the simplest was the best.

In addition, Anderson et al. (2006) indicated that smoothing methods generally produce accurate short-range forecasts. However, Zheng et al.'s (2012) study on 50-week forecasting horizon found that simple MA method and single exponential smoothing method performed equally well and both outperformed others. In other words, contrary to what Anderson et al. (2006) defined, smoothing methods could perform well in long-term forecasting. Therefore, they should be included in selection of forecasting models for both short- and long-term forecasting.

8.2.2.6   REGRESSION

Regression analysis is a statistical procedure that examines the relationship among variables. The variable that is being predicted is *dependent variable* (DV) and the variable(s) used to predict the values of DV are *independent variables* (IVs). Regression analysis that examines the relationship between two variables is called *simple regression*, and regression analysis that contains two or more IVs is *multiple regression.* Regression analysis can be used for causal forecasting and time series forecasting and this section focuses on the latter.

The simplest approach of using regression analysis for time series forecasting is choosing time as the IV and the time series as the DV (DV). Using the deseasonalized average quarterly US RevPAR as an example (column 8 of Table 8.1), the regression equation is calculated as

$$\text{Deseasonalized RevPAR} = 50.56 + 1.15\,\text{Time}$$
(Adjusted R^2 = 0.9346; F = 215.48; $p < 0.000$ for Constant & Time)

This regression equation suggests that the deseasonalized RevPAR increases $1.15 every quarter in 2004, 2005, 2006, and 2007. This equation can be used for forecasting quarterly RevPAR beyond 2007. For example,

Deseasonalized 1st Q of 2008 = $50.56 + 1.15 \times 17 = 70.11$
Deseasnoalized 4th Q of 2008 = $50.56 + 1.15 \times 20 = 73.56$.

It is critical to use deseasonalized data for regression analysis whenever seasonal variations present in the time series. After seasonal effects are removed, the time-series dataset shows linear relationship with continuing upward trend, which in turn ensures good regression model fit. In addition, as suggested by Zheng et al. (2012), multiple deseasonalizing approaches may be tried to improve the model fit.

8.2.2.7   BOX–JENKINS PROCEDURE

Box–Jenkins procedure is a statistically sophisticated time-series extrapolating method that fits Autoregressive Integrated Moving Average (ARIMA) Models to historical data (Box, Jenkins, & Reinsel, 2008). Autoregressive (AR) is a process of estimating a time series value based on the weighted average of previous data points; Integrated (I) represents number of times a time series is differenced for stationarity; and MA is a process of estimating a time series value based on the weighted average of estimation error residuals of previous data points (this MA is different from the MA introduced in Section Smoothing Methods). An ARIMA model can be denoted as ARIMA (p, d, q) where:

  p represents the AR p order;
  q represents the MA q order;
  d represents the order of differencing for stationary transforming.

To analyze a time series with seasonality, a seasonal ARIMA model SARIMA (p, d, q) $(P, D, Q)_s$ can be used.

  P represents the seasonal AR P order;
  Q represents the seasonal MA Q order;
  D represents the order of differencing for stationary transforming at seasonal levels;
  "s" represents the number of time periods within a seasonal cycle (e.g., 12 for monthly data and 4 for quarterly data).

Box–Jenkins procedure is considered accurate in model fitting because it models both lagged DVs and estimation error residuals. In addition, ARIMA with Intervention analysis is the only statistical procedure that tests and measures the impact of an exogenous event on time series.

8.2.2.8   STATIONARITY AND DIFFERENCING

Stationarity means the variance and autocorrelation structure of a time series stay constant over time. It is the foundation of Box–Jenkins procedure as Box–Jenkins procedure models time series that is with constant variance, but without seasonal variations. Statistical tests such as Dickey–Fuller (DF) test, augmented DA, and Phillip–Perron tests can be used for stationarity test. However, since the purpose of this chapter is to provide practical easy-to-follow guidelines, none of these tests will be discussed. Instead, a visual inspection technique will be introduced.

Stationarity can be achieved through data transformation procedures known as differencing. As Bowerman et al. (2005) suggested, there are four levels of differencing: predifferencing, first regular differencing, first seasonal differencing, and first regular differencing and first seasonal differencing. A seasonal time series usually will achieve stationarity through one of the four differencing methods or predifferencing and one of the other three methods.

Predifferencing is a process of stabilizing the variance of a time series (transforming time series Y to a new time series Z).

$$Z_t = Y_t$$

First Regular Differencing creates another new time series Z

$$Z_t = Y_t - Y_{t-1}$$

Frist Seasonal Differencing creates another new time series Z

$$Z_t = Y_t - Y_{t-L}$$

(L denotes the number of seasons in a year. For example: $L = 12$ for monthly data.)

First Regular Differencing and First Seasonal Differencing creates another new time series Z

$$Z_t = Y_t - Y_{t-1} - Y_{t-L} + Y_{t-L-1}$$

Below is a demonstration of differencing and ARIMA model fitting using monthly numbers of 5-star hotel rooms sold in Shanghai from 2004 to 2007. The data are listed in Table 8.3. The time series plot of the original rooms sold, Y, shows increasing variance through 48 months (Fig. 8.1). Calculations such as cubic root, quartic root, and natural logarithm reduce the value of the data, which in turn reduce the variance. Figure 8.1 demonstrates the differences between the raw data and log-transformed data. The transformed data ($Ln(Y)$), or the predifferenced data, have relatively constant variance.

Next step is to perform Autocorrelation Analysis to determine whether the time series has achieved stationarity. The general rule of visual inspection is that the time series is considered stationary if (1) the spikes cut off quickly or die down quickly at the nonseasonal level; and (2) the spikes cut off quickly or die down quickly at the seasonal level. Die down and cut off are both measured by the ratio of correlation to the standard error. Spikes between the two red dotted bands represent the ratio is less than 2, which means the autocorrelation is not considered statistically large (i.e., autocorrelation of the data value equals zero, or not statistically significantly different from zero).

TABLE 8.3   Monthly 5-star Hotel Rooms Sold in Shanghai.

	2004	2005	2006	2007	2008
January	149,875	231,650	223,485	304,226	316,378
February	205,200	175,786	223,485	234,064	247,300
March	245,075	263,214	223,485	383,161	319,200
April	238,965	269,467	223,485	381,634	344,395
May	232,621	251,398	223,485	393,668	315,716
June	245,875	254,770	223,485	392,510	295,055
July	238,355	237,302	223,485	389,014	292,910
August	220,373	233,646	223,485	379,379	245,753
September	250,228	261,659	223,485	429,978	291,477
October	263,534	269,751	223,485	496,912	333,599
November	269,468	278,500	223,485	483,014	317,741
December	222,263	217,523	223,485	376,009	230,113

Source: The Yearbook of China Tourism Statistics (2005–2009), Shanghai Municipal Tourism Administration.

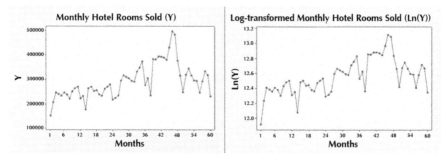

FIGURE 8.1   Raw vs. log-transformed monthly 5-star hotel rooms sold in Shanghai.

Figure 8.2 indicates that the spikes do not cut off or die down quickly at the nonseasonal level (at lags 1, 2, 3, 4, 5, and 6). Therefore, it can be determined that the time series is not stationary and further differencing is needed. Use the same data (Ln(Y)), three other differencing methods are performed to select the one that stationalizes the data. The results suggest that the data transformed with 1st regular differencing and 1st seasonal differencing method achieves stationary. Figure 8.3 shows that spikes cut off quickly at both nonseasonal and seasonal levels (i.e., there is only one spike goes beyond the red color bonds at nonseasonal and seasonal levels).

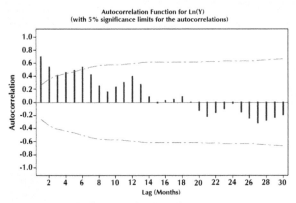

FIGURE 8.2   Autocorrelation analysis of Ln(*Y*).

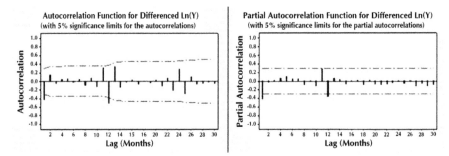

FIGURE 8.3   Autocorrelation and partial autocorrelation analyses of differenced Ln(Y)).

8.2.2.9   ARIMA MODEL FITTING EXAMPLES

After the original monthly average number of rooms sold, time series (*Y*) has been transformed with natural logarithm and differenced with 1st regular differencing and 1st seasonal differencing method, it is ready for model fitting. Bowerman (2005) suggested a three-step model fitting process:

1. Use the results of Autocorrelation and Partial Autocorrelation analyses at the nonseasonal level to identify a nonseasonal model (this is the only step needed for a nonseasonal time series),
2. Use the results of Autocorrelation and Partial Autocorrelation analyses at the seasonal level to identify a seasonal model (this is an optional step for seasonal time series), and

- Create a SARIMA model (or Seasonal ARIMA model for seasonal time series) by combining the nonseasnal model and the seasonal model.

By visual inspection of Figure 8.3, the tentative Seasonal ARIMA model can be estimated to be SARIMA $(1,1,0)(0,1,1)_{12}$, in which:

at the nonseasonal level:

$p = 1$. The spikes cut off after lag 1 (i.e., only the spike at lag 1 is beyond the red dotted lines), which suggests AR order 1 at the nonseasonal level.
$(-0.3435, t = 2.33, p = 0.024)$;
$q = 0$; and
$d = 1$ represents the 1st-order regular differencing.

At the seasonal level:

$P = 0$;
$Q = 1$. The spikes cut off after lag 12, which suggests AR order 1 at the seasonal level. $(0.7908, t = 4.48, p = 0.000)$;
$D = 1$ represents the 1st-order seasonal differencing; and
$s = 12$ represents the number of time periods within a seasonal cycle (12months).

In other words, this SARIMA model uses time series data point at $t - 1$ (AR operator of order 1) and forecasting residual at $t - 1$ (seasonal MA operator of order 1) to forecast value at time t.

The last step of the Box–Jenkins procedure is examining the model adequacy using Ljung–Box test. The Ljung–Box test is used to determine whether significant autocorrelation can be identified in model residuals, also known as forecasting error (residuals are the differences between original time series values and data values "forecasted" by the model for the same period of time). It tests the hypothesis whether the autocorrelation among model residuals are significantly different from zero. As shown in Table 8.4, the high p values suggest the autocorrelation among model residuals are not statistically significantly different from zero. Figure 8.4 also shows the no autocorrelation among model residuals is significant (all spikes are within the red color dotted bonds). Therefore, the model SARIMA $(1,1,0)(0,1,1)_{12}$ is adequacy and can be used for forecasting purpose.

TABLE 8.4   Ljung–Box Chi-Square Statistic for SARIMA $(1,1,0)(0,1,1)_{12}$ Model.

Lag	Chi-square	DF	p
12	3.9	10	0.950
24	9.5	22	0.990
36	24.5	34	0.884

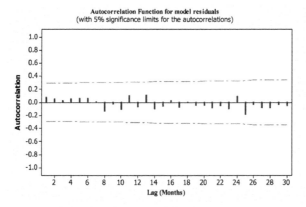

FIGURE 8.4   Autocorrelation function for model residuals.

Once the model is identified and tested for adequacy, it can be used for forecasting. Statistics software packages such as Minitab and SAS calculate the forecasts for the forecasting horizons defined by the researchers.

8.2.2.10   ARTIFICIAL NEURAL NETWORKS (ANN) MODELS

Artificial Neural Networks (ANN) is a group of models for information processing and pattern recognition. Inspired by biological neural systems, ANN consists of many neurons that are connected to each other and receive, process, and send information from and to other neurons in the networks. The major restrictions early ANN had were that they were designed to dealing with linear problems only and without a perceptron-like learning rule (Abdi, Valentin, & Edelman, 1999). To overcome these limitations, hidden layers between the input and the output layers were added and error back propagation function was developed to adjust the weights of neurons of the hidden layers, which helped ANN regained popularity in the 1980s (Abdi, Valentin, & Edelman, 1999). Because of its unique features, ANN was extensively studied and been suggested to be universal approximators of functions (White, 1992).

ANN models have been used to examine time series and considered as a promising alternative to traditional linear methods due to its capability of capturing nonlinear relationships between input variables and output variables (Zhang, Patuwo, & Hu, 1998; Hill, O'Connor, & Remus, 1996). Many have argued that ANN models are able to overcome some limitations observed in traditional statistical time-series forecasting methods. For example, developing ANN models requires less expertise than developing ARIMA models, which makes ANN a less subjective technique (Wasserman, 1998; White 1992). However, mixed results have been presented. Particularly, the M3-Competition didn't find ANN to be superior in comparisons among 24 time-series forecasting methods on 3003 time series of different time intervals (Makridakis & Hibon, 2000).

In addition, Zheng et al. (2012) examined how ANN behaved on the weekly RevPAR data with impact from the recent recession and found that ANN's performance was rather disappointing. Smoothing methods and ARIMA models outperformed ANN. Therefore, given the time and effort required to perform this complicated procedure and its mediocre performance, the author does not recommend ANN models for time-series analysis or forecasting, at least not with small data sets.

8.3   TIME SERIES MODELS IN THE HOSPITALITY AND TOURISM RESEARCH

8.3.1   RECENT STUDIES USING TIME SERIES MODELS

Li, Song, and Witt (2005) examined 84 post-1990 tourism demand modeling and forecasting studies and found most studies used time series approach. ARIMA and Seasonal ARIMA modeling was the most popular technique used in univariate time-series-based papers. On the other hand, only a very limited number of capacity management related studies have been identified in the lodging and gaming industries from the past decade. Some recent studies used time-series analysis to detect and assess the impact of 2008 recession.

8.3.2   IMPACT OF INTERVENTION

Once an ARIMA or a SARIMA model is developed, it can be used to assess the impact of an exogenous intervention on the data by detecting the structural breaks of the data and measuring the magnitude of changes of data-pattern trends before and after the intervention (McDowall, McCleary, Meidinger, & Hay, 1980; Bowerman et al., 2005; Box et al., 2008). Specifically, a time series needs to be split into two data sets at the intervention point and the (S) ARIMA model developed based on the time series before the intervention point can be applied to the original time series (the whole data set) to examine the impact. (S)ARIMA with Intervention analysis determines whether an exogenous intervention has statistically significant impact on a time series and quantifies the impact, if any. An identified and quantified impact, which is the amount more or less than expected, represents the difference between the actual time series and what the time series would have been if there was no intervention.

Many hospitality related studies used this technique to examine the impact of exogenous events such as the terrorist attacks on September 11, 2001 and the outbreak of Severe Acute Respiratory Syndrome (SARS) in 2003. For example, Coshall (2003) examined the impact of the September 11 terrorist attack on international travel flows; Eisendrath, Bernhard, Lucas, and Murphy (2008) measured the impact of the September 11 terrorist attack on Las Vegas strip gaming volume; Lee, Oh, and Leary (2005) quantified the decrease of US air-transport passenger demand after the September 11 terrorist attack; Ming, Lim, and Kung (2011) analyzed the impact of SARS on Japanese tourism demand for Taiwan; and Zheng et al. (2012) examined the impact of the 2007 recession on US restaurant stocks.

In addition, Zheng (2014) strategically used ARIMA with Intervention analysis technique to identify the overdevelopment of the US lodging industry and measure its impact on weekly RevPAR through the recession. It was identified that, after the 2007 recession started, the weekly US room supply was 9878 more than expected and the weekly US RevPAR was $0.16 lower than expected. The study further identified that the overdevelopment of the hotel industry caused approximately $0.10 decrease in weekly RevPAR, which means the true impact from the recession was only approximately $0.06.

8.3.3   ECONOMETRICS MODELS VS. TIME SERIES MODELS

There are two categories of quantitative forecasting models: univariate forecasting models (time series models) and causal forecasting models (econometrics models). Unlike time-series models, casual forecasting models require two or more variables (one DV and one or more IVs). The DV is the one to be examined and forecasted and the IVs are the ones related to the DV. Once the IVs are identified, a statistical model can be developed that describes the relationship between the DV and IVs. The model can be used to forecast the future values of the DV. For example, an econometrics model can be developed based on monthly marketing expenses and monthly sales in past ten years. The model can then be used to predict the changes in monthly sales for given amount of monthly marketing expenses.

The biggest advantage of econometrics models is that they allow managers to examine the impact of a specific factor while time-series models simply evaluate the fluctuations of the data without examining the causes. On the other hand, econometrics models are not without disadvantages. First, more data are required to develop econometrics models. Historical data are needed for all variables that are included in a model. Second, the selections of IVs are often arbitrary. For example, since many macro- and microeconomic factors affect the tourism industry, it is difficult to determine the IVs for an econometric model for tourism demand forecast. Lastly, the future values of all IVs in an econometric model need to be forecasted before the future values of the DV can be forecasted. In other words, the forecasts of DVs are based on the forecasts of several other variables, which are likely to increase the forecasting error.

While time-series forecasting ignores the casual relationship between an IV and the factors that affect it, it makes many challenging studies doable by examining only one variable. As Howrey (1980) indicated, time series analysis can be used for econometric research when little prior knowledge is available. In other words, time series analysis is an unmatched approach that provides much more practical and flexible methods in demand forecasting and capacity management related study.

8.3.4 CHOOSING THE BEST METHODS

Trend, cycle, seasonal variations, and irregular fluctuations are the four time-series components and a time series can have one or more of these at any level in any combination. Therefore, the universal best time-series forecasting model does not exist. The best forecasting model for a time series is the one that models the unique patterns of the time series data. In other words, every time series forecasting task should start with identifying the most appropriate forecasting model for the data through testing multiple forecasting techniques. The author strongly suggests that simple techniques such as simple MA method and single exponential smoothing method should always be included in model selection. Multiple studies have found that the sophisticated methods are not necessarily the accurate ones.

Another factor needs to be considered for model selection is the purpose of forecasting. Different purposes of forecasting require different levels of forecasting accuracy. From a practical point of view, the best forecasting model is the one that serves the purpose most effectively and efficiently. In other words, the least amount of time and effort should be invested in producing forecasts that satisfy the purpose. Striving for high level of forecasting accuracy without considering the resources needed for data collection and model building will lead to inefficiency.

8.4 CONCLUSION

Due to the capital intensive and labor incentive nature of the hospitality industry, effective capacity management is critical for hospitality operations. Both over- or under-supply will directly affect the financial performance of a hospitality firm and are undesired. The foremost step of effective capacity management is knowing the market through accurate forecasting of future market demand and fluctuations. Given their uniqueness and overall performance demonstrated in existing literature, time series analysis and forecasting techniques can be considered as an effective and efficient market forecasting tool for the hospitality industry.

In addition to the methods introduced in this chapter, a combined approach can also be considered for time-series forecasting. Bates and Granger (1969) combined the forecasts of airline passengers generated by different forecasting methods and found that the combined forecasts had lower mean square error. Oh and Morzuch (2005) examined the performance of four time-series forecasting methods on forecasting tourism demand in Singapore and found that the simple average of the four forecasts always outperformed the least accurate method and sometimes outperformed that the most accurate method. Wong, Song, Witt, and Wu (2007) examined the combined approach in predicting Hong Kong inbound tourists and found that the combined forecasts generally were more accurate than the least accurate individual forecasts. However, few studies have been identified that examined the combination of forecasts from time series models and econometric models. In addition, the optimal way of selecting methods to combine different forecasts from different methods have not been thoroughly investigated. Therefore, in the future, a hybrid approach that includes both time-series techniques and econometric models should be examined and the combination techniques need to be more thoroughly scrutinized to achieve higher forecasting accuracy.

KEYWORDS

- **time series analysis**
- **forecasting methods**
- **simple moving average**
- **single exponential smoothing method**
- **multiplicative hold-winters method**
- **regression**
- **Box–Jenkins procedure**
- **tourism and hospitality industry**

REFERENCES

Abdi, H.; Valentin, D.; Edelman, B. *Neural Networks.* SAGE Publications: Thousand Oaks, CA, 1999.

Anderson, D. R.; Sweeny, D. J.; Williams, T. A. *Quantitative Methods for Business* (10th ed.). Thomson Higher Education: Mason, OH, 2006.

Bates, J. M.; Granger, C. W. J. The Combination of Forecasts. *Operational Res.* **1996,** *20*(4), 451–468.

Bowerman, B. L.; Connell, R. T.; Koehler, A. B. *Forecasting, Time Series, and Regression: An Applied Approach.* Brooks/Cole: Belmont, CA, 2005.

Box, G. E. P.; Jenkins, G. M.; Reinsel, G. C. *Time Series Analysis, Forecasting and Control* (4th ed.). John Wiley & Sons: Hoboken, NJ, 2008.

Coshall, J. T. The Threat of Terrorism as an Intervention on International Travel Flows. *J. Travel Res.* **2003,** *42*(4), 4–12.

Eisendrath, D.; Bernhard, B. J.; Lucas, A. F.; Murphy, D. J. Fear and Managing in Las Vegas: An Analysis of the Effects of September 11, 2001, on Las Vegas Strip Gaming Volume. *Cornell Hospitality Q.* **2008,** *49*(2), 145–162.

Hill, T.; O'Connor, M.; Remus, W. Neural Network Models for Time Series Forecasts. *Manage. Sci.* **1996,** *42*(7), 1082–1092.

Howrey, E. P. *The Role of Time Series Analysis in Econometric Model Evaluation.* The National Bureau of Economic Research. 1980 (retrieved on August 12, 2013 from http://www.nber.org/chapters/c11706.pdf).

Lee, S.; Oh, C.; O'Leary, J. T. Estimating the Impact of the September 11 Terrorist Attacks on the U.S. Air Transport Passenger Demand Using Intervention Analysis. *Tourism Anal.* **2005,** *9,* 355–361.

Li, G.; Song, H.; Witt, S. Recent Development in Econometric Modeling and Forecasting. *J. Travel Res.* **2005**, *44*(1), 82–99.

Makridakis, S.; Chatfield, C.; Hibon, M.; Lawrence, M. J.; Mills, T.; Ord, K. The M2 Competition: A Real-Time Judgmentally Based Forecasting Competition. *J. Forecasting* **1993**, *9*(1), 5–22.

Makridakis, S.; Hibon, M. The M3-Competition: Results, Conclusions and Implications. *Int. J. Forecasting* **2000**, *16*(4), 451–476.

McDowall, D.; McCleary, R.; Meidinger, E. E.; Hay, R. A. Jr. *Interrupted Time Series Analysis,* SAGE Publications: Thousand Oaks, CA, 1980.

Ming, J. C. H.; Lim, C.; Kung, H. Intervention Analysis of SARS on Japanese Tourism Demand for Taiwan. *Qual. Quantity* **2011**, *45*(1), 91–102.

Oh, C. O.; Morzuch, B. Evaluating Time-Series Models to Forecast the Demand for Tourism in Singapore: Comparing Within-Sample and Post-Sample Results. *J. Travel Res.* **2005**, *43*(4), 404–413.

Wasserman, P. D. *Neural Computing: Theory and practice.* Van Nostrand Reinhold: New York, 1998.

White, H. Connectionist Nonparametric Regression: Multilayer Feedforward Networks Can Learn Arbitrary Mappings. In *Artificial Neural Networks: Approximations and learning Theory*; White, H., Ed.; Blackwell: Oxford, UK, 1992.

Wong, K. K. F.; Song, H.; Witt, S. F.; Wu, D. C. Tourism Forecasting: To Combine or Not to Combine?. *Tourism Manage.* **2007**, *28*(4), 1068–1078.

Zhang, G. P.; Patuwo, E. B.; Hu, M. Y. Forecasting with Artificial Neural Networks: The State of the Art. *Int. J. Forecasting* **1998**, *14*(1), 35–62.

Zheng, T. What Caused the Decrease in RevPAR During the Recession? An ARIMA with Intervention Analysis of Room Supply and Market Demand. *Int. J. Contemp. Hospitality Manage.* **2014**, *26*(8), 1225–1242.

Zheng, T.; Bloom, B. A. N.; Wang, X.; Schrier, T. How Do Less Advanced Forecasting Methods Perform on Weekly RevPAR In Different Forecasting Horizons Following the Recession?. *Tourism Anal.* **2012**, *17,* 459–472.

Zheng, T.; Farrish, J.; Wang, X. How Did Different Restaurant Segments Perform Differently through the Recession? An ARIMA with Intervention Analysis on US Restaurant Stock Indices. *J. Hospitality Financial Manage.* **2012**, *20*(2), Article 1.

Zheng, T.; Gu, Z. Shanghai's High-End Hotel Overcapacity in 2011 and Beyond: How Bad It Could Be and Why?. *Tourism Anal.* **2011**, *16*, 571–581.

other factors, such as public and private sector structures supporting tourism flows (Prideaux, 2005). Specifically, these factors may include natural and cultural resources, as well as general and tourism infrastructures. Moreover, considering its successful history of explaining bilateral flows and the ease of application to tourism, it is necessary to provide a gravity model extended by a concept that can generally explain these factors as a whole rather than focusing on specific regions or events. A recently developed concept, destination competitiveness, includes factors that influence tourism flows (Ritchie & Crouch, 2003; Crouch, 2011; Dwyer et al., 2000; Dwyer & Kim, 2003; Enright &Newton, 2004; Prideaux, 2005).

Therefore, the primary purpose of this study is to improve upon present gravity models in a way that can explain tourism flows more generally and supplement the limitations in both traditional and existing extended gravity models. Specifically, the objectives of this study are: (1) to propose an extended gravity model that includes the components of destination competitiveness; (2) to verify whether the extended gravity model with the components of destination competitiveness has greater explanatory power than traditional gravity models; and (3) to provide empirical implications for policymakers regarding which components of destination competitiveness can increase international tourist arrivals to a destination. By fulfilling these objectives, this study provides both theoretical and academic contributions. Theoretically, this extended gravity model contributes to overcoming the variable issues in previous research by adding various factors of destination competitiveness. It also introduces a new possibility for utilizing destination competitiveness. By empirically analyzing the effect of destination competitiveness components that can be improved or modified by tourism policymakers, this study provides practical guidance for further improvements to attract more visitors to a country.

9.2   LITERATURE REVIEW

9.2.1   GRAVITY MODEL

Gravitation was originally discovered by Newton, and it is known as a physical force that increases with mass and decreases with distance. Newton's concept of gravitation was later adopted in the field of economics. Tinbergen (1962) and Pöyhönen (1963) were the first to adopt gravity equations in their studies, which examined trade flows between two regions. Since then, the gravity model has become a popular instrument in empirical foreign-trade analysis. It has been applied to various types of flows, such as migration (Gallardo-Sejas et al., 2006; Karemera et al., 2000), foreign direct investment (Bergstrand & Egger, 2007; Eichengreen & Tong, 2007), and international trade flows (Armstrong, 2007; Martínez-Zarzoso & Nowak-Lehmann, 2003). The basic rationale behind the gravity model is that flows between importers and exporters depend directly on their economic size and inversely on the distance between them. Simply, it can be expressed as follows:

$$Y_{ijt} = \beta_0 \frac{X_{it}^{\beta_1} X_{jt}^{\beta_2}}{D_{ij}^{\beta_3}} u_{ijt} \qquad (9.1)$$

where Y_{ijt} is the flow from exporter i to importer j at time t. X_{it} and X_{jt} are the economic sizes of the two locations at time t. D_{ij} is the distance between them, and u_{ijt} is a log-normally distributed error term. If Y is measured as monetary flow (such as trade), then X is generally the gross domestic product (GDP). Initially, theoretical support for the gravity model was not very solid, but Anderson (1979), Bergstrand (1985, 1989, 1990), and Helpman and Krugman (1985) derived the gravity equation from a general equilibrium model in which a country's income represents the productive capacity of the exporter and the absorptive capacity of the importer, and distance approximates transport costs. Later, Deardorff (1998) identified that the gravity equation characterizes many models and can be justified based on standard trade theories.

During the theoretical development of initial gravity models, few limitations were identified. One critical limitation is related to explanatory variables. The basic concept of initial gravity models relies heavily on so-called gravity variables (i.e., economic size and physical distance). Yet, international flow does not merely rely upon these gravity variables, which are almost impossible for policy makers to change or improve. Furthermore, these variables cannot provide any further empirical implications. Hence, researchers tried to refine gravity models by adding more variables to initial gravity models (e.g., Bergstrand, 1985; Helpman, 1987; Bougheas et al., 1999). Another concern with initial gravity models is the econometric specification of the gravity equation. To avoid miss-specified econometric models and biased parameter estimates, researchers largely agreed that the effect of time should be included in the model by analyzing the gravity model with panel data framework (Mátyás, 1997, 1998; Breuss & Egger, 1999; Egger, 2000).

9.2.2 GRAVITY MODELS IN TOURISM

Prior to the application of gravity models in tourism, a concern about the effect of spatial distance on consumer travel already existed. Reilly's Law of Retail Gravitation (1931) suggested that distance can influence a consumer's shopping behavior. In other words, distance was identified as an important factor when people plan for shopping travel (Huff & Rust, 1984). Later, the importance of distance was transmitted to the field of tourism along with the introduction of gravity models.

Similar to traditional gravity models in economics, the basic idea of gravity models in tourism is that the magnitude of travel projected from an origin to a destination location is conceived to be proportionately related to the size of the two places and inversely proportional to some function of the distance between them. In earlier versions of gravity models, the main focus of the model was physical distance between origin and destination because distance was viewed as a surrogate measure for all of the various costs associated with travel (Mayo et al., 1988). Though its theoretical foundation was criticized (Uysal & Crompton, 1984), the gravity model has been extensively applied in tourism due to the simplicity of the equation and its effectiveness in forecasting (Getz, 1986).

In general, tourists demand not only natural and cultural resources, but also services associated with leisure and business (i.e., infrastructure, accommodations, etc.). Thus, simple gravity models with size of two places and physical distance could not explain these influential components. Therefore, researchers in tourism attempted to replace initial gravity models with more complex models that typically contain more variables. For example, Khadaroo and Seetanah (2008) included variables for transportation infrastructure in their extended gravity model and found that transportation infrastructure had a significant role in tourism flows. Gil-Pareja et al. (2007) tried to explain the effect of embassies and consulates on tourism flows by including additional variables, such as the number of embassies and general consulates within the gravity model framework. Specifically, they added few variables (i.e., the number of embassies and general consulates of origin countries in destination countries) and found that these embassies and consulates indeed stimulated the tourist flows from G7 countries to 156 other destinations. Moreover, other research included dummy variables to examine the effect of specific events on tourism demand. Fourie and Santana-Gallego (2011) adopted dummy variables for mega-sports events such as the Olympic Games or the World Cup. Similarly, Gil-Pareja et al. (2007) included dummy variables such as common official language and sharing a common border.

Besides issues related to the explanatory variable, researchers adopted complex econometric analysis in an attempt to overcome another limitation of initial gravity models—time effect. Previous studies often adopted panel-data framework. Specifically, fixed effect models (e.g., Fourie & Santana-Gallego, 2011; Yang et al., 2010) and dynamic panel models (e.g., Massidda & Etzo, 2012; Khadaroo & Seetanah, 2008) are the two most commonly adopted models.

Even though various explanatory variables and analysis methods have been adopted to overcome the limitations of traditional gravity models, these extended gravity models still have limitations in terms of generalizability. First, previous studies focused on a small numbers of countries. For example, Gil-Pareja et al. (2007) examined tourist flows from G7 countries (i.e., Canada, France, Germany, Italy, Japan, United Kingdom (UK), and the United States (US)) to 156 destinations. Even though G7 countries generate a great amount of travelers, they only account for 36.2% of recent average international tourist departures from 1995 to 2009 (The World Bank, 2011). Furthermore, Fourie and Santana-Gallego (2011) examined the effect of mega-sports events on tourist flows with data from 169 origins, but their focus was limited to merely 15 countries that held such events during the sample period (1995–2006). A recent study by Yang et al. (2010) included international travelers from nine countries to China. While the inclusion of a limited number of countries may satisfy the purpose of their studies, it is still problematic in terms of generalizability.

Second, previous extended gravity models included extra variables that only reflect specific events or components of tourism, such as adding extra dummy variables for sports events (Fourie & Santana-Gallego, 2011) or extra variables for transportation infrastructure (Khadaroo & Seetanah, 2008). However, the tourist flows between two countries are a function of a matrix of interrelated factors that includes common demand factors (i.e., income, relative price, and transport cost), public and private sector structures, as well as economic and non-economic factors (Prideaux, 2005). Therefore, focusing on specific components of tourism cannot provide a holistic explanation of tourist flows. In addition, even though the importance of the time effect in gravity models has been stressed (Mátyás, 1998), previous studies ignored the time effect in their models. These models generally analyzed the panel data as cross-sectional data, adopting pooled Ordinary Least Squares (OLS) Regression (e.g., Vietze, 2008).

Based on a thorough investigation, it can be concluded that previous research largely adopted extended gravity models with very specific focuses (i.e., particular regions, events, or components of tourism), and time effects were often omitted in these models. Combining these notions, a gravity model must be extended with a concept that can be generally be accepted as a determinant of tourism flows and with a proper model specification. As a concept to explain general tourists' flows, destination competitiveness provides a holistic view of destination characteristics (Ritchie & Crouch, 2003; Crouch, 2011; Dwyer et al., 2000; Dwyer & Kim, 2003; Enright & Newton, 2004; Prideaux, 2005).

9.2.3 DESTINATION COMPETITIVENESS

The success of tourism destinations in world markets lies in the competitiveness of a destination (Enright & Newton, 2004). According to Ritchie & Crouch (2003: p. 2), destination competitiveness is defined as the "ability of [a] destination to increase tourism expenditure, to increasingly attract visitors while providing them with satisfying, memorable experiences, and to do so in a profitable way, while enhancing the well-being of destination residents and preserving the natural capital of the destination for future generations". More succinctly, a destination is considered competitive if it can attract and satisfy potential tourists, and a wide range of components is necessary to satisfy tourists. In other words, destination competitiveness is determined by a wide range of factors because being competitive requires superiority in several aspects (Enright & Newton, 2004).

Three common types of research related to destination competitiveness exist: diagnosing the competitiveness of a specific destination (e.g., Botha et al., 1999; Chon & Mayer, 1995), diagnosing certain components of destination competitiveness (e.g., Baker et al., 1996; Dwyer et al., 2000), and conceptualizing destination competitiveness with a holistic view (e.g., Ritchie & Crouch, 2003; Dwyer & Kim, 2003; Enright & Newton, 2004). Only the third type of research was considered in this study, because it provides a general perspective of destination competitiveness, which is consistent with our research objective—to construct a gravity model that can be applied more generally.

Researchers agreed to the notion that destination competitiveness can contribute to identifying a destination's position in the world market. However, included components vary by researcher. Claiming the importance of destination competitiveness in tourist inflows, Ritchie and Crouch (2003) conceptualized destination competitiveness as being made up of seven sub-components: (1) global (macro) environment; (2) competitive (micro) environment; (3) core resources and attractors; (4) supporting factors and resources; (5) destination policy, planning and development; (6) destination management; and (7) qualifying and amplifying determinants. In a recent study, Crouch (2011) conducted Analytic Hierarchy Process (AHP) to derive a ranking for each component and attribute, and concluded that core resources and attractors were the most important and determinant factors in destination competitiveness.

Compared to Ritchie and Crouch's (2003) study, Dwyer and Kim (2003) provided an example of a more detailed conceptualization. In their study, destination competitiveness was divided into six components: (1) endowed resources, (2) supporting factors, (3) destination management, (4) situational conditions, (5) demand factors, and (6) market performance indicators. However, unlike the previous study, they provided more specific attributes under each component as well as specific measurements. For example, price competitiveness consisted of value for money in destination, exchange rate, price of destination visit relative to competitor destinations, and so forth.

In terms of specific measurements in each category of destination competitiveness, the World Travel and Tourism Council (WTTC) conducted an empirical study that measured each country's competitiveness and provided a ranking according to competitiveness. WTTC published the Competitiveness Monitor (CM) until 2006. Then, the World Economic Forum (WEF) published CM from 2007. In their study, they divided the destination competitiveness index into three different sub-indexes: (1) travel and tourism regulatory framework; (2) travel and tourism business environment and infrastructure; and (3) travel and tourism human, cultural, and natural resources. Each sub-index has four or five different indexes, for example, travel and tourism business environment and infrastructure consist of air transport infrastructure, ground transport infrastructure, tourism infrastructure, ICT infrastructure, and price competitiveness in the travel and tourism industry.

In sum, destination competitiveness is an important concept that can explain tourist flows and consists of various components beyond demand factors. Thus, this study complements traditional gravity models by adding components from destination competitiveness that can explain a destination's attractiveness and characteristics. Prior to applying destination competitiveness to a gravity model, it was necessary to identify common components that vary by researcher (Crouch, 2011; Dwyer & Kim, 2003; Mazanec et al., 2007; WEF, 2009) because including many similar indexes in a category can result in a redundancy (Mazanec et al., 2007). For example, the Human Tourism dimension in the WTTC system is calculated by taking the average of the Tourism Participation Index and the Tourism Impact

Index, which are related to each other. In other words, instead of calculating the compound index, Mazanec et al. (2007) stressed the importance of constructing a parsimonious model when conceptualizing destination competitiveness, and confirmed the effectiveness of having a parsimonious model. Thus, by grouping similar concepts in previous studies, six common components were derived (i.e., physiology and climate, culture and history, tourism infrastructure, general infrastructure, openness, and price competitiveness). These common categories are presented in Table 9.1.

TABLE 9.1   Common Categories of Destination Competitiveness.

	Crouch (2011)	Dwyer and Kim (2003)	Mazanec et al. (2007)	WEF (2009)
1[a]	Physiography & climate	Environmental management	Environmental preservation	Environmental sustainability
		Natural resource	Natural heritage	Natural resources
2	Culture & history	Culture & heritage	Cultural heritage	Cultural resources
3	Tourism superstructure	Tourism infrastructure	–	Tourism infrastructure
4	Mix of activity	Range of activities	–	–
5	Awareness & image	Demand factor	–	–
6	Special events	Special events & festivals	–	–
7	Entertainment	Entertainment	–	–
8	Infrastructure	General infrastructure	Infrastructure	Air transport Ground transportation
			Communication	ICT infrastructure
9	Accessibility	Accessibility	Openness	Tourism openness
10	Positioning & branding	–	–	–
11	Location	Destination location	–	–
12	Market ties	Market ties	–	–
13	Safety & security	Safety & security	–	Safety & security
14	Cost & value	Price competitiveness	Price competitiveness	Price competitiveness
15	Political will	Destination policy, planning, & development	–	Policy rules & regulations

Note: Grey area is the common components examined in four different studies.
[a] This number is the ranking of each attribute's determinance by Crouch (2011).

9.3   METHODOLOGY

9.3.1   DESTINATION COMPETITIVENESS ADDED GRAVITY MODEL

As explained earlier, both initial gravity models and existing extended gravity models lack important explanatory variables that would allow their results to apply to countries or phenomena beyond their specific research interests. Hence, to overcome explanatory variable issues, this study employed six common components of destination competitiveness from a review of previous studies (Crouch, 2011; Dwyer & Kim, 2003; Mazanec et al., 2007; WEF, 2009). Furthermore, to construct as a parsimonious model as possible, only one or two variables were included for each factor after confirming data availability. The proposed extended gravity model takes the following form:

$$\ln Arrival_{ijt} = \beta_0 + \beta_1 \ln GDP_{it} + \beta_2 \ln GDP_{jt} + \beta_3 \ln Dist_{jt} + \beta_4 \ln CO2_{jt} + \beta_5 WHN_{jt} + \beta_6 WHC_{jt}$$
$$+ \beta_7 CommLang_{ij} + \beta_8 \ln Rooms_{jt} + \beta_9 \ln PPP_{jt} + \beta_{10} \ln Air_{jt} + \beta_{11} \ln Road_{jt}$$
$$+ \beta_{12} \ln Trade_{jt} + \beta_{13} \ln Internet_{jt} + \alpha_i + \lambda_t + u_{ijt} \qquad (9.2)$$

where ln denotes natural logarithms, i indicates origin country, j indicates destination country, and t is time. Variables, such as WHN_{jt}, WHC_{jt}, and $CommLang_{ij}$, were not converted to natural log because these variables included "zero."

The dependent variable, $Arrival_{ijt}$ is the tourist arrivals from origin i to destination j in year t. GDP_{it}, and GDP_{jt} are the GDP of origin i and destination j in year t. $Dist_{ij}$ is the distance between origin i and destination j, which was measured as the simple distance between most populated cities. These variables were included as traditional gravity variables. In various studies that utilized a gravity model, GDP of both the origin and destination countries were included and found to increase bilateral flows between two countries (Fourie & Santana-Gallego, 2011; Gil-Pareja et al., 2007). Accordingly, this study expects that GDP of both destination and origin countries would increase tourist arrivals but physical distance would decrease tourist arrivals.

Ten extra variables were added while maintaining as parsimonious of a model as possible. First, it was necessary to determine a destination's natural environment and resources. The importance of natural resources has been stressed in various studies (Cho, 2010; Dwyer & Kim, 2003; WEF, 2009). Accordingly, Crouch (2011) suggested that physiology and climate are the most important and determinant components of destination competitiveness.

To explain the condition of natural resources, two variables were employed: carbon dioxide emission levels ($CO2_{jt}$) and the number of World Heritage Natural Sites (WHN_{jt}) in the destination country. CO_2 emission levels are often adopted to reflect a country's level of industrialization as well as its efforts to preserve nature (Cho, 2010).

In general, there are three different types of World Heritage Sites (i.e., natural, cultural, and mixed). However, previous studies employed total number of World Heritage Sites in their models (Mazanec et al., 2007; Yang et al., 2010). Considering the selection criteria used by United Nations Educational, Scientific and Cultural Organization (UNESCO), it was necessary to distinguish natural sites from cultural sites. For example, natural sites are often selected by criteria such as "the place contains superlative natural phenomena or areas of exceptional natural beauty and aesthetic importance" (see http://whn.unesco.org/en/criteria). However, the selection of a cultural site is based more on a country's prominence in culture—"an outstanding example of a type of building, architectural, or technological ensemble or landscape which illustrates a significant stage in human history" (see http://whc.unesco.org/en/criteria). World Mixed Heritage Sites were not considered because the number itself is relatively small and these sites are limited to a few countries. Thus, the number of World Heritage Natural Sites (WHN_{jt}) and the number of World Heritage Cultural Sites (WHC_{jt}) were adopted separately to more accurately capture the prominence of a destination's natural and cultural resources. A higher level of CO_2 is expected to decrease tourist arrivals to a destination, while the number of World Heritage Natural Sites is expected to increase tourist arrivals.

In addition to natural resources, culture is an influential component of tourist arrivals (Getz & Brown, 2006; Gearing et al., 1974). Specifically, having a rich cultural and historical heritage was ranked as the second most important determinant factor in a study by Crouch (2011). Furthermore, other studies have consistently stressed the importance of cultural aspects of destination countries (Dwyer & Kim, 2003; Mazanec et al., 2007). This study adopted two variables that represent these heritages: the number of World Heritage Cultural Sites (WHC_{jt}) in a destination country and the usage of a common official language between origin i and destination j ($CommLang_{ij}$). Language is often considered an important representation of culture (Ritchie and Zins, 1978), and empirical studies have proved the effect of a common official language on tourist arrivals (Fourie & Santana-Gallego, 2011; Gil-Pareja et al., 2007). These two variables were expected to increase tourist arrivals.

The number of hotel rooms ($Rooms_{jt}$) was adopted as a proxy for tourism infrastructure. Even though Mazanec et al. (2007) did not consider tourism infrastructure, its effect on attracting more travelers cannot be ignored (Dwyer & Kim, 2003; WEF, 2009). Considering the causality between the number of hotel rooms and tourist arrivals, it was suggested that the size of hotel accommodations is necessary for a destination to reach the so-called "critical mass" (Christie & Crompton, 2001). Accordingly, Crouch (2011) listed tourism infrastructure as a third important determinant component in destination competitiveness. Empirically, Yang et al. (2010) utilized the number of hotels in their gravity model to determine the impact of tourism infrastructure on international tourist demands, because hotels or hotel rooms are necessary to convince airlines to establish routes, as well as to justify investment in complementary infrastructure such as roads (Naude & Saayman, 2005). Thus, this study included the number of hotel rooms in destination j at time t, which is expected to generate a greater volume of tourist inflows.

Purchasing Power Parity (PPP) conversion factor to market exchange ratio (PPP_{jt}) was included to capture price competitiveness. Generally, the PPP conversion factor represents the relative cost of living in the destination country with respect to the origin and is commonly adopted as a price indicator (Fourie & Santana-Gallego, 2011; Gil-Pareja et al., 2007; Eilat & Einav, 2004). Furthermore, adopting PPP conversion factor enables us to account for cross-sectional variation in the price of tourism as well as variations in real exchange rates over time (Gil-Pareja et al., 2007). Thus, a high-PPP conversion factor is expected to decrease tourist arrivals to a destination country.

General infrastructures, such as transportation and communication, have been considered influential on bilateral flows for both ordinary trading goods (Bougheas et al., 1999) and tourism flows (Khadaroo & Seetanah, 2008; WEF, 2009). Generally, there are three different types of transportation related to tourism (i.e., air, port, and ground), but port transportation was excluded because its most common form is the cruise that accounts for a relatively small portion of tourism (Khadaroo & Seetanah, 2008). Hence, air and ground transportation were considered in this study—the number of registered international carrier departures (Air_{jt}) and the ratio of paved roads to entire roads (ln$Road_{jt}$). Instead of the number of international terminals, the total number of registered international departures (Air_{jt}) was adopted due to the possibility of invariability during the sample period. Even if it varies across time, the variability would be relatively small. Road density is commonly used to represent ground transportation conditions (Mazanec et al.,

2007), but the ratio of paved roads was adopted instead because countries like Russia or China would not have a high-road density considering the size of the land area. The number of Internet users ($Internet_{jt}$) was adopted to reflect the degree of information technology and communication facilities. For openness to destination country, visa index is often suggested as a measurement (Mazanec et al., 2007; WEF, 2009). However, this study adopted trade openness ($Trade_{jt}$) due to data availability, which was calculated as a ratio of the sum of imports and exports to GDP. Having better general infrastructure and a higher level of openness are expected to increase inbound tourists. Finally, α_i represents the fixed effects (FE) for origin countries, λ_t refers to year FE, and u_{ijt} is a disturbance term. These terms were included to satisfy the specification for FE models, as suggested by Mátyás (1997).

9.3.2 DATA

First, the dependent variable, the annual number of tourist arrivals by nationality, was acquired from the Tourism Statistics Yearbook by the UNWTO. The sample period was from 1995 to 2009 due to data availability. Second, to identify the countries included in the analysis it was necessary to include countries that account for a large proportion of international travel. Hence, total number of international tourist arrivals and departure data during the sample period were required, but the data from UNWTO did not provide aggregated values for the entire sample period. Thus, this study acquired the total number of international arrivals and departures from the World Bank's World Development Indicators (WDI) and calculated the average of both international tourist arrivals and departures from 1995 to 2009. The 30 countries that had both high international tourist arrivals and departures were selected and included for further analysis. The included countries explained nearly 75% of total international arrivals and 82% of total international departures during the sample period (1995–2009). The included countries and the average number of international tourist arrivals and departures for each country during the sample period are provided in Table 9.2.

For explanatory variables, physical distance between two countries was acquired from the dataset provided by Centre d'Etudes Prospectives et d'Informations Internationales (see http://www.cepii.fr). This dataset has been adopted by previous studies (e.g., Mazanec et al., 2007; Fourie & Santana-Gallego, 2011). Furthermore, this dataset provided a dummy variable, which had a value of "1" if two countries had a common official language. This variable was adopted to reflect cultural components

TABLE 9.2   Included Countries and Average Number of Tourist Arrival.

Rank	Country	Arrival	Departure
1[a] (10)[b]	France	73,396,400	20,305,500
2 (3)	United States	48,728,000	58,900,000
3 (26)	Spain	48,574,400	6532,067
4 (7)	Italy	38,303,467	23,631,571
5 (8)	China	36,665,667	23,631,571
6 (4)	Great Britain	25,186,067	57,821,533
7 (18)	Mexico	20,503,467	11,718,133
8 (9)	Russia	20,064,214	21,306,500
9 (2)	Germany	19,430,600	71,823,077
10 (22)	Austria	18,882,533	7713,154
11 (11)	Canada	18,270,667	20,065,500
12 (5)	Poland	15,997,333	46,305,286
13 (27)	Turkey	14,347,000	6436,933
14 (6)	Malaysia	13,167,867	28,144,600
15 (1)	Hong Kong	12,389,917	73,380,250
16 (16)	Ukraine	12,384,600	12,816,000
17 (12)	Portugal	11,139,154	18,654,500
18 (45)	Thailand	10,598,333	2554,200
19 (15)	Hungary	9660,000	14,422,467
20 (14)	Netherlands	9326,000	15,483,667
21 (33)	Saudi Arabia	8538,273	4557,375
22 (19)	Switzerland	7440,714	11,457,200
23 (37)	South Africa	6777,000	3712,667
24 (31)	Ireland	6682,267	4920,533
25 (21)	Belgium	6518,000	7876,071
26 (41)	Egypt	6492,533	3501,417
27 (26)	Croatia	6446,933	2427,000
28 (32)	Singapore	6377,267	4710,400
29 (23)	Romania	5938,667	7649,200
30 (13)	Japan	5574,133	16,354,133
	Sample total	543,801,472	608,812,506
	Population total	724,555,038	743,353,047
	Percentage	75.05	81.90

[a] Ranking in terms of international tourist arrivals from 1995 to 2009.
[b] Ranking in terms of international tourist departures from 1995 to 2009.

of a destination (Fourie & Santana-Gallego, 2011). The number of World Heritage Sites by country was acquired from UNESCO (see http://whc.unesco.org/en/list). As of the end of 2009, a total of 890 World Heritage Sites (689 cultural sites, 175 natural sites, and 27 mixed sites) were designated by UNESCO. The number of hotel rooms was acquired from the Yearbook of Tourism Statistics provided by UNWTO. Finally, other variables were acquired from the World Bank's World Development Indicators (WDI). Definitions and sources for variables are presented in Table 9.3.

TABLE 9.3   Definition and Source of Variables.

Variable	Definition	Source
$Arrival_{ijt}$	International tourist arrivals by nationality per year	UNWTO
GDP_{it}, GDP_{jt}	Gross Domestic Product (GDP) constant (2000 USD)	WDI
$Dist_{ij}$	Distance between most populated cities (km)	CEPII
$CO2_{jt}$	CO_2 emission (metric tons per capita)	WDI
WHN_{jt}	The number of World Heritage Natural sites classified by UNESCO	UNESCO
WHC_{jt}	The number of World Heritage Cultural sites classified by UNESCO	UNESCO
$CommLang_{ij}$	The use of common official language between two countries	CEPII
$Rooms_{jt}$	The number of hotel rooms	UNWTO
PPP_{jt}	Purchase power parity conversion factor to market exchange ratio	WDI
$Trade_{jt}$	Ratio of international trade to GDP	WDI
Air_{jt}	Registered carrier departures worldwide	WDI
$Road_{jt}$	Percentage of paved roads	WDI
$Internet_{jt}$	Sum of internet users	WDI

9.3.3   ANALYSIS

Generally, gravity models are estimated by taking natural logarithms on both sides of Equation (9.1) and are expressed as follows:

$$\ln X_{ij} = \beta_0 + \beta_1 \ln Y_i + \beta_2 \ln Y_j + \beta_3 \ln D_{ij} + \alpha_i + \gamma_j + \lambda_t + u_{ijt} \qquad (9.3)$$

where β_0 is constant, Y_i and Y_j are GDP of origin i and destination j. α_i is the source country effects, and γ_j is the target country effects. These effects allow countries to have differing propensities to export after controlling for divergence across GDP. Furthermore, λ_i are the time effects, and u_{ijt} is the error term. When $\alpha_i = \gamma_j = \lambda_t = 0$, in other words, if no specific effects are considered, this is a "traditional (basic) gravity model." When origin country and time effects are considered (i.e., $\gamma_j = 0$) it is a "standard panel gravity model." When all effects are considered ($\alpha_i \neq \gamma_j \neq \lambda_t \neq 0$) it is a "triple indexed gravity model" (Mátyás, 1997).

In constructing our empirical model, we considered a sample of 30 countries that account for a high proportion of total international tourist arrivals and departures. The time period of this study ranges from 1995 to 2009. Our data consists of balanced panel data of 870 pairs after excluding 30 pairs where origin and destination countries are the same (e.g., from England to England). In total, 13,050 observations were used for analysis. The proposed extended gravity model was analyzed with panel data framework. Specifically, a standard panel gravity model that includes origin and time effects was used (Mátyás, 1997). Using panel data methodology has several advantages over cross-section analysis (Kennedy, 2008). Firstly, panel data makes it possible to capture relevant relationships among variables over time. Secondly, panel data creates more variability by combining variation across individual units with variation over time, alleviating multi-collinearity problems. Thirdly, a major advantage of using panel data is the ability to monitor potentially unobservable individual effects. When these individual effects are omitted, OLS estimates are biased. An FE model or random-effects model (RE) is commonly used when dealing with these unobservable individual effects.

FE models (FE) are often used when controlling for omitted variables that are constant over the period of time and vary across the unit. Specifically, fixed effect models are commonly used to estimate typical trade flows between an *ex ante* predetermined selection of countries (Egger, 2000). However, an FE model does not allow for estimating coefficients of time-invariant variables such as distance or sharing a common language. One way to deal with this problem is to include individual country FEs in the gravity model (Kandogan, 2008; Mátyás, 1997).

An RE model allows for different individual effects but requires stricter assumptions that the individual effects cannot be correlated with the covariates. In other words, observations on different countries must have no correlation between their error terms. An RE model is more appropriate than FE model when estimating trade flows between randomly selected samples of trading partners from a larger population (Martínez-Zarzaso & Nowak-Lehmen, 2003). The RE model generates more efficient estimators of the slope coefficients than the FE model when these assumptions are satisfied. However, the purpose of including an RE model in studies of gravity models was to identify which model is more appropriate (Egger & Pfaffermayr, 1997). A Hausman test is generally used for model selection criteria (Kennedy, 2008). The Hausman test helps to determine whether the RE estimate is insignificantly different from the unbiased FE estimate. Thus, if the null hypothesis is not rejected, the RE model estimator is a better option. Otherwise, the fixed effects model estimator is suggested.

9.4   RESULTS

Originally, three different models were constructed: (1) traditional (basic) gravity model, (2) extended gravity model with fixed effects, and (3) extended gravity model with random effects. First of all, the gravity variables (i.e., $\ln Dist_{ij}$, $\ln GDP_{it}$, and $\ln GDP_{jt}$) for traditional gravity model (Model 1) were significant, meaning that the assumptions of the traditional gravity model were satisfied in our data. Second, to select the more efficient model a Hausman test was conducted. The results suggested that the FE model (Model 2) provided unbiased estimators ($\chi^2 = 86.74$, $p < 0.000$).

Before confirming the model for further interpretation, we conducted bivariate correlation analysis to find possible multicollinearity problems (Table 9.4). The results suggested that $\ln GDP_{jt}$ and $\ln Air_{jt}$ were highly correlated. In general, multicollinearity reduces the overall R^2 and negatively affects the statistical significance tests of coefficients by inflating the variance of independent variables (Hair et al., 2010). However, compared to Model (9.1) the R^2 change statistic was significant ($F = 31.985$, $p < 0.000$), meaning that Model (9.3) had greater explanatory power. Moreover, even though multicollinearity was present in Model (9.3), all independent variables except $\ln Road_{jt}$ were significant. In addition, all variables except $\ln CO2_{jt}$ and $\ln PPP_{jt,}$ turned out to have the same sign with correlation coefficients. The negative signs on CO_2 and PPP level can be interpreted as suppression effects, which can be described as instances when the "true" relationship between the dependent and independent variables has been hidden in the bivariate correlation (Hair et al., 2010). Thus, multicollinearity may not be a problem in this analysis.

To test for heteroskedasticity, we conducted a Breusch–Pagan χ^2 test. The results suggested that heteroskedasticity exists ($\chi^2 = 148.16$, $p < 0.000$) implying that an additional analysis was necessary. Thus, an FE model with robust variance (Model 3), which is known to be a solution for heteroskedasticity

TABLE 9.4 Correlation Table.

	1	2	3	4	5	6	7	8	9	10	11	12	13	14
ln$Arrival$	1.000													
ln$Dist_{ij}$	-0.440***	1.000												
lnGDP_{jt}	0.266***	0.170***	1.000											
lnGDP_{it}	0.443***	0.194***	-0.028	1.000										
ln$CO2_{jt}$	0.031**	0.206***	0.737***	-0.069***	1.000									
WHC$_{jt}$	0.402***	-0.135***	0.588***	0.047***	0.473***	1.000								
WHN$_{jt}$	0.137***	0.145***	0.597***	-0.032**	0.688***	0.294***	1.000							
lnAir_{jt}	0.312***	0.163***	0.926***	-0.005	0.707***	0.560***	0.688***	1.000						
ln$Rooms_{jt}$	0.271***	0.122***	0.883***	-0.029*	0.726***	0.625***	0.618***	0.825***	1.000					
ln$Internet_{jt}$	0.216***	0.139***	0.760***	0.015	0.600***	0.520***	0.592***	0.760***	0.637***	1.000				
lnPPP_{jt}	0.301***	-0.004	0.660***	0.011	0.066***	0.297***	0.162***	0.614***	0.478***	0.430***	1.000			
CommLang$_{jt}$	0.288***	-0.093***	0.058***	0.062***	-0.096***	-0.028	0.012	0.114**	-0.046***	0.066***	0.184***	1.000		
ln$Trade_{jt}$	0.117***	-0.129***	-0.567***	0.065***	-0.732***	-0.274***	-0.424***	-0.428***	-0.593***	-0.366***	-0.103***	0.144***	1.000	
ln$Road_{jt}$	0.125***	-0.056***	0.030**	0.009	-0.182***	0.099***	-0.181***	0.089***	0.008	0.011	0.294***	0.130***	0.304***	1.000

Note: * $p < 0.05$, ** $p < 0.01$, *** $p < 0.001$.

(Greene, 2003), was conducted and included in Table 9.5. It had the same coefficients as Model (9.2). However, the t-value of the independent variables changed due to decreased standard error. Moreover, compared with Model (9.1) the R^2 change statistic was significant ($F = 31.985$, $p < 0.000$), meaning that Model (9.3) had greater explanatory power. In other words, it verifies our research objective that the extended gravity model with destination competitiveness had a higher explanatory power than a traditional (basic) gravity model.

Similar to Model (9.1), $\ln GDP_{it}$, $\ln GDP_{jt}$, and $\ln Dist_{ij}$ were significant in all other models, satisfying the assumptions of a traditional gravity model. Considering the coefficient of each country's GDP, the coefficient of the origin countries was greater than the coefficient of the destination countries, meaning that the economic size of the origin country is more important in determining tourist arrivals than the destination country. In other words, travelers are more likely to be from richer countries than less rich countries. Physical distance had the expected negative sign, meaning that international tourist arrivals decrease as transportation costs increase, *ceteris paribus*. Summing up the results of the gravity variables, if a destination has rich countries nearby it has a higher chance of attracting more travelers.

As indicators of physiology and climate, $\ln CO2_{jt}$ and WHN_{jt} were significant, implying the importance of environment and natural resources. From the negative sign of $\ln CO2_{jt}$ it can be inferred that travelers prefer less polluted destinations. Cultural indicators (i.e., WHC_{jt} and $CommLang_{ij}$) were positively significant, implying the importance of cultural components in stimulating tourism demand. Having more World Heritage Cultural Sites increases tourist arrivals to the country. The effect of a common official language can be interpreted in two different ways. From a cultural perspective, travelers prefer destinations with a culture similar to their own. Yet from the language perspective, educating citizens in commonly used languages, like English or Chinese, contributes to an increase of tourist arrivals to the country. Importantly, the coefficients of World Heritage Sites were significant, implying that this study can provide evidence that having more World Heritage Sites can increase international tourist inflows.

From the perspective of tourism infrastructures, $\ln Rooms_{jt}$ was significant, implying that destinations with more accommodation facilities can attract more travelers. Further, $\ln PPP_{jt}$ as a price competitiveness index was significant, meaning that an increase in the relative price level of the destination country decreases the number of tourist arrivals. In terms of transportation infrastructure, $\ln Air_{jt}$ was significant, meaning that having more airline departures can make the destination itself more accessible to travelers.

TABLE 9.5 Results of Gravity Models.

	Model (9.1) Traditional gravity model		Model (9.2) Fixed effect model		Model (9.3) FE with robust variance	
	Coef.	t-value	Coef.	t-value	Coef.	t-value
$lnDist_{ij}$	-1.292***	-67.316	-1.228***	-57.669	-1.228***	-11.951
$lnGDP_{it}$	0.586***	44.179	0.764***	13.465	0.764***	8.324
$lnGDP_{it}$	0.911***	62.550	1.747***	7.520	1.747***	7.181
$lnCO2_{jt}$			-0.914***	-20.757	-0.914***	-7.505
WHC_{jt}			0.031***	11.070	0.031***	3.888
WHN_{jt}			0.028*	2.120	0.028	1.147
$lnAir_{jt}$			0.484***	9.363	0.484***	5.940
$lnRooms_{jt}$			0.398***	10.882	0.398***	4.804
$lnInternet_{jt}$			0.133***	3.874	0.133*	2.325
$lnPPP_{jt}$			-1.780***	-18.129	-1.780***	-11.286
$CommLang_{ji}$			0.723***	11.811	0.723***	4.017
$lnTrade_{ij}$			0.573***	9.760	0.573***	4.854
$lnRoads_{ij}$			0.001	0.666	0.001	0.281
Constant	-18.222***	-35.127	-49.487***	-7.905	-49.487***	-7.493
Obs	4564		4564		4564	
R^2	0.634		0.683		0.683	

Note: * $p < 0.05$, ** $p < 0.01$, *** $p < 0.001$.
Individual effects of origin and time were included but not recorded.

However, ln$Road_{jt}$ was not significant, implying that air transportation may be a more critical component of being a competitive destination than road transportation. This study adopted the number of Internet users (ln$Internet_{jt}$) as an indicator of general infrastructure. In terms of general trade, having better information communication technology is often considered a determinant in increasing exports (Clarke & Wallsten, 2006). In tourism, the importance of ICT is consistently examined. In tourism settings, export means having inbound tourists, and our results suggest that having more Internet users increases tourist arrivals similar to the general trade. The openness indicator, ln$Trade_{jt}$, was significant. It implies that an open atmosphere toward international travel and trade can eventually increase the volume of tourist arrivals to the country.

9.5 CONCLUSION

For decades tourism has been considered one of the most rapidly developing areas in the world even as the global economy has experienced several downturns. Moreover, significant economic impact of tourism has spurred a series of studies related to tourism demand, and gravity models have been widely adopted to explain the tourist flows between two countries. Despite enormous efforts, these extended gravity models still have a few limitations—a narrow scope of sample countries and a failure to include more general variables and the time effects in their models.

Given this fact, the primary purpose of this study was to provide an extended gravity model that can overcome the limitations of previous models. In terms of scope, this study included 30 countries that explained a high percentage of total international tourist arrivals and departures. Furthermore, to explain time effect, 15 years of panel data were employed and analyzed by an FE model with robust variance. Specifically, the sample period (from 1995 to 2009) was relatively longer than that of previous studies (e.g., Khadaroo & Setanah, 2008; Massidda & Etzo, 2012; Yang et al., 2010). Finally, as complementary variables, this study adopted six components of destination competitiveness from previous studies with a holistic perspective (Crouch, 2011; Dwyer & Kim, 2003; Mazanec et al, 2007; WEF, 2009).

The empirical results suggested that the traditional gravity model still holds high explanatory power in explaining tourism flows, meaning that transportation costs and GDP can explain the large portion of inbound tourists. In other words, the simplicity of traditional gravity models was not as severe a problem as we expected. Hence, traditional gravity models can be considered appropriate when other explanatory variables are not available. However, traditional gravity models still have a limitation in that these gravity variables cannot explain the role of specific components of tourism. Originally, one of this study's research objectives was to provide empirical implications for policymakers by suggesting which components of destination competitiveness contribute to increase inbound travelers to a destination. Even though our proposed model only explained five more percent of inbound tourists' arrivals than the traditional gravity model, the extra variables enabled us to provide further implications to make a destination more attractive.

First, our results indicated that physiology and climate of destination countries significantly affected tourist arrivals as suggested by studies in destination competitiveness (Crouch, 2011; Dwyer & Kim, 2003). Specifically, if a country does not make an effort to preserve its natural environment, for example, an effort to reduce CO_2 levels, it would lead to a considerable loss in international tourist inflows. Furthermore, the number of World Heritage Natural Sites was significant, implying that a destination with globally renowned natural resources can attract more tourists.

Second, culture and heritage played an important role in attracting more international tourists. The number of World Heritage Cultural Sites and usage of a common official language positively affected the number of inbound tourists. Indeed, fear of foreign languages can be a psychological barrier to travelers when they are planning for international travel (Cohen & Cooper, 1986). In other words, if a destination puts effort into language education, for example English or Chinese, it could lower psychological barriers for travelers. This could eventually increase the volume of travelers. Furthermore, having globally renowned cultural heritage can attract more travelers. Hence, countries should utilize their heritages as destination marketing tools. Recently, there has been debate over the role of World Heritage Sites in tourist arrivals (Yang et al., 2010; Cellini, 2011). With a wider scope in terms of countries included and sample period, this study provided evidence that having more World Heritage Sites increases international tourist arrivals.

Third, developing general infrastructure must be seriously considered when a destination country seeks to increase tourist arrivals. The importance of air transportation has often been stressed in tourism (Khadaroo & Setanah, 2008), especially for a country like Australia that cannot be reached by ground transportation (Prideaux & Witt, 2000). Considering the positive effect of air transportation on tourism flows, it is suggested that countries make developing air transportation infrastructure a priority to attract more travelers. However, having good road transportation does not contribute to the volume of tourism flows. Additionally, this study included an indicator for information and communication technology, which significantly affected the number of tourist arrivals. The importance of information and communication technology can be interpreted from two different perspectives (i.e., demand and supply). From the demand side (travelers), travelers may consider Internet conditions as a decision-making criterion when planning to travel, due to the proliferation of mobile Internet devices. From the supply perspective (destination), having highly developed Internet conditions makes it possible for travelers to place a reservation more easily (Buhalis & Law, 2008) and would increase the number of travelers. Thus, to attract more travelers a destination should reconsider developing their general infrastructure.

Fourth, this study examined the effect of tourism infrastructure, but it is important to consider the effect of price at the same time. Having more hotel rooms can definitely increase the number of inbound tourists (Naude & Saayman, 2005; Yang et al., 2010), but relatively high prices can act in the opposite direction. Thus, maintaining a reasonable price along with having sufficient rooms is important in order to be a competitive destination. Moreover, this study examined the role of openness on the inflow of tourists. It was significant, meaning that having an open attitude toward an influx of foreign products and cultures can eventually attract more inbound travelers.

Finally, in addition to these empirical implications, this study provides important theoretical implications. By including various components from destination competitiveness in a traditional gravity model, this study showed a possible way to overcome the variable issues in traditional gravity models. Furthermore, in an attempt to derive components for the proposed model, this study identified six common components and measurements for each component from previous studies. Combining these, this study provided evidence that our proposed model suggests a new way to utilize various components from destination competitiveness and to overcome the explanatory variable issues in traditional gravity models.

9.5   LIMITATIONS AND SUGGESTIONS FOR FUTURE STUDY

Despite contributions, this study is not free from limitations. First, the purpose of this study was to construct as parsimonious a model as possible. Yet, the traditional gravity model turned out to explain a large portion of inbound tourist arrivals, meaning that a traditional gravity model is still appropriate if the research objective is to construct as parsimonious a model as possible. Conversely, if the research aims to identify the role of specific components of tourism and their indexes are available, it is suggested that our model should be utilized in future studies. Second, the causality between GDP and other variables can be a problem. For instance, GDP can represent industrialization and the level of development, which are related to tourism infrastructure. Third, the data for this study was based on country-level, implying that analysis with more detailed data would be helpful in identifying the effect of variables more thoroughly. Lastly, we adopted the distance between most populated cities as the overall distance between two countries. This distance may not clearly reflect the distance that tourists have traveled.

Based on the results and limitations, there can be few suggestions for future studies. First of all, in order to resolve possible causality issues, more advanced models (i.e., dynamic-panel model, dynamic-panel model with instrument variable, etc.) would be applicable. Second, analysis with more specific data (i.e., city-level data or specific purpose for travel) would provide more precise results. In addition, utilizing several other distance measures, such as the distance between airport at origin and airport at travel destination, would be valuable as well. Lastly, even though this study introduced a new research direction for understanding destination competitiveness and gravity models, a great deal of further research exploring other critical explanatory variables of tourism flows (i.e., mega-events or economic recession) is still necessary.

ACKNOWLEDGEMENT

This work originally published in *Journal of Travel & Tourism Marketing* in 2014, vol., 31, pp. 799-816. With the Publisher's permission dated March, 5, 2015 this work as Chapter 9 with minor changes is reprinted in the book.

KEYWORDS

- gravity model
- tourism flow
- destination competitiveness
- tourism infrastructure
- natural and cultural resources

REFERENCES

Anderson, J. E. A Theoretical Foundation for the Gravity Equation. *Am. Econ. Rev.* **1979**, *69*(1), 106–116.

Armstrong, S. *Measuring Trade and Trade Potential. A Survey. Asia Pacific Economic Papers*, 2007.

Baker, M.; Hayzelden, C.; Sussmann, S. Can Destination Management Systems Provide Competitive Advantage? A Discussion of the Factors Affecting the Survival and Success of Destination Management Systems. *Progress Tourism Hospitality Res.* **1996**, *2*(1), 1–13.

Barbosa, L. G. M; Oliveira, C. T. F; Rezende, C. Competitiveness of Tourist Destinations: The Study of 65 Key Destinations for the Development of Regional Tourism. *Rev. Admin. Públ.* **2010**, *44*(5), 1067–1095.

Bergstrand, J. H.; Egger, P. A Knowledge-and-Physical-Capital Model of International Trade Flows, Foreign Direct Investment, and Multinational Enterprises. *J. Int. Econ.* **2007**, *73*(2), 278–308.

Bergstrand, J. H. The Gravity Equation in International Trade: Some Microeconomic Foundations and Empirical Evidence. *Rev. Econ. Stat.* **1985**, *67*(3), 474–481.

Bergstrand, J. H. The Generalized Gravity Equation, Monopolistic Competition, and the Factor-Proportions Theory in International Trade. *Rev. Econ. Stat.* **1989**, *71*(1), 143–153.

Bergstrand, J. H. The Heckscher–Ohlin–Samuelson Model, the Linder Hypothesis and the Determinants of Bilateral Intra-Industry Trade. *Econ. J.* **1990**, *100*(403), 1216–1229.

Botha, C.; Crompton, J. L.; Kim, S. S. Developing a Revised Competitive Position For Sun/Lost City, South Africa. *J. Travel Res.* **1999**, *37*(4), 341–352.

Bougheas, S.; Demetriades, P. O.; Morgenroth, E. L. W. Infrastructure, Transport Costs and Trade. *J. Int. Econ.* **1999**, *47*(1), 169–189.

Breuss, F.; Egger, P. How Reliable Are Estimations of East-West Trade Potentials Based On Cross-Section Gravity Analysis. *Empirica* **1999**, *26* (2), 81–94.

Buhalis, D.; Law, R. Progress in Information Technology and Tourism Management: 20 Years on and 10 Years after the Internet—the State of eTourism Research. *Tourism Manage.* **2008**, *29*(4), 609–623.

Cellini, R. Is UNESCO Recognition Effective In Fostering Tourism? A Comment on Yang, Lin and Han. *Tourism Manage.* **2011**, *32*(2), 452–454.

Cho, V. A Study of the Non-Economic Determinants in Tourism Demand. *Int. J. Tourism Res.* **2010**, *12*(4), 307–320.

Chon, K. S.; Mayer, K. J. Destination Competitiveness Models in Tourism and Their Application to Las Vegas. *J. Tourism Syst. Qual. Manage.* **1995**, *1*(2), 227–46.

Christie, I. T.; Crompton, D. E. Tourism in Africa. *Africa Region Working Paper Series no, 12.* The World Bank: Washington, DC, 2001.

Clarke, G. R. G; Wallsten, S. J. Has the Internet Increased Trade? Developed and Developing Country Evidence. *Econ. Inquiry* **2006**, *44*(3), 465–484.

Cohen, E.; Cooper, R. L. Language and Tourism. *Ann. Tourism Res.* **1986**, *13*(4), 533–563.

Crouch, G. I. Destination Competitiveness: An Analysis of Determinant Attributes. *J. Travel Res.* **2011**, *50*(1), 27–45.

Deardorff, A. Determinants of Bilateral Trade: Does Gravity Work in a Neo-Classic World? In *The Regionalization of the World Economy*; Frankel, J. Ed.; University of Chicago Press: Chicago, 1998; pp 7–22.

Dwyer, L.; Forsyth, P.; Rao, P. The Price Competitiveness of Travel and Tourism: A Comparison of 19 Destinations. *Tourism Manage.* **2000**, *21*(1), 9–22.

Dwyer, L.; Kim, C. Destination Competitiveness: Determinants and Indicators. *Curr. Issues Tourism* **2003**, *6*(5), 369–414.

Egger, P.; Pfaffermayr, M. The Proper Panel Econometric Specification of the Gravity Equation: A Three-Way Model with Bilateral Interaction Effects. *World Econ.* **1997**, *20*(3), 363–368.

Egger, P. A Note on the Proper Econometric Specification of the Gravity Equation. *Econ. Lett.* **2000**, *66*(1), 25–31.

Eichengreen, B.; Tong, H. Is China's FDI Coming at The Expense of Other Countries?. *J. Japanese Int. Econ.* **2007**, *21*(2), 153–172.

Eilat, Y.; Einav, L. Determinants of International Tourism: A Three-Dimensional Panel Data Analysis. *Appl. Econ.* **2004**, *36*(12), 1315–1327.

Enright, M. J.; Newton, J. Tourism Destination Competitiveness: A Quantitative Approach. *Tourism Manage.* **2004**, *25*(6), 777–788.

Fourie, J.; Santana-Gallego, M. The Impact of Mega-Sport Events on Tourist Arrivals. *Tourism Manage.* **2011**, *32*(6), 1364–1370.

Gallardo-Sejas, H.; Pareja, S. G.; Llorca-Vivero, R.; Martínez-Serrano, J. A. Determinants of European Immigration: A Cross-Country Analysis. *Appl. Econ. Lett.* **2006**, *13*(12), 769–773.

Gearing, C. E.; Swart, W. W.; Var, T. Establishing a Measure of Touristic Attractiveness. *J. Travel Res.* **1974**, *12*(4), 1–8.

Getz, D.; Brown, G. Critical Success Factors for Wine Tourism Regions: A Demand Analysis. *Tourism Manage.* **2006**, *27*(1), 146–158.

Getz, D. Models in Tourism Planning: Towards Integration of Theory and Practice. *Tourism Manage.* **1986**, *7*(1), 21–32.

Gil-Pareja, S.; Llorca-Vivero, R.; Martínez-Serrano, J. A. The Impact of Embassies and Consulates on Tourism. *Tourism Manage.* **2007**, *28*(2), 355–360.

Greene, W. H. *Econometric Analysis* (5th ed.). Prentice Hall: New Jersey, 2003.

Hair, J. F; Black, W. C.; Babin, B. J.; Anderson, R. E. *Multivariate Data Analysis* (7th ed.). New Jersey: Pearson Education, Inc. 2010.

Helpman, E.; Krugman, P. R. *Market Structure and Foreign Trade: Increasing Returns, Imperfect Competition, and the International Economy.* MIT Press: Cambridge, 1985.

Helpman, E. Imperfect Competition and International Trade: Evidence from Fourteen Industrial Countries. *J. Japanese Int. Econ.* **1987**, *1*(1), 62–81.

Huff, D. L.; Rust, R. T. Measuring the Congruence of Market Areas. *J. Mark.* **1984**, *48*(1), 68–74.

Kandogan, Y. Consistent Estimates of Regional Blocs' Trade Effects. *Rev. Int. Econ.* **2008**, *16*(2), 301–314.

Karemera, D.; Oguledo, V. I.; Davis, B. A Gravity Model Analysis of International Migration to North America. *Applied Econ.* **2000**, *32*(13), 1745–1755.

Kennedy, P. *A Guide to Econometrics*. Blackwell Publishing: Malden, MA, 2008.

Khadaroo, J.; Seetanah, B. The Role of Transport Infrastructure in International Tourism Development: A Gravity Model Approach. *Tourism Manage.* **2008**, *29*(5), 831–840.

Martínez-Zarzoso, I.; Nowak-Lehmann, F. Augmented Gravity Model: An Empirical Application to Mercosur-European Union Trade Flows. *J. Appl. Econ.* **2003**, *6*(2), 291—316.

Massidda, C.; Etzo, I. The Determinants of Italian Domestic Tourism: A Panel Data Analysis. *Tourism Manage.* **2012**, *33*(3), 603–610.

Mátyás, L. Proper Econometric Specification of the Gravity Model, *World Econ.* **1997**, *20*(3), 363–368.

Mátyás, L. The Gravity Model: Some Econometric Considerations. *World Econ.* **1998**, *21*(3), 397–401.

Mayo, E.; Jarvis, L.; Xander, J. Beyond the Gravity Model. *J. Academy Mark. Sci.* **1988**, *16*(3), 23–29.

Mazanec, J. A.; Woöber, K.; Zins, A. H. Tourism Destination Competitiveness: From Definition to Explanation?. *J. Travel Res.* **2007**, *46*(1), 86–95.

Naude, W. A.; Saayman, A. The Determinants of Tourist Arrivals in Africa: A Panel Data Regression Analysis. *Tourism Econ.* **2005**, *11*(3), 365–391.

Pöyhönen, P. A Tentative Model for the Volume of Trade Between Countries. *Weltwirtschaft. Archiv* **1963**, *90*(1), 93–100.

Prideaux, B.; Witt, S. An Analysis of Tourism Flows between Australia and ASEAN Countries: An Australian Perspective. In *Tourism in Southeast Asia: A New Direction* Chon, K. Ed., Horworth Press: New York, 2000, pp.87–106).

Prideaux, B. Factors Affecting Bilateral Tourism Flows. *Ann. Tourism Res.* **2005**, *32*(3), 780–801.

Reilly, W. J. *The Law of Retail Gravitation.* WJ Reilly: New York, 1931.

Ritchie, J. R. B.; Crouch, G. I. *The Competitive Destination: A Sustainable Tourism Perspective.* CABI: Wallingford, UK, 2003.

Ritchie, J. R. B.; Zins, M. Culture as Determinant of the Attractiveness of a Tourism Region. *Ann. Tourism Res.* **1978**, *5*(2), 252–267.

Smith, S. L. J.; Brown, B. Directional Bias in Vacation Travel. *Ann. Tourism Res.* **1981**, *8*(2), 257–270.

Song, H.; Li, G. Tourism Demand Modelling and Forecasting—A Review of Recent Research. *Tourism Manage.* **2008**, *29*(2), 203–220.

The World Bank. *World Development Indicators,* 2011.(Available at http://data.worldbank. org/data-catalog/world-development-indicators).

Tinbergen, J. An Analysis of World Trade Flows. In *Shaping the world economy* Tinbergen, J. Ed., Twentieth Century Fund: New York, 1962.

Uysal, M.; Crompton, J. L. Determinants of Demand for International Tourist Flows to Turkey. *Tourism Manage.* **1984**, *5*(4), 288–297.

Vietze, C. Cultural Effects on Inbound Tourism into the USA: A Gravity Approach. *Jena Econ. Res. Paper* **2008**, *37*, 1–25.

WEF (World Economic Forum). In *the Travel & Tourism Competitiveness Report 2009.* Geneva, Switzerland, 2009.

World Tourism Organization. *UNWTO Tourism Highlights 2011 Edition*, 2011Available at http://www.unwto.org.

Yang, C. H.; Lin, H. L.; Han, C. C. Analysis of International Tourist Arrivals in China: The Role of World Heritage Sites. *Tourism Manage.* **2010**, *31*(6), 827–837.

CHAPTER 10

EFFICACY OF STATIC SHIFT–SHARE ANALYSIS IN MEASURING TOURISM INDUSTRY'S PERFORMANCE IN SOUTH CAROLINA

TARIK DOGRU[1,2] and ERCAN SIRAKAYA-TURK[3]

[1]*School of Hospitality Administration, Boston University, 928 Commonwealth Avenue Boston, MA 02215 USA.*

[2]*The Faculty of Economics and Administrative Sciences, Ahi Evran University, Bagbasi Kampusu, Merkez, Kirsehir 40100, Turkey. Email: dogru@email.sc.edu*

[3]*College of Hospitality, Retail and Sport Management, University of South Carolina, Columbia, SC 29208, USA. E-mail: ercan@hrsm.sc.edu*

CONTENTS

10.1 INTRODUCTION

When we talk about tourism development, we usually refer to desirable changes in the socioeconomic base of communities via increased levels of tourist activity. For example, increases in employment, real per capita income, tax revenues, or access to tourism and recreational resources and opportunities are all considered indicators of tourism development in any community. The level of changes of these indicators over time gives policy makers a feel for tourism development in their region and might help them identify problem areas so strategies or policies can be recommended to increase the likelihood of effective decisions. Evaluating these changes requires a reference point; implicitly, an area such as the entire nation or a region within a nation is usually taken as a norm (Hoover & Giarratani, 1971; Perloff, Dunn Jr, Lampard, & Keith, 1960). From a macroeconomic point of view, tourism development is a comparative assessment process by which a community attempts to equalize or surpass other tourist regions or the national average. Of course, as most of us would agree for many policy makers, the process of tourism development may merely mean more jobs. More jobs are expected to bring greater socioeconomic benefits: lower unemployment, higher wages, greater property value, increased income and profits for local businesses, more tax revenues for the state, and of course possible re-election for the politician who can take credit for these changes (Bartik, 1991). From a policy perspective, to introduce new tourism activities, or to expand the existing tourism base of a region, policy makers and planners ought to know the strength, composition, and performance of their local tourism economy relative to the economy of an area taken to be the norm (usually the average national tourism economy). It is the purpose of this chapter to illustrate the efficacy of a classic but infrequently used model known as the shift–share analysis (SSA) to regional and spatial economists, which is typically used to analyze competitiveness of a region's various industries relative to a nation's general level of economic development.

SSA is a relatively simple technique for describing regional economic growth, measuring policy effects, and forecasting future growth of a region and has been around with little or no change since early 1960s (Sirakaya et al., 1995). It has been especially popular in the fields of spatial economics (Barff & Knight III, 1988; Brown, 1969; Casler, 1989; Curtis, 1972), political economy (Glickman & Glasmeier, 1989), marketing (Huff & Sherr, 1967), geography (Plane, 1987), and urban studies (Stilwell, 1969) for decades. With the exception of a few studies (see e.g., Sirakaya, Uysal, & Toepper, 1995; Sirakaya, Choi, & Var, 2002; Toh, Khan, & Lim, 2004) and more recently by Yasin, Alavi, Koubida, and Small (2011), tourism scholars have not taken full advantage of such a simple and widely used technique.

One of the benefits of using the shift–share method in its classical form is that it reduces the need for primary data collection (e.g., surveying businesses), a costly and time-consuming activity. Thus, many impact assessment studies including SSA are conducted based on secondary data that are usually mandated by law and collected by various governmental organizations such as the US Department of Labor or US Department of Commerce. Many local decision makers can obtain the required data with relative ease but may lack the theoretical and statistical expertise to conduct an extensive study determining the economic impacts of tourism in their region without the use of such rigorous techniques as time-series analysis, computable general equilibrium or econometrics methods. Accordingly, the shift–share technique is suggested as an alternative modus operandi for policy makers, who need a quick and inexpensive analytical tool to evaluate the performance and composition of their local tourism economy.

This method helps evaluate the change in a region's performance relative to the nation over a given period of time (Andrikopoulos, Brox, & Carvalho, 1990; Doeringer, Terkla, & Topakian, 1987; Kurre & Weller, 1989; Ledebur & Moomaw, 1983; Mead & Ramsay, 1982). Its popularity stems mainly from the fact that it requires data that are relatively easy and inexpensive to obtain, usually employment and income figures will suffice, yet it provides researchers and/or policy-makers useful information regarding the likely reasons for differential growth rates among different regions (Beck & Herr, 1990). Since its original formulation by Perloff et al. (1960) in early 1960s, variations of the shift–share technique have found useful applications in the fields of regional economics and geography. Notwithstanding of different variations, this method measures the change in a region's performance relative to the nation over a given period of time (Andrikopoulos et al., 1990; Doeringer et al., 1987; Kurre & Weller, 1989; Ledebur & Moomaw, 1983; Mead & Ramsay, 1982). SSA requires employment data at industry levels, and accessibility and affordability of the data on employment for industries other than tourism makes the model popular among other fields of studies (Sirakaya et al., 1995). However, conducting SSA for tourism industry requires laborious work that involves combining sectors that constitute tourism industry, because a separate tourism employment data is not readily available. With more states and countries creating tourism satellite accounts (TSA), data collection problems will be eliminated. Nevertheless, SSA results provide researchers and policymakers vital information that allows them comparison of regional growth based on industry, and develop strategies based on strength and weaknesses of the regions (Beck & Herr, 1990). Although theoretical advancement of this, rather, accounting tool is less likely in the near future, recent attempts with newer regression based models show promise.

The purpose of this chapter is to illustrate the efficacy of a SSA in examining the tourism industry performance in a region. For this purpose, the state of South Carolina was examined as a case to exhibit the application of SSA. In this chapter, we further attempted to assess whether any specific sectors of tourism exhibited competitive advantages relative to other sectors in South Carolina.

10.2   CONCEPTUAL MODEL

To measure economic growth in a particular region, some surrogate variables are usually selected that are considered to reflect that growth—Employment figures are the most frequently used proxy variables, since they are easy to obtain and constitute appropriate data for SSA (Bendavid-Val, 1991). Although there are variations of the same model, the basic accounting identities and calculations are similar across models. Accordingly, in its well-known form, the change of employment in a region is viewed as the result of three components: the national growth effect (NGE), the industrial mix effect (IME), and the competitive share effect (CSE).

The NGE attempts to measure the employment change in a region that would have occurred in the region if employment had grown at precisely the same rate as the national average (Tervo & Okko, 1983); in other words, the implicit assumption here, though simplistic, is that the structure of the local economy is identical to the economic structure of the national economy. Hence, if the region grows at the same rate as the national average, it does not possess any comparative advantage in terms of its resource endowments (such as tourist attractions) or human capital (such as trained hospitality labor force); it is neither better nor worse off than its counterparts. This type of attribution to one factor seems simplistic, but it is useful when policy makers evaluate their region based on comparative analysis between it and other regions or the nation's average. If, for example, the job gains in the region under study are attributed mostly to the gains due to the national trend, decision makers must understand how else they can differentiate their tourism industry so it can lead to competitive advantage in the market. According to the model used by (Sirakaya et al., 1995), the NGE is computed by multiplying the regional base-year employment in each sector by the average national employment growth rate and then summing the products. The resulting figures illustrate the quality of newly created jobs that are attributable to the national economic trends and nothing else.

The second of the three components, the IME, associates the differential growth rate in tourism employment between the region in question and the nation with overall strengths and weaknesses of tourism sector. Ideally, it is expected that a large proportion of the region's employment should be concentrated in faster growing industries and by the same token, a smaller percentage of a region's employment should be in slower growing sectors of the regional economy. In other words, it is reasonable to expect that industries with a high propensity to grow will grow faster than the national economy. The IME is calculated by multiplying the local employment in each tourism sector by the difference in the national growth rate for that sector and the growth rate for the entire economy. Accordingly, this effect weighs the source of new tourism employment growth (decline) in slow or fast growing sectors. For example, South Carolina's tourism industry may be highly concentrated in sectors such as transportation and lodging, which may be growing faster than national average. A positive number for the IME would mean that the local economy had relatively more jobs in fast-growth sectors of tourism than the national average, thus exhibiting structural strength (Hustedde, Shaffer, & Pulver, 1993).

The third component, the CSE (also called the "differential shift effect"), indicates that the region under study (e.g., South Carolina) is more or less efficient (competitive) in securing a larger share of employment than its counterpart (the nation). The differential shift effect (also called *local competitive effect*) is calculated by multiplying the regional employment in each tourism sector by the difference in the growth rate of that sector nationally and regionally. In other words, this accounting identity is the difference between the actual expected change in employment if each industrial sector grew at the national rate (Barff & Knight III, 1988). After completing this process for all tourism sectors, the resulting figures are added to generate differential shift effect. It is this component that makes a real difference in a region's ability to draw more tourists; thus, it can be considered as a measurement of the strength of the competitiveness of the tourism industry in a region. However, the CSE cannot provide an explanation for regional employment growth (Sirakaya et al., 1995). In other words, the model cannot be used for explaining the reasons (e.g., the tourism resource endowments, entrepreneurial and management ability, effective management, and governmental policies) for the change in employment. It can only be used as an indicator of the existence or absence of such factors within a region that provide a region with competitive advantage or disadvantage (Bendavid-Val, 1991). Of course, once this has been determined more elaborate studies can be undertaken to determine the actual reasons for the positive or negative competitive effect.

The classical shift–share model is summarized in the following equation:

$$e_{ij}^{t} - e_{ij}^{t-1} = \Delta e_{ij} = NGE + IME + CSE \tag{10.1}$$

where i is the index referring to the industries in the national or benchmark economy; j is the index referring to the regions of the national economy; Δe_{ij} is total change in employment in the ith industry in the jth region; e_{ij}^{t} is employment in the ith industry in the jth region at time t; NGE: national growth effect; IME: industrial growth effect; and CSE: competitive share effect (local competitive effect).

The three accounting identities are computed as follows:

$$NGE_{i}^{r} = E_{i}^{r} g^{n} \tag{10.2}$$

$$IME_{i}^{r} = E_{i}^{r} (g_{i}^{n} - g^{n}) \tag{10.3}$$

$$CSE_{i}^{r} = E_{i}^{r} (g_{i}^{r} - g_{i}^{n}) \tag{10.4}$$

where the national growth component, NGI^{r}, is given by base period regional employment in the ith industry, E_{i}^{r}, times the overall rate of employment change in the nation, g^{n}; the industrial mix component, IME , given by base period regional employment in the ith industry, E_{i}^{r}, times the national rate of employment change in the ith industry, g_{i}^{n}, less the overall rate of employment change in the nation, g^{n}; and the competitive component, CSE$_{i}^{r}$, is given by base period regional employment in the ith industry, E_{i}^{r}, times the regional rate of employment change in the ith industry, g_{i}^{r}, less the national rate of employment change in the ith industry, g_{i}^{n}.

10.3   METHODOLOGY

Tourism industry is a composite of various industries, such as hotels, restaurants, attractions, entertainment, and so on. Therefore, measuring tourism employment is a demanding work since the contribution of industries to tourism not clear. Although, United Nations World Tourism Organization (UNWTO) has attempted to create a TSA to measure tourism industry related economic activities, such as employment, its contribution to the economy, and so on, since 1980s, TSA is yet to be adopted by nations. A version of TSA, Travel and Tourism Satellite Accounts (TTSA), was developed by the United States, approved by UNWTO in 2002, and has become the international standard by which travel and tourism is measured[1]. However, the TTSA data is only available at the national level, and is not available at state level. Thus, a methodology is required to obtain state level data that is compatible with the national level so that policy makers and stakeholders in the region could understand the dynamics of tourism and take an action where necessary.

Smith (1995) and Sirakaya et al. (1995) have argued that tourism consists of two distinct categories, one of which is termed "Tier 1." Basically, the Tier 1 category of the tourism industry for a community includes business that would not survive if there were no tourism activity. The business in this category may earn as low as 75% of their income from tourism activity. The second category, Tier 2, consists of business that would continue to exist in the absence of tourism activity, but at diminished degree such as taxis, restaurants, and gift shops, in which local patronage is vital for the survival of the businesses in this category. The Tier 2 portion of the tourism industry does not, however, reflect the actual number of employees in the tourism industry, since the contribution of Tier 2 industries to the tourism industry is unclear. It is estimated, however, that the Tier 2 contribution may run as high as 90% for some heavily tourism oriented communities (Smith, 1995) like Charleston, SC or Antalya, Turkey. There is no solid reference in the literature that displays the contribution of each sector to the overall tourism industry. We found only one report by The Economic Contribution of Tourism in South Carolina, published in 2005 with cooperation of Travel Industry Association (TIA), and Tourism Economics, a division of Oxford Economics Company that shows somewhat arbitrary percentage contributions. According to the report, 80%, 15%, and 90% of the air passenger and related industries, bus transportation, and travelers' accommodation can be attributed to tourism activity for Tier 1 category, respectively. The rest of the industries, such as travel agencies, scenic and sightseeing transportation, in Tier 1 category were considered as solid tourism industries, and hence the

---

[1]Please visit Office of Travel and Tourism Industries, Travel and Tourism Satellite Account Program at http://travel.trade.gov/research/programs/satellite/ for detailed information on Travel and Tourism Satellite Account.

whole portions were included in the analysis. Similar to Tier 1 industries' attribution, the report includes the percentage contributions of Tier 2 industries to overall tourism industry. According to the report, food and beverage, arts, entertainment and recreation, taxi services, and retail stores contribute 30%, 50%, 15%, and 15% to the tourism industry, respectively.

The data for this study were obtained from County Business Patterns, a publication of the U.S. Department of Commerce (2014). Annual employment data of South Carolina for the years 1998, 2003, 2008, and 2012 were used as calculations in the shift–share model (SSM). The classification system, Standardized Industrial Classification (SIC), was replaced with the North American Industry Classification System (NAICS) in 1997. The NAICS is more detailed and comprehensive than the previous SIC system. According to the Washington State Department of Revenue, NAICS now includes 358 new industries compared to SIC system, and these are mostly service producing industries. Furthermore, since SIC system was replaced by NAICS, its publication was stopped in 1997, and because the classification methodology had changed, SIC and NAICS codes are not compatible. Therefore, NAICS is now used commonly to classify sectors of the economy. Since the tourism industry comprises many different economic sectors, the levels that would provide such detailed information for the purpose of this study are the six-digit levels of the NAICS. Therefore, the levels of NAICS were utilized, where appropriate, to represent the tourism industry and classify the employment figures into appropriate tourism sectors. However, in order to facilitate an easy comparison with other sectors of the economy, only two-digit NAICS codes were used for comparison purposes.

The data presented in this study have some limitations. The NAICS employment data do not contain a separate tourism industry. However, the industries that comprise the tourism industry such as hotel and motel sector, passenger travel sector, and air transportation sector are listed in NAICS. Simply aggregating the employment data of such industries that constitute the tourism industry would not be appropriate because it is crucial to determine how much of that employment is attributable to tourism. Therefore, this study applied the respective attributions of the sectors when creating the aggregate tourism industry figures based on the aforementioned report by TIA. Hence, sectors that were considered part of the tourism industry were extracted and aggregated into two broad categories, Tier 1 and Tier 2. Table 10.2, column 1 displays the industry categories used in creating the Tier 1 and Tier 2 portions of the tourism industry. The summation of these two categories then represents the entire tourism industry. Data were adjusted by summing all portions of the employment that were deemed to represent the tourism industry and then subtracting the sum from its major category. For example, the hotels and motels sector (NAICS 721110), bed and breakfast inns (NAICS 721191) were summed and then subtracted from the total number representing the accommodation and food services (NAICS 72) so that the accommodation and food services contained only those components that were not considered part of the tourism industry. In other words, sectors were purified with respect to tourism industry.

10.4   RESULTS AND DISCUSSION

10.4.1   DESCRIPTIVE RESULTS

South Carolina's employment by tourism sectors and its tourism growth rate versus the nation as a whole are represented in Tables 10.1–3. South Carolina's employment figures by major industry groups are presented in Table 10.1 for the years 1998, 2003, 2008, and 2012.

An examination of Table 10.2 indicates that for the period 1998–2003, 2003–2008, 2008–2012, and 1998–2012, total employment in South Carolina expanded 1.2%, 6.6%, −6.6%, and 0.7%, respectively. Overall, total employment in South Carolina shows positive growth with the exception of the 2008–2012 period. The negative growth rate between 2008 and 2012 can be attributable to the ongoing economic recession that had started by the financial crisis in late 2007 in the United States, and spread over many other countries in the world. The number of people employed in industrial sectors such as manufacturing and construction declined by 38% and 39.1%, respectively, while employment in the service related sector accounted for the largest absolute gain. For example, transportation and warehousing, educational services, and heath care and social assistance industries increased 49%, 53.6%, and 34.8%, respectively. The tourism industry employed 85,859 people in 1990, or almost 6% of the state's total employment, a figure that reflects an increase of 15.7% from the year 1998. However, the Tier 1 category (the core) of the tourism industry in the state decreased by 1180 jobs (−4.4%) for the same period.

TABLE 10.1   South Carolina's Employment by Economic Sector.

NAICS code	Major industry groups	1998	2003	2008	2012
	Tourism employment	74,220	81,524	88,719	85,859
	Tier 1	26,796	29,819	28,641	25,616
	Tier 2	47,424	51,705	60,078	60,243
11	Forestry, fishing, hunting, and agriculture support	5231	5376	4551	4236
21	Mining	1348	1436	1220	1094
22	Utilities	11,774	11,088	12,030	11,958
23	Construction	111,427	108,422	111,971	67,833
31	Manufacturing	343,295	283,244	256,729	212,845
42	Wholesale trade	60,762	62,877	67,040	63,340
44	Retail trade	210,189	211,579	233,116	218,946
48	Transportation & warehousing	31,643	42,706	51,032	47,143
51	Information	27,099	30,184	35,150	32,789
52	Finance & insurance	58,771	70,662	69,830	64,790
53	Real estate & rental & leasing	20,382	24,515	29,560	23,359
54	Professional, scientific & technical services	58,476	68,072	80,101	79,146
55	Management of companies & enterprises	25,845	27,321	25,878	22,501
56	Admin, support, waste mgt, remediation services	121,400	121,748	131,041	155,127
61	Educational services	19,864	24,377	29,493	30,520
62	Health care and social assistance	161,581	188,025	204,184	217,774
71	Arts, entertainment & recreation	14,978	14,430	18,603	17,279
72	Accommodation & food services	87,415	97,575	123,909	113,930
81	Other services (except public administration)	67,783	74,887	80,072	77,978
99	Unclassified establishments	1002	556	175	70
	Total Excluding Tier 1 and 2	1451,886	1469,080	1565,695	1462,657

TABLE 10.2 South Carolina's Employment by Economic Sector, Percent Changes.

NAICS Code	Major industry groups	1998–2003 (%)	2003–2008 (%)	2008–2012 (%)	1998–2012 (%)
	Tourism employment	9.8	8.8	−3.2	15.7
	Tier 1	11.3	−4.0	−10.6	−4.4
	Tier 2	9.0	16.2	0.3	27.0
11	Forestry, fishing, hunting, and agriculture support	2.8	−15.3	−6.9	−19.0
21	Mining	6.5	−15.0	−10.3	−18.8
22	Utilities	−5.8	8.5	−0.6	1.6
23	Construction	−2.7	3.3	−39.4	−39.1
31	Manufacturing	−17.5	−9.4	−17.1	−38.0
42	Wholesale trade	3.5	6.6	−5.5	4.2
44	Retail trade	0.7	10.2	−6.1	4.2
48	Transportation & warehousing	35.0	19.5	−7.6	49.0
51	Information	11.4	16.5	−6.7	21.0
52	Finance & insurance	20.2	−1.2	−7.2	10.2
53	Real estate & rental & leasing	20.3	20.6	−21.0	14.6
54	Professional, scientific & technical services	16.4	17.7	−1.2	35.3
55	Management of companies & enterprises	5.7	−5.3	−13.0	−12.9
56	Admin, support, waste mgt, remediation services	0.3	7.6	18.4	27.8
61	Educational services	22.7	21.0	3.5	53.6
62	Health care and social assistance	16.4	8.6	6.7	34.8
71	Arts, entertainment & recreation	−3.7	28.9	−7.1	15.4
72	Accommodation & food services	11.6	27.0	−8.1	30.3
81	Other services (except public administration)	10.5	6.9	−2.6	15.0
99	Unclassified establishments	−44.5	−68.5	−60.0	−93.0
	Total Excluding Tier 1 and 2	1.2	6.6	−6.6	0.7

Furthermore, national average growth rate for Tier 1 category was 3.25% (Table 10.3). The inadequate performance of the Tier 1 industry group of South Carolina compared with the US average can be ascribed to regional competitive disadvantages (competitive share component < 0). On the other hand, the Tier 2 category of the tourism industry in the state increased by 12,819 jobs (27%) for the same period. Nonetheless, national average growth rate for Tier 2 category was 26.2% (Table 10.3). The performance of the Tier 2 industry group of South Carolina compared with the US average can be ascribed to regional competitive advantages (competitive share component >0).

TABLE 10.3 Growth Rate of Employment in Economic Sectors in the United States and South Carolina 1998–2012.

NAICS codes	Industries	US growth rate (%)	SC growth rate (%)
	Tourism employment	16.42	15.70
	Tier 1	3.25	−4.40
	Tier 2	26.27	27.00
	Tier 1 industries		
481111	Scheduled passenger air transportation	−22.04	0.00
481211	Nonscheduled chartered passenger air transportation	58.45	−51.43
481219	Other nonscheduled air transportation	12.88	500.00
483112	Deep sea passenger transportation	59.45	0.00
483114	Coastal and great lake passenger transportation	26.67	0.00
483212	Inland water passenger transportation	−10.95	−83.33
485210	Interurban and rural bus transportation	−25.36	5.14
485510	Charter bus industry	−3.18	−18.59
487110	Scenic and sightseeing transportation, land	−10.86	7.56
487210	Scenic and sightseeing transportation, water	−2.19	−13.73
487990	Scenic and sightseeing transportation, other	43.10	500.00
488111	Air traffic control	134.29	500.00
488119	Other airport operations	39.54	−54.93
488190	Other support activities for air transportation	52.89	−78.62
561510	Travel agencies	−47.60	−73.12
561520	Tour operators	−34.66	22.06
561591	Convention and visitors bureaus	−18.50	25.86
721110	Hotels (except casino hotels) and motels	8.23	7.23

TABLE 10.3 *(Continued)*

NAICS codes	Industries	US growth rate (%)	SC growth rate (%)
721120	Casino hotels	40.51	0.00
721191	Bed-and-breakfast inns	−18.41	−53.33
721199	All other traveler accommodation	59.45	−83.33
721211	RV (recreational vehicle) parks and campgrounds	12.81	18.60
721214	Recreational and vacation camps (except campgrounds)	10.82	59.23
Tier 2 Industries			
485310	Taxi services	18.59	−42.31
488210	Support activities for rail transportation	45.92	114.29
443130	Camera & photographic Supplies Stores	−100.00	−100.00
445310	Beer, wine, and liquor stores	16.91	15.42
447110	Gasoline stations with convenience stores	11.46	1.06
447190	Other gasoline stations	−52.73	−34.87
448320	Luggage and leather goods stores	−48.69	−50.00
451110	Sporting goods stores	24.22	59.68
453220	Gift, novelty, and souvenir shops	−28.76	−29.82
561599	All other travel arrangement and reservation services	49.10	280.71
722310	Food service contractors	28.92	−84.21
722320	Caterers	23.88	−97.73
722511	Full service restaurants	41.74	57.01
722513	Limited service restaurants	83.11	3074.49
722514	Cafeterias, grill buffets, buffets	49.86	1239.07
722515	Snack and nonalcoholic beverages bars	51.55	475.40
722410	Drinking places (alcoholic beverages)	9.24	48.17
711110	Theater companies and dinner theaters	10.98	28.39
711120	Dance companies	−8.83	191.67
711212	Racetracks	10.84	16.67
711219	Other Spector sports	1.89	−4.82
711310	Promoters of performing arts, sports, and similar events with facilities	225.60	1520.37
711320	Promoters of performing arts, sports, and similar events without facilities	17.15	7.01
711410	Agents and managers for artists, athletes, entertainers, and other public figures	23.14	0.00

TABLE 10.3   *(Continued)*

NAICS codes	Industries	US growth rate (%)	SC growth rate (%)
711510	Independent artists, writers, and performers	37.76	10.29
712110	Museums	31.16	74.57
712120	Historical sites	31.58	−0.80
712130	Zoos and botanical gardens	88.60	152.00
712190	Nature parks and other similar institutions	47.50	330.00
713110	Amusement and theme parks	9.68	−53.33
713120	Amusement arcades	39.29	19.07
713210	Casinos (except hotel casinos)	−12.96	525.00
713290	Other gambling industries	9.44	−76.22
713910	Golf courses and country clubs	13.73	7.58

The employment figures resulting from the SSA are provided in Table 10.4. An examination of employment figures in Table 10.4 indicates that overall Tier 1 category displayed a negative CSE and the industries in this category grew slower than the national average industry growth rate, with the exception of scheduled passenger air transportation, other nonscheduled passenger air transportation, interurban and rural bus transportation, and few other industries (please see Table 10.4 for detailed information). The negative CSE may be due to a lack of new technology or management's inability to increase productivity. Therefore, this analysis merely suggests that the Tier 1 category of tourism industry is not regionally competitive; the study does not, however, attempt to seek normative answers for the reasons for competitive disadvantages. The negative effects of these competitively disadvantaged industries of the tourism sector were not offset by the sectorial makeup (structural strength) exhibited by the same industries. Indeed, the NGE has been positive (1853 jobs) indicating that most of the employment gains were secured due to NGE in Tier 1 category. However, the employment gains due to NGE were also not sufficient to offset the negative effects of these competitively disadvantaged industries of Tier 1 category of the tourism sector. This means that the state of South Carolina's employment rate was lower then the growth rate of national growth rate. For example, the employment gains in hotels and motels industry due to NGE is 1608, and the employment gain due to IME (structural strength) is 221. However, employment gains due to CSE were negative, −220. That is, hotels and motels sector exhibited strength in their sectorial composition but showed disadvantages in competitiveness. Furthermore, employment gains in air traffic control were larger in IME and CSE than NGE. That is, air traffic control sector showed both competitive advantages and structural strength in South Carolina. Also, employment gains in recreational vehicle parks and campgrounds were positive in all components. Thus, South Carolina appears to be advantageous in these sectors, and could further benefit from its competitive advantages in these sectors by further strengthening them via more investments and by developing policies (e.g., introducing tax incentives to the firms) that would allow the growth of these sectors.

TABLE 10.4 Shift–Share Analysis for South Carolina's Tourism Industry: 1998–2012.

	Tourism industries	NGE	IME	CSE
	Tier 1	1,938	−1,066	−2,052
	Tier 2	3,430	9,026	361
NAICS				
Codes	Tier 1 industries			
481111	Scheduled passenger air transportation	43	−176	132
481211	Nonscheduled chartered passenger air transportation	10	72	−154
481219	Other nonscheduled air transportation	1	0	39
483112	Deep sea passenger transportation	1	5	−6
483114	Coastal and great lake passenger transportation	1	2	−3
483212	Inland water passenger transportation	4	−11	−43
485210	Interurban and rural bus transportation	2	−9	8
485510	Charter bus industry	2	−3	−5
487110	Scenic and sightseeing transportation, land	12	−31	32
487210	Scenic and sightseeing transportation, water	15	−19	−24
487990	Scenic and sightseeing transportation, other	1	4	46
488111	Air traffic control	1	10	29
488119	Other airport operations	22	97	−283
488190	Other support activities for air transportation	158	998	−2,873
561510	Travel agencies	77	−583	−272
561520	Tour operators	10	−57	77
561591	Convention and visitors bureaus	8	−30	51
721110	Hotels (except casino hotels) and motels	1,499	206	−206
721120	Casino hotels	1	3	−4
721191	Bed-and-breakfast inns	24	−87	−118
721199	All other traveler accommodation	4	28	−77

TABLE 10.4 *(Continued)*

	Tourism industries	NGE	IME	CSE
721211	RV (recreational vehicle) parks and campgrounds	34	26	27
721214	Recreational and vacation camps (except campgrounds)	8	4	57
	Tier 2 industries			
485310	Taxi services	3	5	−28
488210	Support activities for rail transportation	13	68	120
443130	Camera & photographic supplies stores	3	−39	–
445310	Beer, wine, and liquor stores	13	17	−3
447110	Gasoline Stations with convenience stores	160	93	−229
447190	Other gasoline stations	34	−280	83
448320	Luggage and Leather Goods Stores	1	−10	0
451110	Sporting Goods Stores	19	44	92
453220	Gift, novelty, and souvenir shops	33	−162	−5
561599	All other travel arrangement and reservation services	14	82	456
722310	Food service contractors	1,220	3,659	−19,087
722320	Caterers	1,133	2,607	−19,052
722511	Full service restaurants	39	185	82
722513	Limited service restaurants	52	541	21,323
722514	Cafeterias, grill buffets, buffets	100	589	16,425
722515	Snack and non-alcoholic beverages bars	15	92	879
722410	Drinking places (alcoholic beverages)	71	20	383
711110	Theater companies and dinner theaters	23	12	56
711120	Dance companies	2	−5	60
711212	Racetracks	2	1	2
711219	Other Spector sports	9	−7	−8
711310	Promoters of performing arts, sports, and similar events with facilities	4	118	699
711320	Promoters of performing arts, sports, and similar events without facilities	10	13	−14
711410	Agents and managers for artists, athletes, entertainers, and other public figures	2	5	−7
711510	Independent artists, writers, and performers	6	27	−24
712110	Museums	17	56	102
712120	Historical sites	14	46	−61
712130	Zoos and botanical gardens	6	71	55

TABLE 10.4   *(Continued)*

	Tourism industries	NGE	IME	CSE
712190	Nature parks and other similar institutions	0	2	14
713110	Amusement and theme parks	14	5	−118
713120	Amusement arcades	27	120	−76
713210	Casinos (except hotel casinos)	2	−6	161
713290	Other gambling industries	76	23	−899
713910	Golf courses and country clubs	294	264	−250

Although the Tier 1 category of tourism sector did not, overall, exhibit structural strength or CSE, Tier 2 category of tourism industry showed high-structural strength and CSE in the state of South Carolina. An examination of Figure 10.1 shows that the employment gains in Tier 2 category were mostly due to IME. Indeed, the IME was positive (9026 jobs) indicating that most of the employment gains were secured due to industrial mix component. The employment growth rate due to CSE was positive, but much smaller than NGE and IME. While Tier 2 category of tourism industry assumed to be secondary compared to the Tier 1 category, which is considered to be the bulk of the tourism industry, Tier 2 category exhibited higher structural strength and competitive advantages relative to Tier 1 category for the state of South Carolina.

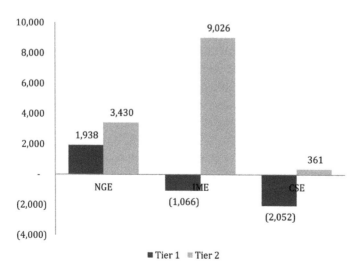

FIGURE 10.1   Shift–share results for Tier 1 and Tier 2 tourism industries.

Moreover, the employment growth rates for both South Carolina and the United States were significantly higher for Tier 2 category than Tier 1 category. Thus, contribution of Tier 2 category to tourism industry should not be underestimated and further resources should be allocated to this category. Overall, industries in Tier 2 category, such as food services and drinking places, exhibited strength in their sectorial composition and showed advantages in competitiveness. Since the first study, things have not changed much in SC, the results were similar to the original study conducted by Sirakaya and his colleagues in 1995. Accordingly, tourism industry South Carolina could benefit from such advantages in further expanding and/or strengthening these particular industries. The industries that showed such healthy growth could be attributed to South Carolina's location, attractions, investments, and climate (Sirakaya et al., 1995).

10.5 CONCLUSION

The study findings show that the entire tourism industry of South Carolina grew in line with the national average. According to the SSA results, the Tier 1 category of South Carolina's tourism industry could not keep pace with national growth rates because the travel industry exhibited regional disadvantages. Overall, in Tier 1 category lost 1180 jobs (4.4%) in 2012 compared to 1998, mostly due to competitive disadvantages of the region. The region also exhibited weak structural strength (IME). Owing to the strength of the national economic growth, the employment did not decrease dramatically. That is, national economic growth offset the decrease in employment by 1938 jobs. That is, the national growth mitigated the decrease in employment due to the regional disadvantaged competitiveness. However, more people were employed in faster growing industries, which are mostly classified under the Tier 2 category, such as full-service restaurants, limited-service restaurants, and drinking places, displaying positive structural strength and regional advantage. Tier 2 of the tourism industry gained, beyond the national growth trend, extra 5958 jobs because of its strength in sectorial composition and its competitive advantages.

In light of these findings, we can make several recommendations. First, the actual reasons for decline in Tier 1 industry, and the relatively weak competitive advantages in Tier 2 industry should be investigated via behavioral and econometric models. Second, it seems that tourism in South Carolina would benefit greatly if policies were designed and support were given to structurally weak and competitively disadvantaged tourism industries, especially to Tier 1 industries. Third, we carefully investigated the industries that constitute the tourism industry individually, instead of mere aggregation of the tourism sectors. In this way, the analyses are not limited to the core industries such as air transportation and hotels and motels, in which similarly, the employment data is constrained to aggregated levels. Thus, policy makers and practitioners could benefit from our findings using the results in industry levels.

In conclusion, this chapter delineated the contribution of industries to tourism industry including Tier 1 and Tier 2 categories of tourism industry by applying the figures published in The Economic Contribution of Tourism in South Carolina to eliminate subjectivity. However, the same figures were applied to both national level (United States) and regional level (South Carolina). Although it is difficult to estimate the contribution of industries to general tourism for a specific region, it is recommended that further studies should attempt to find ways to delineate the exact relationships of supportive industries to tourism in a particular region. Moreover, this chapter aimed to introduce the application and efficacy of shift–share method analyzing the performance of the tourism industry in a region by using the classical form of a SSA. SSA in this presentation format manifests a deterministic relationship rather than statistically testable relationships: it cannot answer the perplexing questions of whether the model explains the significant changes in employment in the tourism industry, and if it is a valid model to examine such changes. Therefore, SSA is open to criticism, as it has been since its development. As Fothergill and Gudgin (1979, p. 309) have noted three decades ago, "shift-share fits the expectation that, when a technique is simple and apparently useful, it will be both widely used and heavily criticized." To address the concerns related to the shift–share method adequately, improved versions of shift–share models that can provide probabilistic measures of employment change (e.g., the ANOVA-based shift–share model) should be applied (Andrikopoulos et al., 1990; Beck & Herr, 1990; Patterson, 1991). However, we have not applied these models in this chapter, mainly because it was not the purpose of this chapter to statistically test and propose an empirical model, but merely to illustrate the reapplication of shift–share method in tourism industry. Accordingly, developing stochastic models that can be tested empirically remain a challenge for future research. For comparison of results, further studies might extend the analysis to another US state or to other sectors in South Carolina or other regions in the world.

ACKNOWLEDGMENTS

Much of the content of this chapter is an amalgamation of two papers that have been published elsewhere (see Sirakaya, Choi, & Var, 2002; Sirakaya, Uysal, & Toepper, 1995). With the permission of the publishers, dated February 3, 2014, within this chapter, we have updated the data, analyses, and results section using the current SC data and changed the language for better flow for the reader.

KEYWORDS

- **shift–share analysis**
- **tourism industry performance**
- **South Carolina**

REFERENCES

Andrikopoulos, A.; Brox, J.; Carvalho, E. Shift–Share Analysis and the Potential for Predicting Regional Growth Patterns: Some Evidence for the Region of Quebec, Canada. *Growth Change* **1990,** *21*(1), 1–10.

Barff, R. A.; Knight III, P. L. Dynamic Shift–Share Analysis. *Growth Change* **1988,** *19*(2), 1–10.

Bartik, T. J. *Who Benefits From State and Local Economic Development Policies?* W.E. Upjohn Institute for Employment Research: Kalamazoo, MI. Books from Upjohn Press, 1991.

Beck, R. J.; Herr, W. M. Employment Linkages from a Modified Shift–Share Analysis: An Illinois Example. *Rev. Reg. Stud.* **1990,** *20*(3), 38–45.

Bendavid-Val, A. *Regional and Local Economic Analysis for Practitioners* (4th ed.). Praeger Publishers: Westport, CT, 1991.

Brown, H. J. Shift and Share Projections of Regional Economic Growth: An Emprirical Test. *J. Reg. Sci.* **1969,** *9*(1), 1–18.

Casler, S. D. A Theoretical Context for Shift and Share Analysis. *Reg. Stud.* **1989,** *23*(1), 43–48.

Curtis, W. C. Shift–Share Analysis as a Technique in Rural Development Research. *Am. J. Agric. Econ.* **1972,** *54*(2), 267–270.

Doeringer, P. B.; Terkla, D. G.; Topakian, G. C. *Invisible Factors in Local Economic Development*: Oxford University Press: New York, 1987.

Fothergill, S.; Gudgin, G. In Defence of Shift–Share. *Urban Stud.* **1979,** *16*(3), 309–319.

Glickman, N. J.; Glasmeier, A. K. The International Economy and The American South. *Deind. Reg. Econ. Transform.* **1989**, 60–80.

Hoover, E. M.; Giarratani, F. *An Introduction to Regional Economics.* Alfred A Knopf: New York, NY, 1971.

Huff, D. L.; Sherr, L. A. Measure For Determining Differential Growth Rates of Markets. *J. Mark. Res.* **1967**, 391–395.

Hustedde, R. J.; Shaffer, R.; Pulver, G. *Community Economic Analysis: A How To Manual.* Iowa State University Printing Services: Ames, IA, 1993.

Kurre, J. A.; Weller, B. R. Forecasting the Local Economy, Using Time-Series and Shift–Share Techniques. *Environ. Plann. A* **1989**, *21*(6), 753–770.

Ledebur, L. C.; Moomaw, R. L. A Shift–Share Analysis of Regional Labor Productivity in Manufacturing. *Growth Change* **1983**, *14*(1), 2–9.

Mead, A. C.; Ramsay, G. A. Analyzing Differential Responses of a Region to Business Cycles. *Growth Change* **1982**, *13*(3), 38–42.

Patterson, M. G. A Note on the Formulation of Full-Analogue Regression Model of the Shift–Share Method. *J. Reg. Sci.* **1991**, *31*(2), 211–216.

Perloff, H. S.; Dunn Jr, E. S.; Lampard, E. E.; Keith, R. F. *Regions, Resources, and Economic Growth.* Johns Hopkins Press: Baltimore, MD, 1960.

Plane, D. A. The Geographic Components of Change in a Migration System. *Geogr. Anal.* **1987**, *19*(4), 283–299.

Sirakaya, E.; Choi, H.-S.; Var, T. Shift–Share Analysis in Tourism: Examination of Tourism Employment Change in a Region. *Tourism Econ.* **2002**, *8*(3), 303–324.

Sirakaya, E.; Uysal, M.; Toepper, L. Measuring Tourism Performance Using a Shift–Share Analysis: The Case of South Carolina. *J. Travel Res.* **1995**, *34*(2), 55–61.

Smith, S. L. J. *Tourism Analysis: A handbook*, second ed. Longman Group Limited: London and New York, 1995.

Stilwell, F. J. B. Regional Growth and Structural Adaptation. *Urban Stud.* **1969**, *6*(2), 162–178.

Tervo, H.; Okko, P. A Note of Shift–Share Analysis as a Method of Estimating the Employment Effects of Regional Economic Policy. *J. Reg. Sci.* **1983**, *23*(1), 115–121.

Toh, R. S.; Khan, H.; Lim, L.-L. Two-Stage Shift–Share Analyses of Tourism Arrivals and Arrivals by Purpose of Visit: The Singapore Experience. *J. Travel Res.* **2004**, *43*(1), 57–66.

U.S. Department of Commerce. *County Business Patterns.* U.S. Bureau of the Census, 2014. Retrieved from http://www.census.gov/econ/cbp/download/.

Yasin, M.; Alavi, J.; Koubida, S.; Small, M. H. An Assessment of the Competitiveness of the Moroccan Tourism Industry: Benchmarking Implications. *Benchmarking: Int. J.* **2011**, *18*(1), 6–22.

CHAPTER 11

DESTINATION ATTRACTIVENESS BASED ON SUPPLY AND DEMAND EVALUATIONS

SANDRO FORMICA[1] and MUZAFFER UYSAL[2]

[1]*Managing Self & Others, Leadership, and Personal Empowerment, Florida International University, Biscayne Bay, 3000 N.E. 151 Street, North Miami, FL 33181, USA.*

[2]*Department of Hospitality and Tourism Management, Virginia Tech, 362 Wallace Hall (0429), 295 West Campus Drive, Blacksburg, VA 24061, USA. E-mail: samil@vt.edu*

CONTENTS

11.1 INTRODUCTION

The pressure exerted by competition is compelling international, national, state, and local governments to re-evaluate, manage the existing tourism resources and to capitalize on them in order to reposition themselves to attract more visitors and also gain competitive advantage. Tourism, as a socioeconomic activity, does not occur randomly. Some regions, destinations, or sites appear to be more successful than others in offering tourism activities and in attracting travelers. The identification and analysis of existing patterns of tourism resources are critical steps in assessing the potential for attracting tourists to a given area (Gunn, 1988; Cracolici & Nijkamp, 2008, Iatu & Bulai, 2011; Crouch & Ritchie, 2012; Pearce, 2012).

The theoretical basis and empirical research on assessing tourism potential for development and tourism attractiveness are derived from multiple disciplines and bodies of knowledge. Those scholars who consider tourism as a landscape industry possess a spatial analysis and planning perspective (Lundgre, 2004; Gunn, 1994; Young, 1999; Walmsley & Jenkins, 1992; Smith, 1983). Others, more concerned with the demand or market outcomes of attractiveness, have built knowledge in the field by borrowing from the marketing literature (Yaprakli & Rasouli, 2013; Vengresayi, 2003; Hu & Ritchie, 1993) and management science and operation research (Enright & Newton, 2004; Var, Beck, & Loftus, 1977). Nyberg (1995) claims that, in addition to the supply and demand approaches, the entire tourism system—visitors, destination, and the linkage between the two—needs to include a definition of attractiveness. Some research, for example, the study by Cracolici and Nijkapm (2008) focused on assessing the relative competitiveness of tourist destinations based on tourists' judgments or perceptions of attractiveness profiles of tourist regions. This type of attractiveness assessment is also consistent with destination image analysis (Pike, 2002) as an indirect assessment of destination attractiveness as perceived by consumers. The current body of knowledge in tourism attractiveness suggests that the main concern of scholars, researchers, and practitioners is not related to the theoretical investigation of the attractiveness concept itself but to the possibility of finding a universal method for its measurement.

A recent study by Lee and Huang (2012) using the analytic hierarchy process (AHP) method examined the relative importance of supply elements such as comfortable climate, segregated bicycle facilities, and road surface and pavement as the most important determinants of attractiveness of a bicycle tourism destination. The use of AHP is a useful and rational way of determining weightings for the various destination attributes—supply—factors through prioritization using pairwise comparisons (Deng, King, & Bauer, 2002). This current study investigates the relationships between the supply and demand elements which contribute to the overall evaluation of destination attractiveness in a specific area.

The theoretical underpinning of this research is imbedded in the tourism system approach. The very nature of the production and consumption of tourism goods and services clearly implies that the functioning tourism system consists of an origin and a destination in its simplest form (Gunn, 1988; Leiper, 1979; Mill & Morrison, 1985). An origin represents the demand side of tourism from which visitors generate. A destination, on the other hand, refers to the supply side of tourism that may have certain attractiveness power. The tourist and tourism attractions are the central elements of the system. The transportation, information, and marketing components are the "linkages" which enable the tourist to make decisions concerning where to go, how long to stay, and what to do. These linkages also enable the industry through promotion, product development, and pricing strategies to affect directly the decisions of prospective customers (Uysal, 1998; Fesenmaier & Uysal, 1990). The interaction between the two is reciprocal and impacts the direction and, in some cases, the magnitude of demand and supply interactions.

According to Rugg (1973), a traveler does not derive utility from possessing or consuming travel destinations; rather, the traveler derives utility from being in a particular destination for some period of time. This demonstrates the influence of attractions at destinations in shaping the overall travel experience. However, the interaction between market and destination will change over time based upon the types of visitors attracted and their behavioral characteristics (Plog, 2001). The very existence of tourism depends on the availability and perceived importance of resources at the destination. The resources which attract tourists are numerous, varied, and limited in number, as well as in distribution and degree of development, and to what extent they are known to the tourist market (Pearce, 1987). Jafari (1982) divides the supply side of tourism into three elements; tourism-oriented products, resident-oriented products, and background tourism elements. Tourism-oriented products include accommodations, food service, transportation, travel agencies and tour operators, recreation and entertainment, and other travel trade services. As tourists extend their stay at destination sites, they may increase their use of resident-oriented products which include hospitals, bookstores, barber shops, and so forth. As they patronize local businesses, tourists also are exposed to or experience the background tourism elements such as natural, socio-cultural, and manmade attractions that frequently constitute their main reasons for travel. These elements collectively produce the ultimate tourism experience and can be examined simultaneously in the same context (Pyo, Uysal & McLellan, 1991). The elements composing tourism supply, therefore, are not mutually exclusive but are complementary in nature.

A behavioral perspective on the nature of the interaction between demand and supply suggests that people travel or participate in leisure activities because they are "pushed or pulled" by travelers' motivations and destination attributes. Push factors are considered to be the socio-psychological constructs of the tourists that predispose the individual to travel or to participate in leisure activities (Crompton, 1979, Dann, 1981; Uysal, Li, & Sirakaya-Turk, 2008). This, of course, influences demand. Pull factors, on the other hand, emerge as a result of the attractiveness of a destination and are believed to help establish the chosen destination. In order for a destination to respond meaningfully to demand or reinforce push factors, however, it must be perceived and valued (Brayley, 1990). The interaction between demand and supply is essential for the vacation and leisure experience to take place.

The review of previous research has shown that destination attractiveness is a function of the resource base—*attraction*—and of demand—those who are *attracted*. Some scholars claim that without attractions tourism is impossible (Gunn, 1994; Pearce, 2012) while others believe that it is demand that propels tourism (Dale, 1990). The reality lies in the reciprocal relationship between these two key elements, which is essential to the very existence of tourism. In order to advance the current knowledge of tourist regional and destination attractiveness, the present study makes use of the regional resource models (destination or supply) in conjunction with demand (origin) preferences. Literature suggests that demand and supply independently or collectively may be used to measure tourism attractiveness. The demand driven approach is based on the assumption that "the travel destination reflects the feelings, beliefs, and opinions that an individual has about a destination's perceived ability to provide satisfaction in relation to his or her special vacation needs" (Hu & Ritchie, 1993, p. 25). Similarly, Mayo and Jarvis (1981) argue that tourism attractiveness is dependent on the personal benefits of travelers and on the perceived delivery of those benefits. The supply approach, alternatively, is best defined by Kaur (1981). He considers tourism attractiveness as the drawing force generated by the overall attractions existing in a given place at a certain time.

Based on the reviewed literature, the following assumptions are established to guide the theoretical and methodological analyses of this study: Demand and supply factors collectively and simultaneously influence the production and development of tourism goods and services, and the components of demand and supply generate the tourist experience. Thus, an analytical technique to measure the development of attractiveness should combine the evaluation of existing resources and their perceived attractiveness.

In sum, the tourist product is comprised of elements such as attractions, services, and infrastructures. Together these elements encompass the total appeal of natural and manmade characteristics that may exist in the area. Because their nature is different, researchers have found it difficult to develop a measurement that is capable of examining, evaluating, and comparing many diverse resources, such as theme parks and historical monuments. However, several scholars have investigated and evaluated destination attractiveness of countries and regions such as South Africa (Ferrario, 1979), Turkey (Gearing, Swart, & Var, 1974), Greece (Piperoglou, 1966), British Columbia (Var, Beck, & Loftus, 1977), Thailand (Tang & Rochananond, 1990), Sweden, (Lundgren, 2004), Italy (Cracolici & Nijkapm, 2008), and Romania, (Iatu & Bulai, 2011). Some researchers have concentrated on exploring a single aspect of destination attractiveness of a region (Ritchie & Zins, 1978). According to Lew (1987), there are three major approaches to determine the attractiveness of a destination: ideographic, organizational, and cognitive. The first relates to a specific characteristic of a site and is represented by descriptive groups of attributes. The ideographic approach is linked with the supply component of tourism. The second approach (organizational) best describes spatial and temporal relationships between attractions. The cognitive approach is based on the experiential characteristics that relate to the attractions and focuses on the demand component of tourism. The method applied in this study uses both the ideographic and the cognitive approaches to represent supply and demand, respectively.

11.2 METHODOLOGY

Despite the growing need for a measure of tourism attractiveness, the prominent literature addressing this topic dates back to the 1960s and 1970s. However, other more recent studies investigating tourism resources offer methodological tools that appear particularly useful for the advancement of tourism attractiveness research (Smith, 1987; Lovingood & Mitchelle, 1989; Uysal & Potts, 1990). Measuring tourism attractiveness needs to be carried out in a process that begins with establishing a framework for existing resources and evaluating such resources. The present study uses different methodological techniques to develop a comprehensive measurement of tourism attractiveness and to test the relationships between its components to complement the existing body of knowledge. Specifically, the present method adopts nine steps to measure the overall attractiveness of tourism regions of Virginia.

1. Content analysis of the tourist guides of Virginia to determine the attraction variables that are associated with the attractiveness construct.
2. Data collection of attraction variables using Virginia's counties and independent cities as units of measurement.
3. Factor analysis of attraction variables to identify tourism attraction dimensions.
4. Cluster analysis of counties and independent cities based on the attraction dimensions. If successful, tourist regions are delineated using the "homogeneous" resource regionalization criterion. If not, on the "a-priori" regionalization criterion applied by the Virginia Tourist Corporation.[1]
5. Addition of the standardized scores of attraction dimensions belonging to each county/independent city part of the region.
6. Determination of the supply weights of the attraction dimensions results from the sum of squared loadings (eigenvalues) of each attraction factor.
7. Selection of a team of experts to determine the attraction dimension weights of Virginia regions. The same team of experts determines the attraction dimension evaluations from a demand perspective.
8. Tourist regions are ranked in order of importance based on supply and demand evaluations of identified attraction dimensions using a classification algorithm.
9. The scores of attraction dimensions generated from demand and supply are objectively and subjectively weighted and added. The resulting measure indicates the overall attractiveness of Virginia regions as a function of demand and supply interaction.

The selection procedure of the attraction variables is based upon Lew's (1986) work. He performed a content analysis of guidebooks to define the resources that were considered as tourist attractions in the area under investigation. The studies in regional analysis of tourism resources (Backman,

---

[1]Stephen, L.J. Smith (1995) in his book "Tourism analysis: a handbook" provides extensive discussion on types of regions and regionalization approaches. An a priori region is an area that is predetermined, drawn by someone. Thus, it is not the result of methodological regionalization and may not use a set of objective indicators. On the other hand, a homogeneous region is a region that is defined by a set of objective, internal similarities (p. 177). The difference between the two is that homogeneous regions are defined on the basis of objective analysis and a priori regions are not.

Uysal, & Backman, 1991; Cha & Uysal, 1994; Smith, 1987; Spotts, 1997; Uysal & Potts, 1990) are instrumental in the development of this methodology. Particularly, these previous works provide the base for: using counties as units of measurement, grouping resource variables into dimensions with the help of factor analysis, and identifying tourist regions based on attraction patterns in space. The literature on regional analysis of tourism resources provides an established methodology for the investigation of destination attractiveness; however, the implementation of that methodology is new to destination attractiveness studies.

There are two distinct weighting procedures: subjective and objective. The first, which is a modified version of the Multiattribute Attitude Model (Fishbein, 1963), has been extensively used in destination attractiveness literature (Hu & Ritchie, 1993; Smith, 1995) and utilizes tourism experts to measure the importance of the attraction dimensions. The objective weighting procedure that is applied in this study is new to destination attractiveness research and results from the sum of squared loadings of each attraction factor.

The notion of attraction availability is applied from a supply and a demand perspective. Supply is achieved by adding the standardized attraction dimension scores of the counties composing the tourist regions. This technique has been successfully applied by previous works on regional analysis of tourism resources (Backman, Uysal, & Backman, 1991; Cha & Uysal, 1994; Smith, 1987; Spotts, 1997; Uysal & Potts, 1990). The demand side of evaluation is measured by tourism experts. This is a common methodology and it is based on a number of destination attractiveness studies (Gearing et al., 1974; Liu, 1988; Var et al., 1977). Finally, the measure of attractiveness resulting from the sum of weighted supply and demand evaluations is found in some attractiveness studies (Lew, 1987; Nyberg, 1995) and is mostly based on the seminal work of Gearing et al. (1974).

Tourist attractiveness poses the challenge of matching tourism resources with tourist preferences (Piperoglou, 1966). The body of literature on regional analysis of tourist resources offers a scientific assessment of quantitative regional variations of tourist attractions. However, visitors' decisions to travel are not only affected by quantitative considerations but also by qualitative considerations (Leiper, 1990). To fill this methodological gap, Spotts (1997) suggests: "One approach may be to conduct a quantitative analysis and then adjust the results, to the extent possible, by incorporating qualitative information provided by the representatives of the target market" (p. 14).

11.3   ANALYSIS AND RESULTS

Secondary and primary data were collected for the purpose of this study. First, a content analysis of secondary data on destination attractiveness was performed during the summer of 2000. Five Virginia tourist guides were included in the analysis. The results of the content analysis were used to identify the general attractions in the state of Virginia. Destination attractions data were collected on a county and independent city level. The units of measurement were the political subdivisions of the 95 counties and 40 independent cities in Virginia. The secondary data were then coded and tabulated on a spreadsheet. Primary data were collected to represent the demand perception of destination attractiveness. The study participants were tourism experts who reside in Virginia. Although the study data were generated in the 2000s, since the focus of this chapter is on the approach, the study did not attempt to update the data structure.

11.3.1   CONTENT ANALYSIS

In order to assess the nature and magnitude of tourist attractions in Virginia, text and pictorial analyses were conducted. The entire content of the five Virginia tourism guidebooks was investigated. A set of attraction variables was created to detect the attractions/services that appear to be the most frequently mentioned in the textbooks and represented in pictures. When a certain tourist attraction or service was discussed, it was recorded on the spreadsheet under its representative category. Overall, the results of the pictorial analysis emphasized the same variables that were identified in the text analysis. Twenty attraction variables were identified as measurable and available through secondary sources. All the inventoried attractions have characteristics and features that can be physically recognized and geographically located within Virginia.

11.3.2   FACTOR ANALYSIS

The statistical analysis of this study consisted of factor analysis, cluster analysis, and data refinement. The twenty attraction variables were factor analyzed to determine the overall attraction underlying the dimensions of Virginia. Four factors explaining 66.1% of the overall variance were identified as attraction dimensions. The identified dimensions were labeled as (1) tourism services & facilities; (2) cultural/historical; (3) rural lodging; and (4) outdoor recreation. Each dimension was labeled based upon the characteristics of the attraction variables that are part of the different factors. For example, the first dimension identified was entitled "tourism services & facilities" because it consisted of six variables that stress the importance of necessary tourism components, such as travel agencies, retail facilities, and hotels, eating and drinking places.

Factor analysis generated the important weights of the four tourist attraction dimensions. Specifically, the importance or weights assigned to each dimensions were captured by the rotation sums of squared loadings (eigenvalues). All the loadings pertaining to each dimension were added. Therefore, the sum of the squared loadings indicates the entire variance in tourist attractions that is explained by that attraction dimension. The four dimensions resulting from the factor analysis explained 66.10% of the variance in supply attractions.

To verify the validity of the sum of squared loadings used as a method to determine the importance of attraction dimensions, four multiple regression analyses were performed. Virginia's counties and independent cities' economic indicators of tourism—tourism receipts, tourism employment generated, tourism state taxes, and tourism local taxes—were used as dependent variables and the four attraction dimensions represented the independent variables. Regression analysis was used to shed light on the relationship between the regional availability of attractions and the economic benefits generated by tourism in the same regions. The purpose of this analysis is to detect the magnitude of each attraction dimension to explain county or regional variations in travel spending (Spotts, 1997). All four regression analyses were significant at the 0.00 level and the adjusted R-squares varied from 0.550 to 0.944. Overall, the findings of the multiple regression analyses are related to the weights generated by the sums of squared loadings. The Beta coefficients were consistent in terms of individual contributions of the single attraction dimensions to the economic benefits of tourism. The highest beta weight was achieved by the tourism services and facilities dimension, followed by the cultural/historical dimension. The last two dimensions, rural lodging and outdoor recreation received the lowest beta weights and were not significant at the 0.05 level.

11.3.3   CLUSTER ANALYSIS

Cluster analysis was used to classify Virginia's counties and independent cities into mutually exclusive tourist regions. Using the SPSS Hierarchical and

Quick Cluster techniques, it was expected that clusters of contiguous counties with similar attraction dimensions would be found. Unfortunately, the outcomes of the cluster analyses that were performed with the 20 variables and repeated with the four factor scores were not satisfactory. In both cases, the analysis offered by the hierarchical clustering agglomeration schedule showed that the largest increase of within-cluster sum of squares is from one to two clusters. As a consequence, the quick cluster analysis resulted in one cluster representing over 95% of the counties and independent cities and other geographically scattered clusters made of one or few political subdivisions. Because of the lack of contiguity among clustered counties and cities and of the imbalance between clustered regions, the homogeneous method had to be discarded. Therefore, the analysis continued using a modified version of the tourist regions defined by the Virginia Tourism Corporation. They are Northern Virginia, Shenandoah Valley, Chesapeake Bay, Eastern Shore, Tidewater and Hampton Roads, North Central, South Central, and Blue Ridge Highlands. The regional modification consisted of dividing Central Virginia in two distinct regions, South Central and North Central. This change resulted from a visual analysis of the standardized scores of tourist attraction dimensions. These scores revealed substantial differences between the southern and northern counties and independent cities. This most likely occurred because of the large size of the central region, which is composed of 33 counties and 11 independent cities. From a research standpoint, it is vital to identify major attraction differences within a region when comparing that region to others. A high degree of attraction heterogeneity within the same region may indicate a poorly defined region. As a result, tourists might be unable to evaluate and compare the attractiveness of a region made of substantially diverse subareas.

11.3.4 STANDARDIZED SCORES

Factor scores resulting from the factor analysis were computed for each unit of measurement—counties and independent cities—and assigned to the appropriate tourist region. The standardized scores that were assigned to each political subdivision are the indicators measuring each county and independent city's ability to provide the four attraction dimensions. Therefore, the supply evaluation of attractiveness in each one of the eight tourist regions of Virginia is measured by the sum of the standardized scores of each county and independent city. From a visual analysis of the standardized scores, the independent cities are richer in tourism services and facilities than counties.

Likewise, counties offer more outdoor recreation attractions as well as rural lodging accommodations than independent cities. Cultural and historical attractions are more easily found in urban rather than rural settings. Regions characterized by densely populated areas, such as Northern Virginia and Tidewater and Hampton Roads, scored very high in terms of tourism services and facilities whereas all the other regions received negative scores.

11.3.5 TOTAL SUPPLY ATTRACTIVENESS

The final supply attractiveness score is obtained by multiplying the evaluation scores of each region by the importance scores of each dimension. Table 11.1 illustrates the evaluation scores by tourist regions, and Table 11.2 shows the total supply attractiveness scores of the eight tourism regions. The sums of squared loadings (eigenvalues) that indicate the importance of the delineated dimensions have been translated into percentages. The weighting procedure has caused some shifts in the ranks of the eight Virginia regions. Northern Virginia increased its distance from North Central Virginia because it had very high scores in the first two attraction dimensions, which bear the highest weights. The Shenandoah Valley was the most penalized by the weighting procedure and shifted from third to fifth rank. Its negative score on tourism services and facilities was the cause of such negative change. Tidewater benefited from the weights because it had relatively high scores

TABLE 11.1 Summary of Supply Evaluation Measures of Destination Attractiveness.

	Tourist service and facilities	Cultural/ Historical	Rural loading	Outdoor recreation	Total	Rank
NVA	9.37	10.74	−3.93	0.53	16.71	1
THR	7.39	2.80	4.61	−9.19	5.61	4
CB	−3.35	−2.81	1.10	−6.10	−11.16	7
ES	−0.96	−0.56	10.82	−1.25	8.05	5
NCV	−0.09	13.86	−3.02	4.75	15.50	2
SCV	−5.66	−12.27	−6.67	−13.81	−37.78	8
SV	−4.58	1.26	1.42	8.13	6.23	3
BRH	−2.13	−13.02	−4.33	16.94	−2.54	6

Note: NVA: northern Virginia; THR: Tidewater and Hampton Road; CB: Chesapeake Bay; ES: eastern shore; NCV: northern central Virginia; SCV: south central Virginia; SV: Shenandoah Valley; BRH: Blue Ridge Highlands; TSF: tourist service and facilities; C/H: cultural/historical; RL: rural loading; OR: outdoor recreation

TABLE 11.2 Overall Supply Measure of Attractiveness.

	TSF	Evaluation c weight (41.75%)	C/H	Evaluation c weight (23.75%)	RL	Evaluation c weight (18.46%)	OR	Evaluation c weight (16.04%)	Total	Rank
NVA	9.37	3.91	10.74	2.55	-3.93	-0.72	0.53	0.08	5.82	1
THR	7.39	3.08	2.80.	0.66	4.61	0.85	-9.19	-1.47	3.12	3
CB	-3.35	-1.40	-2.81	-0.67	1.10	0.20	-6.10	-0.98	-2.58	7
ES	-0.96	-0.40	-0.56	-0.13	10.82	1.99	-1.25	-0.20	1.26	4
NCV	-0.09	-0.04	13.86	3.29	-3.02	-0.56	4.75	0.76	3.45	2
SCV	-5.66	-2.36	-12.27	-2.91	-6.67	-1.23	-13.81	-2.21	-8.71	8
SV	-4.58	-1.91	1.26	0.30	1.42	0.26	8.13	1.30	-0.05	5
BRH	-2.13	-0.88	-13.02	-3.09	-4.33	-0.79	16.94	2.72	-2.04	6

Note: NVA: northern Virginia; THR: Tidewater and Hampton Road; CB: Chesapeake Bay; ES: eastern shore; NCV: northern central Virginia; SCV: south central Virginia; SV: Shenandoah Valley; BRH: Blue Ridge Highlands; TSF: tourist service and facilities; C/H: cultural/historical; RL: rural loading; OR: outdoor recreation.

in the first three dimensions and a below average score in the dimension that resulted having the lightest weight. Eastern Shore advanced one position and the remaining regions did not modify their earlier rankings.

11.3.6 PRIMARY DATA ANALYSIS

Forty Virginia's tourism experts were used as a representative of tourist demand. All tourist regions of Virginia are represented by one or more experts, with the exception of Eastern Shore. Those experts were academicians, destination management executives, state tourism organizations and associations, marketing media, and tourism planners. Two-thirds of the experts lived in Virginia for 11 or more and had at least 6 years of experience in the tourism field.

Destination attractiveness studies are dependent on two measurement tools: importance and availability (Brayley, 1990). Measuring how important the natural dimension is in relation to the cultural dimension in a given destination is critical. However, it does not answer the question of how many natural and cultural resources are available. Likewise, being acquainted with the tourist attractions in a given area is not sufficient if there is no awareness about their importance. Therefore, both notions of importance and availability are necessary elements for measuring attractiveness. The experts were asked to define the importance of the four Virginia attractiveness dimensions and to evaluate the availability of attractions in the eight tourist regions.

11.3.7 DEMAND IMPORTANCE OF ATTRACTION DIMENSIONS

Respondents indicated the percentage of variance of tourist attractions, which were represented by tourism services, culture and history, rural lodging, and outdoor recreation attractions. An examination of the results reveals that the cultural/historical attraction dimension is the most valued and captures 38.74% of Virginia's attractiveness importance. The tourism services and facilities dimension is second in order of importance with 28.74%, whereas outdoor recreation and rural lodging are third and fourth with, respectively, 19.70% and 12.82%. A t-test was performed to determine whether significant statistical differences existed between the attractiveness importance ratings of those experts who have spent fewer and those who have spent more than 10 years in Virginia. There was no statistical difference between the two groups with the exception of "rural lodging," which revealed a significant difference at the 0.05 level. A possible explanation for this is that newer residents tend to explore the surrounding environment more often than long standing residents. The test was repeated to identify possible differences between the most experienced and the least experienced experts. The *t*-tests indicated that there are no differences between those who have worked in the tourism industry for fewer than 10 years and those who have worked for more than that time. Both *t*-tests demonstrate that, overall, there are no differences between experts based on the years spent in Virginia and years worked in the tourism industry. This analysis suggests that despite differences in length of residence and experience in the tourism field the group of experts was consistent overall in evaluating the importance of the four attraction dimensions.

11.3.8 DEMAND EVALUATION OF TOURIST REGIONS

When asked to rate the availability of attraction dimensions in the eight tourist regions of Virginia, the experts were provided with a map which identified counties and independent cities in relation to the tourist regions. To relate the demand attractiveness evaluations to the corresponding supply attractiveness evaluations, the mean scores resulting from the responses of the 40 experts were translated into standardized scores. Table 11.3 illustrates the changes in regional scores based on attraction dimensions.

11.3.9 TOTAL DEMAND ATTRACTIVENESS

In comparison of the changes which occurred from the supply evaluation scores to the supply weighted evaluation scores, the effect of the weights on the demand evaluations had a relatively modest impact on the regional scores and no impact on the final rankings. Table 11.4 reports the weighted demand measures of attractiveness by tourist regions and their relative ranking. The last step in measuring tourist attractiveness involved the sum of supply and demand measurements. Table 11.5 shows the overall supply and demand scores of attractiveness by Virginia tourist regions. A visual analysis of the table reveals that the range of supply scores is significantly broader than that of demand scores. In fact, the lowest standardized supply score is −8.71 and the highest is 5.82. By contrast, the lowest demand score is −0.77 and the highest is 0.82. This difference was generated by the regional variations in availability of tourist attractions. For example, the differences were

TABLE 11.3 Demand Evaluation Mean Transformation of Attraction Destinations by Region.

	Tourist services and facilities (TSF)	z-Scores of TSF	Cultural/Historical (C/H)	z-Scores of CH	Rural lodging (RL)	z-Scores of RL	Outdoor recreation (OR)	z-Scores of OR
NVA	6.40	1.73	5.75	1.41	2.83	-1.85	3.20	-1.53
THR	5.80	1.20	5.15	0.76	3.75	-0.48	4.53	-0.06
CB	4.13	-0.25	3.78	-0.71	4.08	0.01	4.70	0.12
ES	3.60	-0.72	3.30	-1.22	4.35	0.41	4.90	0.34
NCV	4.30	-0.10	5.00	0.60	4.05	-0.03	4.05	-.059
SCV	3.38	-0.91	3.75	-0.74	3.80	-0.41	3.78	-0.89
SV	4.55	0.11	5.20	0.82	5.10	1.53	5.85	1.39
BRH	3.20	-1.06	3.58	-0.92	4.63	0.83	5.68	1.20

Note: NVA: northern Virginia; THR: Tidewater and Hampton Road; CB: Chesapeake Bay; ES: eastern shore; NCV: northern central Virginia; SCV: south central Virginia; SV: Shenandoah Valley; BRH: Blue Ridge Highlands; TSF: tourist service and facilities; C/H: cultural/historical; RL: rural loading; OR: outdoor recreation.

very large in retail sales or hotel rooms from some northern Virginia counties and independent cities and other south central political subdivisions. Again by comparison, the demand standardized scores were contained because the regional availability was measured on a Likert-type scale ranging from 1 to 7. Despite those discrepancies, which will be adjusted later in this section, it is important to compare and analyze the differences in direction of regional evaluations of supply and demand. A rank-order correlation test was performed to identify whether a significant direct association between the overall demand and supply measure of tourist attractiveness exists. The Spearman rank-order correlation coefficient was 0.64 and it was significant at the 0.08 level. This finding denotes a relatively strong association between the demand and supply measures of destination attractiveness. The scores of Northern Virginia, Tidewater, and North Central Virginia were positive from both perspectives. However, while the first two regions received strong positive scores from both perspectives, the last received a sound supply score and a slightly above average demand score. This difference suggests that the North Central region has more to offer than what is actually perceived by demand. This region, therefore, has potential for further development.

Concordant negative scores were found in relation to the following regions: Chesapeake Bay, South Central, and Blue Ridge Highlands. Both supply data and demand evaluations were consistent in considering those regions less attractive overall compared to the average. These findings do not imply that the aforementioned regions are not attractive: instead they suggest that the attraction offer may be limited to one or two attraction dimensions. Blue Ridge Highlands, for example, obtained very high outdoor recreation evaluations, and the Chesapeake Bay obtained above average outdoor recreation and rural lodging scores. Two regions had scores with different directions, Shenandoah Valley and Eastern Shore. The change in direction of the first region was mostly caused by the negative supply score of tourism services and facilities. Demand evaluation of the same dimension was neutral whereas all the other dimensions received similar scores by demand and supply. One of the possible reasons for such a difference is the presence of interstate U.S. 81, which allows the traveler to notice a concentration of available services and facilities just outside the highway. The Shenandoah Valley is also made of other regions that are more isolated and less equipped with tourism services and facilities. By the same token, perhaps the most isolated region of the state, the Eastern Shore, has obtained the opposite results with a positive supply score and a negative demand evaluation. This region is made up of only two counties and is home to approximately 50,000 residents. Because of the very limited area covered by this peninsular region and because of its unique flora and fauna, it is particularly rich in rural lodging facilities, especially campgrounds. The availability of campgrounds, B&Bs, cottages and cabins in the Eastern Shore region has compensated for the deficiency of other attractions, resulting in a positive supply score. Demand is probably unaware of that availability and assigned slightly above average evaluations to outdoor recreation and rural lodging. This did not compensate for the negative evaluations of the other two dimensions.

The measurement of the overall attractiveness implies adding the supply and demand scores. However, adding the two scores as they are presented in Table 11.5 would result in assigning an excessive weight to the supply measures and a negligible weight to the demand measures. Evidently, the measurement required further refinement because the two groups of scores were not fully comparable. Therefore, the demand scores would have had little impact in the overall measurement of attractiveness. In order to solve this measurement problem, two score transformations were performed. The first involved the transformation of the lowest supply and demand scores into a zero value, thus making it a reference point. All the other scores were adjusted accordingly. For example, assigning a value of 0 to -0.77 would transform the next lowest score of -0.55 into 0.22 ($0.77 - 0.55 = 0.22$). The second step was to transform the new scale into a percentage scale. As a consequence, the highest numbers in the new scales (14.53 for supply and 1.33 for demand) were assigned 100 and the lowest numbers maintained a 0 score. Table 11.6 shows the two steps used to balance the score magnitude of supply and demand scores.

The final measure of destination attractiveness as a result of the supply and demand attraction measures is shown in Table 11.6. Northern Virginia ranked first because of its high scores in the two most important dimensions, which are tourism services and facilities and cultural/historical. Tidewater performed well above average in the first two dimensions and had a positive supply evaluation of the rural lodging dimension. This region appears to be one of the most complete in terms of tourist attractions. It offers the history of Williamsburg, well developed shores, and the services and facilities of the most densely populated independent cities of the entire state. The Shenandoah region, which ranked third, possesses most of the attractions, especially outdoor recreation, cultural/historical and rural lodging. The regions that ranked from fourth to the seventh share one characteristic: they have more available attractions than what is perceived by demand. The fourth most attractive region was North Central Virginia, which is the richest in terms of cultural/historical attractions. Eastern Shore and Blue Ridge Highlands ranked fifth and sixth, respectively, despite their above-average

TABLE 11.4 Overall Demand Measure of Attractiveness.

	TSF	Evaluation c weight (28.74%)	C/H	Evaluation c weight (38.74%)	RL	Evaluation c weight (12.82%)	OR	Evaluation c weight (19.70%)	Total	Rank
NVA	1.73	1.41	1.41	0.55	-1.85	-1.53	-1.53	-0.30	0.51	3
THR	1.20	0.76	0.76	0.29	-0.48	-0.06	-0.06	-0.01	0.56	2
CB	-0.25	-0.07	-0.71	-0.27	0.01	0.00	0.12	0.02	-0.32	6
ES	-0.72	-0.21	-1.22	-0.47	0.41	0.05	0.34	0.07	-0.55	7
NCV	-0.10	-0.03	0.60	0.23	-0.03	0.00	-0.59	-0.12	0.08	4
SCV	-0.91	-0.26	-0.74	-0.29	-0.41	-0.05	-0.89	-0.17	-0.77	8
SV	0.11	0.03	0.82	0.32	1.53	0.20	1.39	0.27	0.82	1
BRH	-1.06	-0.30	-0.92	-0.36	0.83	0.11	1.20	0.24	-0.31	5

Note: NVA: northern Virginia; THR: Tidewater and Hampton Road; CB: Chesapeake Bay; ES: eastern shore; NCV: northern central Virginia; SCV: south central Virginia; SV: Shenandoah Valley; BRH: Blue Ridge Highlands; TSF: tourist service and facilities; C/H: cultural/historical; RL: rural loading; OR: outdoor recreation.

TABLE 11.5 Score Transformation to Compare the Overall Measure of Attractiveness.

	Supply			Demand		
	Standard scores	Lowest score = 0 transformation	%	Standard scores	Lowest score = 0 transformation	%
Northern Virginia	5.82	14.53	100	0.51	1.28	80.50
Tidewater and Hampton Road	3.12	11.83	81.41	0.56	1.33	83.64
Chesapeake Bay	−2.85	5.86	40.33	−0.32	0.45	28.30
Eastern Shore	1.26	9.97	68.62	−0.55	0.22	13.84
Northern Central Virginia	3.45	12.16	83.69	0.08	0.85	53.46
South Central Virginia	−8.71	0	0	−0.77	0	0
Shenandoah Valley	−0.05	8.66	59.60	0.82	1.59	100
Blue Ridge Highlands	−2.04	6.67	45.90	−0.31	0.46	28.93

availability of rural lodging and outdoor recreation attractions. Chesapeake Bay obtained positive rural lodging scores and because of the poor availability of other attractions ranked seventh. South Central Virginia concluded last. The final scores illustrated in Table 11.6 were calculated to compare and add the supply and demand dimensions of attractiveness. Therefore, 100 and 0 should not be interpreted as representing destinations having all the possible attractions or no attractions at all. Instead they are the maximum and minimum relative scores assigned for evaluation purposes only.

TABLE 11.6   Overall Measure of Destination Attractiveness.

	Supply	Demand	Total attractiveness	Final rank
Northern Virginia	100	80.50	180.50	1
Tidewater and Hampton Road	81.41	83.64	164.81	2
Chesapeake Bay	40.33	28.30	68.63	7
Eastern Shore	68.62	13.84	81.97	5
Northern Central Virginia	83.69	53.46	137.15	4
South Central Virginia	0	0	0	8
Shenandoah Valley	59.60	100	159.60	3
Blue Ridge Highlands	45.90	28.93	74.83	6

11.4   CONCLUSION

The present study proposed a tourist destination attractiveness model that builds on previous investigations by using new theoretical and analytical models. This process includes the use of established analytical tools and new weighting schemes to identify tourism attraction dimensions, determine tourism regions, and simultaneously measure and compare attractiveness from both a demand and supply perspective (Appendix A).

First, it allows for an objective comparison of supply and demand measures of attractiveness. The possibility of obtaining scores from two different perspectives offers an opportunity to investigate the interplay between demand and supply in determining the overall tourist attractiveness of multiple regions. The availability of supply and demand measures of attractiveness and the possibility of analyzing them simultaneously have many potential applications. For example, in exploring only the supply or demand evaluations of destination attractiveness, Northern Virginia performed well in terms of tourism services and facilities but was weak when outdoor recreation and rural lodging were evaluated. By comparison, the Blue Ridge

Highlands region received a poor evaluation in terms of tourism services and facilities, cultural/historical, and rural lodging but earned a high outdoor recreation score.

The differences in evaluations and weights that emerged between demand and supply suggest that gaps exist between the objective and subjective measurement of attractiveness. Shenandoah Valley, for example, ranked first in overall demand scores and fifth in overall supply scores. Among the possible explanations for this is Interstate U.S. 81, which runs throughout the entire state of Virginia but is mostly located in the Shenandoah area. The more exposed and accessible the destination, the more likely that demand will be attracted by it (Nyberg, 1995). In addition, the Shenandoah area extends from Roanoke to Winchester and thus may be perceived as offering a wider variety of activities and attractions than smaller regions.

There are substantial managerial implications of this study. For example, the Shenandoah Valley region is a good case in point. This region ranked first based on demand attractiveness measured and fifth based on supply measures. Neither one of the two approaches, considered separately, would be usable for tourism planning or marketing purposes. The major difference between supply and demand focuses on the tourism services and facilities dimension. Demand representatives thought that the region had an average availability of tourism services and facilities whereas supply measures were notably below average. The other three dimensions obtained positive scores from both supply and demand perspectives; however, the demand scores were higher than those of supply. It appears that Shenandoah Valley was seen as a leading tourism region in Virginia but it may not deliver what it promises. Therefore, the task of planners should be geared toward the creation and/or improvement of all four dimensions to ensure that demand perceptions are matched by supply. Shenandoah destination marketers have a competitive advantage because demand is significantly influenced by what the region has to offer. However, because the region is perceived as having more attractions than what the supply analysis indicates, the region might be unable to provide what is expected.

By contrast, all the counties that received higher supply scores than demand scores, such as North Central Virginia, Eastern Shore, Blue Ridge Highlands, and Chesapeake Bay, have untapped potential. This is particularly true for those regions that received high availability of attractions included in dimensions that are deemed as the most important, such as "Cultural/Historical" and "Tourism Services and Facilities." For example, North Central Virginia is abundant in cultural/historical attractions but demand does not perceive this. In this case, the role of destination marketers is critical in creating awareness of those attractions to the potential travelers. Likewise, Blue Ridge Highlands led the "Outdoor Recreation" dimension but was not identified as such by demand. In this case, however, marketers need to consult with planners to create opportunities for overnight stays as well as strengthen the "Tourism Services and Facilities" dimension and the "Rural Lodging" dimension. Eastern Shore offers a unique view of a supply–demand attractiveness discrepancy. Demand scores revealed that the rural lodging and the outdoor recreation dimensions were slightly above average. Supply has only one positive dimension, rural lodging, but its weight positively influenced the overall attractiveness score of this region. On one hand, Eastern Shore is in a precarious position because it has much availability of rural lodging facilities, which are not being perceived by demand representatives as very important. This might result in low occupancy rates of those facilities and eventually to their divestment. On the other hand, this region can build upon the positive perception of outdoor recreation resources to attract more "See and Do" travelers and fill the rural lodging facilities.

It is apparent that Virginia, as a tourist destination, is comprised of eight diverse regions that possess a unique blend of attractions. It was noted that even the regions that have a lower level of general attractiveness are rich in one or more attraction dimensions. State tourism organizations need to identify the unique attractiveness components of each region and refrain from considering all of the regions as a single product. It is also necessary to calculate the degree of appeal of attraction dimensions among different market segments. Finally, tourism marketing efforts should be directed toward each segment by emphasizing the most appealing attraction dimension(s).

In conclusion, the research findings enable tourist regions to design and develop more effective planning, development, and marketing programs by using an integrative or systems approach. By applying this approach, tourism regions will be able to maximize the potential of their attractions and optimize the effectiveness of their resource allocation.

This study furthers the body of knowledge on destination attractiveness measurement; however, it is not without its limitations. The first limitation is the use of the 20 attraction variables. They have been recognized by literature as important attractiveness indicators, but they might not be comprehensive. Because the observations were the counties and independent cities in Virginia, they could not be increased to accommodate more attraction variables. However, it is acknowledged that the four attraction dimensions explained a little over 66% of the attraction variance. Second, the geographic representation of judges was not evenly distributed among tourist regions. Some regions were represented by one respondent and others by four. It is possible that the uneven geographical distribution of respondents might have influenced the demand findings. Third, the use of actual tourist regions requires a thorough knowledge of every single one of those regions. Although tourism experts are generally more knowledgeable of actual or potential visitors, some of them might have had some difficulty in articulating the perceived differences and similarities among regions. To avoid this problem, Brayley (1990) used destination types instead of actual regions. In this study, the use of destination types would have defeated the purpose and objectives of the investigation. Fourth, the substantial differences that emerged among regions based on the delineated attraction dimensions can be affected by the exceptional availability of one or more attraction types. For example, the presence of an extremely high number of campsites in the Eastern Shore region has significantly increased its "Rural Lodging" availability score. Therefore, the ample presence of major campgrounds in that region has resulted in a better overall attractiveness score. While outliers cannot be eliminated from destination attractiveness studies, a sensitivity analysis might help to capture, evaluate, and explain unusual cases and circumstances. Fifth, the sums of squared loadings were first used as an objective weighting method to measure destination attractiveness. However, the applicability of this experimental method has yet to be proven and needs further substantiation.

In summary, despite the above limitations, the results of this study expand the current knowledge on destination attractiveness measurement and supply demand interaction. This study is experimental in nature and additional research is needed to measure destination attractiveness to assess the interrelationship between demand and supply measures. Future research should test the attractiveness model presented here in other destinations, states, and/or countries. A different setting will require different attraction variables and it is likely that additional dimensions will be identified. However, the connection between demand and supply indicators can be always tested using the model offered in this study, regardless of the setting. The number of variables representing destination attractiveness that were included in this study was limited. Other variables should be considered in future destination attractiveness studies, among which are theme and natural parks, rivers and lakes, beaches, and weather variables. It is likely that the increased number of variables will generate additional attraction dimensions which, in turn, will explain a greater amount of attractiveness variance. Additional studies are needed to determine how appropriate and accurate it is to use the opinions of tourism experts as substitutes for tourists (Liu, 1988). It is recommended that a comparison be made of experts' regional evaluations and dimension weights to those of actual and/or potential visitors to verify their degree of accuracy and representation.

ACKNOWLEDGEMENT

This work was originally published in *Journal of Travel Research* in 2006, vol. 44, pp 418–430. With the Publisher's permission dated November 11, 2013, this work as Chapter 11 with some additions and minor changes is reprinted in the book.

KEYWORDS

- **destination attractiveness**
- **demand and supply evaluation measurement**

REFERENCES

Backman, S.; Uysal, M.; Backman, K. Regional Analysis of Tourism Resources. *Ann. Tourism Res.* **1991,** *8*(1), 323–327.

Brayley, R. E. An Analysis of Destination Attractiveness and the Use of Psychographics and Demographics in Segmentation of the Within-State Tourism Market." *Unpublished PhD Dissertation.* Texas A&M University: College Station, TX, 1990.

Cha, S.; Uysal, M. Regional Analysis of Tourism Resources: A Case Study of Korea. *J. Hospitality Leisure Mark.* **1994,** *2*(3), 61–74.

Cracolici, M. F.; Nijkamp, P. The Attractiveness and Competitiveness of Tourist Destinations: A Study of Southern Italian Regions. *Tourism Manage.* **2008,** *30*, 336–344.

Crompton, J. Motivations for Pleasure Vacation. *Ann. Tourism Res.* **1979,** *6*(4), 408–424.

Crouch, I. G.; Ritchie, B. J. R. Destination Competitiveness and Its Implications for Host-Community QOL. In *Handbook of Tourism and Quality-of-Life Research: Enhancing the Lives of Tourists and Residents of Host Communities*; Uysal, M., Perdue, R., Sirgy, M. J. Eds.; Springer: Dordrecht, Netherlands, 2012; pp 491–514.

Dann, M. S. D. Tourism Motivation: An Appraisal. *Ann. Tourism Res.* **1981,** *8*(2), 187–219.

Dale, F. Consumer Perceptions of Tourist Attractions. *J. Travel Res.* **1990,** *28*(4), 3–10.

Deng, J.; King, B.; Bauer, T. Evaluating Natural Attractions for Tourism. *Ann. Tourism Res.* **2002,** *29*(2), 438–2002.

Enright, M. J.; Newton, J. Tourism Destination Competitiveness: A Quantitative Approach. *Tourism Manage.* **2004,** *25*, 777–788.

Ferrario, F. The Evaluation of Tourist Resources: An Applied Methodology. *J. Travel Res.* **1979,** *17* (3), 18–22 and *17*(4), 24–30.

Fesenmaier, D.; Uysal, M. The Tourism System: Levels of Economic and Human Behavior. In *Tourism and Leisure: Dynamics and Diversity*; Zeiger, J. B., Caneday, L. M., Eds.; National Recreation and Park Association: Alexandria, VA, 1990, pp 27–35.

Fishbein, M. An Investigation of the Relationship Between the Beliefs About an Object and Attitude Towards That Object. *Hum. Relat.* **1963,** *16*(2), 232–240.

Gearing, C. E.; Swart, W.; Var, T. Establishing a Measure of Touristic Attractiveness. *J. Travel Res.* **1974,** *12,* 1–8.

Gunn, C. A. *Tourism Planning* (second ed.), Taylor & Francis: New York, 1988.

Gunn, C. A. *Tourism Planning* (third ed.), Taylor & Francis: London, 1994.

Hu, Y.; Ritchie, B. Measuring Destination Attractiveness: A Contextual Approach. *J. Travel Res.* **1993,** *fall,* 25–34.

Iatu, C.; Bulai, M. New Approach in Evaluating Tourism Attractiveness in the Region of Moldavia. *Int. J. Energy Environ.* **2011,** *2*(5), 165–174.

Jafari, J. The Tourism Market Basket of Goods and Services: The Components and Nature of Tourism. In *Studies in Tourism Wildlife Parks Conservation*; Singh, T. V., Kaur, J., Singh, D. P., Eds.; Metropolitan Book Company: New Delphi, 1982; pp 1–12.

Kaur, J. Methodological Approach to Scenic Resource Assessment. *Tourism Recreation Res.* **1981,** *6*(1), 19–22.

Leiper, N. The Model of Tourism. Towards a Definition of Tourism, Tourist, and the Tourist Industry. *Ann. Tourism Res.* **1979,** *6*(4), 390–407.

Leiper, N. Tourist Attraction Systems. *Ann. Tourism Res.* **1990,** *17*(3), 379–381.

Lee, C.-F.; Huang, H. The Attractiveness of Taiwan as a Bicycle Tourism Destination: A Supply-Side Approach. *J. Asia Pac. Tourism Assoc.* **2012,** DOI: 10.1080/10941665.2012.739190.

Lew A. Guidebook Singapore: The Spatial Organization of Urban Tourist Attractions. *Unpublished PhD Dissertation*, Department of Geography, University of Oregon, 1986.

Lew, A. A Model of Tourist Attraction Research. *Ann. Tourism Res.* **1987,** *14,* 553–575.

Liu, J. C. Touristic Attractiveness of Hawaii by County. *Occasional paper, Tourism Research Publications* No. 10, University of Hawaii at Manoa, 1988.

Lovingood, P. E.; Mitchell, L. A Regional Analysis of South Carolina Tourism. *Ann. Tourism Res.* **1989,** *16*(3), 301–317.

Lundgren, A. Micro-Simulation Modelling of Domestic Tourism Travel Patterns in Sweden. *The Seventh International Forum on Tourism Statistics,* Stockholm, Sweden, June 9–11, 2004.

Mayo, E. J.; Jarvis, L. P. *Psychology Leisure Travel.* CBI Publishing Co.: Boston, MA, 1981, 191–223.

Mill, R. C.; Morrison, A. M. *The Tourism System: An Introductory Text.* Prentice-Hall, Inc.: Englewood Cliffs, NJ, 1985.

Nyberg, L. Determinants of the Attractiveness of a Tourism Region. In *Tourism Marketing and Management Handbook*; Witt, S. F., Moutinho, L. Eds.; Prentice Hall: Hertfordshire, 1995, pp 29–38.

Pearce, D. G. *Frameworks for Tourism Research.* CABI: U.K, 2012.

Pearce, D. G. Toward Geography of Tourism. *Ann. Tourism Res.* **1987,** *6*(3), 245–272.

Pike, S. Destination Image Analysis—A Review of 142 Papers from 1973 to 200. *Tourism Manage.* **2002,** *23,* 541–549.

Piperoglou, J. Identification and Definition of Regions in Greek Tourist Planning, *Pap. Regional Sci. Assoc.* **1966,** *18,* 169–176.

Plog, S. Why Destination Areas Rise and Fall in Popularity: An Update of a Cornell Quarterly Classic. *Cornell H. R. A. Q.* **2001,** *42*(3), 13–24.

Pyo, S.; Uysal, M.; McLellan, R. A Linear Expenditure Model for Tourism Demand. *Ann. Tourism Res.* **1991,** *18*(3), 443–454.

Ritchie, B. J. R.; Zins M. Culture as a Determinant of the Attractiveness of a Tourist Region. *Ann. Tourism Res.* **1978,** *5*(2), 252–267.

Rugg, D. The Choice of Journey Destinations: A Theoretical and Empirical Analysis. *Rev. Econ. Stat.* **1973,** *55*(1), 64–72.

Smith, L. J. S. *Recreation Geography.* Longman, 1983.

Smith, L. J. S. Regional Analysis of Tourism Resources. *Ann. Tourism Res.* **1987,** *14*(2), 254–273.

Smith, L. J. S. *Tourism Analysis: A Handbook* (second ed.). Longman: Harlow, 1995.

Spotts, D. M. Regional Analysis of Tourism Resources for Marketing Purposes. *J. Travel Res.* **1997,** *35*(3), 3–15.

Tang, J. C.; Rochananond, N. Attractiveness as Tourist Destination: A Comparative Study of Thailand and Selected Countries. *Socio-Econ. Plann. Sci.* **1990,** 24 (3), 229–236.

Uysal, M. The Determinants of Tourism Demand: A Theoretical Perspective. In *The Economic Geography of the Tourist Industry*; Ioannides, D., Debbage, K. G., Eds.; Routledge: London, 1998; pp 79–98.

Uysal, M.; Li, X.; Sirakaya-Turk, E. Push–Pull Dynamics in Travel Decisions. *Handbook of Hospitality Marketing Management*; Routledge–Taylor & Francis Group: New York, NY, 2008; pp 412–439.

Uysal, M.; Potts, T. An Analysis of Coastal Tourism Resources with Special Reference to Accommodations: A South Carolina Study. In *Proceedings of the 1990 Congress on Coastal and Marine Tourism*, 1990, pp 430–439.

Var, T.; Beck, R. A.; Loftus, P. Determination of Tourist Areas in British Columbia. *J. Travel Res.* **1977,** *15* (Winter), 23–29.

Yaprakli, T. S.; Rasouli, R. Investigating the Effect of Tourist Destination on Attracting Tourist: A Case Study. *Life Sci. J.* **2013,** *19*(7), 218–224.

Young, M. Cognitive Maps of Nature-Based Tourists. *Ann. Tourism Res.* **1999,** *26*(4), 817–839.

Vengresayi, S. A Conceptual Model of Tourism Destination Competitiveness and Attractiveness. In *ANZMAC 2003 Conference Proceedings*, Adelaide, December, 103, Australia, 2003; pp 637–647.

Walmsley D. J.; Jenkins J. M. Tourism Cognitive Mapping of Unfamiliar Environments. *Ann. Tourism Res.* **1992,** *19*, 268–286.

APPENDIX 11.A Steps, objectives, analyses, and results/actions established in measuring attractiveness.

Step	Objective	Analysis	Results/Action
Content analysis of tourist guides	Define the attraction variables	Text and pictorial content analysis of five Virginia guidebooks	Both text and pictorial analyses identified twenty key attraction variables
Collection of the 20 key attraction variables at the county and independent city level (135 units of observation)	Inventory of selected attractions at the county and independent city level to determine their geographic distribution within Virginia	Collection and tabulation of number of attractions located in each of the 135 counties and independent cities. Attraction variables found from different sources, such as Census data and the Virginia Tourist Corporation	Complete supply inventory of attractions at a county and independent city level
Factor analysis of selected attraction variables	Identify attraction dimensions	Principal component factor analysis	Four factors dimensions explaining 66.1% of variance: (1) Tourism Services & Facilities; (2) Cultural/Historical; (3) Rural Lodging; and (4) Outdoor Recreation (Table 11.1)
Cluster analysis	Group Virginia counties and independent cities into mutually exclusive tourist regions based on similar attraction dimensions	Hierarchical and quick cluster analysis	No clear attraction dimension clusters of contiguous counties and independent cities. A modified version of the tourist regions defined by the Virginia Tourism Corporation was adopted
Factor scores	Determine standardized scores of each county and independent city to compare and contrast the availability of attractions at the county, independent city, and regional level	The supply evaluation of attractiveness in each one of the eight tourist regions of Virginia is measured by the sum of the standardized scores of available attractions existing in each county and independent city	Cultural and historical attractions are more easily available in urban rather than rural settings. Regions characterized by densely populated regions, such as Northern Virginia and Tidewater and Hampton Roads, scored very high in terms of availability of tourism services and facilities whereas the sparsely populated regions received negative standardized scores

APPENDIX 11.A   *(Continued)*

Step	Objective	Analysis	Results/Action
Measuring the total supply attractiveness of each tourist region	Destination attractiveness studies are dependent on two measurement tools: importance and availability. The objective of this step is to operationalize these two constructs and calculate the overall attractiveness of each tourist region	From a supply side, the availability is measured by the quantity of the attractions available whereas importance is measured by the eigenvalues resulting from the factor analysis	By multiplying the availability scores of each region by the importance scores of each dimension we obtain the total supply attractiveness scores for each region (Table 11.4)
Determining the availability of demand attraction dimensions	Identify the perception of availability of attraction dimensions in the eight tourist regions	Averages of experts' opinions (measured by a Likert scale) about availability of attraction dimensions existing in the eight Virginia tourist regions	The perception of availability of attraction dimensions differs widely across the eight Virginia tourism regions
Determining the importance of demand attraction dimensions	Ascertain the importance given by demand to the four attraction dimensions	Percentage of variance attributed to the four different attraction dimensions by tourism experts	The cultural/historical attraction dimension is the most valued and captures 38.74% of Virginia's attractiveness importance. The tourism services and facilities dimension is second in order of importance with 28.74%, whereas outdoor recreation and rural lodging are third and fourth with respectively 19.70% and 12.82%
Measuring the total demand attractiveness of each tourist region	Determine total demand attractiveness based on perceived availability and perceived importance of attraction dimensions	Multiply the perceived availability of attractions in each region by the perceived importance assigned by tourism experts to each dimension	Total demand attractiveness scores for each region are different from the total supply attractiveness scores (Table 11.6)

APPENDIX 11.A *(Continued)*

Step	Objective	Analysis	Results/Action
Total attractiveness as a result of supply and demand interaction	Obtain the total measure of tourism attractiveness in each region. Also, to identify attractiveness gaps between supply and demand	Adding the total supply with demand attractiveness scores. However, the range of supply scores is significantly broader than that of demand scores. To solve the problem the lowest supply and demand scores were changed into a zero value, thus making it a reference point. All the other scores were adjusted accordingly	Results are shown in Table 11.6. Northern Virginia ranked first, followed by Tidewater, The Shenandoah, North Central Virginia, Eastern Shore, Blue Ridge Highlands, Chesapeake Bay, and South Central Virginia

CHAPTER 12

OVERBOOKING RESEARCH IN THE LODGING INDUSTRY: FROM ORIGINS IN AIRLINES TO WHAT LIES AHEAD

MATTHEW KRAWCZYK[1], TIMOTHY WEBB[2], ZVI SCHWARTZ[3] and MUZAFFER UYSAL[4]

[1]*Department of Hospitality and Tourism Management, Virginia Tech, 12600 Foxridge Lane Apt. F Blacksburg, VA 24060, USA. E-mail: mattjk@vt.edu*

[2]*Department of Hospitality and Tourism Management, Virginia Tech, 2507 Capistrano St. Blacksburg, VA 24060, USA. E-mail: Timdw89@ vt.edu*

[3]*Department of Hospitality Business Management, Alfred Lerner College of Business & Economics, University of Delaware, 14 W. Main Street, Raub Hall, Newark, DE 19716, USA. E-mail: zvi@udel.edu*

[4]*Department of Hospitality and Tourism Management, Virginia Tech, 362 Wallace Hall (0429), 295 West Campus Drive, Blacksburg, VA 24061, USA. E-mail: samil@vt.edu*

CONTENTS

12.1   INTRODUCTION

The idea of overbooking has historically been a controversial one, both in practice and in research. Originally considered an issue of capacity management in the airline industry, the application of overbooking to the lodging industry has sparked numerous debates as to the legality of its use. In general, concerns arise from a hotel being unable to uphold their part of a reservation, leading to the necessity of the guest being transported to and booked at another property, to say nothing of the potential ill-will and loss of future business that can result (Rothstein, 1974; Williams, 1977). However, empirical studies and reports from major hotels have supported overbooking's role as a tool by which to control potential revenue loss and solidified it as a major component in our understanding of revenue management. Weatherford (1995) mentions the possibility of a gain of $200 million annually for Marriott hotels, directly attributed to overbooking and rate controls. Vinod's (2004) less conservative model of revenue management techniques attributes 20% of the potential total revenue from the rooms department to overbooking practices (Vinod, 2004). Other models featured in earlier academic articles also show other examples of financial positives resulting from proper use of overbooking (e.g., Jain & Bowman, 2005; Lambert, Lambert, & Cullen, 1989).

This potential benefit is subject to the utilization and understanding of overbooking models and how they can be applied to a firm. The earliest models presented in academia were unwieldy for practitioners and would have required decision makers at individual hotels to have a thorough understanding of decision science for proper implementation. As time went on, technological upgrades allowed for models to be built into a revenue management system; changing the requirements of hotel management involvement to an input assessment role. Despite these advances, one fact remains the same: managerial judgment and comprehension is essential to properly calculate a booking policy regardless of the sophistication of a revenue management system. Recent innovations in software have of course made this process much simpler; however, human experience and knowledge of both internal and external factors is required in order to optimize revenue and limit guest dissatisfaction—criteria which is acknowledged throughout the history of overbooking academic studies. As such, this chapter aims to examine the growth of overbooking models by presenting the development of overbooking and related models in the lodging industry, taking a closer look at how some of the more influential models were formed and presented, report on some of the ways hotels manage overbooking in the present day and finally posit as to the direction of overbooking in the future. Table 12.1 offers a selected look at the progression of paradigms in lodging overbooking literature, while representing the research from inception to present day. While the studies presented in this chapter are not an exhaustive list of overbooking research, they represent the most influential works in the area of lodging overbooking.

12.2 ORIGINS OF RESEARCH CONCERNING OVERBOOKING IN HOTELS

Instituted at first in the airline industry, overbooking allows an airline to control for last minute cancellations and no-shows by booking seats in excess of the actual capacity of the airplane. This concept was carried into the lodging industry, in which the booking units represented by seats are replaced by rooms. Regardless of the type of unit being sold, the controversy of the practice remains the same: While attempting to ensure a maximum amount of revenue per time period (one flight or one room night), there is of course the distinct possibility of a customer being denied service due to every unit being filled, despite the previously confirmed sale of the seat or room. The concept was recognized as far back as 1967 by the Civil Aeronautics Board as beneficial to both businesses for the security of revenue and customers for the access to otherwise empty seats, however only when "carefully controlled" (Rothstein, 1971). It has since expanded into a necessary method used by the service industry when applicable, and recognized as crucial to optimizing revenue opportunities.

Academic studies conducted in the airline industry served to lay groundwork in mathematical modeling, as well as identifying the factors which constituted complications in booking policy. Models such as the ones presented in Beckmann (1958) and Kosten (1960) were the first to recognize the need for balancing the costs of denied service against the increased revenue (Beckmann, 1958; Kosten, 1960). Rothstein's study in 1971 also recognized the importance of time as a factor in the determination of booking policy, in that a decision regarding the probabilities of cancellations, no-shows, etc. must be able to be made at any given point in time prior to the actual service (Rothstein, 1971). This was expanded into the lodging industry by a subsequent and influential work by Rothstein in 1974. The presented model utilized dynamic programming, defining each state as the amount of reservations realized at that point of time. Each stage of the system represented the number of days leading up to the date of interest for setting booking policy.

TABLE 12.1 Selected Studies on Overbooking in General.

Article	Authors	Sample & method	Contribution to existing literature
An Airline Overbooking Model. (1971)	Rothstein, Marvin	Reviews existing models to build a new model considering time	Brings time as a decision process into airline overbooking models. Utilizes dynamic programming to optimize solutions
Hotel Overbooking as a Markovian Sequential Decision Process. (1974)	Rothstein, Marvin	Small hotel data applied to existing airline models	Identified two key concepts to apply existing airline model to hotels: multiple-day stays and double occupancy of a unit
Dynamic Operating Rules for Motel Reservations. (1976)	Ladany, Shaul	Rothstein's previous model	Added multiple room rates to further apply to hotels specifically. Also considers overbooking penalty and cancellations to maximize expected revenue per day
Decision Theory and the Innkeeper: An Approach for Setting Hotel Reservation Policy. (1977)	Williams, Fred	Builds a probability model based on historical data and managerial judgment	Considers stay-overs, reservations and walk-ins as priorities in calculation of overbooking. Uses probabilities to consider overbooking costs
On the Hotel Overbooking Problem - An Inventory System with Stochastic Cancellations. (1978)	Liberman, Varda & Yechiali, Uri	Builds a model based on previous studies, using dynamic programming	Attempts to maximize profit considering cancellation penalties on the part of the hotel; while acknowledging that customers may cancel at any time with no penalty
An Inventory Depletion Overbooking Model For the Hotel Industry. (1985)	Toh, Rex S.	New type of model (not using dynamic programming); treats guests as a Bernoulli problem	Proposes a more manager-friendly model that assumes overbooking to be an inventory depletion model; balancing the benefits of booking another room versus the negative connotations of overbooking
Coping with No-shows, Late Cancellations and Oversales: American Hotels Out-do the Airlines. (1986)	Toh, Rex S.	Conceptual paper; no model or study performed	Examines the differences in airline and hotel overbooking, using similarities between the two as criteria

TABLE 12.1 (Continued)

Article	Authors	Sample & method	Contribution to existing literature
The Overbooking Question: A Simulation. (1989)	Lambert, Carolyn U., Lambert, Joseph M & Cullen, Thomas P.	Simulates hotel reservations over a month period; manipulating policies	Using a simulation, the study analyzes how different overbooking limits affect profit as well as when no walking of guests or overbooking was allowed
The Basics of Yield Management. (1989)	Kimes, Sheryl, E.	Conceptual paper; no model or study performed	Introduces the concept of Yield Management and its appropriateness to the hotel industry.
An Application of Yield Management to the Hotel Industry Considering Multiple Night Stays. (1995)	Bitran, Gabriel R. & Mondschein, Susana V.	Uses stochastic and dynamic programming to build models partly based on previous studies	Considers multiple rates based on type of customer. Compares single night to multiple night stays; uses approximation heuristics for multiple night stays in order to maximize hotel occupancy
Managing Hotel Reservations with Uncertain Arrivals. (1996)	Bitran, Gabriel R. & Gilbert, Stephen M.	Uses heuristic models to estimate booking policy	Takes into account guests' ability to not honor reservations by arriving on a different date than expected
Overbooking with Multiple Tour Operators. (1997)	Hadjinicola, George C. & Panayi, Chryso	Actual hotel data over three months is examined by a given equation	Argues that overbooking policy for resorts should be set at the hotel level, not the tour operator level; aggregating multiple operators instead of allocating separately
An Optimal, Dynamic Policy for Hotel Yield Management. (2000)	Badinelli, Ralph, D.	Builds upon earlier models, incorporating Yield Management techniques	Proposes a model using expected yield of guests in setting booking policy; adds potential gain/loss of non-room revenues to equation
Hotel Room-Inventory Management: An Overbooking Model. (2002)	Toh, Rex S. & Dekay, Frederick	Constructed computer equation derived from a simulated hotel	Considers a customer service (opportunity) cost associated with walking a guest in setting booking levels
Non-Performance Penalties in the Hotel Industry. (2004)	DeKay, F, Yates, Barbara & Toh, Rex S.	Surveyed multiple hotels on no-show penalty policies	Argues that non-performance policies are a measure to prevent lost revenue from no-shows, cancellations, etc.

TABLE 12.1 *(Continued)*

Article	Authors	Sample & method	Contribution to existing literature
Pricing and Revenue Optimization. (2005)	Phillips, Robert L.	Book using updated models reflecting latest understanding of overbooking	Presents four major types of overbooking strategies, including customer service policy and risk analysis model
The Effect of Perceived Fairness Toward Hotel Overbooking and Compensation Practices on Customer Loyalty. (2009)	Hwang, Johye & Wen, Li	Used scenario manipulation to test recovery methods on sample	Presented customer service failure recovery effects in specific context of hotel overbooking
Hotel Overbooking: The Effect of Overcompensation on Customers' Reactions to Denied Service. (2011)	Noone, Breffni M. & Lee, Chung Hun		

Note: The studies presented in this table are representative of hotel overbooking literature and does not constitute an exhaustive list. Some studies may have been omitted unintentionally.

The transitions from stage to stage were calculated by using given probabilities based on no-shows, cancelations, and demand at that point in time and are assumed from historical data and managerial judgment.

While the study utilized an innovative Markovian time series as a novel method in lodging research, its chief contribution was the recognition of two factors distinct to the lodging industry that made adaptation from airline models difficult:

(1) The increase in rate and complexity which may result from a higher number of people occupying the room (as opposed to an airline seat, which is for only one person).
(2) The possibility of multiple night stays in a hotel room does not translate into an airline ticket, which can only be compared to one room night.

The first point was addressed by using a weighted average for the room rate to bridge the gap from a single occupancy room to a double occupancy unit; however, occupancies over double were not discussed at this point. The second challenge of multiple-night stays was more profound, and not as easily overcome by use of dynamic programming; thus, the study made assumptions in its model that did not directly address this issue (Rothstein, 1974).

Ladany (1976) extended this model by focusing on the problem of multiple occupancy, but ultimately only controlled for the differences between a single or double occupancy room night (Ladany, 1976). Williams' study (1977) followed by using probability distributions to estimate early departures and walk-ins, which can then be used to assist in incorporating a cost of overbooking to find an optimal booking level (Williams, 1977). The models suggested by Williams were both easier to track and more digestible to practitioners, however suffered from many of the same pitfalls as earlier works, namely the inability to properly compensate for different length of stays and the difficulty of implementing such a mode in the face of constantly changing booking scenarios.

Liberman and Yechiali's work in 1978 took this one step further in introducing a decision process that incorporates the uncertain nature of cancellations and no-shows when calculating overbooking. This in turn drives the model to use given booking benchmarks pre-established by hotel management to determine the course of action with regards to bringing in new reservations or to hold at a given level of inventory. However, the study also makes the assumption that a hotel can cancel confirmed reservations ahead of time in order to prevent walking a guest, which in practice does not happen (Liberman & Yechiali, 1978). It should be noted that with the exception of Rothstein's study (1974) the overbooking models presented may have included input from hotel professionals, but did not acknowledge a model actively utilized in the industry or actual hotel data in their findings.

The previous studies shared a few common themes that made it difficult to transfer findings into the hands of hotel managers. First, they concerned dynamic programming: a mathematics-based process by which the larger problem of determination of booking policy was broken into smaller subsets and given specific values. When the values are considered at a specific state of the system, they can then be combined into the larger concern. As one can imagine, this type of approach requires not only the time to process such an effort, but an understanding of management science generally not possessed by lodging managers. Second, as the studies were adapted from the airline industry, they required adaptation for different concerns due to the nature of the lodging industry. Today's overbooking models can be processed with the aid of revenue management systems; at the times these articles were published, the research was still in a very early phase of development and could not be relied upon to be of immediate use to industry leaders. Lastly, the service industry was outpacing academic understanding much quicker than the limited number of scholars in this area could keep up. With Yield Management beginning in the early 1980s, a rapidly advancing level of technology and a more thorough understanding of how multiple rates could affect revenues, the lodging industry was quickly becoming more and more sophisticated in the pursuit of revenue management.

12.3   OVERBOOKING'S TRANSITION INTO YIELD MANAGEMENT

Research began to move away from the dynamic programming approach through three studies that transitioned into the future outpouring of Yield Management research. These studies also represented works that recognized the limited use methods such as dynamic programming would have for practitioners and adjusted accordingly. The first of these was produced by Toh in 1985. The model presented involved the decision to book another room or not based on weighing the potential cost attributed to walking a guest versus the marginal revenue expected to be gained (Toh, 1985).

Toh (1985) opted to forgo earlier programming and probability models in his mathematical formula for optimal booking policy:

$$\left[1-(p-z)\left(\frac{\sqrt{pq}}{x}\right)\right]X = C$$

where p is the probability of a no-show, early departure or late cancellation; q is the probability of a guest arrival or stayover; x is the number of guests with reservations; X is the authorized booking level. This variable is the unknown and would need to be calculated separately; C is the working inventory of rooms, or the room capacity minus the average number of stayovers; and z is a pre-determined customer service level.

Of note in this model is the inclusion of the "z" variable; comprised of various criteria such as the effect on front-line staff morale due to negative customer interaction resulting from walking a guest and the loss of goodwill resulting from the same. While the model requires significantly less input in determining booking policy, it still lacks concrete values for the monetary and non-monetary costs associated with walking an overbooked guest (Toh, 1985).

A subsequent study presented a simulation used to manipulate different levels of overbooking, as well as how the refusal to overbook affected revenue levels in a given time period (Lambert et al., 1989). This study proposes the use of simulation instead of forecasting methods due to the time and resources involved (which were considerably more limited at the time) as well as the ability to test budgeted values in advance of forming booking policy. Finally, Bitran and Gilbert's study in 1996 showed the unrealistic nature of the assumptions made by previous research including the idea that all reservations arrive to the hotel at the same time. Using a heuristic model, the authors acknowledge the ability of guests to not honor a reservation and in fact arrive a day early or late to the hotel (Bitran & Gilbert, 1996).

12.4   OVERBOOKING IN YIELD AND REVENUE MANAGEMENT

The concept of Yield Management was introduced as a profitable tool to the airline industry, but branched rapidly into lodging when the value of this method was understood to transfer into room nights (Kimes, 1989a,b; Relihan, 1989). At its core, yield management attempts to acquire an optimal amount of revenue by allocating the right inventory to the right market at the right price (Kimes, 1989a). Forecasts are weighed against historical purchase demand and processed according to the hotel management's wishes. In the process, potential consumers are divided into different rate classes according to potential revenue, allowing a hotel to discriminate room sales by segment (Relihan, 1989). To this effect, overbooking is utilized as a safeguard against cancellations, early departures or late arrivals and allows a hotel to have some measure of control over the associated potential loss of revenue.

Relihan's study (1989) introduces a threshold curve approach to yield management that is relatively simple in scope. Limits on consumer demand are compiled on a daily basis for a selected number of days prior to arrival. Should actual demand vary outside of these limits, prices are adjusted accordingly. The limitations of this approach are acknowledged by a later comparison of heuristic methods featured in a separate article; outlining the threshold curve's inability to adjust over time when a room night is already sold out (Baker & Collier, 1999). Relihan's (1989) study is indicative of the infancy of yield management approaches, as overbooking was not as of yet able to be integrated due to the earlier mentioned difficulties of assigning room nights with different prices over dynamic periods of time. However, a separate method was mentioned as potentially being superior: mathematical optimization using algorithms to find the optimal mix between daily rate and total revenues. Recognizing this, subsequent Yield Management studies in this time period fell back on programming as a method to attempt to solve these issues.

With reference to the multiple-night problem of applying overbooking models to the hotel industry, Bitran and Mondschien's (1995) study set out to apply a yield management model with this key consideration. Their heuristics were built upon an optimal single-night model that attempted to implement relatively easy-to-use rules by which to allow multiple room nights (Bitran & Mondschein, 1995). The initial heuristics consider a one-night stay, in which the opportunity cost of accepting an incoming room reservation is weighed against the potential of lost revenue from expected arrivals. As mentioned previously, the possibility of multiple night reservations complicates this optimization. The solution was proposed to include a one-week window, in which capacity constraints were updated after every reservation, giving an optimal solution based on longer stays. The endeavor for an optimal policy was continued in Badinelli's application of dynamic programming which incorporated hidden-market pricing to allow for a better optimization model. Of note in this study was the acknowledgement of the loss of goodwill that must be factored in as its own value when calculating the cost of walking a guest (Badinelli, 2000). This consideration of a non-monetary cost as applies to overbooking practices is a common theme in many articles and often considered separate from the understood costs of transportation and a room night at another property. The long-term effects associated with this loss of goodwill, however, are not well understood and is generally relegated to managerial judgment in calculation of total cost. The continuation of attempting to understand costs associated with the stochastic nature of hotel guests was discussed in the most recent paper to use a management-science approach to overbooking. Phumchusri and Maneesophon (2014) discussed the marginal costs associated with no-shows and the costs of walking a guest by comparing optimal solutions for hotels with one and two types of rooms. The study was limited by the uncertain scope of the costs of walking a guest as well as the assumption of prices remaining static.

Some of the most recent studies to utilize a management science approach to hotel overbooking strove to adopt revenue management policies through acknowledgment of length of stay. Lai and Ng (2005) derived booking models on the premise of the stochastic nature of arrivals and departures in hotels. While overbooking was only used as a constraint in their model, the study emphasizes the uncertainty that needs to be accounted for as a result of displacement of guests on a daily basis. Similarly, Jain and Bowman (2005) focused on length of stay as a control by which revenue managers were able to isolate rate controls, such as length of stay and overbooking. By simulating the way a hotel operates and classifying expected demand through nights of the week, guests staying for more than one-room night were predicted and optimal revenue gains were shown.

12.5 OVERBOOKING'S EFFECTS ON CUSTOMER SATISFACTION

Notable research performed more recently than the afore-mentioned studies involve customer reactions to overbooking policies. With the importance of maintaining a good relationship with customers being generally understood, the consequences of overbooking are emphasized with outcomes generally expressed by customer satisfaction and/or brand loyalty. Wirtz, Kimes, Theng, and Patterson (2003) identify customer perception as a matter of fairness with consumers treating the situation as unjust. In this context, the study outlines negative reactions to overbooking as a result of the consumer believing that the hotel could have prevented the situation from ever arising (Wirtz, Kimes, Theng, & Patterson, 2003). In the setting of the airline industry, Wangenheim and Bayon (2007) showed a decrease in long term customer loyalty as a result of customers' perceived negative fairness in overbooking transactions. Hwang and Wen (2009) adapted the concept into the hotel industry, finding a direct effect on perceived customer fairness in overbooking practices on their loyalty. Finally, Noone and Lee (2010) reported a very favorable effect on customer satisfaction when the firm offered extra compensation above and beyond what is generally accepted by the industry.

12.6   CURRENT RESEARCH IN HOTEL OVERBOOKING

A current understanding of overbooking models can be broken down into four basic categories as outlined in *Pricing and Revenue Optimization* by Phillips (2005):

(1) *Deterministic heuristic*: As shown earlier, this can be a simple but effective tool in determining booking capacity. By dividing the capacity by the historic show rate, managers are able to see a reasonable number to overbook based on past experience.

(2) *Service-level policy*: A hotel may choose to minimize the effect on customer service that denying a guest a room at the property brings about. As such, this type of booking policy sets a goal of how many guests in a given total number of guests to deny service to.

(3) *Risk-based analysis*: Considered to be the best model for revenue optimization, a risk-based analysis uses the cost of denied service to weigh against the potential in increased revenue from overbooking rooms. Also, this cost can take into account a monetary value related to physical charges of walking a guest such as paying for accommodation at another property, possible meals and amenities as compensation and an estimate for the loss of customer loyalty and satisfaction that arises from the guest being walked.

(4) *Hybrid policy*: A combination of risk-based and service-level, managers will determine overbooking levels by determining an optimal level versus the cost of denial of service, yet constrain the policy at a certain service level.

Whereas the Deterministic Heuristic relies for the most part on accurate recording of past show rates for a booking policy, the other three strategies bear further examination due to their significantly more complex nature. The service-level policy attempts to mitigate the total adverse effect that can stem from denial of service. Subscribers to this method believe that in large numbers the negative impact on customer goodwill might outweigh the need for total revenue optimization and as such, set a quote of denied guests that cannot be breached. An example of this would be a hotel setting a level of one guest in one hundred being denied lodging based on overbooking.

A service-level policy could be demonstrated as an algorithm as follows:

$$s(x) = \frac{E\left[\left(B(x) - C\right)^+\right]}{E\left[B(x)\right]}$$

in which $s(x)$ is defined as the service level of bookings, $B(x)$ is the expected number of shows for x bookings and C is capacity. This service level would then determine the percentage of bookings that are acceptable for denial of service and limit the total bookings to this number (Sulistio, Kim, & Buyya, 2008). Notably missing from the above calculation is any concept of the cost of denial of service, limiting the possibility of total revenue optimization through use of this model. A risk-based analysis addresses this need.

In order to calculate a risk-based model, hotel management must use historical no-show data to determine a percentage of no-shows they expect for the given night. Also, a denial of service cost must be considered as walking a guest will lead to considerable expense for the hotel. Using these, a hotel is able to calculate expected net revenue:

$$E\left[R|b\right] = pE\left[\min(b,d) - x\right] - DE\left[\left(\min(d,b) - x - C\right)^+\right]$$

where $E[R \mid b]$ is expected net revenue from bookings, p is price or rack rate for a room night, $\min(b,d)$ is the minimum of actual bookings or demand for bookings, x is the expected no-show rate, D is the cost for denial of service and C is capacity (Phillips, 2005). While this equation could determine an optimal booking level by finding the highest point of possible net revenue, a simple process is much more useful to management. By dividing price by the cost of denied service and comparing to the probability of no-shows being less than or equal to the number of bookings minus capacity of the hotel, an optimal booking limit is established:

$$p/D \leq G\ (b - C)$$

If p/D is greater than $G(b - C)$, b should be replaced by $b + 1$ until the booking limit is reached.

The preceding models may not represent the exact method used by hotel management in their calculation of overbooking levels, but the concept remains the same: a value for the cost for denial of service must be included in order to have a more accurate representation of the final total revenue potential. What is uncertain is the most common model by which hotels are actively calculating the daily overbooking policy, as empirical surveys have been limited to small sample sets. Rothstein's study in 1974 used a single hotel's data from a one-month period and found that the hotel used historical data based on the day of the week to determine its booking policy. Toh and Dekay (2002) used data from six hotels to form a model based on a service-level policy that corresponded with data from the properties (Toh & Dekay, 2002). A subsequent study from the same authors in 2004 surveying 20 hotels over a one-year period found that smaller properties rely on management experience to adjust overbooking levels while larger properties use computer analysis to reset overbooking levels on a frequent basis, through access to the central reservation system (DeKay, Yates, & Toh, 2004). With the exception of these studies, insights into specific models used in hotel overbooking decisions are scarce; with actual airline overbooking models being used in many cases to perform research.

12.7 CONCLUSION

As seen from the review of studies on overlooking and revenue/yield management, the notion of overbooking stemmed from airline models and found their way into lodging, through management science applications of dynamic/goal programming. The initial applications attempted to adjust for multiple occupancy and multiple night stays with limited success and were very difficult to execute. This approach was later enhanced by including more complicated constraints for late departure, no-shows, cancellations and the like; still utilizing dynamic/goal programming without solid empirical data for support. Starting in the late 1980s, literature began to become more conceptual in its orientations, focusing on algorithms and simulations, with very limited industry applications that did not address the complexity of overbooking. Although there was a shift and encouragement in focus away from classic management science techniques to yield management principles, the movement did not offer comprehensive models that would actively allow for estimation of booking scenarios. However, part of these discussions evolved into a research agenda that stressed the importance of consumer perceptions in overbooking. This may reflect the rise of more sophisticated revenue management systems that were better able to process and handle the complexity of overbooking practice.

As shown in Table 12.1, the evolution of research concerned with overbooking in the lodging industry has paralleled the increased use of technology in hotels, with management science studies becoming scarcer in recent years. This does not discount the value of management science contributions; indeed, the importance of developing optimal booking policies for implementation into revenue management systems is more relevant than ever. Future studies of revenue management should explore industry practices and implications, mainly what overbooking policies and practices are prevalent and what is their relative effectiveness. These systems are relied upon to determine overbooking levels through historical data and management constraints, correlating to the type of risk or service policy the property is employing. As such, the various aspects of how these input decisions are made represent a line of research that has been explored to a small extent.

Another crucial stream of research has begun to emerge for the concept of "Total" Revenue Management (RM). Total RM is concerned not only with the stream of revenue resulting from room sales, but also incorporates subsidiary department revenues such as hotel restaurants and conference room rentals (Kimes, 2011). For overbooking, a Total RM approach may allow overbooking decisions to take not only the traditional costs of walking a guest into account, but also the missed opportunities for spending in other areas of the property. Lastly, the increase in interest in Big Data may allow for a more informed booking policy decision based on individual customer profile. As a larger volume of hotel guests and potential customers' data is gathered in "real time", the ability for management to make profitable overbooking decisions is increased. Specifically, research should explore how the wealth of new information and data analytics methods could assist in better estimating some of the more challenging variables such future demand, no shows and cancellations, overstays etc. Even more exciting is the notion that big data analytics will move us closely to be able to assess these decision variables on individual levels rather than segments or entire hotels as is done currently.

KEYWORDS

- overbooking research
- airline industry
- lodging industry
- overbooking practices
- hotel overbooking
- future research in overbooking

REFERENCES

Badinelli, R. D. An Optimal, Dynamic Policy for Hotel Yield Management. *Eur. J. Oper. Res.* **2000,** *121*(3), 476–503.

Baker, T. K.; Collier, D. A. A Comparative Revenue Analysis of Hotel Yield Management Heuristics. *Decis. Sci.* **1999,** *30*(1), 239–263.

Beckmann, M. J. Decision and Team Problems in Airline Reservations. *Econ.: J. Econ. Soc.* **1958,** 134–145.

Bitran, G. R.; Gilbert, S. M. Managing Hotel Reservations with Uncertain Arrivals. *Oper. Res.* **1996,** *44*(1), 35–49.

Bitran, G. R.; Mondschein, S. V. An Application of Yield Management to the Hotel Industry Considering Multiple Day Stays. *Oper. Res.* **1995,** *43*(3), 427–443.

DeKay, F.; Yates, B.; Toh, R. S. Non-performance Penalties in the Hotel Industry. *Int. J. Hospitality Manage.* **2004,** *23*(3), 273–286.

Hwang, J.; Wen, L. The Effect of Perceived Fairness toward Hotel Overbooking and Compensation Practices on Customer Loyalty. *Int. J. Contemporary Hospitality Manage.* **2009,** *21*(6), 659–675.

Jain, S.; Bowman, H. B. Measuring the Gain Attributable to Revenue Management. *J. Revenue Pricing Manage.* **2005,** *4*(1), 83–94.

Kimes, S. E. The Basics of Yield Management. *Cornell Hotel Restaurant Admin. Q.* **1989a,** *30*(3), 14–19.

Kimes, S. E. Yield Management: A Tool for Capacity-Considered Service Firms. *J. Oper. Manage.* **1989b,** *8*(4), 348–363.

Kimes, S. E. The Future of Hotel Revenue Management. *J. Revenue Pricing Manage.* **2011,** *10*(1), 62–72.

Kosten, L. Een Mathematisch Model Voor Een Reserveringsprobleem. *Stat. Neerland.* **1960,** *14*(1), 85–94.

Ladany, S. P. Dynamic Operating Rules for Motel Reservations. *Decis. Sci.* **1976,** *7*(4), 829–840.

Lai, K. K.; Ng, W. L. A Stochastic Approach to Hotel Revenue Optimization. *Comput. Oper. Res.* **2005,** *32*(5), 1059–1072.

Lambert, C. U.; Lambert, J. M.; Cullen, T. P. The Overbooking Question: A Simulation. *Cornell Hotel Restaurant Admin. Q.* **1989,** *30*(2), 14–20.

Liberman, V.; Yechiali, U. On the Hotel Overbooking Problem—An Inventory System with Stochastic Cancellations. *Manage. Sci.* **1978,** *24*(11), 1117–1126.

Phumchusri, N. & Maneesophon, P. Optimal Overbooking Decision for Hotel Rooms Revenue Management. *J. Hospitality Tourism Technol.* **2014,** *5*(3), 261–277.

Noone, B. M.; Lee, C. H. Hotel Overbooking the Effect of Overcompensation on Customers' Reactions to Denied Service. *J. Hospitality Tourism Res.* **2011,** *35*(3), 334–357.

Phillips, R. Pricing and Revenue Optimization: Stanford University Press, 2005.

Relihan III, W. J. The Yield-Management Approach to Hotel-Room Pricing. *Cornell Hotel Restaurant Admin. Q.* **1989,** *30*(1), 40–45.

Rothstein, M. An Airline Overbooking Model. *Transport. Sci.* **1971,** *5*(2), 180–192.

Rothstein, M. Hotel Overbooking as a Markovian Sequential Decision Process. *Decis. Sci.* **1974,** *5*(3), 389–404.

Sulistio, A.; Kim, K. H.; Buyya, R. Managing Cancellations and No-shows of Reservations with Overbooking to Increase Resource Revenue. In *Cluster Computing and the Grid, 2008. CCGRID'08. 8th IEEE International Symposium on.* IEEE, 2008; pp 267–276.

Toh, R. S. An Inventory Depletion Overbooking Model for the Hotel Industry. *J. Travel Res.* **1985,** *23*(4), 24–30.

Toh, R. S.; Dekay, F. Hotel Room-Inventory Management: An Overbooking Model. *Cornell Hotel Restaurant Admin. Q.* **2002,** *43*(4), 79–90.

Vinod, B. Unlocking the Value of Revenue Management in the Hotel Industry. *J. Revenue Pricing Manage.* **2004,** *3*(2), 178–190.

Wangenheim, F. V.; Bayón, T. Behavioral Consequences of Overbooking Service Capacity. *J. Mark.* 2007, 36–47.

Weatherford, L. R. Length of Stay Heuristics: Do They Really Make a Difference? *Cornell Hotel Restaurant Admin. Q.* **1995,** *36*(6), 70–79.

Williams, F. E. Decision Theory and the Innkeeper: An Approach for Setting Hotel Reservation Policy. *Interfaces* **1977,** *7*(4), 18–30.

Wirtz, J.; Kimes, S. E.; Theng, J. H. P.; Patterson, P. Revenue Management: Resolving Potential Customer Conflicts. *J. Revenue Pricing Manage.* **2003,** *2*(3), 216–226.

CHAPTER 13

EVALUATING FORECASTING PERFORMANCE: ACCURACY MEASURES AND THEIR APPLICATION IN HOSPITALITY

LARISSA KOUPRIOUCHINA[1], JEAN-PIERRE VAN DER REST[2], ZVI SCHWARTZ[3], and DIRK SIERAG[4,5]

[1]Hotelschool The Hague, Hospitality Business School, Brusselselaan 2, 2587 AH, The Hague, The Netherlands. E-mail: l.koupriouchina@hotelschool.nl.

[2]Department of Business Studies, Institute of Tax Law and Economics, Leiden Law School, Steenschuur 25, 2311 ES Leiden, The Netherlands. E-mail: j.i.van.der.rest@law.leidenuniv.nl.

[3]Department of Hospitality Business Management, Alfred Lerner College of Business & Economics, University of Delaware, 14 W. Main Street, Raub Hall, Newark, DE 19716, USA. E-mail: zvi@udel.edu.

[4]Centrum Wiskunde & Informatica (CWI), Stochastics Department, Amsterdam, The Netherlands

[5]VU University Amsterdam, Faculty of Exact Sciences, Science Park 123, 1098 XG, Amsterdam, The Netherlands. E-mail: D.D.Sierag@cwi.nl.

CONTENTS

13.1   INTRODUCTION

Forecasting is a cornerstone of hotel revenue management. Its quality has direct impact on hotels' ability to generate higher revenues and profits. Failure to produce accurate forecasts can lead to applying inappropriate capacity and rate restrictions and/or to making suboptimal staffing, purchasing, and budgeting decisions (Schwartz & Hiemstra, 1997; Weatherford & Kimes, 2003). There are, however, some inherent challenges associated with the evaluation of hotel revenue management forecasts. A crucial yet often overlooked aspect is the intricate nature of the forecasting accuracy measures used to evaluate forecasting performance.

The measure of forecasting accuracy became a point of controversy in operations research especially after the M-competitions (M-1, M-2, and M-3) when commentaries were exchanged on the appropriateness of the various measures (Makridakis & Hibon, 2000). This has led to a growing awareness in the research community that forecasting accuracy measures can produce misleading results when the properties of each measure are not fully understood.

13.2   AN OVERVIEW OF FORECASTING MEASURES

Forecasting accuracy measure can be used for two distinct purposes: (1) in the phase of selecting a forecasting model to screen out a forecasting method that is not appropriate; (2) once the forecasting model is selected, forecasting accuracy measures to monitor the forecasting model's performance. The latter is the focus of this chapter.

Accuracy measures can be applied to a variety of forecasting approaches, and their calculation is independent of the underlying method used to generate the forecasts. For example, forecasts based on extrapolative methods (e.g., using time series), explanatory models, or qualitative techniques can all be assessed using the same accuracy measures. Accordingly, in the realm of hotel revenue management, subjective human (judgmental) forecasts can be compared with machine or model-based forecasts by using the same forecasting accuracy measure(s).

A common way to categorize forecast accuracy measures is based on how they relate to the scale of the corresponding time series.

Scale-dependent measures are those where the scale of the accuracy measure depends on the scale of the data. Scale-dependent measures are applicable for datasets that have the same data scales. They are often employed to evaluate forecast performance of several forecasting techniques on a single time series. When the forecasting accuracy of multiple time series needs to be estimated, these measures can produce distorted results, as the scale of the series impacts the measurement result.

Scale-independent (or Scale-free) measures are those where the scale of the accuracy measures does not depend on the scale of the data. Scale-independent measures are applicable for datasets that have different size (e.g., to compare forecasting performance of multiple hotels each with a different number of rooms). Scale-independent measures, however, do bring in their own challenges as they "may at times be infinite, not defined, extremely skewed or perceived as favoring some errors over the others" (Bodea & Ferguson, 2014, p. 13).

Several forecast accuracy measures have been proposed in the literature. Figure 13.1 provides an overview of the most common measures. In the next section, for every measure a formula is given together with a step-by-step computation example. When more than one example is provided for the same measure, this is to illustrate some intricate characteristics of the particular measure. If reported by the research literature, advantage and disadvantages have been described.

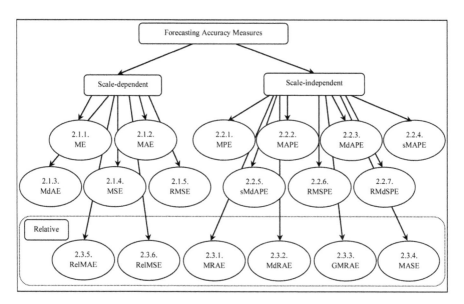

FIGURE 13.1   Overview of forecasting accuracy measures.

There are studies that have tested the performance of forecasting measures in very specific categories. Armstrong and Collopy (1992), who provided an influential study on this topic, ranked forecasting error measures using various characteristics as follows:

- **Reliability**: "Addresses the question whether repeated application of a procedure will produce similar results" (Armstrong & Collopy, 1992, p. 72).
- **Construct validity**: Addresses the questions of whether a measure measures "what it purports to measure" (Armstrong & Collopy, 1992, p. 73).
- **Outlier protection**: Addresses the degree to which a measure is affected by outliers.
- **Sensitivity**: Is the measure responsive to changes in the model's parameters?
- **Relationship to decisions**: Addresses the usefulness to decision makers.

13.2.1   SCALE-DEPENDENT FORECASTING ACCURACY MEASURES

Scale-dependent measures are calculated using various transformations of the forecasting error (e_t) Let us denote Y_t as actual value and F_t as forecast. Forecast error can be defined as $e_t = Y_t - F_t$ where $t = 1, 2, ..., n$.

13.2.1.1   MEAN ERROR

The formula for mean error (ME) is

$$ME = \frac{1}{n} \sum_{t=1}^{n} e_t.$$

(13.1)

ME is computed as illustrated in Table 13.1.

Some important considerations need to be made when interpreting ME results. In the illustration above, the negative sign might be an indication of systematic over-forecasting (i.e., F_t is higher than Y_t). Consequently, an opposite sign (positive ME) might be a systematic under-forecasting. However, while ME provides information about systematic under- or over-forecasting (called forecast bias), it does not give much information about the size of the typical errors (Makridakis, Wheelwright & Hyndman, 1998). In fact, one of the major drawbacks of ME is that positive and negative errors tend to offset one another and might lead to misleading conclusions, as is illustrated in Table 13.2.

TABLE 13.1 Computations of the Mean Error (ME).

Period	Actual	Forecast	Error
t	Y_t	F_t	$e_t = Y_t - F_t$
1	64	90	−26
2	76	101	−25
3	35	44	−9
4	33	32	1
5	29	31	−2
6	35	44	−9
7	47	102	−55
Total			−125
	ME = −125/7 = −17.86	using Equation (13.1)	

TABLE 13.2 Example of ME with Positive and Negative Errors.

Period	Actual	Forecast	Error
t	Y_t	F_t	$e_t = Y_t - F_t$
1	110	120	−10
2	100	90	10
Total			0
	ME = 0/2 = 0	using Equation (13.1)	

As we can see, an ME of zero does not necessarily imply that there are no forecasting errors. A large (positive or negative) ME might be a useful indication of forecasting bias. That is, under- or over-forecasting due to a larger number of small errors of a certain sign, or a small number of large errors of a certain sign. However, the opposite reasoning (the smaller ME, the more accurate is forecast) does not necessarily hold. Another difficulty with this measure is to establish what constitutes a "large" or a "small" error.

13.2.1.2   MEAN ABSOLUTE ERROR

The formula for mean absolute error (MAE) is

$$\text{MAE} = \text{mean}\left(\left|e_t\right|\right) = \frac{1}{n}\sum_{t=1}^{n}\left|e_t\right|.$$

$$\text{where } t = 1, \ldots, n \qquad\qquad (13.2)$$

Using the same data as for ME, MAE is as illustrated in Table 13.3.

TABLE 13.3   Computations of the Mean Absolute Error (MAE).

Period	Actual	Forecast	Error	Absolute error
t	Y_t	F_t	$e_t = Y_t - F_t$	$\left|e_t\right| = \left|Y_t - F_t\right|$
1	64	90	−26	26
2	76	101	−25	25
3	35	44	−9	9
4	33	32	1	1
5	29	31	−2	2
6	35	44	−9	9
7	47	102	−55	55
Total			−125	127
	MAE = 127/7 = 18.14		using Equation (13.2)	

By taking the absolute value of error, MAE overcomes some of the issues related to ME. For example, where positive and negative errors may offset each other in ME, MAE does not have this disadvantage, as illustrated in Table 13.4.

TABLE 13.4   Example of MAE with Positive and Negative Errors.

Period	Actual	Forecast	Error	Absolute error
t	Y_t	F_t	$e_t = Y_t - F_t$	$\left|e_t\right| = \left|Y_t - F_t\right|$
1	110	120	−10	10
2	100	90	10	10
Total			0	20
	MAE = 20/2 = 10		using Equation (13.2)	

Another advantage of MAE is that it is interpretable and easy to explain to non-specialists. However, it shares some of the general disadvantages of scale-dependent measures. For example, MAE results depend on the scale of the data and do not facilitate comparison across different time series and for different time intervals.

13.2.1.3 MEDIAN ABSOLUTE ERROR

The formula for median absolute error (MdAE) is

$$MdAE = \text{median of } |e_t|.$$

$$\text{where } t = 1, \ldots, n \tag{13.3}$$

MdAE is computed as illustrated in Table 13.5.

TABLE 13.5   Computations of the Median Absolute Error (MdAE).

Period	Actual	Forecast	Error	Absolute error
t	Y_t	F_t	$e_t = Y_t - F_t$	$|e_t| = |Y_t - F_t|$
1	64	90	−26	26
2	76	101	−25	25
3	35	44	−9	9
4	33	32	1	1
5	29	31	−2	2
6	35	44	−9	9
7	47	102	−55	55
Total			−125	127
MdAE = median of (1, 2, 9, 9, 25, 26, 55) = 9			using Equation (13.3)	

The median absolute error shows that 50% of the errors are less than MdAE. However, the measure does not give any information on the errors that are larger than MdAE, or on the tail of the error, that is, how large the error can get. The errors could be large, but MdAE does not take them into account. Therefore, MdAE is not affected by outliers.

13.2.1.4   MEAN SQUARE ERROR

The formula for mean square error (MSE) is

$$MSE = mean\left(e_t^2\right) = \frac{1}{n}\sum_{t=1}^{n} e_t^2 \;.$$

$$where\ t = 1,\ ...,\ n \tag{13.4}$$

This scale-dependent measure is computed as illustrated in Table 13.6.

TABLE 13.6   Computations of the Mean Square Error (MSE).

Period	Actual	Forecast	Error	Absolute error	Squared error
t	Y_t	F_t	$e_t = Y_t - F_t$	$\|e_t\| = \|Y_t - F_t\|$	$(Y_t - F_t)^2$
1	64	90	−26	26	676
2	76	101	−25	25	625
3	35	44	−9	9	81
4	33	32	1	1	1
5	29	31	−2	2	4
6	35	44	−9	9	81
7	47	102	−55	55	3025
Total			−125	127	4493
		MSE = 4493/7 = 641.86		using Equation (13.4)	

MSE squares each error, and, therefore, avoids the issues of ME where positive and negative errors may offset each other. Compared to MAE, it is easier to handle mathematically and is often used in statistical optimization (Makridakis et al., 1998). However, MSE cannot be easily interpreted and cannot be as easily explained to non-specialists as MAE (Makridakis, 1993). For example, what does a MSE of 641.86 mean?

MSE has been especially criticized for use in comparing forecasting methods across series, as it can be disastrous to average MSE from different series as it is scale-dependent and has poor protection to outliers (Armstrong & Collopy, 1992; Armstrong, 2001). It squares the errors and, therefore, it emphasizes the highest errors (Makridakis, 1993).

The table shown above is a modification of the table used for the first MSE computation. The sum of absolute errors in both tables is equal to 127. However, in the first case MSE = 641.86 and in the second MSE = 330.4. Does it mean that the second forecast is twice as accurate as the first?

13.2.1.5 ROOT MEAN SQUARE ERROR

The formula for root mean square error (RMSE) is

$$\text{RMSE} = \sqrt{\text{MSE}} = \sqrt{\text{mean}\left(e_t^2\right)} = \sqrt{\frac{1}{n}\sum_{t=1}^{n}e_t^2}.$$

where $t = 1, \ldots, n$ \hfill (13.5)

Using the examples of Tables 13.6 and 13.7 the computations result in

$$\text{RMSE} = \sqrt{\text{MSE}} = \sqrt{641.86} = 25.33 \quad \text{using Equation (13.5)}$$

$$\text{RMSE} = \sqrt{\text{MSE}} = \sqrt{330.4} = 18.18 \quad \text{using Equation (13.5)}$$

TABLE 13.7 Modified Example of Computations of the Mean Square Error (MSE).

Period	Actual	Forecast	Error	Absolute error	Squared error
t	Y_t	F_t	$e_t = Y_t - F_t$	$|e_t| = |Y_t - F_t|$	$(Y_t - F_t)^2$
1	64	81	−17	17	289
2	76	94	−18	18	324
3	35	16	19	19	361
4	33	50	−17	17	289
5	29	12	17	17	289
6	35	16	19	19	361
7	47	27	20	20	400
Total			23	127	2313
	MSE = 2313/7 = 330.4		using Equation (13.4)		

RMSE was historically popular due to its theoretical relevance in statistical modeling. It is often preferred to MSE as it is on the same scale as the data (Hyndman & Koehler, 2006). According to Armstrong and Collopy (1992) RMSE was rated "good" on Sensitivity and Relationship to decisions. However, it was rated "poor" on Reliability and Outlier protection (Armstrong & Collopy, 1992). The fact that RMSE is "more sensitive to outliers than MAE or MdAE has led some (e.g., Armstrong, 2001) to recommend against its use in forecast accuracy evaluation" (Hyndman & Koehler, 2006, p. 682).

13.2.2 SCALE-INDEPENDENT FORECASTING ACCURACY MEASURES

Scale-independent forecasting accuracy measures tend to remove the dependency on the measurement units of the time-series data. For the measures based on percentage errors, the percentage error (p_t) is defined as $(Y_t - F_t) / Y_t \times 100 = (100 \times e_t) / Y_t$. For measures based on relative errors, the error is divided by a benchmark error, for example obtained from another method of forecasting.

13.2.2.1 MEAN PERCENTAGE ERROR

The formula for mean percentage error (MPE) is

$$\text{MPE} = \frac{1}{n}\sum_{t=1}^{n} p_t = \frac{1}{n}\sum_{t=1}^{n} \frac{100 \times e_t}{Y_t}.$$

$$\text{where } t = 1, \ldots, n \qquad\qquad (13.6)$$

MPE is computed as illustrated in Table 13.8.

TABLE 13.8 Computations of the Mean Percentage Error (MPE).

Period	Actual	Forecast	Error	Percentage error
t	Y_t	F_t	$e_t = Y_t - F_t$	$p_t = (Y_t - F_t)/Y_t \times 100$
1	64	90	−26	−40.63
2	76	101	−25	−32.89
3	35	44	−9	−25.71
4	33	32	1	3.03
5	29	31	−2	−6.90
6	35	44	−9	−25.71
7	47	102	−55	−117.02
Total			−125	−245.84
	MPE = −245.84/7 = −35.12		using Equation (13.6)	

The disadvantage of MPE is that positive and negative percentage errors tend to offset one another (Makridakis et al., 1998). Also, difficulties arise when the time series contain zeros since the percentage error cannot be computed, which is common for other measures based on percentage error. Moreover, when the time series values are very close to zero, the computation involving percentage error can be meaningless (Makridakis et al., 1998).

13.2.2.2 MEAN ABSOLUTE PERCENTAGE ERROR

The formula for mean absolute percentage error (MAPE) is

$$\text{MAPE} = \text{mean}\left(\left|p_t\right|\right) = \frac{1}{n}\sum_{t=1}^{n}\left|p_t\right| = \frac{1}{n}\sum_{t=1}^{n}\left|\frac{100 \times e_t}{Y_t}\right|.$$

$$\text{where } t = 1, \ldots, n \tag{13.7}$$

MAPE is computed as illustrated in Table 13.9.

TABLE 13.9 Computations of the Mean Absolute Percentage Error (MAPE).

Period	Actual	Forecast	Error	Absolute percentage error
t	Y_t	F_t	$e_t = Y_t - F_t$	$\left|p_t\right| = \left|(Y_t - F_t)/Y_t \times 100\right|$
1	64	90	−26	40.63
2	76	101	−25	32.89
3	35	44	−9	25.71
4	33	32	1	3.03
5	29	31	−2	6.90
6	35	44	−9	25.71
7	47	102	−55	117.02
Total			−125	251.90
	MAPE = 251.90/7 = 35.99		using Equation (13.7)	

In the (hotel) revenue management literature, this measure is widely used. "MAPE is a relative measure that incorporates the best characteristics among the various accuracy criteria. Moreover, it is the only measure (in addition to Percent Better) that means something to decision makers who have trouble even understanding medians, not to mention geometric means" (Makridakis, 1993, p. 528). MAPE is, therefore, the most common accuracy measure used in practice. The measure is easy to communicate and useful to compare forecasts from different situations (Armstrong, 1985). Furthermore, it is rated as "good" on Construct validity and Sensitivity (Armstrong & Collopy, 1992). It is similar to MAE but is dimensionless, which makes it easier for communication purposes and comparing different forecasts. There are, however, also a number of disadvantages. First of all, there is a bias favoring estimates of forecast that are below the actual values as it places a "heavier penalty on positive errors than on negative errors" (Hyndman & Koehler, 2006, p. 683). Second, there are difficulties when the time series contain zeros, since the percentage error cannot be computed and when the time series values are very close to zero, the computation involving percentage error can result in very large numbers and can be meaningless (Makridakis et al., 1998; Hyndman & Koehler, 2006). Third, MAPEs cannot be compared directly with Naive 1 (random walk) or Naive 2 (de-seasonalized random walk) models as is the case with RAE, and, therefore, with Geometric Means and Relative Medians which summarize them. Finally, MAPE is rated "poor" on Outlier protection (Armstrong & Collopy, 1992).

13.2.2.3   MEDIAN ABSOLUTE PERCENTAGE ERROR

The Formula for median absolute percentage error (MdAPE) is

$$\text{MdAPE} = \text{median}\left(|p_t|\right) = \text{median}\left(\left|\frac{(Y_t - F_t)}{Y_t} \times 100\right|\right) = \text{median}\left(\left|\frac{100 \times e_t}{Y_t}\right|\right).$$

$$\text{where } t = 1, \ldots, n \qquad\qquad (13.8)$$

MdAPE is computed as illustrated in Table 13.10.

TABLE 13.10   Computations of the Median Absolute Percentage Error (MdAPE).

Period	Actual	Forecast	Error	Absolute percentage error
t	Y_t	F_t	$e_t = Y_t - F_t$	$\|p_t\| = \|(Y_t - F_t)/Y_t \times 100\|$
1	64	90	−26	40.63
2	76	101	−25	32.89
3	35	44	−9	25.71
4	33	32	1	3.03
5	29	31	−2	6.90
6	35	44	−9	25.71
7	47	102	−55	117.02
Total			−125	251.90

MdAPE = median of (3.03, 6.90, 25.71, 25.71, 32.89, 40.63, 117.02) = 25.71
using Equation (13.8)

As an advantage it has a closer relationship to decision making (Bunn & Taylor, 2001). Also, MdAPE is rated "good" on Construct Validity and Outlier protection (Armstrong & Collopy, 1992). According to Hyndman and Koehler (2006), a disadvantage is that MdAPE can lead to infinite values occurring due to division by zero or could result in very large numbers if divided by numbers close to zero. Also, it places a "heavier penalty on positive errors than on negative errors" (Hyndman & Koehler, 2006, p. 683). Armstrong and Collopy (1992) rate it as "poor" on Sensitivity.

13.2.2.4 SYMMETRIC MEAN ABSOLUTE PERCENTAGE ERROR

The formula for the symmetric mean absolute percentage error (sMAPE) is

$$\text{sMAPE} = \text{mean}\left(\frac{200 \times |Y_t - F_t|}{Y_t + F_t}\right) = \frac{1}{n}\sum_{t=1}^{n}\left(\frac{200 \times |Y_t - F_t|}{Y_t + F_t}\right).$$

$$\text{where } t = 1, \ldots, n \qquad\qquad (13.9)$$

sMAPE is computed as illustrated in Table 13.11.

TABLE 13.11   Computations of the Symmetric Mean Absolute Percentage Error (sMAPE).

Period	Actual	Forecast	Error	Absolute error	Symmetric absolute percentage error
t	Y_t	F_t	$e_t = Y_t - F_t$	$|e_t| = |Y_t - F_t|$	$200x|Y_t - F_t|/(Y_t + F_t)$
1	64	90	−26	26	33.77
2	76	101	−25	25	28.25
3	35	44	−9	9	22.78
4	33	32	1	1	3.08
5	29	31	−2	2	6.67
6	35	44	−9	9	22.78
7	47	102	−55	55	73.83
Total			−125	127	191.15
		sMAPE = 191.15/7 = 27.31		using Equation (13.9)	

This measure's advantage that it avoids the problem of large errors when the actual values are close to zero and the large difference between the absolute percentage errors when the actual is greater than forecast and vice versa. Moreover, it fluctuates between −200% and 200% while the non-symmetric measure does not have limits (Makridakis & Hibon, 2000). As a disadvantage "sMAPE can take negative values, although it is meant to be an 'absolute percentage error'" (Hyndman & Koehler, 2006, p. 682). Moreover, sMAPE, originally proposed by Makridakis (1993) to overcome the asymmetry of MAPE, places a heavier penalty when forecasts are low compared to when forecasts are high, and, therefore, is not as "symmetric" as the name suggests (Goodwin & Lawton, 1999; Bunn & Taylor, 2001; Koehler, 2001; Hyndman & Koehler, 2006).

13.2.2.5   SYMMETRIC MEDIAN ABSOLUTE PERCENTAGE ERROR

The formula for symmetric median absolute percentage error (sMdAPE) is

$$\text{sMdAPE} = \text{median}\left(\frac{200 \times |Y_t - F_t|}{Y_t + F_t} \right).$$

$$\text{where } t = 1, \dots, n \qquad\qquad (13.10)$$

sMdAPE is computed as illustrated in Table 13.12.

TABLE 13.12   Computations of the Symmetric Median Absolute Percentage Error (sMdAPE).

Period	Actual	Forecast	Error	Absolute error	Symmetric absolute percentage error
t	Y_t	F_t	$e_t = Y_t - F_t$	$|e_t| = |Y_t - F_t|$	$200x|Y_t - F_t|/(Y_t + F_t)$
1	64	90	−26	26	33.77
2	76	101	−25	25	28.25
3	35	44	−9	9	22.78
4	33	32	1	1	3.08
5	29	31	−2	2	6.67
6	35	44	−9	9	22.78
7	47	102	−55	55	73.83
Total			−125	127	191.15

sMdAPE = Median of (3.08, 6.67, 22.78, 22.78, 28.25, 33.77, 73.83) = 22.78
using Equation (13.10)

sMdAPE's advantage is that is not influenced by extreme values and is more robust than the average absolute percentage error (Makridakis & Hibon, 2000). However, it can lead to infinite values occurring due to division by zero or could result in very large numbers if divided by numbers close to zero (Hyndman & Koehler, 2006). Similarly to sMAPE, it is not as "symmetric" as the name suggests.

13.2.2.6 ROOT MEAN SQUARE PERCENTAGE ERROR

The formula for root mean square percentage error (RMSPE) is

$$\text{RMSPE} = \sqrt{\text{mean}\left(p_t^2\right)} = \sqrt{\frac{1}{n}\sum_{t=1}^{n}\left(\frac{100 \times e_t}{Y_t}\right)^2}.$$

$$\text{where } t = 1, \ldots, n \qquad (13.11)$$

RMSPE is computed as illustrated in Table 13.13.

TABLE 13.13 Computations of the Root Mean Square Percentage Error (RMSPE).

Period	Actual	Forecast	Error	Square percentage error
t	Y_t	F_t	$e_t = Y_t - F_t$	$(p_t)^2 = ((Y_t - F_t)/Y_t \times 100)^2$
1	64	90	−26	1650.39
2	76	101	−25	1082.06
3	35	44	−9	661.22
4	33	32	1	9.18
5	29	31	−2	47.56
6	35	44	−9	661.22
7	47	102	−55	13,693.98
Total			−125	17,805.63

$$\text{RMSPE} = \sqrt{\text{mean}(17805.63)} = \sqrt{17,805.63 / 7} = 50.43$$

using Equation (13.11)

Hyndman and Koehler (2006, p. 683) report a disadvantage for RMSPE as it can be infinite or undefined if actual equals to zero in the period of interest, "having an extremely skewed distribution when any value of Y_t is close to zero".

13.2.2.7 ROOT MEDIAN SQUARE PERCENTAGE ERROR

The formula for root median square percentage error (RMdSPE) is

$$RMdSPE = \sqrt{median\left(p_t^2\right)}.$$

$$where \ t = 1, \ ..., \ n \qquad\qquad (13.12)$$

RMdSPE is computed as illustrated in Table 13.14.

TABLE 13.14   Computations of the Root Median Square Percentage Error (RMdSPE).

Period	Actual	Forecast	Error	Square percentage error
t	Y_t	F_t	$e_t = Y_t - F_t$	$(p_t)^2 = ((Y_t - F_t)/Y_t \times 100)^2$
1	64	90	−26	1650.39
2	76	101	−25	1082.06
3	35	44	−9	661.22
4	33	32	1	9.18
5	29	31	−2	47.56
6	35	44	−9	661.22
7	47	102	−55	13,693.98
Total			−125	17,805.63

$$RMdSPE = \sqrt{median\left(p_t^2\right)} = \sqrt{661.22} = 25.71$$

using Equation (13.12)

Similar to the previous measure, RMdSPE can be infinite or undefined if actual equals to zero in the period of interest, "having an extremely skewed distribution when any value of Y_t is close to zero" (Hyndman & Koehler, 2006, p. 683).

13.2.3 RELATIVE VERSUS NON-RELATIVE MEASURES

Some scale-independent and scale-dependent measures apply a benchmark to determine a relative error which can be defined as $r_t = e_t / E_t$, where E_t is the forecast error obtained from the benchmark error. Usually naïve forecast is taken as a benchmark method.

13.2.3.1   MEAN RELATIVE ABSOLUTE ERROR

The formula for mean relative absolute error (MRAE) is

$$MRAE = \text{mean}(|r_t|)$$
$$\text{where } t = 1, ..., n \tag{13.13}$$

MRAE is computed as illustrated in Table 13.15.

TABLE 13.15   Computations of the Mean Relative Absolute Error (MRAE).

Period	Actual	Forecast	Error	Benchmark forecast	Benchmark forecast error	Absolute relative error
t	Y_t	F_t	$e_t = Y_t - F_t$	BF_t	$E_t = Y_t - BF_t$	$|r_t| = |e_t|/|E_t|$
1	64	90	−26	68	−4	6.50
2	76	101	−25	75	1	25.00
3	35	44	−9	33	2	4.50
4	33	32	1	54	−21	0.05
5	29	31	−2	37	−8	0.25
6	35	44	−9	38	−3	3.00
7	47	102	−55	50	−3	18.33
Total			−125			57.63
		MRAE = 57.63/7 = 8.23		using Equation (13.13)		

The advantage of this measure is its ease of interpretation relative to Theil's U (Armstrong & Collopy, 1992). As a disadvantage Hyndman and Koehler (2006) argue that an error of a benchmark method can be small but a relative error can have infinite variance. According to Makridakis (1993, p. 528), "RAE-based measures mean *absolutely* nothing to decision makers who cannot understand either their meaning or grasp the non-linear scales being reported".

13.2.3.2   MEDIAN RELATIVE ABSOLUTE ERROR

The formula for the median relative absolute error (MdRAE) is

$$MRAE = \text{median}(|r_t|)$$

$$\text{where } t = 1, \ldots, n \tag{13.14}$$

MdRAE is computed as illustrated in Table 13.16.

TABLE 13.16   Computations of the Median Relative Absolute Error (MdRAE).

Period	Actual	Forecast	Error	Benchmark forecast	Benchmark forecast error	Absolute relative error
t	Y_t	F_t	$e_t = Y_t - F_t$	BF_t	$E_t = Y_t - BF_t$	$|r_t| = |e_t|/|E_t|$
1	64	90	−26	68	−4	6.50
2	76	101	−25	75	1	25.00
3	35	44	−9	33	2	4.50
4	33	32	1	54	−21	0.05
5	29	31	−2	37	−8	0.25
6	35	44	−9	38	−3	3.00
7	47	102	−55	50	−3	18.33
Total			−125			57.63

MdRAE = median of (0.05, 0.25, 3.00, 4.50, 6.50, 18.33, 25.00) = 4.50
using Equation (13.14)

MdRAE, according to Makridakis and Hibon (2000, p. 462), "is de-signed to be easy to interpret and it lends itself easily to summarizing across horizons and across series as it controls for scale and for the difficulty of forecasting". The measure is rated "good" on Construct validity and Outlier protection (Armstrong & Collopy, 1992). As a specific disadvantage, in ad-dition to common disadvantages of RAE-based measures, MdRAE may be appropriate only in "specific cases when the number or series involved is neither very small nor very large, when *no* winsorizing is required *and* when the results are reported exclusively for statistical audiences" (Makridakis, 1993, p. 528). Moreover, MdRAE does not perform better than MAPE over the criteria of reliability, validity, outlier protection, sensitivity, and value to decision making (Makridakis, 1993). It is rated "poor" on Sensitivity and Relationship to decisions (Armstrong & Collopy, 1992).

13.2.3.3   GEOMETRIC MEAN RELATIVE ABSOLUTE ERROR

The formula for geometric mean relative absolute error (GMRAE) is

$$\text{GMRAE} = \text{gmean}\left(|r_t|\right) = \sqrt[n]{\frac{|e_1|}{|E_1|} \times \cdots \times \frac{|e_n|}{|E_n|}} = \sqrt[n]{\prod_{t=1}^{n} \frac{|e_t|}{|E_t|}}.$$

$$\text{where } t = 1, \ldots, n \qquad (13.15)$$

GMRAE is computed as illustrated in Table 13.17.

TABLE 13.17 Computations of the Geometric Mean Relative Absolute Error (GMRAE).

Period	Actual	Forecast	Error	Benchmark forecast	Benchmark forecast error	Absolute relative error
t	Y_t	F_t	$e_t = Y_t - F_t$	BF_t	$E_t = Y_t - BF_t$	$|r_t| = |e_t|/|E_t|$
1	64	90	−26	68	−4	6.50
2	76	101	−25	75	1	25.00
3	35	44	−9	33	2	4.50
4	33	32	1	54	−21	0.05
5	29	31	−2	37	−8	0.25
6	35	44	−9	38	−3	3.00
7	47	102	−55	50	−3	18.33
Total			−125			57.63

$$\text{GMRAE} = \sqrt[7]{6.50 \times 25 \times 4.50 \times 0.05 \times 0.25 \times 3 \times 18.33} = \sqrt[7]{478.8} = 2.41$$
$$\text{using Equation (13.15)}$$

The geometric mean relative absolute error compares the geometric average of the forecasting error with the geometric average of the benchmark error. We consider three cases: if GMRAE = 1, then the forecasting measures are equally good in terms of the geometric average; if GMRAE < 1 the forecasting method performs better than the benchmark; and, finally, if GMRAE > 1 the forecasting method performs worse than the benchmark, in terms of the geometric average.

This measure is rated "poor" on Relationship to decisions and "good" construct validity and sensitivity (Armstrong & Collopy, 1992) and shares some of the previously described disadvantages of MRAE and MdRAE. Another disadvantage of GMRAE is that the geometric mean can only be computed for positive non-zero values.

13.2.3.4   MEAN ABSOLUTE SCALED ERROR

The mean absolute scaled error (MASE) is the average value of $|q_t|$:

$$MASE = \text{mean}\left(|q_t|\right) = \frac{1}{n-1}\sum_{t=2}^{n}|q_t|$$

$$q_t = \frac{e_t}{\dfrac{1}{n-1}\sum_{i=2}^{n}|Y_i - Y_{i-1}|}$$

where

and $t = 2,\ldots,n$ (13.16)

MASE is computed as illustrated in Table 13.18.

TABLE 13.18   Computations of the Mean Absolute Scaled Error (MASE).

Period	Actual	Naïve	Absolute error of naïve forecast	Forecast	Error	Scaled error	Absolute scaled error
t	Y_t	Y_{t-1}	$|Y_i - Y_{i-1}|$	F_t	$e_t = Y_t - F_t$	q_t	$|q_t|$
1	64			65	−1	−0.08	0.08
2	76	64	12	67	9	0.70	0.70
3	35	76	41	36	−1	−0.08	0.08
4	33	35	2	34	−1	−0.08	0.08
5	29	33	4	100	−71	−5.53	5.53
6	35	29	6	36	−1	−0.08	0.08
7	47	35	12	48	−1	−0.08	0.08
Total			77		−67		

$$\frac{1}{n-1}\sum_{i=2}^{n}|Y_i - Y_{i-1}| = \frac{1}{6}(12+41+2+4+6+12) = \frac{77}{6} = 12.83$$

The values of q_t are calculated by dividing e_t by 12.83. For example q_2 is calculated as follows:

$$q_2 = \frac{9}{12.83} = 0.70$$

Then MASE is computed using Equation (13.16):

$$MASE = \text{mean}\left(|q_t|\right) = \frac{0.70+0.08+0.08+5.53+0.08+0.08}{6} = 6.55/6 = 1.09$$

The measure has a meaningful scale and is easy to interpret. We can consider the following distinct cases:

If MASE = 1, then the forecasting method performs just as well as the naïve method.

If MASE < 1, then the forecasting method performs better than the naïve method.

If MASE > 1, then the forecasting method performs worse than the naïve method.

As Hyndman and Koehler (2006, p. 685) explain, when MASE is smaller than 1, "the proposed method gives, on average, smaller errors than the one-step errors from a naïve method". Values of MASE greater than one indicate that the forecasts are worse, on average, than in-sample one-step forecasts from the naïve method.

Hyndman and Koehler (2006) find that MASE is not subject to degeneracy problems. Furthermore, the only circumstance under which MASE "would be infinite or undefined is when all historical observations are equal" (Hyndman & Koehler, 2006, p. 686).

Moreover, the measure is "less sensitive to the outliers and more easily interpreted than RMSSE, and less variable on small samples than MdASE"(Hyndman & Koehler, 2006, p.686). However, in some circumstances, an asymmetric loss function may be preferred in which case some other (asymmetric) function of the scaled errors may be appropriate (Lawrence & O'Connor, 2005; Diebold, 2001; Hyndman & Koehler, 2006).

13.2.3.5   RELATIVE MEAN ABSOLUTE ERROR OR CUMRAE

The formula for relative mean absolute error (RelMAE) or CumRAE as referred to by Armstrong and Collopy (1992) is

$$RelMAE = \frac{MAE}{MAE_b}.$$

$$where \; t = 1, \ldots, n \qquad\qquad (13.17)$$

where MAE_b is MAE from a benchmark method. The most commonly used benchmarks methods are the random walk or "**naïve**" and "**naïve 2**."

RelMAE (or CumRAE) is computed as illustrated in Table 13.19.

TABLE 13.19 Computations of the Relative Mean Absolute Error (RelMAE) or CumRAE.

Period	Actual	Forecast	Error	Absolute error	Benchmark forecast	Absolute Bench-mark forecast error
t	Y_t	F_t	$e_t = Y_t - F_t$	$|e_t| = |Y_t - F_t|$	BF_t	$|E_t| = |Y_t - BF_t|$
1	64	90	−26	26	68	4
2	76	101	−25	25	75	1
3	35	44	−9	9	33	2
4	33	32	1	1	54	21
5	29	31	−2	2	37	8
6	35	44	−9	9	38	3
7	47	102	−55	55	50	3
Total			−125	127		42

$$\text{MAE} = 127/7 = 18.14 \qquad \text{using Equation (13.2)}$$
$$\text{MAE}_b = 42/7 = 6 \qquad \text{using Equation (13.2)}$$
$$\text{RelMAE} = 18.14/6 = 3.02 \qquad \text{using Equation (13.17)}$$

An advantage of these methods is their interpretability. For example, relative MAE measures the improvement possible from the proposed forecast method relative to the benchmark forecast method. When RelMAE < 1, the proposed method is better than the benchmark method, and when RelMAE > 1, the proposed method is worse than the benchmark method. However, they require several forecasts on the same series to enable a MAE (or MSE) to be computed. One common situation where it is not possible to use such measures is where one is measuring the out-of-sample forecast accuracy at a single forecast horizon across multiple series. It makes no sense to compute the MAE across series (due to their different scales) (Hyndman & Koehler, 2006, p. 684).

13.2.3.6   RELATIVE MEAN SQUARED ERROR

There a various measures similar to RelMAE which can be devised, for example relative mean squared error (RelMSE):

$$\mathrm{RelMAE} = \frac{\mathrm{MAE}}{\mathrm{MAE}_b}.$$

where $t = 1, \ldots, n$ (13.17)

RelRMSE is also known as Theil's U statistic and is sometimes called $U2$.

13.3   CASE ILLUSTRATION

To illustrate the inherent difficulties of applying forecasting accuracy measures in practice, real-life manual and machine-based hotel occupancy forecasts data were obtained. The data was provided by a large international chain hotel in the Netherlands and a small and recent set of data was collected at the segment level. For ease of illustration, only two segments are presented—Transient and Group—which make up a Total Hotel column. Per segment two independent forecasts were generated: daily occupancy forecasts by a commercial (3rd party) RMS, and subjective (manual) assessments of the daily occupancy by the revenue management team. The occupancy for a specific date was forecasted six times before the date. Specifically, the forecasting horizons included: over 2 months (i.e., 2 months plus several days), over a month, 4, 3, 2 and 1 week ahead. See Table 13.20, where two forecasting horizons: 1 month ahead and 3 weeks ahead were selected for illustrative purposes.

To compute the relative accuracy measures, a benchmark forecasting method was required. Naïve methods (e.g., random walk, seasonal random walk) are commonly used as benchmark methods. The *random walk* (Naïve Forecast 1 or NF1) as defined by Makridakis et al. (1998) uses the last observation as the future forecast. An example of a *seasonal random walk* (Naïve Forecast 2 or NF2) would be to use the actual from a year ago as the forecast for the corresponding period this year.

Naïve 2 instead of Naïve 1 forecast was selected as a benchmark because typical hotel demand displays seasonality patterns. Since annual seasonality as well as weekly patterns are often present (demand for Sunday night for a business hotel can be drastically different from Wednesday night demand), it was not appropriate to take April 1 of the previous year data as a forecast for April 1 the current year. They would fall at different days of the week. Therefore, the same day of week was considered as presented in Table 13.21.

For example, if April 1 of the previous year (Friday) would be blindly selected, it would serve as forecast for April 1 (Sunday) of the current year. Therefore, the same day of week (Sunday) around the beginning of April of the previous year was considered: Sunday April 3 and Sunday March 27. Initially, it felt more intuitive to select April 3 as it was closer to the calendar date to be forecasted (April 1). However, if April 3 was selected as a start date and taking 30 days (number of days in April) it would result in the inclusion of May 1 and May 2 in the dataset as well. These days are, however, European holidays with different demand patterns. Therefore, March 27, 2011–April 25, 2011 was selected as a data range for the Naïve 2 forecast. Results of the forecasting accuracy calculations and preliminary analysis are presented in the next table.

In Table 13.22 accuracy measures are presented per segment and total hotel. While in some cases (e.g., *Group segment, 1 month before arrival*; *Group segment, 3 weeks before arrival*) interpretation of forecasting accuracy evaluation results is relatively straightforward, other cases show an inconsistency between measures, for example, for the *Transient segment, 3 weeks before arrival*.

According to ME, MAE, MSE, RMSE, MPE, MAPE, sMAPE, RMSPE, MRAE, RelMAE, and RelMSE, the manager was more accurate than the system. When MdAE, MdAPE, sMdAPE, RMdSPE, and MdRAE are used for the same segment and forecasting horizon, the conclusion is that the System was more accurate. As can be noticed, the measures that identifies the system as more accurate, were based on a variety of median calculations. Median is a numerical value separating the higher half of the data sample, from the lower half. Median is used primarily for skewed distributions, and it might be seen as a better indication of a central tendency than the arithmetic mean and is more robust in the presence of outlier values. Thus, the question of how outliers should be considered is important to address.

An outlier can be defined as any observation that exceeds the mean with three standard deviations (Weatherford & Kimes, 2003). A distinction should be made, however, between outliers at the stage of forecast development (holiday, special events, and unusual days) and outliers in the forecast accuracy evaluation. As can be seen from the result table, several measures were not computable for all segments and forecast horizons (MPE, MAPE, MdAPE, sMAPE, sMdAPE, RMSPE, RMdSPE, and GMRAE). There are distinct cases where the measures cannot be computed.

TABLE 13.20 Forecasted and Actual Occupancy for the Month of April at the Segment and Total Hotel Level.

Day of week	Date (Current year)	Forecast: 1 months before arrival						Forecast: 3 weeks before arrival						Actual			Reference day of week	Reference date (previous year)	Naïve 2		
		Transient		Group		Total hotel		Transient		Group		Total hotel		Transient	Group	Total hotel			Transient Benchmark forecast	Group Benchmark forecast	Total hotel Benchmark forecast
		Sys F_t	Mgr F_t	Sys F_t	Mgr F_t	Sys F_t	Mgr F_t	Sys F_t	Mgr F_t	Sys F_t	Mgr F_t	Sys F_t	Mgr F_t	Y_t	Y_t	Y_t			BF_t	BF_t	BF_t
Sun	April 1	65	72	73	89	138	161	64	65	86	91	150	156	49	84	133	Sun	March 27	98	37	135
Mon	April 2	134	113	44	38	178	151	86	76	45	44	131	120	64	44	108	Mon	March 28	60	46	106
Tue	April 3	136	130	65	63	201	193	117	118	59	59	176	177	80	54	134	Tue	March 29	101	104	205
Wed	April 4	109	136	71	56	180	192	80	90	52	53	132	143	71	48	119	Wed	March 30	96	111	207
Thu	April 5	163	128	32	6	195	134	111	98	9	6	120	104	48	4	52	Thu	March 31	126	40	166
Fri	April 6	194	180	8	3	202	183	203	178	1	3	204	181	131	1	132	Fri	April 1	82	37	119
Sat	April 7	202	185	0	15	202	200	204	199	0	5	204	204	195	0	195	Sat	April 2	125	37	162
Sun	April 8	181	134	17	19	198	153	159	126	2	5	161	131	140	0	140	Sun	April 3	173	47	220
Mon	April 9	87	83	27	17	114	100	76	91	23	20	99	111	54	1	55	Mon	April 4	115	45	160
Tue	April 10	163	90	24	27	187	117	135	95	18	12	153	107	69	10	79	Tue	April 5	56	45	101
Wed	April 11	172	88	23	29	195	117	144	91	27	19	171	110	87	15	102	Wed	April 6	99	46	145
Thu	April 12	147	118	50	64	197	182	119	95	49	44	168	139	99	31	130	Thu	April 7	69	30	99
Fri	April 13	170	157	29	37	199	194	157	150	18	14	175	164	106	23	129	Fri	April 8	58	36	94
Sat	April 14	180	169	22	37	202	206	167	162	36	36	203	198	96	24	120	Sat	April 9	82	46	128
Sun	April 15	147	104	44	49	191	153	145	116	46	41	191	157	90	38	128	Sun	April 10	93	47	140
Mon	April 16	101	100	101	117	202	217	99	101	105	117	204	218	111	95	206	Mon	April 11	68	102	170
Tue	April 17	74	92	128	140	202	232	88	84	116	138	204	222	99	123	222	Tue	April 12	91	82	173
Wed	April 18	74	92	128	140	202	232	82	83	122	138	204	221	95	113	208	Wed	April 13	73	67	140
Thu	April 19	130	134	49	41	179	175	106	105	52	38	158	143	175	34	209	Thu	April 14	103	42	145
Fri	April 20	154	141	20	26	174	167	147	147	53	58	200	205	179	50	229	Fri	April 15	163	51	214
Sat	April 21	183	189	14	25	197	214	171	189	33	27	204	216	189	32	221	Sat	April 16	78	87	165
Sun	April 22	115	91	19	29	134	120	103	89	45	32	148	121	107	42	149	Sun	April 17	73	96	169

TABLE 13.20 *(Continued)*

Day of week	Date (Current year)	Forecast: 1 months before arrival						Forecast: 3 weeks before arrival						Actual					Naïve 2		
		Transient		Group		Total hotel		Transient		Group		Total hotel		Transient	Group	Total hotel	Reference day of week	Reference date (previous year)	Transient Benchmark forecast	Group Benchmark forecast	Total hotel Benchmark forecast
		Sys F_t	Mgr F_t	Sys F_t	Mgr F_t	Sys F_t	Mgr F_t	Sys F_t	Mgr F_t	Sys F_t	Mgr F_t	Sys F_t	Mgr F_t	Y_t	Y_t	Y_t			BF_t	BF_t	BF_t
Mon	April 23	143	106	59	93	202	199	136	112	67	46	203	158	159	46	205	Mon	April 18	102	56	158
Tue	April 24	159	123	43	88	202	211	156	148	46	43	202	191	161	38	199	Tue	April 19	114	54	168
Wed	April 25	160	123	41	100	201	223	154	144	44	43	198	187	178	34	212	Wed	April 20	108	36	144
Thu	April 26	155	113	38	86	193	199	152	126	38	24	190	150	170	24	194	Thu	April 21	68	51	119
Fri	April 27	177	132	22	61	199	193	175	149	27	17	202	166	177	22	199	Fri	April 22	83	99	182
Sat	April 28	192	199	10	12	202	211	181	189	23	19	204	208	233	11	244	Sat	April 23	96	57	153
Sun	April 29	202	131	0	26	202	157	189	158	15	20	204	178	218	24	242	Sun	April 24	135	50	185
Mon	April 30	199	135	3	28	202	163	191	142	13	25	204	167	178	12	190	Mon	April 25	119	53	172
Total		4468	3788	1204	1561	5672	5349	4097	3716	1270	1237	5367	4953	3808	1077	4885			2907	1737	4644

TABLE 13.21   Actual Occupancy Information for the Month of April (previous year) at the Segment and Total Hotel Level.

Previous year		Transient	Group	Total hotel
Day of week	Date			
Sun	March 27	98	37	135
Mon	March 28	60	46	106
Tue	March 29	101	104	205
Wed	March 30	96	111	207
Thu	March 31	126	40	166
Fri	April 1	82	37	119
Sat	April 2	125	37	162
Sun	April 3	173	47	220
Mon	April 4	115	45	160
Tue	April 5	56	45	101
Wed	April 6	99	46	145
Thu	April 7	69	30	99
Fri	April 8	58	36	94
Sat	April 9	82	46	128
Sun	April 10	93	47	140
Mon	April 11	68	102	170
Tue	April 12	91	82	173
Wed	April 13	73	67	140
Thu	April 14	103	42	145
Fri	April 15	163	51	214
Sat	April 16	78	87	165
Sun	April 17	73	96	169
Mon	April 18	102	56	158
Tue	April 19	114	54	168
Wed	April 20	108	36	144
Thu	April 21	68	51	119
Fri	April 22	83	99	182
Sat	April 23	96	57	153
Sun	April 24	135	50	185
Mon	April 25	119	53	172
Tue	April 26	157	81	238
Wed	April 27	135	123	258

TABLE 13.21   *(Continued)*

Previous year		Transient	Group	Total hotel
Day of week	Date			
Thu	April 28	139	117	256
Fri	April 29	129	52	181
Sat	April 30	148	34	182
Sun	May 1	174	41	215
Mon	May 2	101	38	139

Case 1: At least one actual (Y_t) is equal to zero. Then the following measures will present computation errors due to division by zero: MPE, MAPE, MdAPE, RMSPE, and RMdSPE.

Case 2: Both the actual (Y_t) and the forecast (F_t) are equal to zero for at least one t. Then sMAPE and sMdAPE will present computation errors due to division by zero.

Case 3: At least one forecast error (e_t) is equal to zero. Then GMRAE could not be computed because some of the entries (e_t) were equal to zero.

There are various methods to work around these issues (Habib, 2012). However, caution should be used when workaround methods are selected and applied in practice since they may alter the measure.

One of the commonly observed mistakes in practice is to compute forecasting accuracy measure at total level, for example, by taking the total monthly number of room nights instead of the daily numbers to calculate forecasting error, or to compute measures only on total hotel level instead of segment level:

> *If only overall error is calculated, it would mean that all arrivals for a given night were lumped together (all rate categories and lengths of stay) and that only the forecast error for this aggregate number was reported. Therefore, the impacts on the detailed rate and availability controls created by the revenue management system, that attempts to manage accept/reject decisions at the rate category/lengths of stay level will be ignored.* (Weatherford & Kimes 2003, p. 407).

Finally, it is difficult to know whether forecasts for the Group segment are more or less accurate than for the Transient segment, especially for the Group forecast generated by the system at 1 month and 3 weeks out. As emphasized at the beginning of the Section 13.2, scale-dependent measures can be used only for the data sets that have the same data scales. In order

TABLE 13.22 Forecasted Accuracy Measures for the Month of April at the Segment and Total Hotel Level.

Forecasting accuracy measure	Forecast: 1 months before arrival						Forecast: 3 weeks before arrival					
	Transient		Group		Total Hotel		Transient		Group		Total hotel	
	System	Manager	System	Manager	System	Manager	System	Manager	System	Manager	System	Manager
ME	-22.00	0.67	-4.23	-16.13	-26.23	-15.47	-9.63	3.07	-6.43	-5.33	-16.07	-2.27
MAE	38.00	35.60	12.10	19.47	42.97	34.73	30.43	29.00	7.83	7.53	30.73	29.73
MdAE	29.00	38.00	11.00	14.50	41.00	28.50	22.00	27.00	7.50	5.00	22.00	26.50
MSE	2320.60	1834.93	220.90	671.73	3153.30	1856.60	1421.37	1199.13	98.30	95.33	1574.07	1282.60
RMSE	48.17	42.84	14.86	25.92	56.15	43.09	37.70	34.63	9.91	9.76	39.67	35.81
MPE	-33.52	-13.71	–	–	-33.17	-20.03	-18.54	-7.57	–	–	-20.60	-10.01
MAPE	43.82	34.68	–	–	40.78	29.02	30.85	26.94	–	–	27.15	23.40
MdAPE	25.48	24.79	–	–	16.87	17.87	16.17	19.66	–	–	13.89	16.94
sMAPE	31.52	29.49	–	61.85	28.26	23.60	25.44	24.48	–	41.52	21.45	20.52
sMdAPE	26.81	27.12	–	44.64	18.43	17.75	16.97	21.81	–	20.34	13.74	17.01
RMSPE	66.78	48.39	–	–	68.91	43.34	43.03	34.88	–	–	41.89	33.95
RMdSPE	25.48	24.80	–	–	16.87	17.94	16.26	19.67	–	–	13.94	16.94
MRAE	2.58	1.47	2.14	3.83	2.74	2.42	1.79	1.18	1.26	1.14	1.90	1.67
MdRAE	0.79	0.76	0.36	0.47	0.70	0.63	0.49	0.61	0.30	0.16	0.52	0.60
GMRAE	–	–	–	0.64	–	0.77	0.62	–	–	–	0.55	–
MASE	0.78	0.73	0.40	0.64	0.91	0.74	0.62	0.59	0.26	0.25	0.65	0.63
RelMAE	0.78	0.73	0.39	0.63	0.94	0.76	0.62	0.59	0.25	0.24	0.67	0.65
RelMSE	0.66	0.52	0.16	0.49	1.04	0.61	0.40	0.34	0.07	0.07	0.52	0.42

to compare Group and Transient segments, scale-independent forecasting accuracy measures have to be used. As can be seen from the table, for the Group forecast generated by the system at 1 month and 3 weeks out, scale-independent measures (MPE, MAPE, MdAPE, sMAPE, sMdAPE, RMSPE, and RMdSPE) are incomputable. This lack of information illustrates a possible practical challenge in answering a question "on which segment the forecasting efforts need to be intensified?" A possible work-around could be considering importance of each segment in terms of revenue and profit and prioritizing based on this information, yet what happens if two segments are equally important?

13.4   CONCLUSION

It is widely accepted that forecasting is a complex and crucial part of successful hotel operations. "Detailed forecasts are the major input to most revenue management systems, and without accurate detailed forecasts, the rate and availability recommendations produced by the revenue management system may be highly inaccurate" (Weatherford & Kimes, 2003, p. 401). However, little attention is given in the literature and by practitioners to the systematic and consistent evaluation of the quality of produced and adjusted forecasts (Schwartz, 1999; Schwartz & Cohen, 2004a,b). Whilst forecasting accuracy evaluation is a complex data-intense process, Revenue Management Systems currently do not offer a wide choice and flexibility in selecting and applying measures of forecasting accuracy. The proper evaluation and interpretation of those evaluations are critical for the entire forecasting process.

The aim of this chapter is to demonstrate how various widely used forecasting accuracy measures are calculated, what the known and recorded advantages and disadvantages of each measure are, and to warn against unconsidered usage of measures by illustrating how different measures may generate contradictory results and lead to misjudgment in evaluating forecasting accuracy. Over time incorrect conclusions about forecasting accuracy may impact which forecasting models are used and how their components are calibrated. They also affect our understanding of whether forecast adjustments performed by Revenue Managers improve or reduce forecasting accuracy, "leading to a potential cascade of misguided decisions related to pricing, inventory control, operational planning and even strategy formulation" (Koupriouchina, Van der Rest & Schwartz, 2014, p. 110). As was illustrated, forecasting accuracy measure is not a straightforward task. It requires understanding of the underlying data and advantages and disadvantages of the various forecasting accuracy measures. However, if applied properly it promises to inform the decision-making process and helps to avoid making costly mistakes. There are ample future opportunities to work on appropriate measures of forecasting accuracy with the RMS providers/developers and train managers to choose, compute, and interpret the forecasting accuracy measures and to expand their application beyond room occupancy, including ADR and RevPAR forecasts and perhaps not only considering rooms' revenue, but a total spend (as in Casino hotel practices) and improving even further inventory pricing and allocation decisions. Moreover, as Granger and Pesaran (2000, p. 537) state "in the real, non-academic world forecasts are made for a purpose and the relevant purpose in economics is to help decision makers improve their decisions. It follows that the correct way to evaluate forecasts is to consider and compare the realized values of different decisions made from using alternative sets of forecasts". However, this topic has been widely ignored in the generic and hospitality research literature with the exception of Leitch and Tanner (1991) and Pesaran and Timmermann (1994, 1995).

There is little consensus about the accuracy measures to be used in hotel revenue management research. In fact, the reasoning behind the selection of a measure is often even omitted. Armstrong and Collopy (1992) recommended MdRAE and GMRAE for a small number of data series and MdAPE for a moderate to large number of data series. Weatherford and Kimes (2003) warn that the small numbers associated with some of the detailed forecasts may lead to higher errors, and if the error is measured as a percentage, it may appear unusually high. Therefore, it may be that the MAE is the error measure which is most meaningful and relevant to the financial losses incurred from inaccurate forecasts. However, if MAE is used to set up different forecasting accuracy targets for different rate categories, it is more difficult to set them up compared to setting the targets as a percentage. In other words, MAE is scale-dependent and if a segment is large, than it is reasonable to expect a higher MAE. Another disadvantage if MAE is used is that it cannot be used to compare across properties.

Some forecasting accuracy measures consider absolute error, which avoids the problem of forecasting errors cancelling each other out. An important point in the interpretation of forecasting accuracy measure is over- and under-forecasting. Some measures provide an indication whether systematic over- or under-forecasting took place. However, there is no consensus on whether over-forecasting errors caused a larger decline in revenue than under-forecasting errors (for a detailed discussion, refer to Weatherford & Kimes, 2003).

As the nature of hotel revenue management forecasting is very complex it require various systematic re-forecasting on each rate category and length of stay. This adds to the complexity and it is not uncommon for hotels to produce high numbers of forecasts. For example, referring to Marriott Hotels and Hyatt Hotels, Weatherford and Kimes (2003, p. 406) reported that a hotel can "perform over 200 forecasts for each stay night (10 different rate categories, seven different lengths of stay and three different room types." Evaluating 200 forecasts for just one stay night might be a cumbersome task. A related question then arises: at which time horizon point are the forecasts more critical in terms of decision-making? Related to this issue is a lack of research attention to the impact of manual adjustments to a forecasting system. When are overrides detrimental for a forecasting model's accuracy, and are revenue managers aware of this phenomenon?

In hotel revenue management, it is important that managers can forecast not only the number of guests per night, but make a prediction regarding customers' duration of use. "Although most hotels rely on room night forecasts, most sophisticated revenue management systems rely on arrival-based forecasts. Arrivals-based forecasts are more appropriate for revenue management because the type of rate and availability controls usually imposed are applied to guests arriving on a particular night. Once an arrival-based forecast is developed, a room-night based forecast can easily be derived as long as length of stay information is available" (Weatherford & Kimes, 2003, p. 405). As Weatherford, Kimes and Scott (2001:p. 54) state: "most major hotel chains use linear-programming-based models that require detailed forecasts by day of arrival, length of stay (LOS), and rate category." However, the forecasting accuracy assessment are often made on room-night basis.

As an important and often overlooked area, volatility of data is also crucial for accuracy measure. Sanders and Ritzman (1992) define and measure volatility by the coefficient of variation of the raw data. They categorized time series into two groups: low (<30%) and high (>30%) coefficient of variation. Fildes, Goodwin, Lawrence and Nikolopoulos (2009) propose an alternative approach to measuring volatility based on the coefficient of variation of the system forecast absolute error. These two studies, however, yield contradictory results. According to Sanders and Ritzman (1992), when series have a high coefficient of variation judgmental forecasters outperform statistical time series methods. Fildes et al. (2009, p. 10) conclude that "while there is a significant association between volatility and forecast improvement, the improvements are greater for low volatility series." The example reported in Table 13.23 illustrates this volatility debate as defined by Sanders and Ritzman (1992) for two hotels:

The coefficient of variation is defined as the ratio of the standard deviation σ to the mean μ:

$$C_v = \frac{\sigma}{\mu}$$

TABLE 13.23   Computations of Coefficient of Variation.

Period	Hotel 1 actual	Hotel 2 actual
t	Y_t	y_t
1	64	90
2	76	101
3	35	95
4	33	90
5	29	97
6	35	70
7	47	102
Standard deviation σ	16.58	10.05
Mean μ	45.57	92.14
Coefficient of variation	**36.38%**	**10.91%**

If the volatility of time series is high, it is in general harder to forecast and therefore expectations for the forecast accuracy should take it into account. In other words if two hotels have similar or the same forecasting accuracy measures results (say MAPE for Hotel 1 and Hotel 2 are 35.99) should it be concluded that their forecasting performance is equal? Moreover, for the same property volatility may even differ per segment and per length of stay. Therefore, it might be advisable to assess volatility per segment and to consider it in a process of interpretation of forecasting accuracy measures, yet another direction for future research.

Finally, and a nearly forgotten aspect of hotel revenue management forecasting, forecasting accuracy is only one of the many ways to evaluate forecasting performance. Other important indicators include forecast efficiency and forecast bias. Bodea and Ferguson (2014) suggest also computing Bias and Tracking Signal. Gilliland (2010) proposes a Forecast Value Added measure and Koupriouchina et al. (2014) indicate a need for comprehensive forecast *quality* assessment.

KEYWORDS

- **Revenue Management**
- **Hotel Forecasting**
- **Accuracy**
- **Error Measures**

REFERENCES

Armstrong, J. S. *Long Range Forecasting: From Crystal Ball to Computer*. John Wiley and Sons: New York, 1985.

Armstrong, J. S. *Principles of Forecasting: A Handbook for Researchers and Practitioners*. Kluwer Academic Publishers: Norwell, MA, 2001.

Armstrong, J. S.; Collopy, F. Error Measures for Generalizing about Forecasting Methods: Empirical Comparisons. *Int. J. Forecast.* **1992,** *8*(1), 69–80.

Bodea, T.; Ferguson, M. *Segmentation, Revenue, Management, and Pricing Analytics*. Routledge: New York, 2014.

Bunn, D. W.; Taylor, J. W. Setting Accuracy Targets for Short-Term Judgmental Sales Forecasting. *Int. J. Forecast.* **2001,** *17*(2), 159–169.

Diebold, F. X. *Elements of Forecasting*. South-Western: Cincinnati, OH, 2001.

Fildes, R.; Goodwin, P.; Lawrence, M.; Nikolopoulos, K. Effective Forecasting and Judgmental Adjustments: An Empirical Evaluation and Strategies for Improvement in Supply-Chain Planning. *Int. J. Forecast.* **2009,** *25*(1), 3–23.

Goodwin, P.; R. Lawton. On the Asymmetry of the Symmetric MAPE. *Int. J. Forecast.* **1999,** *15*(4), 405–408.

Gilliland, M. *The Business Forecasting Deal*. John Wiley & Sons Inc.: Hoboken, NJ, 2010.

Granger, C. W. J.; Pesaran, M. H. Economic and Statistical Measures of Forecast Accuracy. *J. Forecast.* **2000,** *19*(7), 537–560.

Habib, E. A. E. Geometric Mean for Negative and Zero Values. *Int. J. Res. Rev. Appl. Sci.* **2012,** *11*(3), 419–432.

Hyndman, R. J.; Koehler, A. B. Another Look at Measures of Forecast Accuracy. *Int. J. Forecast.* **2006,** *22*(4), 679–688.

Koehler, A. The Asymmetry of the sAPE Measure and Other Comments on the M3-Competition. *Int. J. Forecast.* **2001,** *17*(2), 570–574.

Koupriouchina, L.; Van der Rest, J. I.; Schwartz, Z. On Revenue Management and the Use of Occupancy Forecasting Error Measures. *Int. J. Hospitality Manage.* **2014,** *41*, 104–114.

Lawrence, M.; O'Connor, M. Judgmental Forecasting in the Presence of Loss Functions. *Int. J. Forecast.* **2005,** *21*(1), 3–14.

Leitch G.; Tanner J. E. Economic Forecast Evaluation: Profits versus the Conventional Error Measures. *Am. Econ. Rev.* **1991,** *81*(3), 580–590.

Makridakis, S. Accuracy Measures: Theoretical and Practical Concerns. *Int. J. Forecast.* **1993,** *9*(4), 527–529.

Makridakis, S.; Hibon, M. The M3-Competition: Results, Conclusions and Implications. *Int. J. Forecast.* **2000,** *16*(4), 451–476.

Makridakis, S.; Wheelwright, S.; Hyndman, R. *Forecast. Methods Appl.* John Wiley & Sons, Inc.: Hoboken, NJ, 1998.

Pesaran, M. H.; Timmermann, A. Forecasting Stock Returns: An Examination of Stock Market Trading in The Presence of Transaction Costs. *J. Forecast.* **1994,** *13*(4), 335–367.

Pesaran, M. H.; Timmermann, A. Predictability of Stock Returns: Robustness and Economic Significance. *J. Finance* **1995,** *50*(4), 1201–1228.

Sanders, N. R.; Ritzman, L. P. The Need for Contextual and Technical Knowledge in Judgmental Forecasting. *J. Behav. Decis. Making* **1992,** *5*(1), 39–52.

Schwartz, Z. Monitoring the Accuracy of Multiple Occupancy Forecasts: A Corporate Office Perspective. *FIU Hospitality Rev.* **1999,** *17*(1–2), 29–42.

Schwartz, Z.; Cohen, E. Hotel Revenue-Management Forecasting. *Cornell Hotel Restaurant Admin. Q.* **2004a,** *45*(1), 85–98.

Schwartz, Z.; Cohen, E. Subjective Estimates of Occupancy Forecast Uncertainty by Hotel Revenue Managers. *J. Travel Tourism Mark.* **2004b,** *16*(4), 59–66.

Schwartz, Z.; Hiemstra, S. Improving the Accuracy of Hotel Reservations Forecasting: Curves Similarity Approach. *J. Travel Res.* **1997,** *36*(1), 3–14.

Weatherford, L. R.; Kimes, S. E. A Comparison of Forecasting Methods for Hotel Revenue Management. *Int. J. Forecast.* **2003,** *19*(3), 401–415.

Weatherford, L. R.; Kimes, S. E.; Scott, D. A. Forecasting for Hotel Revenue Management: Testing Aggregation against Disaggregation. *Cornell Hotel Restaurant Admin. Q.* **2001,** *42*(4), 53–64.

CHAPTER 14

FRONTIER APPROACHES FOR PERFORMANCE MEASUREMENT IN THE HOSPITALITY AND TOURISM INDUSTRIES

A. GEORGE ASSAF[1] and FRANK WOGBE AGBOLA[2]

1Isenberg School of Management, University of Massachusetts-Amherst, 90 Campus Center Way, 209A Flint Lab, Amherst, MA 01003, USA. E-mail:assaf@isenberg.umass.edu

[2]Economics Discipline, Newcastle Business School, University of Newcastle, SRS 152, 1 University Drive, Callaghan, NSW 2308, Australia. E-mail: frank.agbola@newcastle.edu.au

CONTENTS

14.1   INTRODUCTION

In recent years, there has been a strong shift in the literature focusing on performance measurement in the tourism and hotel literature (Assaf & Dwyer, 2013). Specifically, simple performance measures such as return on assets (ROA), revenue per available rooms (RevPAR), and occupancy rate that were previously used in the literature have been replaced with more powerful and comprehensive metrics of performance measurement such as technical efficiency (TE) (Anderson et al., 1999; Barros & Dieke, 2008; Assaf & Agbola, 2011). There are now a large number of studies using TE across many sectors of the tourism and hospitality industries (Assaf & Josiassen, 2014; Barros, 2005; Chen, 2007; Reynolds & Thompson, 2007; Assaf, Barros, & Dieke, 2011; Botti et al., 2010).

TE offers at least two advantages over simple performance metrics. First, the method is derived based on multiple inputs and outputs, therefore allowing a more comprehensive measure of performance. For example, a hotel with higher RevPAR is not necessarily a better performing hotel, as it might be achieving this at the expense of higher input costs. Unfortunately, measures such as RevPAR only account for one input (i.e., the number of available rooms) and one output (i.e., total revenue) at one time, therefore ignoring other key inputs (e.g., labor costs, material costs) and outputs (e.g., sales, number of rooms sold), which are vital for hotel operations. The second advantage is that "simple performance measures are only meaningful when compared to a benchmark, and finding a suitable benchmark may be difficult" (O'Donnell & Der Westhuizen, 2002, p. 486). For example, while a hotel may have a strong RevPAR compared to the industry average or other close competitors, it may still be far from achieving its maximum potential. Unfortunately, measures such as ROA or RevPAR do not reflect the gap between a hotel's current performance and its maximum (i.e., optimal) performance (Coelli et al., 2005).

TE can address this limitation, as it measures a firm's performance relative to a frontier of best practice (i.e., frontier of maximum performance). For example, a TE of 60% indicates that a firm is 40% away from achieving its maximum efficiency; this 40% represents the level of wastage or operational inefficiency (Barros & Dieke, 2008). Not only is such information vital for management in allocating resources and managing capacity, but it can also facilitate comparison with competitors in the industry (Assaf & Josiassen, 2012). For example, when all competitors are measured relative to the same benchmark and using the same inputs and outputs, the comparison between them becomes more meaningful and realistic (Barros, 2005).

Thus far, different methods have been used in the literature on hospitality and tourism to measure TE. The two most common methods are the non-parametric data envelopment analysis (DEA) and the parametric stochastic frontier (SF). While both methods provide measures of TE by first estimating a benchmark of best practice and then measuring the distance between the first actual performance and its optimal performance, they differ in the assumption they make in estimating this frontier. The selection between the two methods remains an issue of debate in the literature due to the advantages and disadvantages of both approaches (Barros & Dieke, 2008; Anderson et al., 1999). The principal limitation of DEA is that it does not differentiate between TE and noise in the data (Coelli et al., 2005). While the SF approach can handle noise given its parametric nature, its principal limitation is that it requires "the definition of a specific functional form for the frontier technology and for the inefficiency error term. This functional form requirement causes both specification and estimation problems" (Murillo-Zamorano, 2004, p. 36).

Considering the strengths and weaknesses associated with these two approaches, our aim in this chapter is to provide a description of both approaches and illustrate their advantages and disadvantages. We provide researchers in tourism and hospitality with guidance on how to estimate both methods using an interesting application on Australian hotels. We discuss the various software available and the advantages and limitations of each type. We also discuss how to analyze the determinants of TE in both DEA and SF contexts. Finally, we highlight some of the latest methodological advances in the DEA and SF literature, and provide some guidance for future research in the field.

This chapter proceeds as follows: the following section provides further theoretical details about the concept of TE, which leads to the discussion of frontier methods. We then provide an application that compares between different frontier methods for the estimation of TE. The last section provides some concluding remarks and directions for future research.

14.2   CONCEPT OF TECHNICAL EFFICIENCY

The TE concept was first introduced in the literature by Debreu (1951) and Farrell (1997), and later developed by several other researchers in the field (Kumbhakar & Lovell, 2003; Coelli et al., 2005). The basic aim of TE is to capture the difference between a firm's current performance and its optimal performance. For a producer to be technically efficient, it must operate at the boundary of its production–possibility set or frontier, which depending on the behavior of the firm can occur in two special cases: (1) if the producer is able to minimize input usage of a given output vector, or (2) if the producer is able to maximize its outputs given its input vector (Kumbhakar & Lovell, 2003). These two cases are also known in the literature as the input-oriented and output-oriented TE measures (Coelli et al., 2005).

To illustrate, let $x = (x_1,\ldots,x_N) \in R_+^N$ be the vector of inputs used by the firm to produce the following vector of outputs, $y = (y_1,\ldots,y_M) \in R_+^M$. The production technology set corresponding to these input and output vectors can be expressed as follows:

$$P(x) = \{(y,x) : "x" \text{ can produce } "y"\} \qquad (14.1)$$

which describes the set of feasible inputs that are used to the produce output vector. The concept of the frontier for the output-oriented case is best illustrated in Figure 14.1, where we graph the production set in (14.1) using a simple example of two outputs y_1, y_2 and an input vector x. As presented in Figure 14.1, the production set in (14.1) is the area that is bounded from above by the frontier of best practice PPC-P(x). That is, the frontier represents the boundary of the production set T. Firms that sit on this boundary are known to be 100% technically efficient, as it is not possible to produce beyond this boundary. Conversely, the further a firm is from the frontier, the less technically efficient it is.

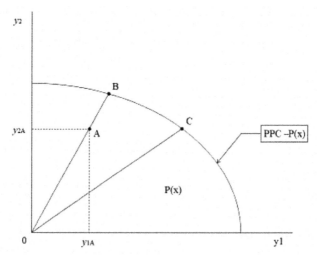

FIGURE 14.1   Output oriented technical efficiency (adapted from Coelli et al., 2005).

In Figure 14.2, we present the input-oriented case. To illustrate, we assume that we have two inputs x_1 and x_2 that are used to produce the output vector y. We can see that the production set in (14.1) is now bounded from below by the frontier Isoq-$P(y)$. Again, firms that sit on the frontier are fully technically efficient. However, as mentioned, the difference between the output-oriented and the input-oriented cases is that the first seeks output expansion to achieve full efficiency, while the second seeks input minimization to achieve full efficiency. The decision about which orientation to follow depends on the overall behavior of the firm being analyzed. For example, some not-for-profit firms are more interested in minimizing input usage than expanding outputs (Coelli et al., 2005). In the hotel and tourism contexts, while both orientations have been used, most studies have used the output-oriented approach (e.g., Assaf & Agbola, 2014; Barros, 2005).

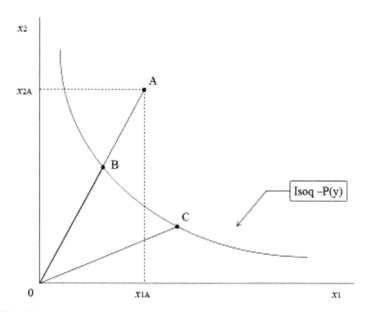

FIGURE 14.2   Input oriented technical efficiency (adapted from Coelli et al., 2005).

14.3   FRONTIER METHODS FOR ESTIMATING TECHNICAL EFFICIENCY

As demonstrated above, the estimation of efficiency is based on first identifying a frontier of best practice and measuring firm performance relative to this frontier. However, such frontier is not observed in practice and must be estimated from the data. The available methods proposed in the literature to estimate this frontier can be grouped into two categories: the non-parametric DEA approach and the parametric SF approach. Both methods have been used extensively in the hotel and tourism literature (Assaf & Josiassen, 2012; Assaf & Agbola, 2012; Barros & Dieke, 2008; Anderson et al., 1999). The following two subsections present further details on these methods, illustrating their advantages and disadvantages.

14.3.1   DATA ENVELOPMENT ANALYSIS

The DEA method was first introduced by Charnes et al. (1978). It is a linear-programming approach for estimating the "frontier." Depending on the orientation needed, DEA can be estimated using input-oriented or output-oriented models. An input-oriented DEA model can be specified as follows:

$$\hat{\theta}_i = \min\left\{\theta \middle| y_i \leq \sum_{i=1}^{n} \lambda_i y_i, \theta_{xi} \geq \sum_{i=1}^{n} \lambda_i x_i, \sum_{i=1}^{n} \lambda_i = 1\right\} \tag{14.2}$$

where y_i is the outputs of form I, x_i is the observed inputs, and u and v are unknown vectors of non-negative output and input weights. θ_i is a scalar and λ is a $I \times 1$ vector of constants. The value of θ_i obtained is the TE score for the i-th firm, and ranges between 0 and 1, with the former being the least efficient and the latter being the most efficient.

The output-oriented DEA model can be expressed as follows:

$$\hat{\theta}_i = \max\left\{\theta \middle| x_i \geq \sum_{i=1}^{n} \lambda_i x_i, \theta_{xi} \leq \sum_{i=1}^{n} \lambda_i y_i, \sum_{i=1}^{n} \lambda_i = 1\right\} \tag{14.3}$$

where all the terms are as defined in (14.2). However, the difference is that the model in (14.2) seeks maximization of outputs instead of minimization in inputs. Overall, the models expressed in (14.2) and (14.3) present important advantages in the estimation of TE. For example, they can incorporate multiple inputs and outputs without imposing any functional form on the data (Coelli et al., 2005). In addition, they do not necessitate a large number of observations, as does the parametric approach. Being non-parametric, however, their main disadvantage is that they do not account for measurement error in the data. They require a homogenous and clean sample; for example, any strong outlier in the data can bias the TE results.

Such limitations can be addressed through the use of the bootstrap approach, which consists of repeating the estimation of the DEA model using thousands of random samples from the data. TE estimates can then be derived from each of these samples, where the researcher can take the average of all these TE estimates as the new TE efficiency score. This may partially address the problem with outliers in the data. In addition, using the thousands of TE efficiency scores, the researcher can approximate the underling sampling distribution and conduct statistical inferences on the efficiency scores (Simar & Wilson, 1998, 2000). Due to these advantages, the DEA bootstrap has become highly popular in the literature across several service industries (Pergelova et al., 2010; Luo & Donthu, 2006).

14.3.2 STOCHASTIC FRONTIER APPROACH

The SF approach uses a parametric approach to estimate TE. The mathematical formulation of the SF model can be written as follows:

$$y_{it} = f(x_{it}', \beta) + v_{it} - u_{it}, \ i = 1, \ldots, n, \ t = 1, \ldots, T, \tag{14.4}$$

where y_{it} represents a vector of outputs, x_{it} represents inputs, β_i is a vector of parameters, v_{it} is a random error term, and u_{it} is a inefficiency term that measures the gap (i.e., technical inefficiency) from the frontier of best practices. This term has a positive distribution such as half-normal, truncated, exponential, or gamma. The parameters of the model in (14.4) can be estimated using either a maximum likelihood (ML) or Bayesian approach.

Overall, the model in (14.4) provides several advantages for estimating TE. For example, in contrast to DEA, we have now the random error v_{it}, which allows for measurement error. The SF model thus distinguishes between TE and measurement error. In DEA, any measurement error is usually wholly attributed to TE because the model does not account for any measurement error in the data. An important advantage of the SF model is that it can also account for the panel structure of the data. For example, if the researcher has panel data and is interested in analyzing the changes in TE over time, the SF can provide TE for each period in the sample. Conversely, because of its non-parametric nature, DEA does not differentiate between panel or non-panel data. If panel data is available, DEA simply treats each period as another observation in the data (Coelli et al., 2005).

However, SF also presents problems. For example, since it is a parametric technique, it requires a much larger sample size than the DEA model

(Cullinane et al., 2006). SF also requires imposing a distributional-assumption term on the technical-inefficiency term u_{it}. The DEA is more flexible in that it estimates TE without any distributional assumption. With the SF method, the researcher must decide in advance which distributional assumption to impose on the technical-inefficiency term u_{it}. Different distributions are available (e.g., half-normal, gamma, exponential, truncated) and they do not necessarily lead to the same results (Kumbhakar & Lovell, 2003). In the hotel and tourism literature, some of the most common distributions have been the exponential and half-normal. However, few studies have compared the results of the different distributional assumptions reporting mixed conclusions (Assaf & Josiassen, 2014).

14.4   WHICH FRONTIER APPROACH IS PREFERABLE?

Given the advantages and disadvantages of the two methods, the researcher may encounter difficulty choosing between the DEA and SF approaches. As noted, even within the same method, there are different specifications that can lead to different efficiency results (Coelli et al., 2005; Kumbhakar & Lovell, 2003). While the business literature has placed considerable focus on this issue (Assaf, Barros, & Josiassen, 2010; Assaf & Gillen, 2012; Cullinane et al., 2006), it is surprising that most studies in the hotel and tourism literature have ignored the comparison between the different frontier methods. As neither approach is deemed to be necessarily better than the other (Murillo-Zamorano, 2004), it is important to consider the characteristics and the industry under analysis prior to the implementation of these techniques. For example, when the sample size is small and the data is homogenous, DEA is certainly the clear choice.

In many cases, however, the decision is not obvious, and conducting a comparison between the two methods becomes necessary to validate the findings (Murillo-Zamorano, 2004). There is currently lack of empirical evidence in the hotel and tourism literature about such issues. In our application, which is presented below, we provide a detailed comparison of the two approaches. We also provide directions on how to estimate each method, and compare and validate the findings. Given the advantages and disadvantages of each approach, comparing them "is not only necessary, but potentially yields important results and conclusions with respect to the relative merits of the two alternative approaches and the circumstances under which each is most appropriately applied" (Cullinane et al., 2006, p. 356).

14.5 EMPIRICAL APPLICATION

In this section, we discuss the two methodologies outlined above using the data employed in the study by Assaf and Agbola (2011). The data employed in this study consist of a sample data of 31 hotels overs a period of four years ($31 \times 4 = 124$ observations). Thus, the sample is large enough to allow for both DEA and SF estimation.

A key step in the DEA or SF estimation is to first identify a list of input and output variables that best describe the industry or firms under analysis. Following the extant literature, for the purposes of illustration, we use six inputs, namely, total payroll in the room division department, total payroll in other departments, the cost of food, cost of beverages, cost of maintaining rooms, and the number of rooms available, and two outputs, namely, total room revenue and total food and beverage revenue. As Barros and Dieke (2008) notes, these are the most common input and outputs used by previous studies in the tourism literature. Table 14.1 provides a summary of the key input and output variables used in the literature.

TABLE 14.1 Some Key Input and Outputs Used in the Hotel Literature.

Study	Input variables	Output variables
Sigala et al. (2005)	1. Number of rooms	1. Average room rate
	2. Front office payroll	2. Number of room nights
	3. Administration and general material and other expenses	3. Non-room revenue
	4. Other payroll	
	5. Other material and other expenses	
	6. Demand variability	
Sun and Lu (2005)	1. Total operating expenses	1. Total operating revenues
	2. Number of employees	2. Average occupancy rate
	3. Number of guest rooms	3. Average daily rate
	4. Total area of the catering department	4. Average production value per employee in the catering department
Barros and Santos (2006)	1. Number of employees	1. Sales
	2. Capital (book value of the assets)	2. Added value
		3. Earnings

TABLE 14.1   *(Continued)*

Study	Input variables	Output variables
Chiang (2006)	1. Hotel rooms 2. F&B capacity 3. Number of employees 4. Operating cost	1. Yielding index 2. F&B revenue 3. Miscellaneous revenue
Wang et al. (2006a)	1. Number of full-time employees 2. Guest rooms 3. Total area of meal department	1. Room revenue 2. F&B revenue 3. Other revenue
Wang et al. (2006b)	1. Number of rooms 2. Number of full-time employees in room departments 3. Total floor area of F&B departments 4. Number of full-time employees in F&B departments	1. Revenue from room department 2. Revenue from F&B 3. Other revenue
Wöber (2007)	1. Personnel costs 2. Occupancy costs marketing costs 3. Other variable costs 4. Other fixed costs 5. Number of employees 6. Average job experience of employees	1. Number of contracts 2. Turnover 3. Contribution margin
Reynolds and Biel (2007)	1. Cost of goods sold 2. Labor cost 3. Employee satisfaction 4. Rent 5. Tax and insurance 6. Square footage 7. Number of seats	1. Revenue 2. Controllable income 3. Guest satisfaction 4. Retention equity
Reynolds & Thompson (2007)	1. Server wage 2. Seats 3. Square footage 4. Parking 5. Stand alone	1. Sales 2. Tips

TABLE 14.1 *(Continued)*

Study	Input variables	Output variables
Barros and Dieke (2008)	1. Total costs 2. Investment expenditure	1. RevPAR
Shang et al. (2008a)	1. Number of guest rooms 2. F&B capacity 3. Number of employees 4. Operating expenses	1. room revenue 2. F&B revenue 3. Miscellaneous revenue
Shang et al. (2008b)	1. Number of guest rooms 2. F&B capacity 3. Number of employees 4. Operating expenses	1. Room revenue 2. F&B revenue 3. Miscellaneous revenue
Botti et al. (2009)	1. Costs 2. Territory coverage 3. Chain duration	1. Sales
Neves and Lourenco (2009)	1. Current assets 2. Net fixed assets 3. Shareholders' equity 4. Cost of goods and services	1. Total revenue 2. EBITDA
Yu and Lee (2009)	1. Number of employees in the room service department 2. Number of employees in the F&B department 3. Number of rooms 4. Total floor area in the F&B service department 5. Total expenses for each service sector	1. Total revenue generated from rooms 2. Total revenue generated from F&B 3. Other revenue

14.6 RESULTS

This section consists of three parts. The first part discusses the empirical results from the DEA method, the second discusses the empirical results from the SF method, and finally, the third part compares and contrasts the empirical results of the two approaches.

14.6.1 DEA ESTIMATION

One important step in the DEA estimation is to first ensure that the data is free from any outliers. We carefully checked here our data set for this issue before estimation. As described above, the DEA method can be estimated using either input or output orientation. We select here the output-orientation in line with most studies in the literature (Barros, 2005; Barros & Dieke, 2008; Assaf & Josiassen, 2012; Assaf & Agbola, 2014). In addition to estimating a traditional DEA method, we also bootstrapped the DEA scores in order to account for possible bias in the data and to make the comparison with the SF method more reasonable (Assaf & Agbola, 2012).

For the estimation of the DEA models, we use the FEAR software which is freely available from http://www.clemson.edu/economics/faculty/wilson/Software/FEAR/fear.html. The software is highly popular (Barros & Dieke, 2008; Assaf & Josiassen, 2012) as it can bootstrap the DEA scores using the Simar and Wilson (1998) bootstrap procedure. While there are many other DEA software available on the web, only few can bootstrap the DEA scores. Table 14.2, provides the TE estimates of Australian hotels. The first column reports the non-bootstrapped DEA scores, the second column reports the bootstrapped DEA scores[1], the third column reports the bias which is simply the difference between the non-bootstrapped and the bootstrapped DEA scores, and finally the last two columns report the 95% confidence intervals of the DEA efficiency scores. Due to space limitation, we only report results for the first 50 observations in our sample.

TABLE 14.2 Non-Bootstrapped and Bootstrapped DEA Scores.

Hotel	Non-Boot DEA	Boot-DEA	Bias	95% Confidence interval	
1	0.951	0.920	0.031	0.873	0.950
2	0.924	0.893	0.031	0.848	0.922
3	1.000	0.941	0.059	0.868	0.998
4	1.000	0.911	0.089	0.783	0.998
5	1.000	0.693	0.307	0.609	0.998
6	1.000	0.706	0.294	0.609	0.998
7	1.000	0.959	0.041	0.909	0.998
8	1.000	0.669	0.331	0.606	0.998
9	1.000	0.622	0.378	0.606	0.998
10	1.000	0.682	0.318	0.608	0.998
11	1.000	0.966	0.034	0.932	0.998

[1]These bootstrapped scores were obtained by replicating the DEA estimation 2000 times.

TABLE 14.2   *(Continued)*

Hotel	Non-Boot DEA	Boot-DEA	Bias	95% Confidence interval	
12	0.993	0.968	0.025	0.940	0.991
13	1.000	0.687	0.313	0.610	0.998
14	0.990	0.941	0.050	0.801	0.989
15	1.000	0.656	0.344	0.607	0.998
16	1.000	0.973	0.027	0.948	0.998
17	0.887	0.864	0.023	0.840	0.886
18	0.895	0.872	0.023	0.845	0.893
19	0.949	0.922	0.026	0.878	0.947
20	0.867	0.849	0.017	0.832	0.865
21	0.361	0.352	0.009	0.334	0.360
22	0.351	0.346	0.005	0.337	0.351
23	0.482	0.478	0.005	0.470	0.482
24	0.526	0.522	0.005	0.513	0.526
25	1.000	0.942	0.058	0.894	0.998
26	1.000	0.945	0.055	0.892	0.998
27	1.000	0.958	0.042	0.914	0.998
28	0.071	0.069	0.002	0.065	0.070
29	1.000	0.978	0.022	0.953	0.998
30	0.962	0.942	0.020	0.922	0.960
31	1.000	0.957	0.043	0.918	0.998
32	1.000	0.961	0.039	0.925	0.998
33	1.000	0.606	0.394	0.605	0.998
34	1.000	0.712	0.288	0.608	0.998
35	1.000	0.931	0.069	0.838	0.998
36	1.000	0.689	0.311	0.611	0.998
37	1.000	0.666	0.334	0.609	0.998
38	0.986	0.922	0.064	0.749	0.984
39	1.000	0.677	0.323	0.608	0.998
40	1.000	0.660	0.340	0.606	0.998
41	0.683	0.668	0.015	0.650	0.681
42	0.705	0.690	0.015	0.672	0.704
43	0.712	0.704	0.008	0.694	0.711
44	1.000	0.647	0.353	0.607	0.998
45	1.000	0.672	0.328	0.611	0.998
46	0.546	0.530	0.016	0.501	0.545
47	0.656	0.639	0.017	0.619	0.654
48	0.653	0.637	0.016	0.622	0.652
49	0.926	0.899	0.027	0.860	0.924
50	0.971	0.937	0.035	0.888	0.970

Overall we can see that both DEA estimations (i.e., non-bootstrap and bootstrap) indicate high-level TE for Australian hotels. In fact, most hotels in the sample operate close to 90% efficiency level (i.e., around 10% in-efficiency level). In terms of the difference between the bootstrapped and non-bootstrapped DEA scores, we can "see that while the non-bootstrapped DEA scores always lie outside the lower and upper bounds of the confidence intervals, the bootstrapped scores are always within the intervals" (Assaf & Agbola, 2011, p.80). The difference between the non-bootstrapped and bootstrapped DEA scores seem also to be large in some cases, as indicated by the bias column. We also conducted a t-test to confirm the differences in averages between the bootstrapped and non-bootstrapped model, and found significant differences in the results ($t = 4.38$, $p < 0.05$). These results are not surprising and confirm previous findings in the literature (Simar & Wilson, 1998). Overall, we recommend using the bootstrap model at it can provide measures of efficiency scores adjusted for possible bias. In other words, it can reveal more accurately the efficiency score of each hotel in the data.

14.6.2   STOCHASTIC FRONTIER ESTIMATION

As mentioned above, before conducting the SF estimation, the researcher needs to decide on the functional form $f(.)$ as well as the distribution of the technical inefficiency term u_{it}. For the functional form we select here the translog form as it is the most common choice in the literature, and is known to provide TE scores that are more in line with economic theory (Coelli et al., 2005). For the distributional choice of u_{it}, we estimate here two models, one that allows for exponential distribution and one that allows for half-normal distribution. These have been the two most common distributions in the hotel literature (Anderson et al., 1999; Assaf & Agbola, 2014) and as they can provide different efficiency results (Kumbhakar & Lovell, 2003), comparing between them is essential to validate the findings.

For the estimation of the SF model we use here the STATA software. Many studies in the hotel literature used the FRONTIER Software provided by Tim Coelli (http://www.uq.edu.au/economics/cepa/frontier.php). However, the advantage of the STATA software is that it provides different distribu-tional assumptions for the technical inefficiency term u_{it}. The FRONTIER software on the other hand only allows for half-normal estimation.

Table 14.3 provides the results from the SF estimation. Again, we only provide results for the first 50 observations in the sample. The first col-umn provides the results for the exponential model and the second column provides the results for the half-normal model. The results from both models seem be in line with the DEA results. We can see that most hotels in the sample operate at a high-efficiency level, and there is high homogeneity between the exponential and half-normal models ($t = 1.65$, $p = 0.02$). In comparison to the DEA results, one important difference is that with the SF estimation none of the hotels receive a perfect efficiency score (i.e., 100%). This is because the method accounts for random error in the data. Importantly, we also see that the variation between efficiency across hotels is smaller for the SF models than it is for the DEA models. For example, we present in Figure 14.3, the boxplot for two DEA and two SF models. As it is clear the variation of efficiency across hotels is much larger in the DEA context. Such finding confirms previous studies in the literature (Cullinane et al., 2006) and is attributed to the fact that DEA does not differentiate between the random error and inefficiency. It simply treats all noise in the data as sources of technical inefficiency (Cullinane et al., 2006).

TABLE 14.3   Half-Normal and Exponential SF Models.

Hotel	Half-normal	Exponential
1	0.947	0.947
2	0.960	0.966
3	0.945	0.944
4	0.953	0.956
5	0.949	0.951
6	0.947	0.947
7	0.937	0.927
8	0.940	0.933
9	0.959	0.964
10	0.956	0.960
11	0.958	0.964
12	0.959	0.965
13	0.942	0.937
14	0.951	0.954
15	0.942	0.937
16	0.933	0.916
17	0.940	0.933
18	0.940	0.931
19	0.937	0.926

TABLE 14.3   *(Continued)*

Hotel	Half-normal	Exponential
20	0.947	0.946
21	0.959	0.965
22	0.965	0.972
23	0.961	0.967
24	0.962	0.969
25	0.954	0.956
26	0.949	0.949
27	0.949	0.949
28	0.960	0.965
29	0.966	0.973
30	0.969	0.976
31	0.953	0.958
32	0.951	0.953
33	0.956	0.960
34	0.960	0.965
35	0.962	0.968
36	0.965	0.971
37	0.955	0.960
38	0.953	0.956
39	0.945	0.943
40	0.957	0.960
41	0.949	0.950
42	0.955	0.960
43	0.962	0.968
44	0.965	0.972
45	0.965	0.971
46	0.951	0.954
47	0.940	0.933
48	0.951	0.954
49	0.945	0.945
50	0.953	0.958

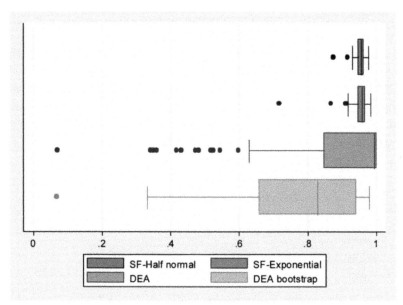

FIGURE 14.3 Efficiency variation of various DEA and SF models.

14.6.3 COMPARISON BETWEEN THE DEA AND SF RESULTS

To provide further insights into the difference between the DEA and SF models, we also conducted a direct comparison between the two methods. For example, an ANOVA analysis revealed significant difference between the average efficiency estimates obtained from the DEA and SF models ($F = 2.62$, $p < 0.05$). Between the two SF models and the two DEA models, the DEA bootstrap method yielded the lowest average inefficiency score, followed by the non-bootstrapped DEA. The half-normal SF model provided slightly higher average inefficiency score than the exponential model but both average inefficiency scores were higher than those reported for the DEA techniques.

When comparing between the DEA and SF methods, it is also common to validate if firms retain the same rank in terms of their efficiency score. For this purpose, we conducted a Spearman rank-order correlation test to check the ranking level of efficiency scores generated by the various DEA and SF models. A high value of the correlation coefficient indicates high similarity between the rankings of the various approaches. Table 14.4 reports the Spearman rank-correlation coefficient. The results show that while there is a strong correlation between the two SF models, as well as those of the DEA models, there appears to be a very weak correlation between the efficiency scores obtained from the SF and DEA models. This finding is important as it demonstrates that the efficiency ranking of hotels using the two methods, SF and DEA, is not necessarily the same (Cullinane et al., 2006; Coelli et al., 2005; Saleh et al., 2012). Of course, when such finding exists it would be difficult to draw direct conclusions from the results. The researcher has to decide which method is more suitable for a particular context. We provide in the next section more discussions on these findings as well as some directions for future research.

TABLE 14.4   Spearman Rank Order Correlation Between the Various DEA and SF Models.

	SF-half-normal	SF-exponential	Non-boot DEA	Boot DEA
SF-half-normal	1			
SF-exponential	0.9954	1		
Non-boot DEA	−0.0710	−0.0538	1	
Boot DEA	−0.0477	−0.0392	0.4155	1

14.7   CONCLUSION

We showed in this application that DEA and SF do not always necessarily lead to the same results. Hence, this illustrates the importance of comparing between the two methods prior to making some conclusions about the efficiency standing of the firm or industry under analysis. Unfortunately, most studies in the hotel industry do not conduct such analysis and use only either of the two methods (Assaf & Josiassen, 2014). As mentioned in some situations the researcher has limited choice but to select either of the two methods. For example, in the context of small sample size, it becomes highly difficult to apply the SF method.

In line with recent suggestions from the literature (Odeck & Brathen, 2012) we focus on the following recommendations.

1. First, we always recommend comparing between the two methods in order to validate the findings. Of course, there are situations in which one method is better than the other. For example, if the researcher is interested to estimate the efficiency change over time, and if panel data is available, we recommend using the SF as DEA does not account for the panel characteristics of the data. The SF

may also be more appropriate where there the data set involves a lot of noise.

2. Second, there are many alternatives available to validate the results. For example, in the context of DEA, we illustrated above the advantage of the bootstrap approach. Most recent studies in the tourism literature or other-related fields have started using the bootstrap approach (Barros & Dieke, 2008; Merkert & Hensher, 2011; Saleh et al., 2012). In the past, bootstrapping was difficult due the need of complicated computer programming (Simar & Wilson, 2007). However, with the availability of the FEAR software which can easily bootstrap the DEA scores, there is no reason why tourism researchers should avoid the bootstrap method. It can provide statistical properties for the DEA scores, and also accounts for bias in the estimation.

3. For SF, there also several methodological advances that can improve the robustness of estimation. For example, most tourism researchers still largely use the ML approach to estimate the SF model (Anderson et al., 1997; Saleh et al., 2012). In other fields, however, there is a strong shift toward using the Bayesian approach (Chen, 2007; Saleh et al., 2012; Tsionas & Assaf, 2014). In contrast to the ML approach, the Bayesian approach performs better in small samples (Coelli et al., 2005). It can also handle more complicated versions of the SF model, such as the dynamic and random effect SF models. For more detail on this issue, refer to Coelli et al. (2005) and Tsionas (2006).

4. Finally, we recommend using a second stage estimation to identify the main causes of why inefficiency exists. For example, both DEA and SF only provide the efficiency scores but do not identify the reasons of high of low efficiency in the sample. In the hotel literature, some studies have already explained the differences in efficiency between hotels in terms of factors such as size, location, ownership (Assaf & Cvelbar, 2011; Assaf & Agbola, 2012). We encourage more studies in these directions as this has the potential to inform companies "on the provision or implementation of appropriate incentives or policies for enhancing their competitiveness" (Cullinane et al., 2006, p. 367). The efficiency estimation is one step, but further analysis is required to enrich the implications the findings and to provide some strategies for efficiency improvement.

KEYWORDS

- **parametric and non-parametric frontier methods**
- **software application**
- **technical efficiency**
- **performance measurement**
- **data envelopment analysis (DEA)**

REFERENCES

Anderson, R. I.; Fish, M.; Xia, Y.; Michello, F. Measuring Efficiency in the Hotel Industry: A Stochastic Frontier Approach. *Int. J. Hospitality Manage.* **1999,** *18*(1), 45–57.

Assaf, A. G.; Josiassen, A. Frontier Analysis: A State-of-the-Art Review and Meta-Analysis, *J. Travel Res.* **2014,** in press.

Assaf, A. G.; Agbola, F. W. Efficiency Analysis of the Australian Accommodation Industry: A Bayesian Output Distance Function. *J. Hospitality Tourism Res.* **2014,** *38*(1), 116–132.

Assaf, A. G.; Dwyer, L. Benchmarking International Tourism Destinations. *Tourism Econ.* **2013,** *19*(6), 1233–1247.

Assaf, A. G, & Gillen, D. Measuring the Joint Impact of Governance form and Economic Regulation on Airport Efficiency. *Eur. J. Oper. Res.* **2012,** *220*(1), 187–198.

Assaf, A. G.; Josiassen, A. Identifying and Ranking the Determinants of Tourism Performance: A Global Investigation. *J. Travel Res.* **2012,** *51*(4), 388–399.

Assaf, A. G.; Agbola, F. W. Modelling the Performance of Australian Hotels: A DEA Double Bootstrap Approach. *Tourism Econ.* **2011,** *17*(1), 73–89.

Assaf, A., & Cvelbar, K. L. (2011). Privatization, market competition, international attractiveness, management tenure and hotel performance: Evidence from Slovenia. *International Journal of Hospitality Management, 30*(2), 391-397.

Assaf, A.; Barros, C. P.; Josiassen, A. Hotel Efficiency: A Bootstrapped Metafrontier Approach. *Int. J. Hospitality Manage.* **2010,** *29*(3), 468–475.

Assaf, A. G.; Barros, C. P.; Dieke, P. U. Portuguese Tour Operators: A Fight for Survival. *J. Air Transport Manage.* **2011,** *17*(3), 155–157.

Barros, C. P.; Dieke, P. U. Technical Efficiency of African Hotels. *Int. J. Hospitality Manage.* **2008,** *27*(3), 438–447.

Barros, C. A. P.; Santos, C. A. The Measurement of Efficiency in Portuguese Hotels Using Data Envelopment Analysis. *J. Hospitality Tourism Res.* **2006,** *30*(3), 378–400.

Barros, C. P. Measuring Efficiency in the Hotel Sector. *Ann. Tourism Res.* **2005,** *32*(2), 456–477.

Botti, L.; Briec, W.; Cliquet, G. Plural Forms versus Franchise and Company-Owned Systems: A DEA Approach of Hotel Chain Performance. *Omega* **2009,** *37*(3), 566–578.

Botti, L.; Briec, W.; Peypoch, N.; Solonandrasana, B. Productivity Growth and Sources of Technological Change in Travel Agencies. *Tourism Econ.* **2010,** *16*(2), 273–285.

Charnes, A.; Cooper, W. W.; Rhodes, E. Measuring the Efficiency of Decision Making Units. *Eur. J. Oper. Res.* **1978**, *2*(6), 429–444.

Chen, C. F. Applying the Stochastic Frontier Approach to Measure Hotel Managerial Efficiency in Taiwan. *Tourism Manage.* **2007**, *28*(3), 696–702.

Chiang, W. E. A Hotel Performance Evaluation of Taipei International Tourist Hotels—Using Data Envelopment Analysis. *Asia-Pacific J. Tourism Res.* **2006**, *11*(1), 29–42.

Coelli, T. J.; Rao, D. S. P.; O'Donnell, C. J.; Battese, G. E. *An Introduction to Efficiency and Productivity Analysis.* Springer: New York, USA, 2005.

Cullinane, K.; Wang, T. F.; Song, D. W.; Ji, P. The Technical Efficiency of Container Ports: Comparing Data Envelopment Analysis and Stochastic Frontier Analysis. *Transport. Res. A: Policy Practice* **2006**, *40*(4), 354–374.

Debreu, G. The Coefficient of Resource Utilization. *Econometr.: J. Econometr. Soc.* **1951**, *19*(3), 273–292.

Kumbhakar, S. C.; Lovell, C. K. *Stochastic Frontier Analysis.* Cambridge University Press: Cambridge, 2003.

Luo, X.; Donthu, N. Marketing's Credibility: A Longitudinal Investigation of Marketing Communication Productivity and Shareholder Value. *J. Mark.* 2006, *70*(4), 70–91.

Merkert, R.; Hensher, D. A. The Impact of Strategic Management and Fleet Planning on Airline Efficiency—A Random Effects Tobit Model Based on DEA Efficiency Scores. *Transport. Res., A: Policy Practice* **2011**, *45*(7), 686–695.

Murillo-Zamorano, L. R. Economic Efficiency and Frontier Techniques. *J. Econ. Surv.* **2004**, *18*(1), 33–77.

Neves, J. C.; Lourenço, S. Using Data Envelopment Analysis to Select Strategies That Improve the Performance of Hotel Companies. *Int. J. Contemporary Hospitality Manage.* **2009**, *21*(6), 698–712.

Odeck, J.; Bråthen, S. A Meta-Analysis of DEA and SFA Studies of the Technical Efficiency of Seaports: A Comparison of Fixed and Random-Effects Regression Models. *Transport. Res. A: Policy Practice* **2012**, *46*(10), 1574–1585.

O'Donnell, C. J.; Westhuizen, G. Regional Comparisons of Banking Performance in South Africa. *S. Afr. J. Econ.* **2002**, *70*(3), 224–240.

Pergelova, A.; Prior, D.; Rialp, J. Assessing Advertising Efficiency. *J. Advertis.* **2010**, *39*(3), 39–54.

Reynolds, D.; Biel, D. Incorporating Satisfaction Measures into a Restaurant Productivity Index. *Int. J. Hospitality Manage.* **2007**, *26*(2), 352–361.

Reynolds, D.; Thompson, G. M. Multiunit Restaurant Productivity Assessment Using Three-Phase Data Envelopment Analysis. *Int. J. Hospitality Manage.* **2007**, *26*(1), 20–32.

Saleh, S A.; Assaf, A. G.; Son Nghiem, H. Efficiency of the Malaysian Hotel Industry: A Distance Function Approach. *Tourism Anal.* **2012**, *17*(6), 721–732.

Shang, J. K.; Hung, W. T.; Lo, C. F.; Wang, F. C. Ecommerce and Hotel Performance: Three-Stage DEA Analysis. *Serv. Ind. J.* **2008a**, *28*(4), 529–540.

Shang, J. K.; Hung, W. T.; Wang, F. C. Service Outsourcing and Hotel Performance: Three-Stage DEA Analysis. *Appl. Econ. Lett.* **2008b**, *15*(13), 1053–1057.

Sigala, M. Integrating Customer Relationship Management in Hotel Operations: Managerial and Operational Implications. *Int. J. Hospitality Manage.* **2005**, *24*(3), 391–413.

Simar, L.; Wilson, P. W. Estimation and Inference in Two-Stage, Semi-Parametric Models of Production Processes. *J. Econ.* **2007**, *136*(1), 31–64.

Simar, L.; Wilson, P. W. Statistical Inference in Nonparametric Frontier Models: The State of the Art. *J. Product. Anal.* **2000**, *13(1)*, 49–78.

Simar, L.; Wilson, P. W. Sensitivity Analysis of Efficiency Scores: How to Bootstrap in Nonparametric Frontier Models. *Manage. Sci.* **1998**, *44(1)*, 49–61.

Sun, S.; Lu, W. M. Evaluating the Performance of the Taiwanese Hotel Industry Using a Weight Slacks-Based Measure. *Asia-Pacific J. Oper. Res.* **2005**, *22*(04), 487–512.

Tsionas, E. G.; Assaf, A. G. Short-run and Long-run Performance of International Tourism: Evidence from Bayesian Dynamic Models. *Tourism Manage.* **2014**, *42*, 22–36.

Tsionas, E. G. Inference in Dynamic Stochastic Frontier Models. *J. Appl. Econ.* (2006), *21*(5), 669–676.

Wang, F. C.; Hung, W. T.; Shang, J. K. Measuring the Cost Efficiency of International Tourist Hotels in Taiwan. *Tourism Econ.* **2006a**, *12*(1), 65–85.

Wang, F. C.; Hung, W. T.; Shang, J. K. Measuring Pure Managerial Efficiency of International Tourist Hotels in Taiwan. *Serv. Ind. J.* **2006b**, 26(1), 59–71.

Wöber, K. W. Data Envelopment Analysis. *J. Travel Tourism Mark.* **2007**, *21*(4), 91–108.

Yu, M. M.; Lee, B. C. Efficiency and Effectiveness of Service Business: Evidence from International Tourist Hotels in Taiwan. *Tourism Manage.* **2009**, 30(4), 571–580.

CHAPTER 15

MANAGING TOURIST SATISFACTION: AN INDEX APPROACH

JASON LI CHEN[1], GANG LI[1,2], and HAIYAN SONG[3]

[1]*School of Hospitality and Tourism Management, University of Surrey, Guildford GU2 7XH, United Kingdom. E-mail: l.chen@surrey.ac.uk*

[2]*Research fellow in Tourism Research in Economic Environs and Society, North-West University, South Africa. E-mail: g.li@surrey.ac.uk*

[3]*School of Hotel and Tourism Management, The Hong Kong Polytechnic University, 17 Science Museum Road, TST East, Kowloon, Hong Kong. E-mail: haiyan.song@polyu.edu.hk*

CONTENTS

15.1   INTRODUCTION

Customer satisfaction has been attracting significant research interests for over three decades. It is a central construct in marketing research (Luo & Homburg, 2007). The importance of customer satisfaction has been well recognized by both practitioners and academics. A good understanding of customer satisfaction is imperative for a firm to establish a long-term relationship with customers and to maintain long-term competitiveness (Hennig-Thurau & Klee, 1997). Customer satisfaction leads to consumer behavior patterns that positively affect business performance (Keiningham, Perkins-Munn, & Evans, 2003). For example, customer satisfaction is commonly accepted as a key antecedent to loyalty and repurchase across a range of organizations operating in various industries (Seiders, Voss, Grewal, & Godfrey, 2005). Some evidence suggests that there is a positive effect of customer satisfaction on the increase of a firm's market share and profitability (Anderson, Fornell, & Lehmann, 1994), rising financial return on investment and return on assets (Rust, Moorman, & Dickson, 2002), boosting shareholder value by increasing cash flow growth, and reducing its volatility (Fornell, Johnson, Anderson, Cha, & Bryant, 1996; Gruca & Rego, 2005), and even the firm's excellence in human capital (Luo & Homburg, 2007). Therefore, measuring, understanding, and managing customer satisfaction is a crucial cornerstone for all customer-oriented businesses and sectors, especially in increasingly competitive market environment. Mittal and Kamakura (2001, p. 131) point out that "customer satisfaction management has emerged as a strategic imperative for most firms."

Tourism supply is characterized by a series of interrelated service businesses in the form of a supply chain (Song, 2012), whose products are mostly intangible. Meanwhile, tourism markets are becoming increasingly competitive. Such features of tourism supply emphasize the particular importance of tourist satisfaction management. Sirakaya, Petrick, and Choi (2004, p. 518) stress that "measuring and managing customer satisfaction is crucial for the survival, development, and success of service industries like tourism." In addition to financial benefits for tourism businesses and sectors, tourist satisfaction plays an essential role in destination management. Satisfied tourists are more likely to recommend the destination to their friends and relatives. Word of mouth is the most effective way to promote a tourist destination. In addition, tourist satisfaction could contribute to the increased rates of retention of tourists' patronage, loyalty and acquisition (Li & Carr, 2004), which will have important impact on the destination's economic growth in general.

Firms and destinations aim to achieve sustained success and performance improvements in such increasing competitive environment. It is important to know the changes of performance over time, comparative performance against key competitors, benchmarking the performance against industry average. Hence, a consumer-based system of evaluating tourism service performance that focuses on tourist satisfaction will be of great importance for tourist destination management.

An evaluation system that can objectively inform tourism authorities and related stakeholders about the performance of various service sectors and effectively assist service providers in enhancing their performance needs to be both backward- and forward-looking (Fornell et al., 1996). In other words, this consumer-based evaluation system should be able to capture the cause and effect relationships regarding tourist satisfaction. For example, if data show a decline in tourist satisfaction, tourism practitioners can identify possible causes (e.g., tourists' expectations, perceived performance or assessed value) and suggest immediate remedies.

At the same time, the consequences of a decline in satisfaction, such as negative tourist voices and declining consumer loyalty, should be indicated by the evaluation system too. In addition, by adopting a universal framework for performance evaluation and reporting, such as a tourist satisfaction index (TSI) system, service providers can establish internal targets to assess their performance over time and to provide useful comparisons with other organizations. Furthermore, by facilitating increased transparency and accountability, the performance measures will enable service providers to establish a platform on which they can clearly articulate their contribution to their stakeholders and the local community. In other words, the evaluation system should be able to identify the relationship between the performance of individual service providers and a destination's overall performance as perceived by its received tourists. This chapter aims to introduce such a universal system of tourism service evaluation from a consumer's point of view, that is, a TSI system.

15.2 THEORETICAL FRAMEWORKS OF CONSUMER/TOURIST SATISFACTION

Given the importance of customer satisfaction, various approaches to its measurement have been developed. However, a consensus has not yet been reached. Among various customer satisfaction theories, two approaches attract extensive debates in the literature: the expectation–perception paradigm such as the SERVQUAL model developed by Parasuraman, Zeithaml, and Berry (1985), and the performance-only theory represented by the SERVPERF model (Cronin & Taylor, 1992). According to the expectation–perception theory, a customer has established certain expectation of the performance of the good or service before a purchase decision, and he or she tends to make comparison between the perceived performance of the good or service and his/her initial expectation after consumption. If the perceived performance of the good or service surpasses the expectation, a positive gap is formed, which would then lead to the consumer's satisfaction and willingness to re-purchase. If the actual performance fails to meet the initial expectation, a negative gap is shaped. The expectation–perception approach is criticized because consumers' expectations may be updated once they receive further information about the good or service (Boulding, Kalra, Staelin, & Zeithaml, 1993; Kozak & Rimmington, 1999). Therefore, the SERVPERF model is proposed which discards the expectations portion of SERVQUAL in favor of just the performance measurements included in the scale. It has been argued that the service quality measurements are based only on customers' perceptions of the service performance, rather than the gap between the customers' perceptions and their expectations of performance. However, the removal of the expectation construct makes it impossible using the performance-only model "to interpret high levels of customer satisfaction as the results of low expectations or superior quality of service provider" (Fuchs & Weiermair, 2004, p. 215).

Within the expectation–perception paradigm, a number of models have been applied to customer satisfaction studies. LaTour and Peat (1979) introduce the norm theory, according to which, "norms serve as reference points for judging the product, and dissatisfaction comes into play as a result of disconfirmation relative to these norms" (Yoon & Uysal, 2005, p. 47). Sirgy (1984) replaces "norm" with "ideal standard" and further develops the congruity model, which suggests that customer satisfaction depends on the comparison of the perceived performance of the product or service concerned relative to customers' hypothetical ideal product. A comprehensive review of the above approaches can be seen in Oh and Parks (1997).

In the tourism literature, most of the above approaches have been applied to examine tourist satisfaction in various empirical contexts. Some studies focus on the overall levels of tourist satisfaction with a destination (e.g., Kau & Lim, 2005), while the others pay attention to specific attributes at service encounter level such as a hotel, restaurant, travel agent, attraction, transport, and retail shop (e.g., Heung, 2000; Wang, Vela, & Tyler, 2008).

The expectation–perception paradigm has been the most commonly applied theoretical foundation in tourist satisfaction research, given its broadly applicable conceptualization. In addition to the importance for tourism service providers, the direct relevance of tourist satisfaction to destination competitiveness is well noted (Wong & Law, 2003).

With regard to the measurement of tourist satisfaction, earlier studies use traditional single-item scales to obtain tourists' responses from "very dissatisfied" to "very satisfied." The drawbacks of this approach have been noted in the general customer satisfaction literature, such as failure to capture the complexity of satisfaction evaluation, and higher possibility of measurement errors in a survey (Chan et al., 2003; Yi, 1990). As a result, the reliability of the findings is challenged (Yi, 1990). More recent satisfaction research regards satisfaction as a theoretical construct or latent variable, which cannot be measured directly (Fornell, 1992). Therefore, multi-item scales are more desirable to measure satisfaction. Oliver (1980) shows that the multi-item scales are significantly more reliable than single-item scales in an empirical study. In the tourism literature, many tourist satisfaction studies still employ single-item scales to measure the overall satisfaction, with few exceptions such as Yoon and Uysal (2005).

15.3 DEVELOPMENT OF THE TOURIST SATISFACTION INDEX FRAMEWORK

15.3.1 CUSTOMER SATISFACTION INDEX AND STRUCTURAL EQUATION MODELING

To systematically and comparably assess the customer satisfaction and thus evaluate the financial performance of economies or industries, a number of customer satisfaction index (CSI) models have been developed, such as the American customer satisfaction index (ACSI, Fornell et al., 1996) and the Hong Kong consumer satisfaction index (Chan et al., 2003). As a measure of overall customer satisfaction, a CSI has uniform and comparable attributes (Fornell et al., 1996). Unlike the single-item method, the latent constructs in the model represent different types of customer assessments that cannot be measured directly. The result is an index that is general enough to be comparable across firms, industries, sectors, and countries.

As CSIs use the multiple-indicator approach to measure the customer satisfaction as a latent variable, structural equation modeling (SEM) has been the most commonly used method to build CSIs in the literature. CSIs are usually aggregated from lower levels. For instance, in the ACSI model, an industry-level ACSI is an aggregate of the firm-level ACSIs weighted by firm sales; a sector-level ACSI is an aggregate of the industry-level ACSIs weighted by industry sales; the overall ACSI is an average of the sector-level ACSIs weighted by each sector's contribution to the gross domestic product (Fornell et al., 1996). As the lowest level in the system, the firm-level ACSI is a weighted average of a number of satisfaction indicators. One of the purposes of using SEM is to obtain these weights.

The rationale of SEM is similar to multiple regressions, yet SEM provides more information which simultaneously estimates path coefficients between multiple latent variables, and factor loadings or outer weights between each construct and its indicators. As such, SEM is a comprehensive method with the features of multiple regressions, path analysis, and factor analysis. Within a structural equation model, the internal structural relationships between constructs are explained by a set of linear regression equations, known as latent structural equations, while the external relationship between each construct and its indicators are described by factor analysis equations, known as measurement equations (Chan et al., 2003; Fornell & Cha, 1994; Fornell et al., 1996). Latent variables are measured by their corresponding indicators. As such, a structural equation model can be considered as a combination of a factor analysis model, which measures the relationships between latent variables and their indicators, and a regression or path analysis model, which accounts for the relationships between latent variables.

Two widely used methods in SEM estimation are covariance structure analysis (CSA) such as the well-known maximum likelihood (ML), and the partial least squares (PLS) approach. The PLS method has been widely used to estimate CSI models in the literature due to its advantages over ML such as its good performance under small samples, the ability of using formative indicators, and it is free of strict assumptions.

15.3.2 DEVELOPMENT OF THE TOURIST SATISFACTION INDEX FRAMEWORK

The first attempt to develop a satisfaction index in the tourism context was made by Song et al. (2009a,b, 2010, 2011, 2012) who developed The Hong

Kong Polytechnic University tourist satisfaction index (PolyU TSI) based on a dual-model framework. Song et al. (2011) evaluate Mainland Chinese tourists' satisfaction with SEM-based models at both sector and destination levels. A pilot survey was carried out in 2008 involving three tourism-related service sectors in Hong Kong. The proposed framework at sector level (Fig. 15.1) is consistent with the Hong Kong consumer satisfaction index model. The measurements of the sectoral model are presented in Table 15.1. To allow tourists to better discriminate their response to each survey question, an 11-point Likert scale, from 0 to 10, is adopted. The scales ranged from "extremely poor" to "extremely good" or from "completely disagree" to "completely agree."

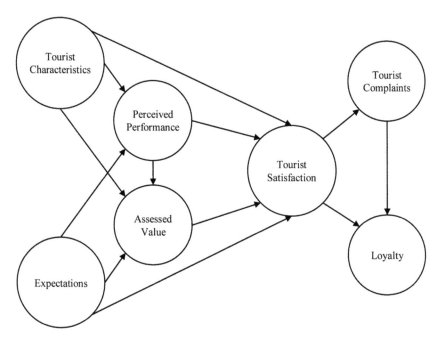

FIGURE 15.1   The Hong Kong Polytechnic University tourist satisfaction index model at sector level, 2011. **Source**: Adapted from Song et al. (2011).

TABLE 15.1 Measurements of the Sectoral Model.

Construct	Indicator
Tourist characteristics	Gender
	Education
	Age
	No. of visits
Expectations	Overall expectations
	Customization
	Reliability
Perceived performance	Overall performance
	Customization
	Reliability
Assessed value	Price given quality
	Quality given price
Loyalty	Revisit intentions
	Recommendation to others
Complaint intention	Intentions to complain to employees
	Intentions to complain to others
Tourist satisfaction	Overall satisfaction
	Comparison with expectations
	Comparison with ideal

Where multiple service levels are concerned, index aggregation through a scientific weighting scheme will be necessary. A dual-model system is developed in the TSI framework. In the first stage, the sector-level structural equation model is estimated. The tourist satisfaction index for each key tourism sector is calculated as an average of the indicators of the Tourist Satisfaction construct weighted by factor loadings. The structural relationships between the constructs are also examined. The model is expected to be applicable to various service sectors because the constructs in the model are designed to provide the necessary levels of generality. The multiple indicator approach is sufficiently universal to be comparable across firms, industries, sectors, and nations (Fornell et al., 1996).

The second stage applies an aggregation model to synthesize the service performance metrics across source markets and across tourism-related sectors to visualize their contributions to the performance of the destination as a whole. Unlike the aggregation approach used in the CSI models which utilize firm sales or contributions to GDP as the weights, Song et al. (2011)

propose an overall model based on a second-order confirmatory factor analysis model which aggregates tourists' satisfaction with each service sector by using factor loadings as weights. The aggregate overall satisfaction is a reflective construct which determines tourists' satisfaction with each service sector.

On the basis of Song et al.'s (2011) pilot study, Song et al. (2012) improved the theoretical models and included six tourism-related sectors based on a survey conducted in 2010. At the sector level, the construct of tourist characteristics has been removed, as the pilot study suggests that none of the relationships between tourist characteristics and its consequences is significant. As shown in Figure 15.2, the sectoral model is modified by excluding tourist characteristics from Figure 15.1.

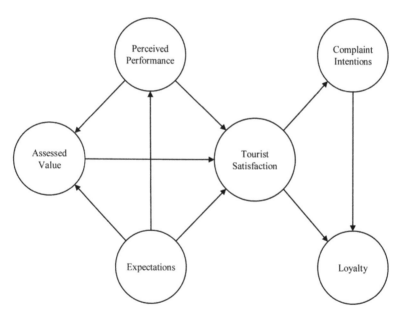

FIGURE 15.2   The Hong Kong Polytechnic University tourist satisfaction index model at sector level, 2012. **Source**: Adapted from Song et al. (2012).

In terms of the aggregation at destination level, Song et al. (2012) argue that the overall satisfaction should be a formative construct rather than reflective to reveal the logic that tourists' satisfaction with each service sector contributes to the overall tourist satisfaction. The overall model at destination level in Song et al.'s (2012) study is equivalent to a multiple indicator multiple cause (MIMIC) model in PLS (as shown in Fig. 15.3). The dual-construct model is developed to measure aggregate service satisfaction and overall destination satisfaction separately. Aggregate service satisfaction is a formative construct which is measured by variables of sectoral TSIs calculated from the model at the sector level. While the reflective construct of overall destination/experience satisfaction is measured by its three satisfaction indicators reflecting the influence of particular non-service attributes of a destination, such as culture and climate. Hence, the improved aggregate service satisfaction index has more useful managerial implications because services can be managed and controlled and improved, while there is not much that practitioners can do about the climate or overall culture. Nevertheless, taken together the aggregate service satisfaction index and the overall destination satisfaction index are useful as far as tourist experience is concerned.

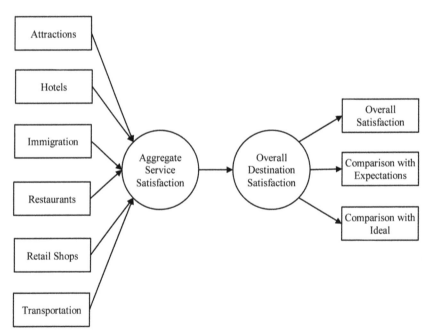

FIGURE 15.3   The Hong Kong Polytechnic University tourist satisfaction index model at destination level, 2012. **Source**: Adapted from Song et al. (2012).

As the aggregate service satisfaction construct is formative, the outer model on the left-hand side of the equation is similar to a multiple regression. The weights used to calculate the aggregate service satisfaction index are the outer weights, or regression weights, derived from the estimated

MIMIC model. This helps with the interpretation, in that the current weights are regression weights rather than factor loadings, and hence represent the influence of each service sector on the overall satisfaction level. These weights are then used to obtain the overall TSI for the destination based on the six measured service sectors. Overall satisfaction with the destination is estimated by building a reflective construct that is measured by its own three satisfaction indicators. Given its reflective nature, factor loadings are adopted as the weights for this construct. The gap between aggregate service satisfaction and overall destination satisfaction is due to the non-service attributes of the destination which contribute (mostly positively) to tourists' overall satisfaction with their tourism experiences at the destination. However, it is necessary to understand tourists' overall satisfaction with their entire travel experience in a destination in addition to their aggregate satisfaction with manageable services.

The TSI theoretical framework can be applied to various levels of aggregation, from a service unit within an organization (such as rooms or food and beverage departments of a hotel), to a whole company (e.g., a hotel, a restaurant, or a theme park), to a company group (e.g., a hotel group, a chained restaurant), to a tourism sub-sector (accommodation, restaurants, transport, and so on), and to the destination as a whole. For example, a hotel is interested to evaluate the performance and customer satisfaction about each service department as well as the performance of the hotel overall; a destination management organization would like to know tourist satisfaction with each service sector and with the destination as a whole.

15.4 CASE STUDIES

The TSI framework has been empirically tested first based on a pilot study on mainland Chinese tourists' satisfaction with three selected service sectors including hotels, retail shops, and local tour operators in 2008. The computed sectoral TSIs are 76.78, 73.01, and 72.82 out of 100, respectively. The aggregated overall TSI is 74.04, with the retail sector satisfaction contributing the most to Chinese tourists' overall satisfaction, followed by the hotel sector satisfaction and then the local tour operator sector satisfaction (Song et al., 2011). In the follow-up TSI studies, annual surveys haven been conducted covering all major source markets and six-key tourism sectors including attractions, hotels, immigration services, restaurants, retail shops, and transportation. The PolyU Tourist Satisfaction Index for Hong Kong is 75.96 in 2013, with an increase of 0.89 points from 75.07 in 2012, which has been so far the highest tourist satisfaction index since the Index was launched in 2009, scoring 1.91 points above the 5-year average of 74.05 (The Hong Kong Polytechnic University, 2013).

By adopting the theoretical framework of Song et al. (2011, 2012), a number of research projects have developed and published tourist satisfaction indexes in various destinations, such as Macau tourist satisfaction index (Macau TSI) and Shenzhen tourist satisfaction index (Shenzhen TSI), among others (The Hong Kong Polytechnic University, 2009, 2010, 2011). Built on a uniform theoretical framework, the TSIs can be benchmarked across different destinations. Table 15.2 shows the TSIs for the attractions, hotels, immigration and restaurants sectors as well as the overall satisfaction with Hong Kong, Macau and Shenzhen.

TABLE 15.2   Comparison of TSIs Across Destinations in 2011.

	Attrac-tions	Hotels	Immi-gration	Restau-rants	Retail shops	Transpor-tation	Overall (aggregate)
Hong Kong	74.6	69.4	69.6	67.4	69.7	77.8	72.6
Macau	71.3	68.1	69.4	65.1	69.5	72.0	68.5
Shenzhen	64.3	63.2	64.0	60.6	61.1	68.9	65.1

Source: The Hong Kong Polytechnic University (2011).

The contrast between destinations shows a uniform pattern across six observed service sectors. All of the tourism-related sectors in Hong Kong received the highest satisfaction scores from the inbound tourists, followed by the tourism services in Macau and Shenzhen. This finding indicates that Hong Kong holds a relative competitive position comparing to its neighboring destinations Macau and Shenzhen. Yet the differences of tourists' satisfaction are only marginal in sectors such as immigration, retail shops, and hotels. In fact, the competitive advantages of the tourism industry in Hong Kong are facing potential challenges from neighboring destinations. For example, the development of Disney Resort in Shanghai, the launch of the pilot tax refund program in Hainan, and the development of resort and business travel industries in Singapore and Macau are considerably increasing the competition in the region. Therefore, initiatives should be taken to improve the industry's service quality and tourist satisfaction for maintaining and enhancing Hong Kong's competitiveness as an international destination.

The results also reveal a pattern of tourists' satisfaction with the tourism-related sectors across three comparable destinations. The tourists were most satisfied with the services of transportation, followed by attractions across the observed destinations. The satisfaction scores for restaurants are consistently ranked bottom among all the service sectors. This can be explained by many factors. Some of these factors are outlined by Anderson (1994), who notes that satisfaction is greater when levels of competition, differentiation, involvement or experience are high or when switching costs, ease of standardization, or ability to evaluate quality are low. As services are co-produced in the customer's presence, at a time and in a place of the customer's choosing and with the customer's input, high levels of service performance are more difficult to achieve (Fornell & Johnson, 1993; Grönroos, 1990). This is particularly true for restaurants, where the nature of the service encounter is different from that in the transportation and immigration sectors. Hong Kong is well known as a culinary center, and it has a large number of hotels. As the competition within these sectors is very intense, it is much easier to switch providers than in the top two sectors. Competition in the attractions and public services sectors in Hong Kong is limited in comparison. These potential factors are also applicable in explaining the differences of tourists' satisfaction between service sectors in other destinations.

Another comparison is conducted by Li, Song, Chen, and Wu (2012) who assess Mainland Chinese tourists' satisfaction with Hong Kong as well as the United Kingdom. Based on the same TSI framework, the empirical results are highly consistent with the previous studies of Song et al. (2011, 2012). The study computes the overall destination TSIs and sectoral TSIs for both Hong Kong and the United Kingdom. Overall, Mainland Chinese tourists were more satisfied with Hong Kong than with the United Kingdom as their travel destination. With respect to individual service sectors, Mainland Chinese tourists were most satisfied with transport services and least satisfied with local tour operators in Hong Kong. Visitor attractions in the United Kingdom received the highest satisfaction score among the seven sectors and hotels received the lowest score. A comparison between the two destinations suggests that Mainland Chinese tourists were more satisfied with six out of seven tourism-related service sectors in Hong Kong than in the United Kingdom. In particular, the TSIs for restaurants, immigration services, and hotels in Hong Kong are more than 10 points higher than the TSIs for their U.K. counterparts. This finding suggests that Hong Kong's tourism industry has gained more competitiveness over the United Kingdom as far as Mainland Chinese tourists are concerned. This can be explained by the fact that many tourism and hospitality operators in Hong Kong have adopted industry-wide and/or internationally recognized service standards to ensure a high level of service, and particular effort has been made in understanding and satisfying this critical market, such as hiring Mandarin-speaking service staff. In comparison, language barriers and cultural differences were more prominent in tourism sectors in the United Kingdom as a more culturally distant destination for Chinese tourists. Given the potential negative relationship between cultural distance and tourist satisfaction, tourism service providers in both Hong Kong and the United Kingdom should continue to improve their understanding of the cultural characteristics of the Chinese tourist market and adopt cross-cultural perspectives in their operations. Service providers need to be more aware of and sensitive to cultural differences. Relevant staff training including intercultural communication skills is necessary. Cultural knowledge will contribute to both service providers' business success and international tourists' satisfaction with their experience in intercultural encounters. The unique research design of such a comparative setting further suggests the wide applicability of the TSI theoretical model.

In addition to more and more applications of the TSI framework, some attempts have been made to further extend the theoretical mode. In 2012, the PolyU tourism service quality index (PolyU TSQI) was launched measuring the performance of tourism-related services in Hong Kong (The Hong Kong Polytechnic University, 2013). The research design of the TSQI model resembles that of the TSI framework. At the sector level, tourism service quality is influenced by three antecedents including Interaction Quality, Servicescape Quality and Outcome Quality (Brady & Cronin, 2001; Grönroos, 1984). Similar to the TSI aggregation approach, the overall TSQI at destination level is based on a MIMIC model, where the Aggregate Service Quality construct is an antecedent of Overall Destination Satisfaction. The gap between these two indices is again caused by the non-service attributes of the destination which (mostly negatively) influence tourists' overall satisfaction at the destination. For example, it has been found that the TQSIs consistently exceed the corresponding TSIs, which suggests that service quality fails to generate tourist satisfaction at the same level due to possible factors such as air pollution, crowdedness, and traffic congestion (The Hong Kong Polytechnic University, 2013).

15.5 CONCLUSION

Given the importance of managing tourist satisfaction, it is necessary to build a system to facilitate the assessments and comparisons over time. The

TSI framework developed by Song, Li, van der Veen, and Chen (2009a,b, 2010, 2011) and Song et al. Chen (2012) is able to provide comparable and continuous assessment of tourist satisfaction. Based on an innovative dual-model design, the indexes at a higher level such as firms, tourism sectors and destinations are aggregated from the corresponding lower level such as departments, firms, and tourism sectors. Government agencies that are responsible for tourism-related activities, various departments within a firm, different sectors of the tourism industry and the general public with much needed information for decision-making and planning purposes will benefit from such system. By examining the structural relationships between constructs, the TSI model is able to address and evaluate the linkages between the performance inputs and strategic outcomes related to tourist satisfaction for all the service sectors considered. By establishing a measure of tourist satisfaction which has reliable and valid links to strategic goals, the model may even help instill a long-term market perspective in regulators, investors and other tourism stakeholders.

As demonstrated in the case studies, the TSI framework is capable of benchmarking and various comparisons. By standardizing the satisfaction scores (as well as the evaluation of other constructs in the model) scientifically, comparisons are allowed across departments, firms, service sectors, source markets and destinations based on a uniform framework. Accordingly, useful implications with regard to service performance improvements can be drawn. In addition, the TSI framework is able to track changes in the service performance of relevant sectors over time by conducting the survey and calculating the indexes on a regular basis. Monitoring the dynamic changes of the TSI scores can help in evaluating the success and effectiveness of relevant business strategies and government policies.

The TSI theoretical framework is flexible, as illustrated by the further extension of the TSQI. Future research should consider further developments from both theoretical and methodological perspectives. Theoretically, the index framework can be potentially extended to cover other relevant concepts, for instance, happiness and subjective wellbeing (Uysal, Perdue, & Sirgy, 2012). Instead of providing descriptive results as is the current practice (e.g., the measuring national well-being project conducted by Office for National Statistics in the United Kingdom), a number of comparable indexes (e.g., tourist happiness indexes) at different levels can be constructed and aggregated based on a more comprehensive, further extended TSI framework, which incorporates the relationships between these additional constructs and tourist satisfaction.

In terms of the model estimation method, PLS has been seen as the best suited approach for prediction purpose as it produces optimal predictions of the dependent variables from the observed explanatory variables. However, because PLS is a limited-information estimation method, its estimates are not as efficient as full-information estimates. More advanced estimation techniques should be explored, such as the Bayesian approach. The Bayesian approach has been introduced into the SEM framework (Lee, 2007; Lee & Song, 2004; Song & Lee, 2006) as an asymptotically unbiased estimation method with many other advantages. For example, prior knowledge can be incorporated in the SEM; it is possible to use dichotomous or binary variables; estimates are reliable even with small sample. The robust performance of the Bayesian approach is particularly helpful for frequent small-scale surveys, and will therefore be particularly useful for small enterprises to implement the TSI framework on a regular basis.

KEYWORDS

- **tourist satisfaction index**
- **structural equation modeling**
- **dual-model system**

REFERENCES

Anderson, E. W. Cross-Category Variation in Customer Satisfaction and Retention. *Mark. Lett.* **1994,** *5*(1), 19–30.

Anderson, E. W.; Fornell, C.; Lehmann, D. R. Customer Satisfaction, Market Share, and Profitability: Findings from Sweden. *J. Mark.* **1994,** *58*(3), 53–66.

Boulding, W.; Kalra, A.; Staelin, R.; Zeithaml, V. A. A Dynamic Process Model of Service Quality: From Expectations to Behavioral Intentions. *J. Mark. Res.* **1993,** *30*(1), 7–27.

Brady, M. K.; Cronin, J. J., Jr. Some New Thoughts on Conceptualizing Perceived Service Quality: A Hierarchical Approach. *J. Mark.* **2001,** *65*(3), 34–49.

Chan, L. K.; Hui, Y. V.; Lo, H. P.; Tse, S. K.; Tso, G. K. F.; Wu, M. L. Consumer Satisfaction Index: New Practice and Findings. *Eur. J. Mark.* **2003,** *37*(5/6), 872–909.

Cronin, J. J.; Taylor, S. A. Measuring Service Quality: A Reexamination and Extension. *J. Mark.* **1992,** *56*(3), 55–68.

Fornell, C. A National Customer Satisfaction Barometer: The Swedish Experience. *J. Mark.* **1992,** *56*(1), 6–21.

Fornell, C.; Cha, J. Partial Least Squares. In *Advanced Methods of Marketing Research*; Bagozzi, R. P., Ed.; Blackwell: Cambridge, MA, 1994; vol. 407, pp 52–78.

Fornell, C.; Johnson, M. D. Differentiation as a Basis for Explaining Customer Satisfaction across Industries. *J. Econ. Psychol.* **1993**, *14*(4), 681–696.

Fornell, C.; Johnson, M. D.; Anderson, E. W.; Cha, J.; Bryant, B. E. The American Customer Satisfaction Index: Nature, Purpose, and Findings. *J. Mark.* **1996**, *60*(4), 7–18.

Fuchs, M.; Weiermair, K. Destination Benchmarking: An Indicator-System's Potential for Exploring Guest Satisfaction. *J. Travel Res.* **2004**, *42*(3), 212–225.

Grönroos, C. *Service Management and Marketing: Managing the Moments Of Truth in Service Competition.* Lexington Books, Lexington, MA, 1990.

Gruca, T. S.; Rego, L. L. Customer Satisfaction, Cash Flow, and Shareholder Value. *J. Mark.* **2005**, *69*(3), 1–130.

Hennig-Thurau, T.; Klee, A. The Impact of Customer Satisfaction and Relationship Quality on Customer Retention: A Critical Reassessment and Model Development. *Psychol. Mark.* **1997**, *14*(8), 737–764.

Heung, V. C. Satisfaction Levels of Mainland Chinese Travelers with Hong Kong Hotel Services. *Int. J. Contemporary Hospitality Manage.* **2000**, *12*(5), 308–315.

Kau, A. K.; Lim, P. S. Clustering Of Chinese Tourists To Singapore: An Analysis Of Their Motivations, Values And Satisfaction. *Int. J. Tourism Res.* **2005**, *7*(4–5), 231–248.

Keiningham, T. L.; Perkins-Munn, T.; Evans, H. The Impact of Customer Satisfaction on Share-Of-Wallet in a Business-To-Business Environment. *J. Serv. Res.* **2003**, *6*(1), 37–50.

Kozak, M.; Rimmington, M. Measuring Tourist Destination Competitiveness: Conceptual Considerations and Empirical Findings. *Int. J. Hospitality Manage.* **1999**, *18*(3), 273–283.

LaTour, S. A.; Peat, N. C. Conceptual and Methodological Issues in Consumer Satisfaction Research. *Adv. Consumer Res.* **1979**, *6*(1), 431–437.

Lee, S. Y. *Structural Equation Modeling: A Bayesian Approach.* Wiley: Chichester, West Sussex, 2007.

Lee, S. Y.; Song, X. Y. Evaluation of the Bayesian and Maximum Likelihood Approaches in Analyzing Structural Equation Models with Small Sample Sizes. *Multivariate Behav. Res.* **2004**, *39*(4), 653–686.

Li, G.; Song, H.; Chen, J. L.; Wu, D. C. Comparing Mainland Chinese Tourists' Satisfaction with Hong Kong and the UK Using Tourist Satisfaction Index. *J. China Tourism Res.* **2012**, *8*, 371–392.

Li, J. W. J.; Carr, N. Visitor Satisfaction: An Analysis of Mainland Chinese Tourists on the Australian Gold Coast. *Int. J. Hospitality Tourism Admin.* **2004**, *5*(3), 31–48.

Luo, X.; Homburg, C. Neglected Outcomes of Customer Satisfaction. *J. Mark.* **2007**, *71*(2), 133–149.

Mittal, V.; Kamakura, W. A. Satisfaction, Repurchase Intent, and Repurchase Behavior: Investigating the Moderating Effect of Customer Characteristics. *J. Mark. Res.* **2001**, *38*(1), 131–142.

Oh, H.; Parks, S. C. Customer Satisfaction and Service Quality: A Critical Review of the Literature and Research Implications for the Hospitality Industry. *Hospitality Res. J.* **1997**, *20*(3), 35–64.

Oliver, R. L. A Cognitive Model of the Antecedents and Consequences of Satisfaction Decisions. *J. Mark. Res.* **1980**, *17*(4), 460–469.

Parasuraman, A.; Zeithaml, V. A.; Berry, L. L. A Concept Model of Service Quality and Its Implications for Future Research. *J. Mark.* **1985**, *49*(3), 41–50.

Rust, R. T.; Moorman, C.; Dickson, P. R. Getting Return on Quality: Revenue Expansion, Cost Reduction, or Both? *J. Mark.* **2002,** *66*(4), 7–24.

Seiders, K.; Voss, G. B.; Grewal, D.; Godfrey, A. L. Do Satisfied Customers Buy More? Examining Moderating Influences in a Retailing Context. *J. Mark.* **2005,** *69*(4), 26–43.

Sirakaya, E.; Petrick, J.; Choi, H. S. The Role of Mood on Tourism Product Evaluations. *Ann. Tourism Res.* **2004,** *31*(3), 517–539.

Sirgy, M. J. A Social Cognition Model of Consumer Satisfaction/Dissatisfaction: An Experiment. *Psychol. Mark.* **1984,** *1*(2), 27–44.

Song, H. *Tourism Supply Chain Management.* London: Routledge, 2012.

Song, H.; Li, G.; Van Der Veen, R.; Chen, J. L. Assessing Mainland Chinese Tourists' Satisfaction with Hong Kong Using the Tourist Satisfaction Index. In *Marketing Innovations For Sustainable Destinations*; Fyall, A., Kozak, M., Andreu, L., Gnoth, J., Lebe, S. S., Eds.; Goodfellow Publishing: Oxford, 2009a; pp 113–122.

Song, H.; Li, G.; Van Der Veen, R.; Chen, J. L. Assessing Mainland Chinese Tourists' Satisfaction with Hong Kong Using the Tourist Satisfaction Index. *Presented at the Third Advances in Tourism Marketing Conference*, Bournemouth, UK, 2009b.

Song, H.; Li, G.; Van Der Veen, R.; Chen, J. L. Hong Kong Tourist Satisfaction Index. Presented at the Eighth Asia-Pacific CHRIE Conference, Phuket, Thailand, 2010.

Song, H.; Li, G.; Van Der Veen, R.; Chen, J. L. Assessing Mainland Chinese Tourists' Satisfaction with Hong Kong Using Tourist Satisfaction Index. *Int. J. Tourism Res.* **2011,** *13*(1), 82–96.

Song, H.; Van Der Veen, R.; Li, G.; Chen, J. L. The Hong Kong Tourist Satisfaction Index. *Ann. Tourism Res.* **2012,** *39*(1), 459–479.

Song, X. Y.; Lee, S. Y. Model Comparison of Generalized Linear Mixed Models. *Stat. Med.* **2006,** *25*(10), 1685–1698.

The Hong Kong Polytechnic University. *The 2009 Hong Kong Polytechnic University Tourist Satisfaction Index*. The Hong Kong Polytechnic University: Hong Kong, 2009.

The Hong Kong Polytechnic University. *The 2010 Hong Kong Polytechnic University Tourist Satisfaction Index*. The Hong Kong Polytechnic University: Hong Kong, 2010.

The Hong Kong Polytechnic University. *The 2011 Hong Kong Polytechnic University Tourist Satisfaction Index*. The Hong Kong Polytechnic University: Hong Kong, 2011.

The Hong Kong Polytechnic University. *The Hong Kong Polytechnic University Tourist Satisfaction Index and Tourism Service Quality Index 2013*. The Hong Kong Polytechnic University: Hong Kong, 2013.

Uysal, M.; Perdue, R. R.; Sirgy, M. J., Eds. *Handbook of Tourism and Quality-of-Life Research: Enhancing the Lives of Tourists and Residents of Host Communities.*: Springer, New York, 2012.

Wang, Y.; Vela, M. R.; Tyler, K. Cultural Perspectives: Chinese Perceptions of UK Hotel Service Quality. *Int. J. Cult., Tourism Hospitality Res.* **2008,** *2*(4), 312–329.

Wong, J.; Law, R. Difference in Shopping Satisfaction Levels: A Study of Tourists in Hong Kong. *Tourism Manage.* **2003,** *24*(4), 401–410.

Yi, Y. A Critical Review of Consumer Satisfaction. In *Review of Marketing 1990*; Zeithaml, V. A. Ed.; Chicago: American Marketing Association, 1990; pp 68–123.

Yoon, Y.; Uysal, M. An Examination of the Effects of Motivation and Satisfaction on Destination Loyalty: A Structural Model. *Tourism Manage.* **2005,** *26*(1), 45–56.

CHAPTER 16

TOWARD INCREASED ACCURACY IN PRODUCTIVITY MEASUREMENT: EVIDENCE-BASED ANALYTICS

CHERYLYNN BECKER

University of Southern Mississippi, Gulf Coast, College of Business, 730 East Beach Boulevard, Long Beach, MS 39560, USA. E-mail: Cheri.becker@usm.edu

CONTENTS

16.1   INTRODUCTION

The belief that the maximization of worker productivity leads to exceptional organizational performance can be tracked back to the earliest period of industrialization. In its simplest form labor productivity is nothing more than a ratio between an organization's labor input and the amount of output in products and services that result from the employees' efforts. Within for-profit industries, an overriding organizational goal is the maximization of output while simultaneously minimizing the associated inputs without sacrificing the organization's established quality standards. In spite of the seeming simplicity and widespread acceptance of this definition of productivity, attempts at measurement continue to present a challenge for researchers and practitioners alike. Existing measures of productivity range from highly quantitative financial computations to more conceptual qualitative ones; they may be aggregated to include multifactor elements or represented by a single factor (Hu & Cai, 2004). It appears that different people perceive productivity differently based upon their "backgrounds, positions of responsibility and goals," (Sigala, 2004) so it makes sense that no single measure serves equally well across all contexts. While some approaches to measuring productivity are effective at identifying relative productivity among industries or businesses, other measures provide a more accurate picture of the specific levels of productivity achieved by a business, by an individual, or by a work unit. In reviewing the broadly based literature on productivity measurement, it is clear that over time the understanding of productivity has evolved and it has become increasingly clear that many of the elements contributing to productivity are tucked away in a "black box" and can only be guessed at. Given that labor expenditures are often an organization's single greatest expense category and also one of the most difficult to control, the importance of this issue cannot be overstated (Combs et al., 2006). For labor-intensive industries such as hospitality and retailing the issue is paramount.

The present chapter draws from across disciplines to present an evolutionary perspective on productivity and issues related to its measurement in management and hospitality studies. The chapter identifies how limitations in traditional productivity measurement have led to the emergence of evidence-based management and analytics, two perspectives that appear to offer a clearer understanding of the relationships between organizational activities and policies and the labor productivity of an organization's workforce.

16.2   HISTORIC PERSPECTIVES

The earliest endeavors related to management science and productivity measurement were introduced by Frederick Taylor in the late nineteenth century. Coined as either "Taylorism" or "Scientific Management," the principles Taylor introduced at that time laid the ground work and foundation for many areas of industrial engineering and management science that are still prevalent today. The primary objective sought by Taylor was the improvement of economic efficiency and labor productivity through the application of empirical measurement, engineering processes, or motivational strategies. Taylor observed and evaluated factory workers to identify the one best way to perform a task and trained the workers accordingly. He noted that although some workers were more capable than others, even the most gifted would slow their work activity to the lowest level acceptable because there were no incentives associated with higher levels of production. Taylor recognized that workers were individuals, that they possessed self-interest, and that they could be motivated to work harder if they were compensated proportionately according to their output. Taylor implemented piece rates and rest breaks both of which contributed to increased worker output (Taylor, 1911).

While Taylor focused on time studies by using stopwatches and slide rules, Lillian and Frank Gilbreth introduced the concept of motion studies by filming workers and later analyzing work motions through a magnifying glass. Together, these methods were used to minimize both time and motion associated with task performance; worker productivity increased in some cases up to 300% (Gilbreth & Gilbreth, 1953; Price, 1990). Although many productivity increases fostered through scientific management continue to influence work practices today others did not endure in the long run, as workers performing de-skilled jobs as part of a rigorously scheduled, mechanized process became increasingly dissatisfied. The strict emphasis on the scientific management approach to labor productivity diminished following worker strikes and congressional investigations which banned Taylor's scientific management in some facilities (Mullins, 2004). These events paved the way for a less controversial approach to secure increased labor productivity; that was by appealing to the humanistic needs of workers.

Although the goals of profit maximization were the same, the human relations movement of the 1930s inspired by the Hawthorne studies communicated the notion that productivity could be maximized with less worker–manager antagonism by appealing to the workers' needs for social relationships, by providing satisfying work environments, and by recognizing and acknowledging the workers' efforts and accomplishments. Under the guidance of Elton Mayo, a group of Harvard professors introduced experimentation into the factory environment to study the effects of various social and environmental factors on worker output. Although these researchers were able to document short-term improvements in productivity, their five-year study found no evidence to support the sustainability of these improvements. Overall, the results of the Hawthorne studies were controversial, yet the human relations movement offered a managerial ideology that was easy to sell to workers and managers alike (Bruce & Nyland, 2011).

In summing up the early era of modern management thinking, it is clear that productivity measurement focused jointly on the individual worker and the process the worker used to complete a task. In either case, the overriding goal focused on eliminating waste and maximizing the organization's profitability and return on investment. The same challenges exist today and several fields of study and research have emerged over the years which continue to study the same issues. Included among these are industrial-organizational psychology, industrial engineering, operations management, and human resources management.

Beginning with a measurement system primarily based on counting and accounting, the emergence of new tools such as high-speed microcomputers have increased the complexity and sophistication of our analyses but have fallen short of providing the answers to age old questions. It is meaningful that the same concepts and relationships that dominated the early research efforts of Taylor, the Gilbreths, and Mayo continue to challenge contemporary researchers who persist in their efforts to document causal relationships between managerial practices and productive output. It could be that the choice of how to manage and motivate workers toward increased productivity has no significant effect (Bloom & Reenen, 2010), or alternatively, it could be that the research designs and measures employed lack the fine grained distinctions needed to document and confirm these relationships.

16.3   ECONOMIC PERSPECTIVES

Evolution in the measurement of productivity has been largely generated through economic research originally developed to provide aggregate models for evaluating productivity at the nation level. These models have exerted meaningful influences on productivity measurement and variants of them continue to be applied in a bottoms-up approach to explain observed differences in productivity among organizations (Hulten, 2000). The Cobb–Douglas production function evolved over a 20-year period (1927–1947) to illustrate the relationship between production output and the inputs used to obtain it (Douglas, 1976). In its simplest form, output (Q) is considered to be a direct product of capital investment (K) and labor (L) and can be written as $Q = f(L, K)$. The conceptual evolution of the model over time allowed for the inclusion of additional inputs to the factors of production, such that an expanded version might be expressed as, for example, $Q = f(L, K, H, M)$ where the additional factor H represents business initiative and M represents managerial expertise (two concepts that cannot easily be converted into the form of a measured continuous variable necessary to operationalize the formula). Alternatively, the function may be expressed more efficiently as $Q = f(L, K, A)$ where A, measures any increase in production output that cannot be directly attributed to capital or labor. In this last example A is identified as total factor productivity (TFP) and is considered to be an intangible component of production that defies direct measurement. Solow (1956) introduced the term "Solow residual" to describe TFP because it consists of the residual that remains after identifiable factors of production have been accounted for. Solow, who received the 1987 Nobel Prize in Economic Sciences for his contributions in this area, originally attributed TFP to labor-augmenting technologies, but his conceptualization was highly influenced by the rapid expansion of technology that took place during the era in which his work was accomplished.

In reality, the composition of TFP cannot be credited to any single factor but represents contributions to productivity which may emerge from any combination of different sources. These may include, for example, research and development expenditures, innovation, creativity, managerial excellence, the financial or organizational structures of a business, educational attainment, work experience, organizational culture, fluctuations in demand, or changes in societal attitudes (OECD, 2008; Hulten, 2000). Mankiw, Romer, and Wells (1992) expanded the productivity function to include the input associated with human capital which has the effect of producing a smaller TFP on the one hand and the additional challenge of providing an accurate measurement of human capital on the other, though level of education, training, or work experience are often used as surrogate measures. Economists have described TFP as a measure of "ignorance" because the actual source from which this component of productivity is generated cannot be sorted out

(Abramovitz, 1956). Nonetheless, the concept continues to provide a consistent intellectual framework to guide economic measurement and in spite of some weaknesses, other techniques available for evaluating productivity have not performed better (Hulten, 2000). The Bureau of Labor Statistics (BLS) adopted the use of TFP in 1983 yet renamed the term multi-factor productivity and applies the measurement to annual economic releases limited to a few select industrial classifications.

It should be noted that the production functions offered in the preceding section have been presented in a very simplified format to provide a basic understanding of production function measurement to a broad audience including those with limited exposure to the application of mathematical formulae to economic models. In spite of this simplistic treatment, meaningful insights emerge from the discussion which appears relevant to the analysis of labor productivity in contemporary research.

In management-oriented research, widely used measures of labor productivity typically rely upon ratio calculations determined by revenue per employee, revenue per labor hour, or revenue per full time equivalent employee. Revenue figures used may be based upon total revenues, gross revenues, or net revenues; the adjustment of revenue figures to exclude the operational expenses unrelated to labor serves to minimize error contributed by extraneous factors. The revenue per employee and its derivatives provide a commonly accepted measure of labor productivity because it mirrors the system used by the BLS in calculating industry productivity measures. Notably, the BLS offers the caveat that their measures do not actually reflect the individual contribution of labor, but rather represent the combined effects of many factors (technology, capital, materials, contract employment, managerial skill, capacity utilization, energy, process efficiency, and unidentified but unique characteristics associated with the workforce).

When the research goal is to evaluate the impact of any management policy which is intended to increase worker productivity, the only relevant productive output is one secured exclusively from the contribution of labor. Although it may be impossible to factor out an accurate value for the contribution of labor, greater accuracy can be secured by controlling for or eliminating factors that impact upon revenues and incur identifiable expenses. While critical control factors may vary according to industry, within the hospitality sector, two major control factors include capital and land.

Although it is typical for researchers to note that hotels are labor intensive, the recognition of capital intensity is less prevalent and it is not unusual to see the costs associated with capital expenditures and capital investments either ignored or underestimated. Although size (based upon the number of guest rooms) is often used as a surrogate measure of capital investment, this ignores public areas and many other important features that differentiate properties and their associated room rates and revenue structures. According to O'Neill (2003) capital expenditure rates for hotels averaged 10.6% of revenue over the period between 1990 and 2002. More recent figures suggest an average range of 8.5 to 9.8 depending upon the hotel segment (Sheehen, 2007). Clearly a major element of the product and service delivered by a lodging property is associated with its original capital investments and the investments incurred by timely refurbishments. The failure to provide an accurate account of this cost seriously undermines the outcome of productivity analysis particularly as it relates to labor. Any analysis that underestimates actual capital expenditures and provides a measure of employee productivity based solely on revenues cannot be considered as a source of valid information regarding labor productivity. Related areas that should be included as cost factors in hotel productivity functions also include franchise and management fees. These areas incur costs along with advantages that are directly related to the market value (i.e., output) of a property and incorporate benefits such as brand recognition, marketing programs, and reservations systems. Research findings generally suggest that franchised units and branded properties outperform independents when productivity studies are undertaken. One wonders if this would be the case if the expenses associated with brand affiliation were incorporated into study designs.

A primary consideration for any customer interactive service operation is its location. This is particularly true within the hotel sector where room rates are set to reflect the desirability of the hotel's location. Premium prices can be demanded for properties with ocean frontage, for those in close proximity to convention facilities and tourist attractions or merely based upon convenience. Just as revenues vary to reflect location attributes, so too do expenses factors. Property taxes are typically in the public domain and can be used to calculate the differential impact of expenses incurred by a property based upon location attributes.

In sum, this section was framed to consider the measurement of labor productivity as it relates to the variation in and implementation of management practices. It reviewed a generalized approach to understanding the various sources that contribute to productivity, identified some shortcomings associated with measuring productivity as a simple ratio between revenues and labor and provided some examples of meaningful control factors that can be applied to increase the accuracy of productivity studies.

16.4   COMPARATIVE PRODUCTIVITY—DATA ENVELOPMENT ANALYSIS

The last two decades have witnessed a tremendous growth in the use of data envelopment analysis (DEA) a mathematical programming approach which shares a tight linkage with economic production theory (Cook, Tone, & Zhu, 2014). According to Hulten (2000), DEA was initially developed to better identify the various unidentified elements that contribute to TFP. Although DEA can be viewed as a production frontier, it is primarily intended as a process "for performance evaluation and benchmarking against best practice" (Cook, Tone, & Zhu, 2014, p. 1). DEA calculates an efficiency measure based on the ratio between inputs and outputs and uses this to identify the most efficient operations from a sample of homogeneously operating units. DEA is effective at combining multiple inputs and multiple outputs into a single measure of performance efficiency and can accommodate both quantitative and qualitative data. The DEA procedure has been used successfully in a number of service-oriented businesses including retail, restaurants, fast food, nursing homes, and banking (Sherman & Zhu, 2006; Hu & Cai, 2004). Wober (2007) provides an extensive review of 35 separate studies that applied DEA to the hospitality and tourism sector. In spite of its potential to provide decision makers with meaningful information, the effectiveness of DEA is heavily reliant on the degree to which the researcher has a clear understanding of the process and selects measures that accurately reflect meaningful variables (Cook, Tone, & Zhu, 2014).

Unlike popular statistical procedures, the model generated by DEA is dependent upon the initial selection of the inputs and outputs, and no provision is offered to test for the best specification (Berg, 2010). DEA cannot identify specific values for the productivity performance of any unit but rather provides a relative assessment of each unit as compared to the sample being evaluated (Jones & Siag, 2009). Although sources contributing to inefficient operations can often be identified, analyzed, and used to improve the productivity of underperforming units (Sherman & Zhu, 2006), the appropriateness of the information of a comparative assessment is contingent upon the degree to which the sample units share the same strategic goals, operate in similar environments with comparable internal resources and expenditures. Several hospitality studies have utilized DEA to evaluate comparative hotel efficiencies and establish benchmark units in samples demarcated by segment affiliation or strategic groups (Assaf & Agbola, 2014; Tsang & Chen, 2013; Sigala, Jones, Lockwood, & Airey, 2005; Hu & Cai, 2004; Sigala,

2004). While this approach increases homogeneity to some extent, in practice, the informative analysis generated through DEA is clearly strengthened when applied to properties within a single chain because the strategies and standards of single chain units should be more homogeneous and practices that lay outside norm are more readily identifiable. Such an example is provided by Sherman and Zhu (2006) who report that a US banking corporation was able to save over $100 million of annual personnel and operating costs by analyzing the results secured through DEA to explore and correct the causes of inefficiency found in its underperforming units.

Although it is common in the application of DEA (as in regression studies) to use number of rooms as a surrogate for capital investment, research that incorporates more precise values should yield more accurate outcomes. In a number of DEA applications, the book value of properties provided a more accurate assessment for capital investment (Barros, 2005a,b; Barros & Alves, 2004). A notable shortcoming in DEA studies is that input variables used in the analyses typically ignore environmental factors. Thus, property location, the relevant economy, and political upheavals which may impact upon operational performance are typically omitted from the actual analysis process. The DEA study by Shyu and Hung (2012) provided a meaningful exception by incorporating property location, years in operation, unemployment rates, and consumer price indices as control variables in their study. The application of these controls created a down shift in resulting efficiency scores. With a similar objective, DeJorge and Suarez (2014) conducted a DEA which incorporated a second level explanatory analysis including variables measuring market concentration share, size as measured by number of beds, quality rating, geographic location, and level of decentralization. The inclusion of the second level analysis provided meaningful results and enhanced the informative value of their study. While it is clear that researchers are progressively pursuing attempts to overcome the deficiencies inherent to this technique, to date the interest in DEA as evidenced by hospitality research appears more concerned with exploring the boundaries of the procedure than exploring the potential of its application in real life scenarios.

16.5   RATIO BENCHMARKING

Although DEA offers a great advantage in that it facilitates competitive benchmarking, the application of benchmarking through ratio analysis has been a mainstay in hospitality firms for decades and it continues to be used extensively in performance and efficiency measurement within the industry.

Ratios assess the relationship between two factors associated with measures of some specific area of organizational performance. They provide benchmarks which allow an operation to compare its performance against external industry data or against the performance of other units operating within its brand or chain affiliation. Used internally ratio benchmarks provide an ongoing evaluation of departmental and organizational performance relative to established internal standards, to chart improvement over time, or to compare actual financial performance to that which was budgeted. Commonly used ratio measures for the lodging industry include measures of operational performance (based upon profit and loss statements), financial performance (using data secured from the balance sheet), and employee performance (e.g., rooms cleaned per hour). Exhibit A provides a sampling of standard ratio measures used in the lodging industry today.

EXHIBIT A Examples of standard ratio measures used as benchmarks for hotel properties.

Operating ratios	Profitability ratios	Activity ratios	Employee ratios
Percent occupancy	ROI (return on investment)	Employee turnover	Rooms cleaned per hour
ADR (average daily rate)	ROE (return on equity)	Daily seat turnover	Customers served per hour
RevPar (revenue per available room)	PM (profit margin)	Fixed asset turnover	Sales revue per month
TrevPAR (total revenue per available room)	GOPPAR (gross operating profit)	Receivables turnover	
Food cost %	RE ratio (price earnings ratio)		
Labor cost %			

Although the ratio approach to benchmarking offers the advantage of providing a quick reference for managers to use to monitor performance on a continuing basis, it often fails to provide sufficient information about the bottom line to stand alone as a decision tool. The example provided below addresses concerns associated with an over reliance on standard industry ratio measurement and provides a very effective summary of the related deficiencies.

Revenue per available room (RevPar) provides an industry standard for evaluating hotel performance. By using the number of guestrooms as a variable unit of measure across properties as the denominator inherent discrepancies apply. For example, a 200 room property that generates $20,000 daily, exhibits a RevPar of $100. The same property undertakes a conversion which combines the existing guestrooms into 100 suites and charges a room rate of $200 generating the same level of revenue. The resulting RevPar after conversion is now $200. Although the reliance on RevPar suggests improved performance, a reality check indicates that the idea of improved performance is merely an artifact of the measurement approach employed. In recent years, newer measures have surfaced such as total revenue per available room (TrevPar) and gross operating profit per available room (GopPar) but both measures are subject to the same distortions associated with the traditional measure of RevPar. Worse because the new measures incorporate non-room revenue in their calculations, they have the potential to increase the distortions related to hotel performance or efficiency based upon the number of units and ignoring any other factor which may be relevant.

While ratios provide insufficient stand-alone measures, used on a continuous and ongoing basis they serve effectively as an internal quality control system by alerting management to problems much in the way statistical control operates under total quality management (TQM). Ratios establish a foundation for meaningful analytical inquiry. They can be used effectively as variables in DEA analysis and appear to be emerging as a core component of evidence-based management and human resource analytics, both of which represent newer approaches which have emerged to rectify deficiencies in tradition approaches addressing issues of measuring labor productivity.

16.6 EVIDENCE-BASED ANALYTICS

A driving force behind evidence-based management is the desire to document the financial outcomes associated with investments made in human capital development (e.g., such as training, enhanced selection, or participative management) to demonstrate the effect these programs have on bottom line results. It was this same objective that inspired the body of research conducted over the decade of 1995 through 2005 that explored the impact of human resource policies on organizational productivity and financial performance. Huselid (1995) summarized the findings of his seminal contribution by inferring (but not substantiating) that a one-standard deviation increase in high performance work practices was associated with a 7.05% reduction in turnover, and per employee generated a $27,044 increase in sales, a $18,641 increase in market value, and an increase of $3,814 in profits. Huselid's study inspired an onslaught of similar studies, replications, and extensions, which taken as a whole produced disappointing results for a number of reasons. Among these are the use of cross sectional data making it impossible to establish causality, the utilization of aggregate organizational productivity measures that aren't controlled for influences on revenues outside of employee influence, an overreliance on subjective data secured from single sources, the failure to establish baseline measures, and a disregard for the inherent time lags associated with the initial implementation of HR initiatives (Wall & Wood, 2005). This is not to imply that contributions have not been forthcoming from this vein of research, but rather to suggest that answers to the questions may be better secured using a different approach.

Evidence-based management is based upon the premise that the most effective decisions are directly related to the decision maker's access to reliable and valid information. Supporters of the evidence-based approach to management feel that it has the potential to close the gap between research and practice by providing managers with accurate and relevant information to improve decision-making outcomes (Kepes, Bennett, & McDaniel, 2014). Based in empiricism evidence-based management is better understood as a systematic process that acquires, reviews, and evaluates an accumulation of information and data which includes input from quantitative, qualitative, and observational sources (Rousseau, 2006; Briner & Rousseau, 2011). When properly executed evidence-based management focuses on internal measures and provides an ongoing data stream analogous to TQM by facilitating a comparative analysis that looks within the organization, the department, or the job, to assess performance over different periods of time. When developed to align with organizational goals such as enhanced profitability or increased performance, an evidence-based data base considers both expenditures and financial gains, and simplifies the process of connecting changes in productivity outputs to inputs related to training, development or incentive structures within an organization. This, in turn, produces evidence which leads to informed decision-making and better organizational investments and practices. Evidence-based management is based upon the premise that when organizational leaders and departmental managers ask for resources they need to be able to demonstrate how the use of these resources relates to meeting organizational goals.

Concurrent with the academic interest in evidence-based management is the growing interest in analytics, a practitioner-oriented approach to management decision making that relies upon the same accumulation of data and information that provides the foundation for evidence-based management. The two perspectives share the common goal of tying investments in organizational policy and human resource practices to outcomes that positively impact on an organization's bottom line. Analytics, like evidence-based management requires breaking data and information down into component parts to increase the understanding of cause and effect. It differs from management science in that it takes a microperspective directed specifically toward the goals and objectives unique to an organization rather than on generalizations and global theory. The idea is that contextual differences count and that aggregate measures often fall short of providing organizational decision makers with the information they need to make better decisions.

One issue that appears particularly relevant in the context of hospitality research is the concept of intangibility. Hospitality researchers are quick to emphasize that intangible components of service are difficult, if not impossible, to measure. Hopefully the earlier discussion on TFP demonstrates that intangible elements drive variances in productivity across most, if not all, industrial sectors. Employee engagement, for example, is clearly intangible, yet will make a meaningful contribution to output regardless of whether an employee is delivering a service to a customer or generating a solution to a problem encountered on the assembly line of the factory floor. According to Fitz-Enz (2009), many of the leading indicators which provide organizations with information about their employees and the return of investment are intangible. The accumulation of data over time and across employees discovers relationships that otherwise may go unnoticed and undocumented. Documentation of these relationships offers the potential to identify the impact of intangibles on productive output and the opportunity to identify intangible components of job performance as important sources of competitive advantage.

To date, analytics is largely focused on human capital development and the relationship between organizational expenses and labor productivity. Common themes in analytics explore the costs and benefits associated with absenteeism, with employee turnover, with employee attitudes and employee engagement, with selection criteria, and with training and development programs (Cascio & Boudreau, 2011). Both analytics and evidence-based management give an organization the opportunity to apply a portfolio approach to workforce management which acknowledges that all employees and all jobs within an organization do not exert an equal influence on organizational performance (Gates & Langevin, 2010). Given this it is easier to understand why aggregate measures of organizational absenteeism, turnover, training expenditures or hiring costs, for example, have been ineffective when applied to productivity research or when used to assess outcomes at the organizational level.

Analytics disaggregates organizational data to facilitate the classification of employees and jobs into segments based upon the degree to which their contributions are considered to be critical to meeting organizational goals. The idea is to identify jobs where talent and performance is most likely to impact on organizational outcomes, and to focus efforts and investments on the retention and development of employees in these jobs. Casio and Boudreau (2012) provide an explicit example in discussing the impact of two different jobs associated with a Disney theme park. Their comparison focuses upon how the level of performance in different jobs might impact differentially upon a guest's experience. Although they noted that "Mickey Mouse" is both valuable and important in the park scheme, they also noted that "Mickey Mouse" is never seen outside of the costumed character, "never talks, and is always accompanied by a supervisor who manages the guest encounters" (p. 224). Their analysis suggests that a well-engineered job such as that filled by "Mickey" is subject to too little performance variability to benefit from any additional expenses associated with training. In contrast, they note that the park sweeper job may have a pivotal impact upon the customer experience which can determine whether the customer evaluates his/her experience in a positive or negative light. Sweepers occupy jobs and identities that are accessible to customers; sweepers can be consulted to provide answers to questions pertaining to directions, to park policies and generally are expected to adjust to meet customer expectations across a variety of areas depending upon whatever customer needs may arise. From this perspective, it becomes clear that training expenditures indiscriminately applied and aggregated across jobs or across departments can potentially obscure the value of meaningful investments in training activities.

According to Fitz-Enz (2010), a CEO of a major bank allocates $250 million annually to training programs but has no idea if the training activities he supports have any impact on productivity or job performance. His experience is not unique. In 2011, US businesses invested almost $172 billion in employee training and development (Cairns, 2012). Yet, according to a survey of 704 mid and senior level executives conducted by the American Society of Training and Development, 92% used participant reaction, rather than performance improvement, to evaluate training effectiveness (Cairns, 2012). Meaningful assessments of training effectiveness cannot be secured in the short run. While an experimental design with pre and post-tests may provide a quick quantitative comparison, it falls short of evaluating the transfer of any new knowledge learned into the work environment. Previous research has documented time lags for the implementation of new practices to generate meaningful outcomes of 1 to 4 years for empowerment and 6 to 9 years for teamwork (Birdi et al, 2008). Because both analytics and evidence-based approaches at the core rely upon the compilation of organization specific data overtime, these methods promise to provide meaningful answers to many uncertainties that undermine effective managerial decision-making activities. Neither approach suggests that there is "one best way" but rather emphasize that contextual factors related to the unique characteristics of organizations and the various workgroups within them will determine what works best.

16.7 CONCLUSION

This chapter has taken a broad perspective in summarizing a century of research related to the measurement of productivity in an organizational context. The review highlighted the dominant approaches that have been used by researchers and pointed out why these traditional approaches have often fallen short of producing actionable results. The last five years have witnessed a slow but steady increase in attention devoted to evidence-based management from both the academic side and from the popular business press. That the two separate but similar concepts have gained some prominence in tandem but independent of one another suggests that both academics and practitioners are invested in the hope that evidence-based analytics may provide a more definitive answer to what drives organizational productivity.

To date, it is unclear whether hospitality leaders are informed of the shift toward evidence-based analytics and if informed the degree to which they are receptive to this change. A dozen executives from major hospitality corporations were contacted about participating in a research project utilizing an evidence-based approach. The goal was to assess the impact of training investments on employee productivity in financial terms. Most of the executives were unfamiliar with the evidence-based or analytic model. Those who were familiar with the model initially expressed interest in participation but eventually withdrew because their organizations lacked the accessible accumulation of data needed to support the research objective. A few of the executives in the latter group were quite knowledgeable about the potential an evidence-based approach could offer and were investigating the availability of commercially available software programs to facilitate an analytic, evidence-based approach for the future. From this scenario several broad-based research questions emerged:

- What percentage of hospitality firms and their HR executives are familiar with the concepts of HR analytics or evidence-based management?
- For those familiar with the concepts, what percentage has plans to develop an organizational database or purchase software to enable their organizations to use an analytic, evidence-based approach?
- For those familiar with the concepts, who have no plans to use an analytic, evidence-based approach, what are their objections or reasons for not wanting to utilize this approach?
- What is the availability of commercial software programs that are designed for use in implementing a database for evidence-based decision making for hospitality firms?
- What percentage of hospitality programs are currently offering courses in analytics and what is the content of the courses being offered?

In moving forward, a key element in bringing evidence-based analytics to fruition is likely to lie in a tighter collaboration between practitioners and academic researchers. Over recent years, the gap between the objectives pursued by the two groups appear to have broadened with academics supporting a "quest for *what's new* rather than *what's true* "(Pfeffer, 2007: 1339). In conclusion it appears that evidence-based analytics holds great promise for increasing organizational opportunities to more accurately measure the effectiveness of multiple inputs that have a direct impact on productivity. Arguments supporting this approach are strongly grounded in logic, implementation will provide the final test.

KEYWORDS

- **productivity**
- **total factor productivity**
- **data envelopment analysis**
- **HR analytics**
- **evidence-based management**

REFERENCES

Abramovitz, M. Resource and Output Trends in the United States Since 1870. *Am. Econ. Rev.* **1956,** *46*(2), 5–23.

Assaf, A. G.; Agbola, F. W. Efficiency Analysis of the Australian Accommodation Industry: A Bayesain Output Distance Function. *J. Hospitality Tourism Res.* **2014,** *38*(1), 116–132.

Barros, C. Measuring Efficiency in the Hotel Sector. *Ann. Tourism Res.* **2005a,** *32*(2), 456–477.

Barros, C. P. Evaluating the Efficiency of a Small Hotel Chain with a Malmquist Productivity Index. *Int. J. Tourism Res.* **2005b,** *7*(3), 173–184.

Barros, C. P.; Alves, F. P. Productivity in the Tourism Industry. *Int. Adv. Econ. Res.* **2004,** *10*(3), 215–225.

Berg, S. *Water Utility Benchmarking: Measaurement, Methodology and Performance Incentives.* University of Florida. Public Utilities Research Centerinternational Water Association, 2010.

Birdi, K.; Clegg, C.; Patterson, M.; Robinson, A.; Stride, C. B.; Wall, T. D.; Wood, S. J. The Impact of Human Resource and Operational Management Practices on Company Productivity: A Longitudinal Study. *Pers. Psychol.* **2008,** *61*(3), 467–501.

Bloom, N.; Reenen, J. V. *Human Resource Management and Productivity.* Cambridge, MA: National Bureau Of Economic Research, 2010.

Briner, R.; Rousseau, D. Evidence-Based I-O Psychology: Not There Yet But Now a Little Nearer? *Ind. Organ. Psychol.* **2011,** *4*, 76–82.

Bruce, K.; Nyland, C. Elton Mayo and the Deification of Human Relations. *Organ. Stud.* **2011,** *32*(3), 383–405.

Cairns, T. Overcoming the Challenges to Developing an ROI for Training and Development. *Employment Relat. Today* **2012,** 23–27.

Cascio, W.; Boudreau, J. *Investing in People: Financial Impact of Human Resource Initiatives* (second Ed.). Pearson Education, Inc.: Upper Saddle River, NJ, 2011.

Cascio, W. F.; Boudreau, J. W. *Short Introduction to Strategic Human Resource Management.* Cambridge University Press: Cambridge, U.K., 2012.

Combs, J.; Liu, Y.; Hall, A.; Ketchen, D. How Much Do High-Performance Work Practices Matter? A Meta-Analysis of their Effects on Organizational Performance. *Pers. Psychol.* **2006,** *59*(3), 501–528.

Cook, W.; Tone, K.; Zhu, J. Data Envelopment Analysis: Prior to Choosing a Model. *Omega* **2014,** *44*, 1–4.

DeJorge, J. D.; Suarez, C. Productivity, Efficiency and its Determinant Factors in Hotels. *Serv. Ind. J.* **2014,** *34*(4), 354–372.

Douglas, P. H. The Cobb–Douglas Production Function Once Again: Its History, its Testing and Some New Empirical Values. *J. Polit. Econ.* **1976,** *84*(5), 903–916.

Fitz-Enz, J. *ROI of Human Capital.* AMACOM: New York City, NY, 2009.

Fitz-Enz, J. *The New HR Analytics: Predicting The Economic Value of Your N company's Human Capital Investments.* AMACOM: New York City, NY, 2010.

Gates, S.; Langevin, P. Strategic Human Capital Measures: Using Leading HCM to Implement Strategy. In *The New HR Analytics: Predicting the Economic Value of Your Company's Human Capital Investments*; Fitz-Enz, J., Ed.; AMACOM: New York City, NY, **2010**; pp 26–38.

Gilbreth, F.; Gilbreth, L. Applied Motion Study. In *The Writings of The Gilbreths*; Spriegel, W., Myers, C., Eds.; Irwin: Homewood, IL, 1953; pp 207–274.

Hu, B.; Cai, L. Hotel Labor Productivity Assessment: A Data Envelopment Analysis. *J. Travel Tourism Mark., 16*(2/3), 27–38, 2004.

Hulten, C. R. *Total Factor Productivity: A Short Biography.* National Bureau Of Economic Research: Cambridge, MA, 2000.

Huselid, M. The Impact of Human Resource Practices on Turnover, Productivity and Corporate Financial Performance. *Acad. Manage. J.* **1995,** *38*(3), 635–672.

Jones, P.; Siag, A. A Re-Examination of the Factors that Influence Productivity in Hotels: A Study of the Housekeeping Function. *Tourism Hospitality Res.* **2009,** *9*(3), 224–234.

Kepes, S.; Bennett, A.; Mcdaniel, M. Evidence-Based Management and the Trustworthiness of Our Cumulative Scientific Knowledge: Implications for Teaching, Research and Practice. *Acad. Manage. Learn. Educ.* **2014,** *13*(3), 446–466.

Mankiw, G.; Romer, D.; Weil, D. A Contribution to the Empirics of Economic Growth. *Q. J. Econ.* **1992,** *107*(2), 407–437.

Mullins, L. *Management and Organizational Behavior.* Prentice Hall Pearson Education Ltd.: Upper Saddle River, NJ, 2004.

OECD. *OECD Compendium of Economic Indicators.* Organization for Economic Co-Operation and Development, 2008.

O'Neill, J. How Fees and Capex Affect Values. *Lodging Today* **2003, August,** *59*(11), P. 20.

Pfeffer, J. A Modest Proposal: How We Might Change the Process and Product of Managerial Research. *Acad. Manage. J.*, 50, 1334–1345, 2007.

Price, B. Frank and Lillian Gilbreth and The Motion Study Controversy, 1907–1930. In *A Mental Revolution: Scientific Management Since Taylor*; Nelson, D., Ed.; The Ohio State University Press: Columbus, OH, 1990.

Rousseau, D. Is There Such a Thing as 'Evidence-Based' Management? *Acad. Manage. Rev.* **2006,** *31*(2), 256–269.

Sheehen, P. Capex 2007: Spending on the Rise. *Lodging Hospitality* **2007, July 15,** 44–45.

Sherman, H.; Zhu, J. *Service Productivity Management: Improving Service Using Data Envelopment Analysis.* Springer Press: New York City, NY, 2006.

Shyu, J.; Hung, S.-C. The True Managerial Efficiency of International Tourist Hotels In Taiwan: Three-Stage Data Envelopment Analysis. *Serv. Ind. J.* **2012,** *32*(12), 1991–2004.

Sigala, M. Using Data Envelopment Analysis for Measuring and Benchmarking Productivity in the Hotel Sector. *J. Tourism Mark.* **2004,** *16*(2/3), 39–60.

Sigala, M.; Jones, P.; Lockwood, A.; Airey, D. Productivity in Hotels: A Stepwise Data Envelopment Analysis of Hotels' Rooms Division Processes. *Serv. Ind. J.* **2005,** *2.5*(1), 61–81.

Solow, R. M. Contribution to the theory of Economic Growth. *Q. J. Econ.* **1956,** *February, 70,* 65–94.

Taylor, F. *The Principles of Scientific Management.* Harper & Brothers: New York, 1911.

Tsang, S.-S.; Chen, Y.-F. Facilitating Benchmarking with Strategic Grouping and Data Envelopment Analysis: The Case of International Tourist Hotels in Taiwan. *Asia Pacific J. Tourism Res.* **2013,** *18*(5), 518–533.

Wall, T.; Wood, S. The Romance of Human Resource Management and Business Performance, and The Case for Big Science. *Human Relat.* **2005,** *58*(4), 429–462.

Wober, K. Data Envelopment Analysis. *J. Travel Tourism Mark.* **2007,** *21*(4), 91–108.

CHAPTER 17

PERFORMANCE MEASURES AND USE IN HOSPITALITY

ERSEM KARADAG

Robert Morris University, Department of Marketing, Massey Hall, #311, Moon Township, PA 15108, USA. E-mail: karadag@rmu.edu

CONTENTS

17.1 INTRODUCTION

Performance measurement of a business organization is one of the main in-struments that enable managers or other stakeholders to understand if the operational results are according to what is set initially. Key performance in-dicators are guidance for decision makers providing them crucial information about profit, products, services, and operational efficiencies. Performance measurement is the basis of most operational, planning, control, and evalu-ation decisions. Therefore, it plays a significant role in the achievement of organizational objectives, evaluating and compensating managers' perfor-mances, improving control over assets, and planning company strategies. The management guru Peter F. Drucker once said "if you can't measure it, you can't manage it" remains true for all business establishments. Without utilizing certain performance measurement tools, a company is unable to make successful plans, control the operation, and measures organizational effectiveness. This is especially true for hospitality organizations since their products are perishable, business environment is more dynamic, more com-petitive, and business volume is changeable from day to day or from season to season. In this dynamic and highly competitive environment, hospitality managers make important decisions based on performance indicators than that of other industry managers.

The success of a hospitality operation is truly dependent on managers' decisions. Performance-measurement systems allow managers to prevent or detect some problem areas in advance so managers can take correct de-viations from established goals and objectives. Unacceptable performances can be noticed quickly through the use of critical performance measure-ment tools so that mangers ensure progress toward goals being settled in advance.

17.2 PERFORMANCE MEASUREMENT AND MANAGERIAL DECISIONS

A performance measure or a metric is a quantitative value that can be em-ployed for purposes of preset comparisons or established standards. Within this context, performance is defined as "the process of quantifying the ef-ficiency and effectiveness of past actions" (Neely, 2002). On the other hand, the performance measurement is described as "the process of mea-suring work accomplishments and output, as well as measuring in-process parameters that affect work output and accomplishments"(Harbour, 1997). Ideally, performance measures are expressed in units of measures that are most meaningful to the user who make decisions based on those measures.

The purpose of financial measurement is to provide a measurable indicator to decision makers so that they can judge the organizational performance and see at what degrees their organizational objectives are met. Performance-measurement systems may be utilized at corporate level and at unit levels. At corporate level, executives use financial measurement tools to see if organizational goals are met. At the property level, managers use financial measurement tools for operational decisions, tactical and for control decisions.

Companies measure business performance for many reasons. The following are most commonly listed reasons (Bititci, Carrie & Turner, 2002).

- To monitor and control the operation or process.
- To drive improvement.
- To maximize the effectiveness of the improvement effort.
- To achieve alignment with organizational goals and objectives.
- To reward and discipline employees and managers.

Performance-measurement systems provide feedback to managers periodically about how to set business goals and provide tools on progress toward achieving goals. Performance of a hospitality organization has traditionally been measured based on financial metrics, such as occupancy, average daily rate (ADR), RevPAR, profitability, food cost, etc. In the hospitality industry, most financial metrics are developed based primarily on most fundamental common denominator in business, such as profitability, number of rooms sold, occupancy ratio, food cost, and so on.

The traditional performance measurement tools based on financial reports serve as the roots of performance metrics. However, in recent years many non-financial metrics were developed and employed together with financial metrics. In many industries, there is a growing tendency utilizing non-financial performance metrics. Financial performance measures are generated from financial statements or financial transaction records. Business performances are generated from other business reports, such as Property Management System reports. Operational performance measures show how efficiently the business resources are used, such as financial resources, human resources, or other assets. Many of the operational performance measures employ ratios that do not involve financial metrics, such as room occupancy, ADR, revenue per available room, etc. For the hospitality industry scholars, usually use two broad categories as financial metrics and non-financial metrics. Traditionally financial metrics are most commonly used however non-financial performance metrics are becoming popular in recent years.

17.2.1 FINANCIAL PERFORMANCE MEASURES

Financial measures are traditional means of performance measurement tools widely used in all kind of operations. Financial measures communicate financial objectives, and provide an overall summary of operational performance. It has been suggested that the hotel industry appears to concentrate on financial measures (Brown and McDonnell, 1965). Companies use financial measurement indicators to measure, manage, and communicate operational results. These indicators often called key performance indicators. Financial measures include, profitability, GOP, NOP, sales growth, customer profitability, etc.

Financial metrics are typically the basis for evaluating management's effectiveness, but can be read in different ways. In addition, some other factors (e.g., customer satisfaction, employee turnover) contribute to the financial outcomes and can be themselves be potential measures of management's success (Denton and White, 2000). Management guru, Peter Drucker once said: "Neither the quantity of output nor the bottom line is by itself an adequate measure of the performance of management and enterprise. Market standing, innovation, productivity, development of people, quality, and financial results—all are crucial to a company's performance and indeed to its survival. Performance has to be built into the enterprise and its management; it has to be measured—or at least judged—and it has to be continuously improved" (Drucker, 1998).

17.2.2 NON-FINANCIAL PERFORMANCE MEASURES

The use of non-financial performance measures is a relatively new area with growing recognition in the research community (Potter and Schmidgall, 1999). By the 1980s, there was a growing realization that the traditional performance measures were no longer sufficient to manage organizations competing in modern markets (Johnson and Kaplan, 1987). Managers and other stakeholders used financial performance measures for a long time, but competitive forces and market dynamics such as information technology, globalization, accountability, corporate social responsibility, transparency, and deregulation in the service industry all have changed the business environment and forced companies to create non-financial measurement tools in order to predict the future performances of an operation.

The traditional management accounting literature advocates the use of financial performance measures as the basis of many decisions. However, it is claimed that financial performance measures give little or no guidance to future performance since they do not include any measures relating to customers' satisfaction and organizational learning. Management accounting literature also advocates the use of non-performance measures as a tool in order to overcome the deficiencies attributed to financial measures. It is argued that non-financial performance measures should be used beside traditional financial performance measures in order to identify the forces that determine financial performance (Solomons, 1965). Furthermore, recent coverage of performance measure has criticized periodic financial measures as being too aggregated, too late, and too backward-looking to help managers understand the root causes of performance problems, initiate timely, corrective actions, encourage cross-functional decision making, and focus on strategic issues (Fisher, 1992). Wöber (2002) stated that performance analysis based on accounting information does not reflect many aspects of operation productivity and neglects important differences between various forms of business. For instance, in the hotel sector, financial reports do not indicate the number of overnights generated during the fiscal year, nor do they give information about the available (maximum) capacities.

There exists no single approach to generate a set of non-financial reports. Non-financial measures usually derive from non-financial resources, such as quality of customers, guest opinions, employee satisfaction surveys, observations, or from other qualitative records. Some non-financial measures are competitiveness, customer loyalty, service quality, guest satisfaction, employee satisfaction, employee turnover rate, customer retention rate, innovation, social responsibility, etc.

17.3   FINANCIAL MEASURES USED IN THE HOSPITALITY INDUSTRY

17.3.1   MEASURES USED BY ALL TYPES OF HOSPITALITY COMPANIES

17.3.1.1   GROSS PROFIT OR CONTRIBUTION MARGIN (CM) OR NET REVENUE

Gross profit indicates the net revenue that is the total revenue minus variable costs. It is an indication of management's ability to produce profits by generating sales and controlling variable costs. It can be calculated as an amount or as a percentage. The amount can be found as follows:

$$\text{Gross Profit} = (\text{Total Revenue} - \text{Variable Costs})$$

Consider the following example:

Serena Hotel's total revenue from all revenue generating departments in July is 145,565. The variable costs incurred for the same period is \$52,620. Then gross operating profit (GOP) as an amount is calculated as

$$\text{Gross Profit} = (\$145,565 - \$52,620) = \$92,945$$

If gross profit or contribution margin is expressed as a percentage, it is referred to as gross profit margin or contribution margin and calculated as follows:

$$\text{Gross Profit Margin or Contribution Margin} = 92,945/145,565 = 63.8\%$$

When calculated on monthly basis for an operation, "gross profit" is a more common term. However, when it is used for expressing a single room's profitability, "contribution margin" is a preferred term.

17.3.1.2   GROSS OPERATING PROFIT PERCENTAGE AND GOP%

GOP and GOP % is the most common financial performance measurement tool used in all hospitality properties. It is calculated at the end of each month and or year. GOP takes into account all variable and operational costs;

however, it does not consider non-operational costs, such as loan interest, depreciation, amortization, taxes, and property rents (if any). GOP provides a perfect measurement for management's overall ability and efficiency. It takes into account all costs that can be controlled by management, therefore, reflects management's control and efficiency. Assume that at Serena Hotel total operating expenses during the month of July is $48,554.

Based on Table 17.1 GOP and GOP% will be calculated as follows:

$$GOP = \text{Total Revenue} - (\text{Variable Costs} + \text{Operating Expenses})$$
$$\$145,565 - (\$52,620 + \$48,555) = \$44,390$$

Based on the figures given above for the Serena Hotel, the GOP percentage is calculated as follows:

$$GOP\% = (\text{Gross Operating Profit/Total Revenue}) \times 100$$
$$GOP\% = \$44,390/145,565 = 30.50\%$$

17.3.1.3   NET OPERATING PROFIT RATIO

Net Operation Profit (NOP) measures an investments' profitability. NOP look at the profit only from the investors' perspective, not from the manager's perspective; since managers have no control over such non-operational expenses. Loan interest, depreciation, amortization, and taxes are such non-operational expenses deducted from the GOP in order to obtain the NOP. The ratio can be calculated as

$$\text{Net Profit Ratio} = (\text{Net Profit/Total Revenue}) \times 100$$

Based on Table 17.2, non-operational expenses for Serena Hotel in July is $24,224.

Therefore, the Net Profit and Net Profit ratio can be calculated as followings:

$$\text{Net Operating Profit} = \text{Gross Operating Profit} - \text{Non-Operational Cost}$$
$$= \$44,390 - \$24,224 = \$20,166.$$

$$\text{Net Operating Profit/Total Revenue} = \$20,166/145,565 = \% \ 13.85\%$$

17.3.1.4   GROSS OPERATING PROFIT PER AVAILABLE ROOM

RevPAR provides useful information to managers from revenue perspective, but it does not reflect operational costs of a room. GOPPAR takes into account operational costs and the allow managers to look at the operation from an ownership perspective. Owners, management companies, real estate experts, and prospective investors can precisely evaluate hotel management's performance and operating efficiency on a per unit basis. GOPPAR provides a more reliable measure to hoteliers in analyzing the operational results both from revenue and operational costs perspective. From the owner's perspective, a hotel investment is a real estate investment and a business investment. Therefore, GOPPAR allows owners to make additional capacity investment decisions, renovation decisions, capital investment decisions, investing in human resources or realizing an enjoyable profit by selling the property to a potential investor. Thus, GOPPAR explains management's capacity to generate a reasonable profit for owners and to meet with their return on investment (ROI) expectations.

GOPPAR is calculated periodically, at the end of a month or a year. It is computed as follows:

GOPPAR = GOP/(Total Number of Rooms × Number of Days of the Period)

Based on Table 17.1 GOPPAR can be calculated as follows:

Gross Operating Profit: $44,390

Total number of rooms available: 64 rooms

Total number of available rooms in the hotel in July = 64 rooms × 31 day = 1984 rooms

GOPPAR = $44,390/1984 = $22, 37.

The amount of $22, 37 shows the average "gross operating profit" or "contribution margin" generated from the room inventory over the month of July.

TABLE 17.1   Financial Metrics at Serena Hotel.

		Amount	Formula
Total revenue	A	145,565	
Variable costs	B	52,620	
Operation expenses	C	48,554	
Non-operational expenses	D	24,224	
Gross profit	E	92,945	$(A - B)$
Gross operation profit (GOP)	F	44,390	$A - (B + C)$
Gross operation profit (GOP %)	G	30.50%	$(F/A) \times 100$
Number of rooms	H	64	
Number of days in July	I	31	
Number of rooms available in July	J	1984	$(H \times I)$
GOPPAR	K	22.37	(F/J)

17.3.2   MEASURES USED IN THE LODGING INDUSTRY

The financial measures used in the hospitality may further be divided into two different categories as traditional metrics and as contemporary metrics. Traditional measures are generally called as Key Performance Indicators (KPI). Traditional metrics are:

- Occupancy Percentage (Occ. %)
- ADR, or Average Room Rate (ARR)
- Revenue per Available Room (RevPAR)

The Contemporary Measures

- Total Revenue per Available Room (TrevPAR)
- Revenue per Available Customer (RevPAC)
- Cost per Occupied Room (CPOR)
- Room Yield Percentage
- Market Indexes

  - Market Penetration Index (MPI) or Market Occupancy (Market Occ)
  - Average Rate Index (ARI)
  - Revenue Generation Index ((RGI) or RevPar Index

17.3.2.1   OCCUPANCY PERCENTAGE

Occ. % is the ratio of occupied rooms to total available rooms at an accommodation property. Mangers use Occ. % to evaluate the operational performance. It is compared to budgeted or forecasted percentages, former month or former years' results or to similar hotels. It gives a comparison to the users about what percentage of units (rooms) were rented (sold) at a specific time; such as a day, week, month, or year. For example; in a hotel with 150 rooms, if 100 rooms are occupied by hotel guests at a night, the Occ. % for that night is calculated as

Occupancy Rate = (Number of Occupied Rooms/Number of Available Rooms) × 100 100/150 = 75%.

If this hotel occupancy is calculated for the month of July as seen on the Table 17.2, the Occ. % can be calculated as follows:

Total numbers of rooms available: 4650 (31 days × 150 rooms)
Total number of rooms sold: 3824
Occupancy Rate: 3824/4650 = 82.23%

One important issue is that it should be given a special consideration is how to determine the number of rooms available for sale. Normally, it is assumed that all rooms at a property are available for sale throughout the year. However, in reality, there are always some rooms, out of inventory (such as under renovation) or out of order. In this case, an adjustment should be made when calculating the number of available rooms. That is, out of inventory rooms or out of order rooms should be deducted from the total room inventory. Only those rooms that are saleable to guests should be considered when figuring out the occupancy rate.

17.3.2.2   AVERAGE DAILY RATE OR AVERAGE ROOM RATE

ADR is a key business metric used in the lodging industry. It refers to the average dollar amount generated from a guestroom. Usually, there is a reverse relationship between the ADR and Occ. %. That is when ADR (price) increases the Occ. % (demand) decreases, or vice versa. ADR itself does not provide an accurate performance snapshot about a hotel's performance. The rate might slightly or greatly differ at different periods depending on the seasons or market segments of a hotel. For instance, in resort hotels the ADR is high in high seasons and low in low seasons. In some business hotels located in big cities, the ADR vary slightly on different seasons, because a big city generally is vibrant and attract visitors in every season. ADR is calculated as daily, weekly, monthly, or yearly. The ADR may also be calculated for each market segment served, such as transitions, groups, and airline crews etc., The ADR is computed by taking the total room revenue and dividing it by the numbers of rooms sold. If there is no revenue generated from a room although occupied (such as complimentary room), it is usually deducted from room inventory. The formula is as follows:

Total Room Revenue/Number of Rooms Sold

For instance based on Table 17.2 the ADR of Moon Star Hotel can be calculated as follow:

Total Room Revenue: $414,616.
The number of rooms sold: 3824.

$$ADR = \$414,616/3824 = \$108.42$$

17.3.2.3   REVENUE PER AVAILABLE ROOM

RevPAR is one of the most crucial ratios employed in the lodging industry to measure the financial performance of room operation. It shows the average room revenue generated from every available room (room inventory) at a property. Although it is a strong financial metric, it does not reflect room profitability, since it does not take operational costs into account. RevPAR combines the room revenue and Occ. % yields as a measure of interaction. When interpreted with ADR and Occ. % it produces a more meaningful metric to users. Managers, who want to maximize the room revenue, need to scan the marketing environment, consider about customer purchase behaviors, and find the best strategy about how to increase room occupancy while also maximizing ADR. While it is not easy, managers always try to find an optimal balance among RevPAR, ADR, and Occ. % in order to maximize room operation performance. RevPAR is also used for external users, such as hotel management companies, financial institutions, and prospective investors as a benchmark to compare performances of similar hotels in a given market. RevPAR is calculated as

$$RevPAR = \text{Total Room Revenue/Number of Available Rooms}$$
or
$$RevPAR = ADR \times \text{Occupancy Rate}$$

Based on Table 17.2, the RevPAR can be calculated as

Total Room Revenue: $414,616.
Number of Rooms Available: 4650.

$$RevPAR = \$414,616/4650 = \$89.16$$

Calculating RevPAR using Occupancy and ADR

$$RevPAR = ADR \times \text{Occupancy Rate}$$
$$\$108.42 \times 82.23\% = \$89.16$$

17.3.3 CONTEMPORARY MEASURES

17.3.3.1 TOTAL REVENUE PER AVAILABLE ROOM

TREVPAR is a more recent metric used in the lodging industry. It is calculated by dividing the total revenue (including room, food and beverage, rentals, and other revenue) by the total number of available rooms.

Let's calculate the TrevPAR based on Table 17.2 figures.
Total Hotel Revenue: $648,472.
Number of Available Rooms: $4650.
Therefore, TRevPAR will be: $648,472/4650 = $139.45.

Revenue per Available Customer

Like TRevPAR, RevPAC takes into account all revenue generated from rooms and other operational departments. The only difference is that RevPAC uses number of customers instead number of rooms as a denominator. RevPAC is meaningful when hoteliers make predictions about future revenue and expect a high double occupancy. High-double occupancy means more customers and more revenue. RevPAC is calculated as

$$RevPAC = \text{Total Hotel Revenue/Number of Customers}$$

Based on Table 17.2, RevPAC will be

Total Hotel Revenue: $648,472
Number of Guests: 5584

$$RevPAC = \$648,472/5584 = \$116.13$$

17.3.3.2   COST PER OCCUPIED ROOM

The variable cost of a hotel room is crucial to managers in order to understand the profit margin of room department. The actual variable costs of occupied rooms enable managers to make precise decision when determining the price of hotel rooms for different markets and in different seasons. Based on the CPOR, managers determine if the room costs are reasonable and competitive to similar hotels.

The formula is as

Cost per Occupied Room (CPOR) = Room Department
Costs/Number of Rooms Sold.

Based on Table 17.2, the CPOR will be calculated as follow:

Total Variable Costs: $54,272.
Number of Rooms Sold: 3824

The CPOR will be: $54,272/3824 = $14.19.

17.3.3.3   ROOM YIELD PERCENTAGE

Room yield or room yield percentage is a new metric used in the lodging industry. It compares the actual revenue to the potential room revenue that could be generated from room sales, based on the assumption that all rooms are sold at the rack rate. The formula is as follows:

Room Yield = (Actual Total Room Revenue/Potential Total Room
Revenue) × 100

Base on Table 17.2 data, the Room Yield Percentage will be

$$\text{Potential Revenue} = (3824 \times 150 = \$573{,}600) \times 100.$$
$$\text{Room Yield Percentage} = \$414{,}616/573{,}600 = 72.28\%$$

In a hotel operation, the room yield is expected to be around 80%. If it is higher than that the room operation is said successful; if not unsuccessful.

TABLE 17.2 Financial Indicators of Moon Star Hotel (July).

Total hotel revenue	A	648,472	
Total room revenue	B	414,616	
Number of rooms available	C	4,650	
Number of rooms sold	D	3,824	
Occupancy %	E	82.23%	(D/C)
Number of guests	F	5,584	
Variable costs	G	54,272	
Rack rate	H	150	
ADR	I	108.42	(B/D)
RevPAR	J	89.16	(B/C)
TRevPAR	K	139.46	(A/C)
RevPAC	L	116.13	(A/E)
CPOR	M	14.19	(F/D)
Room yield %	O	72.28%	(B/(H × D)

17.3.4 MARKET INDEXES

17.3.4.1 MARKET PENETRATION INDEX OR MARKET OCCUPANCY

MPI compares the occupancy of a single hotel to its competitive set. If comparison rate is = 100, the occupancy performance is the same as other comparable hotels. If the rate is bigger than 100; the performance is higher than competitive set; if less, lower than the competitive set. It is calculated as the ratio between the total rooms occupied in a hotel against the total rooms occupied by competitor hotels within a defined area. It helps indicate how you are managing your inventory with demand against your competitive set the formula is as follow:

$$\text{MPI} = \text{Hotel Occupancy \%/Market Set Occupancy \%}$$

For instance, a single hotel's occupancy rate for a time period is 87%, and the occupancy rate of competitive hotels in the market is 72%. The MPI would then be

$$MPI = 90\% / 72\% = 1.25$$

17.3.4.2   AVERAGE RATE INDEX

ARI is a metric that compares the ADR of a hotel to a competitive set. Similar like MPI, if the score is over than 1.0, the performance of the hotel is higher than the competitive set; if below 1.0 the hotel performance rate is lower than the competitive set. It is calculated as following:

$$ARI = Hotel's\ ADR/Market\ Set\ ADR$$

17.3.4.3   REVENUE GENERATION INDEX (RGI) OR REVPAR INDEX

This performance metric compares a hotel's RevPAR to its competitive set. It is calculated by dividing hotel RevPAR by the RevPAR of the competitive set. The RGI score is expected to be over than 100 (or 1.0) in order to stay competitive in the market. An RGI below 100 means the market is outperforming the hotel; whereas an RGI over 100 means that the hotel is outperforming the competitive set. For instance, a hotel's RevPAR is $80 and its competitive SET's RevPAR is the same $80. Then, the subject hotel's RGI would total 100. If the subject hotel's RevPAR totaled $100, its index would be 125. It means that the subject hotel has captured more than its fair share. If the subject hotel's RevPAR totaled $64, its index would be 80, which indicates that the subject hotel has captured less than its fair share. Increase in RGI is often seen as a way to maximize profitability and indicates the competitiveness of an individual hotel

The RGI is calculated as follows:

(Hotel RevPAR/Competitive set RevPAR) × 100 = RevPAR Index.

17.3.5 MEASURES USED IN FOOD SERVICE OPERATIONS

17.3.5.1 FOOD AND OR BEVERAGE COST PERCENTAGE

Food cost and beverage cost percentages are very important to food service operations. This percentage can be compared with a standard percentage in similar food service operations or a preset percentage established by a specific property. Although there is no widely accepted standard food or beverage costs for all types of operations, the cost percentage vary between 24% and 40% for food, and between 8% and 20% for beverage. It should be noted that this is an average percentage. Every food or beverage item cost percentage could be different than each other because of their profit margins are different. For instance, while food cost percentage of an item X would be 25%, the other could be 35%. Similarly the beverage cost percentage of a bottle beer could be 15%, while wine cost percentage could be 27%. According to the National Restaurant Association's yearly report, the food and beverage cost percentage in the USA is between 31.8% for full service restaurants and 31.9% for limited service restaurants (NRA, 2010).

The percentage is calculated as

Food Cost Percentage = Cost of Food Sold/Food Sales × 100
Beverage Cost Percentage = Cost of Beverage Sold/Beverage Sales × 100

For Example:

The Grand View Restaurant food and beverage costs and revenue in April are as follow (see Table 17.3):

TABLE 17.3   Grand View Restaurant Food and Beverage Revenue and Costs.

	Revenue	Cost
Food revenue	102,212	37,364
Beverage revenue	66,338	8446
Food and beverage Combined	168,550	45,810

Based on the above amounts the food and beverage cost percentages will be as follows:

Food cost % = \$37,364/\$102,212 = 36.55%
Beverage cost % = \$8,446/\$66,338 = 12.73%.

Some food service operations use the combination of food and beverage cost together. In this case, the cost of food and beverage is calculated as

Food and Beverage Cost / Food and Beverage Revenue

Using the above figures for the food and beverage costs and revenue the combine F&B cost % will be

Food and Beverage Combine Cost % = $45,810/$168,550 = 27.17%.

17.3.5.2   LABOR COST PERCENTAGE

Food cost and beverage costs are meaningful metrics for food service operation but labor cost cannot be ignored when considering an operation's profitability. Labor cost includes employee wages, salaries, and other benefits provided to food service employees. The food and beverage cost percentage do not fluctuate much but labor cost tend to fluctuate seasonally if sales revenue fluctuate as well. In order to keep labor cost at a minimum level, restaurateurs usually give off employees in low seasons or employ part-time workers. The other way to keep the cost under control is to increase the revenue when possible and if there is a little leeway to reduce the labor cost. (For example, in luxury restaurants managers want to keep good employees and sacrifice labor cost.) When revenue increase the labor cost decrease accordingly.

Assume that the cost of labor at the Grand View restaurant in April is $33,650.

Labor cost percentage is calculated as

Cost of Labor/Total Revenue (food and beverage combined)
$34,392/$168,550 = 20.40%

17.3.5.3   AVERAGE CHECK PER PERSON (OR GUEST)

Average check per person or shortly average check is a useful metric used in food service operations and refers to the average amount of money spent by a guest at a given period. It is calculated by dividing total food and beverage revenues by the total number of persons served. If number of guests served at the Grand View Restaurant in April is 8732, then the average check per guest will be:

Total Food and Beverage Sales/Number of Persons Served.
$$\$168,550/8732 = \$19.30.$$

Foodservice managers use this measure for various purposes. First, it is a significant measure a restaurant's performance to similar restaurants or to competitors. Second, it helps managers to allocate labor dollars, assessing employee productivity, and calculating cost percentage per meal. Lastly, it can be used to compare the current performance with previous periods, budgeted amounts or forecasted values. It is one of the most commonly used and effective comparative analysis tools in the food service industry.

17.3.5.4   SEAT TURNOVER

Seat turnover indicates the ratio of guests served during a meal time period. It measures how often guests occupy tables during a meal period. The seat turnover is a popular metric to measure the effectiveness of the operation. If the total number of seats available at the Grand View restaurant during the entire month of April is 10,480, the seat turnover will be

Number of seats available/Number of guests served
$$10,480/8732 = 1.2.$$

The seat turnover rate may be higher at some meal periods and lower at another meal periods. It is a significant ratio that indicates how a restaurant effectively uses it seats. The seat turnover may be calculated for each meal period, daily, weekly monthly, or yearly.

17.3.6   NON-FINANCIAL MEASURES

Managers of large business organizations believe that when companies focus only on financial metrics ignore the instruments that create value for financial metrics. Financial data when combining with non-financial measures become more meaningful to decision makers, so that when interpreting together managers make more precise and clear decisions about strategic plans, company objectives and develop more meaningful performance systems.

In most areas, there is a strong relationship between financial and non-financial performance measures, so that non-financial indicators influence financial indicators. Non-financial measures sometimes can be better indicators of a firm's future financial performance. For instance, customer satisfaction leads customer loyalty. Loyal customers increase business volume. Increased business volume drives profitability. Non-financial metrics increase the performance of managers by alerting them at early stages before financial metrics obtained from the accounting reports and provide more precise evaluation of their actions.

In some cases, current financial metrics may not lead to high performance or profitability, due to some investment costs that incurred in the current period may yield expected results in the future. For example, investments in customer satisfaction programs, customer loyalty programs, employee training programs yield expected results in future terms. However, the costs of such programs charged in the current accounting period, so that current financial metrics do not reflect long term benefits from such kind of investments. Since financial data cannot capture a link between the current financial results and expected benefits of some investment costs managers may make some wrong assumptions so that lead improper decisions.

17.3.6.1   BALANCED SCORECARD

The balanced scorecard (BSC) concept was pioneered by Robert Kaplan and David Norton in 1992, although the original concept was created by Art Schneiderman in 1987. The deficiencies in traditional financial measurement tools triggered the development of non-financial metrics in 1980s and 1990s. The BSC itself is not purely a non-financial metric; it contains a mixture of financial and non-financial measures. The BSC is not a replacement for traditional financial metrics, but it presents the most relevant performance information to decision makers. The BSC enables companies to track financial results while simultaneously monitoring progress in building the capabilities and acquiring intangible assets they need for future growth. The BSC measures organizational performance across four balanced perspectives:

(1) financial;
(2) customers;
(3) internal business process; and
(4) learning and growth.

Perspective	Dimensions
Financial	The financial objectives focus on the themes of (1) revenue growth and mix, (2) cost reduction and profitability, and (3) asset utilization and investment strategy
Customer	Customers represent the sources that will ultimately deliver financial results. Targets customer-outcome measures (satisfaction, retention, new acquisition) need to achieve desired overall performance
Process	Identify processes (quality, cycle times, innovation) that are most critical for achieving customer and ownership objectives
Learning and growth	Identifies need developments within the organization (employee capabilities, satisfaction, productivity, and empowerment, and information systems) to provide the infrastructure for future growth.

Denton, G. A.; White, B. Implementing a Balanced-scorecard Approach to Managing Hotel Operations: The Cases of White Lodging Services. *Cornell Hotel Restaurant Q.* **2000,** 41, 94.

17.4   RATIO ANALYSIS IN THE HOSPITALITY INDUSTRY

Successful companies are constantly evaluates the operational performances of their companies. Operational results can be compared with previous terms, established standards, competitors set, or with predetermined goals. In any company, the main source of financial information is obtained from financial statements. Financial statements provide a wealth of information to decision makers, such as investors, creditors, managers, and others. Decision makers generate variety of ratios from financial statements in order to compare operational results. A major approach to analyzing financial statement is the use of ratio analysis. A ratio in fact is a comparison of two figures. Ratios express numerical relationships between various parts of financial statements either horizontal or vertical. Comparative ratio analysis helps companies to identify and quantify their strengths and weaknesses, evaluate its financial position, and understand the risks they may be undertaken. There are mainly three different standards that are used to evaluate the ratios for the given period.

1. Comparing ratios to the prior period.
2. Comparing rations to industry averages that provide a useful benchmark.
3. Comparing ratios against budgets or initially settled-goals.

Ratios can be classified in many different ways. One of the common ways classifying ratios is as follows:

    liquidity ratios;
    solvency ratios;
    activity ratios;
    profitability rations; and
    operating ratios.

17.4.1   LIQUIDITY RATIOS

Liquidity ratios have been developed to assess a company's ability to meet its obligations. Current Ratio is the most commonly used ratio for this purpose. It indicates the ability of how a company pays of its short-term liabilities. It is computed as follows:

Current Ratio = Current Assets/Current Liabilities

Assume that a company's current assets is $520,664, and current liabilities (the debts that must be paid less than a year) is 442,720. The current ratio then is calculated as follows:

Current ratio = $520,664/$442,720 = 1.17

A current ratio of $1.17 means that for every one dollar of current liabilities the company has $1.17 of current assets. A ratio of over 1.0 is considered as a safe area.

17.4.1.1   ACID TEST RATIO OR QUICK RATIO

This ratio measures liquidity of a company by taking into account "quick assets" such as "cash and cash equivalents" and some other assets, such as "marketable securities and accounts receivables." It only considers the assets that can be turned into cash quickly. This ratio excludes inventories and prepaid expenses from the total value of current assets, since they are not considered as quick assets. It is calculated as follows:

Acid Test Ratio (Quick Ratio) = (Cash + Marketable Securities + Accounts Receivable)/Current Liabilities.

Assume that a company financial statement contains the following information (see Table 17.4).

TABLE 17.4   Balance Sheet of an Hospitality Operation.

Cash	$30,000	Accounts payable	$50,000
Marketable securities	$90,000	Accrued expenses	$10,000
Accounts receivable	$70,000	Notes payable	$40,000
Prepaid expenses	$10,000	Current portion of	$20,000
Inventory	$100,000	Long-term debt	
Total current assets	$300,000	Total current liabilities	$120,000

Based in the given information, the company's acid test ratio can be calculated as follows:

Cash ($60,000) + Marketable Securities ($90,000) + Accounts Receivable ($70,000)/Total Current Liabilities ($150,000) = 220,000/120,000 = 1.83

As seen here, the value of the ratio is bigger than 1.0. This means that the company can cover all its debts by its quick cash and cash equivalents.

17.4.1.2   ACCOUNTS RECEIVABLE TURNOVER

This ratio measures the speed of the accounts receivable turnover cycle within a given period. It represents the number of times the average amount of accounts receivables are collected. The formula is

Accounts Receivable Turnover = Total Net Credit Sales/Average Accounts Receivable.

In this formula, the average accounts receivable is calculates as "beginning amount of accounts receivables + ending amount of accounts receivables/2".

A high-turnover rate is always desirable. It indicates that a company collects its accounts receivables in a short time. A high rate is also a good indication of a company's effective credit and collection policy.

17.4.2 SOLVENCY RATIOS

Liquidity rations measures a company's ability to pay its short term liabilities. On the other hand, solvency ratios measure a company's ability to pay its long term liabilities. Long-term solvency ratios provide viable information about a company's financial leverage. There are three different versions of solvency rations:

1. Total assets to total liabilities ratios.
2. Total liabilities to total asset ratio.
3. Total liabilities to total stockholder's equity ratio.

Assume that the following figures are taken from the financial statement of a hospitality company.

Total assets: $650,460
Total liabilities: $477,340
Total equity: $244,870

Based on the above figures, let's calculate the three different solvency ratios.

Total assets to total liabilities ratio: $650,460/$477,340 = 1.36 (1)
Total liabilities to total assets ratio: $477,340/$650,460= 0.73 (2)
Total liabilities to total equity ratio: $477,340/$244,870= 1.49 (3)

The first ratio indicates that for each $1.00 of liability, the company has $1.36. The ratio over than 1.00 is always desirable.

The second ratio indicates 73% of company's assets were financed by debt (liabilities). The third ratio tells us that for each dollar stockholder invested, the creditors invested $1.49.

17.4.3 ACTIVITY RATIOS

Activity ratios also known as efficiency or turnover ratios that measure management's effectiveness in using company resources, such as certain assets, inventories, working capital and long term assets. Activity ratios measure the number of times these assets turn over (or replaced) during a certain period. The three most commonly used activity ratios used in the hospitality industry are inventory turnover, fixed asset turnover, and working capital turnover.

17.4.3.1   INVENTORY TURNOVER

This ratio shows how quickly an inventory has been replaced in an accounting period. This ratio can be used for all types of inventory as a whole or can be applied to different inventories, such as food, beverage, and guest supplies inventory. High-inventory turnover normally is an indication of high efficiency. In the hospitality industry food inventory turnover is expected to be 2–4 times a month and beverage inventory one-half to one time a month. However, there could be many variations, internal and external conditions between operations, because of location, product delivery conditions, business volume, the capacity of inventory rooms, inventory conditions, and management's priorities, and so on. Therefore, each company should determine their own turnover ratio and compare the current ratios with the historical ratios.

Here is how to calculate food inventory turnover. Same principles can be applied for all types of inventories.

Food Inventory Turnover = Cost of Food Sold/Average Food Inventory
Beverage Turnover Ratio = Cost of Beverage Sold/Average Beverage Inventory

Let's give an example:

Beginning Food Inventory as of November 1: $56,660
Ending inventory as of November 30: $39,420
Cost of Food Sold in November: $436,222

Calculate the food inventory ratio:

First we need to find the average inventory: ($56,660 + $39,720)/2 = $48,190
Then, divide the Cost of Food Sold to the average inventory:
$436,222/$48,190 = 9.05 times.
This turnover rate is well over the industry standards; however, industry ratios cannot be used as a benchmark because of internal and external conditions.

In an average hospitality company owners and managers prefer high-inventory turnover ratios to low ones. Too low an inventory turnover suggests that food is overstocked or the sales volume is very low. If food overstocked the food may be deteriorated or spoiled. This may increase the cost of food so that indicates a low efficiency.

17.4.3.2   FIXED ASSET TURNOVER

This turnover measures management's effectiveness of the use of fixed assets, such as furniture, operational equipment, vehicle, building, and so on. This turnover ratio examines the use of net fixed assets in relation to total revenues. The formula is as follows:

Fixed Asset Turnover = Total Revenue/Net Value of Fixed Assets

Example: As of December 20XX the total revenue of a hospitality operation is $10,336,824 and total value of net fixed assets (after depreciation) is $16,720,500.

Fixed asset turnover: $10,336,824 /$16,720,500 = 0.61 times.

A limitation of this ratio is that it uses depreciated value of fixed assets, not the historical book value. Second, there could be big differences between different hospitality operations. For instance, in a hotel property the value of fixed assets are higher than a restaurant operation.

17.4.3.3   WORKING CAPITAL TURNOVER

The working capital refers to difference between current assets and current liabilities. This ratio measures the effectiveness of the working capital entrusted to the management. The turnover ratio provides useful information as to how effectively a company is using its working capital to generate revenue. The formula is as follows:

Working Capital Turnover = Total Revenue/Average Working Capital

Based on the figures on Table 17.4, let's find the working capital turnover of a hospitality operation (see Table 17.5).

TABLE 17.5   Working Capital.

	Total	Beginning		Ending	
Total revenue	4,222,476				
Current assets		460,338	A	84,214	X
Current liabilities		396,840	B	42,570	Y
Working capital		63,498	(A − B)	41,644	(X − Y)

Working capital turnover: $4222,476/($63,498 + $41,644) = 80.3$ time

The working capital ratio can vary between hospitality operations. In businesses where credit card transactions are high, the working capital ratio is high; where cash transactions are low, the turnover ratio is high. High-turnover ratio is normally preferred as an indication of management effectiveness of using funds. At the same time high-turnover ratio may also be the indication of tight cash flow or cash budget.

17.4.4 PROFITABILITY RATIOS

The best success measure of a company is its profitability. Profitability ratios measure management's overall effectiveness to generate earnings from the operation. Increasing profit is the best indication that a company can pay to its owners/shareholders. Some of the profitability ratios are, profit margin on sales, gross operating margin on sales, returns on assets, and return on stockholder's equity.

Profit Margin = Net Income/Total Revenue
Gross Operating Profit Margin (GOP) = Earnings before Interest & Taxes/Sales
Return on Assets (ROA) = Net Income/Average Assets
Return on Equity (ROE) = Net Income/Average Common Equity

Assume that a company's financial figures are as follow (see Table 17.6).

TABLE 17.6 Profitability Ratios.

	Total	Beginning	Ending
Net revenue	700,000		
Gross operating profit	60,000		
Net income	40,000		
Assets		200,000	230,000
Common stocks		325,000	325,000
Retained earnings		100,000	150,000

According to the above numbers, the profitability ratios will be calculated as follow:

Profit Margin = $40,000/$700,000 = 5.7%
Gross Operating Profit Margin = $60,000/$700,000 = 8.5%
Return on Assets = $40,000/($200,000 + $230,000)/2 = 9.3%
Return on Equity = $40,000/($325,000 + $325,000)/2 = 12.3%

If the profit margin of a hospitality operation is lower than budgeted number or industry standards, then revenue and expenses should be reviewed. Revenue may be generated from different departments. If so, each revenue generated department should be put under spot light and see what department's revenue is lower than budgeted. Sometimes both revenue and expenses may be disrupted. A careful review of revenue and expenses will show the problem areas. If operated departments' margins are satisfactory, the problem would appear to be with overhead expenses.

17.5   OPERATING RATIOS

Operation rations are examined under financial measurement tools in the chapter. Therefore, they will not be repeated here.

17.6   CONCLUSION

Improvements in technology, competing forces, and globalizations force companies to adapt various management tools in order to monitor, control, evaluate, and improve firm performance. As a management tool, measurement is a crucial element to improve business performance and stay competitive in the market. Improvement in organizations cannot occur without measuring performance or outputs to inputs. Performance-measurement systems help organizations to construct a link between what is measured and the desired goals or standards. Financial and non-financial performance tools provide a clear picture to managers about progress in organizations achieving its goals. Managers at all levels who are leading the efforts of an operation have responsibilities to maximize the efficiency of the operation using all available tools. With the right performance tools managers make well-informed decisions to accomplish continuous improvement. Financial or non-financial performance measurement tools utilized by managers should be used and interpreted wisely. Hospitality organizations need to develop their own performance systems that response to the needs of internal and external decision makers. In the hospitality industry currently there is no a standardized approach to develop and implement performance systems across all the sectors of the industry. Many of the measurement tools adopted by the lodging sector are based on the Uniform Systems of Accounts for the Lodging Industry. Similarly, restaurant sector uses Uniform System of Accounts for Restaurants and clubs use Uniform System of Accounts for Clubs. Other sectors of the industry have no certain guidance.

KEYWORDS

- **performance measures**
- **ratio analysis**
- **financial measures**
- **non-financial measures**
- **contemporary measures**

REFERENCES

Bititci, U.; Carrie, A.; Turner, T. Integrated Performance Measurement Systems: Structure and Dynamics. In *Business Performance Measurement: Theory and Practice*; Neely, A., Ed.; Cambridge University Press: Cambridge, 2002; pp 177–208.

Brown, J. B.; McDonnell, B. The balanced score-card: short-term guest or long-term resident?. *Int. J. Contemporary Hospitality Manage.* **1995,** 7(2/3), 7–11.

Denton, G. A.; White, B. Implementing a Balanced-Scorecard Approach to Managing Hotel Operations: The Cases of White Lodging Services. *Cornell Hotel Restaurant Q.* **2000,** *41*, 94.

Drucker, P. F. *On the Profession of Management,* Free Press: New York, 1998, p 173.

Fisher, J. Use of Nonfinancial performance measures. *J. Cost Manage.* **1992,** *Soring,* 31–38.

Harbour, J. L. *The Basics of Performance Measurement.* Quality Resources: New York, NY, 1997.

Johnson, H. T.; Kaplan, R. S. *Relevance Lost—The Rise and Fall of Management Accounting.* Harvard Business School Press, Boston, MA, 1987.

Neely, A. D. *Business Performance Measurement: Theory and Practice.* Cambridge, U.K., 2002.

NRA. *NRA Operations Report*, National Restaurant Association, 2010.

Potter, G.; Schmidgall, R. Hospitality Management Accounting: Current Problems and Future Opportunities. *Int. J. Hospitality Manage.* **1999,** 18, 387–400.

Solomons, D. *Divisional Performance: Measurement and Control.* Richard D. Irwin, Inc., University Press: Homewood, IL, Cambridge, U.K., 1965.

Wöber, K. *Benchmarking in Tourism and Hospitality Industries: The Selection of Benchmarking Partners.* CABI Publishing, 2002.

INDEX

For Product Safety Concerns and Information please contact our EU
representative GPSR@taylorandfrancis.com
Taylor & Francis Verlag GmbH, Kaufingerstraße 24, 80331 München, Germany

www.ingramcontent.com/pod-product-compliance
Ingram Content Group UK Ltd.
Pitfield, Milton Keynes, MK11 3LW, UK
UKHW021624240425
457818UK00018B/716